UNDERSTANDING
POWER
AN IMPERATIVE FOR
HUMAN
SERVICES

EDITED BY

ELAINE PINDERHUGHES, VANESSA JACKSON, AND PATRICIA A. ROMNEY

NASW PRESS

National Association of Social Workers
Washington, DC

Darrell P. Wheeler, PhD, MPH, ACSW, *President*
Angelo McClain, PhD, LICSW, *Chief Executive Officer*

Cheryl Y. Bradley, *Publisher*
Stella Donovan, *Acquisitions Editor*
Julie Gutin, *Managing Editor*
Sarah Lowman, *Project Manager*
Wayson Jones, *Copyeditor*
Juanita R. Doswell, *Proofreader*
Bernice Eisen, *Indexer*

Cover by Britt Engen, Metadog Design Group
Interior design and composition by Xcel Graphic Services, LLC
Printed and bound by P. A. Hutchison

First impression: January 2017

© 2017 by the NASW Press

Library of Congress Cataloging-in-Publication Data

Names: Pinderhughes, Elaine, editor.
Title: Understanding power : an imperative for human services / edited by
  Elaine Pinderhughes, Vanessa Jackson, and Patricia Romney.
Description: Washington, DC : NASW Press, [2016] | Includes bibliographical
  references and index.
Identifiers: LCCN 2016045084| ISBN 978-0-87101-505-1 (pbk.) | ISBN 978-0-87101-506-8
  (ebook)
Subjects: LCSH: Human services—United States. | Social service and race
  relations—United States. | Ethnic attitudes—United States.
Classification: LCC HV91 .U44 2016 | DDC 361.30973—dc23 LC record available at
    https://lccn.loc.gov/2016045084

Printed in the United States of America

Table of Contents

About the Editors

Elaine Pinderhughes, MSW, is professor emeritus at Boston College, having joined the faculty in 1975. Her 1989 textbook, *Understanding Race, Ethnicity and Power: The Key to Efficiency in Clinical Practice,* substantially changed the language of multiculturalism and human behavior in the practice arena and provided the rubric of culturally competent practice across human services disciplines.

Vanessa Jackson, MSW, is a licensed clinical social worker, Soul Doula, and owner of Healing Circles, Inc., a healing practice based in Atlanta, Georgia. Ms. Jackson earned a master's degree from Washington University, George Warren Brown School of Social Work. She is a nationally recognized speaker on mental health issues, with a focus on culturally conscious therapy and therapy with marginalized populations.

Patricia Romney, PhD, received her doctorate degree from the City University of New York, where she won the Bernard R. Ackerman Award for Outstanding Scholarship in Graduate Psychology. She completed her internship in consultation and education at the Yale University School of Medicine and did postgraduate study at the College of Executive Coaching. Her current work is focused on consulting and coaching for excellence and equity in higher education.

About the Contributors

Makungu M. Akinyela, is an associate professor in the Department of African American Studies at Georgia State University. He is a licensed marriage and family therapist in practice in Atlanta, Georgia, and an approved supervisor of the American Association of Marriage and Family Therapists. He serves on the editorial boards of the *Journal of Marital and Family Therapy*, the *Journal of Systemic Therapy*, and the *International Journal of Narrative Therapy and Community Work*.

The Boston Institute for Culturally Affirming Practices (BICAP) is a multiracial and multicultural group of scholars, researchers, teachers, practitioners, and activists committed to culturally affirming practices that support individuals' and organizations' efforts to build strong, respectful, and productive intercultural relationships. They have worked together on a variety of projects for over 20 years. They include (in alphabetical order) Gonzalo Bacigalupe, MaryAnna Ham, Hugo Kamya, Jay King, Jodie Kliman, Roxana Llerena-Quinn, Patricia Romney, and David Trimble, with Elaine Pinderhughes as a longtime consultant.

Sarita K. Davis, PhD, MSW, is an associate professor in the Department of African American Studies at Georgia State University, where she teaches graduate research methods. She has over 20 years of program evaluation experience. She has published in the areas of evaluation research, social work, Africana studies, anthropology, education, public health, and qualitative research. She received her MSW degree from UCLA and her doctorate in program evaluation from Cornell University.

Scott Drabenstot is assistant professor and director of undergraduate and graduate research in the Department of Psychology and Counseling at Southern Nazarene University in Bethany, Oklahoma.

David Anderson Hooker, JD, is professor of the Practice of Conflict Transformation and Peacebuilding at Kroc Institute for International Peace Studies in the University of Notre Dame's Keough School of Global Affairs. His global practice as mediator, trainer, advocate, and community peacebuilder spans more than 25 years. His research investigates the social and narrative construction of complex identities and the role of multi-generational trauma in the formation of interpersonal and communal relations.

Lani V. Jones, PhD, is an associate professor at the University at Albany, State University of New York, in the School of Social Welfare. Lani's research and scholarship interests are concentrated in the area of evidence-based practice with a focus on reducing depressive and stress symptoms and psychosocial competence enhancement among women of color. She is the author and coauthor of several articles and book chapters. In addition, she is a black feminist therapist in the Albany, New York, community.

Hye-Kyung Kang, PhD, MSW, is associate professor at Seattle University. She is a first-generation immigrant Korean American social worker and received her MSW and PhD at the University of Washington. Kang's research focuses on cultural citizenship, postcolonial social work practice, community organizing in communities of color, and critical pedagogy. She is currently focusing on developing a social-justice-focused and community-based advanced clinical MSW program at Seattle University, where she is director of the MSW program.

Kevin J. Mahoney, PhD, is a professor at Boston College School of Social Work and founding director of the National Resource Center for Participant-Directed Services, which grew out of the Cash & Counseling Demonstration. Kevin has been honored with the Pollack Award from the Gerontological Society of America and the Flynn Prize for social work research affecting policy and programs, and Next Avenue (PBS) designated him one of the 50 Next Avenue Influencers in aging and social justice.

Vanessa McAdams-Mahmoud, LCSW, is a clinical social worker and social justice activist. She has spent the past 30 years developing clinical interventions that focus on the intersection between culture, psychotherapy, and trauma. She has been a contributing author in a number of books and articles focusing on these topics; she also has been mentoring and training advocates and clients to facilitate clinical interventions that pay attention to social justice and promote empowerment of oppressed people.

Erin McGaffigan, PhD, MSW, MS, received her master's of science degree in public policy from the University of Massachusetts, Boston, and her MSW from Boston College. She received her PhD from the University of Massachusetts, Boston, where she focused her dissertation research on the complex factors and related outcomes of consumer engagement practices. She has extensive experience in the area of community-based long-term services and supports for elders and people with disabilities.

Monica McGoldrick, PhD, MSW, LCSW, is cofounder and director of the Multicultural Family Institute in Highland Park, New Jersey, and adjunct faculty at Robert Wood Johnson Medical School. Her books include Genograms: Assessment and Intervention, The Genogram Journey: Reconnecting with Your Family, Living beyond Loss, The Genogram Casebook, Ethnicity and Family Therapy, and The Expanding Family Life Cycle.

Carol Mostow, LICSW, trains interprofessional health care practitioners, staff, and trainees to optimize communication, understanding, inclusion, and support across power differentials with patients, learners, teams, and colleagues. She is a faculty member for the American Academy on Communication in Healthcare and the first social worker to complete their postgraduate training following a long career in community mental health. A Boston University assistant professor of Family Medicine, Carol trains residents at Boston Medical Center.

Mollie Rischard is a doctoral student at an internship in Tulsa, Oklahoma, having finished her masters in community counseling at the University of Oklahoma. She has worked several years counseling children. She also has special interest in multicultural and social justice issues.

Rockey Robbins, PhD, is the training director of the Professional Counseling Program at the University of Oklahoma. He teaches multicultural counseling, behavior disorders, group counseling and psychological assessment. He has published over 50 articles in the past 15 years, all in the area of multicultural counseling. He presents workshops around the United States throughout the year on multicultural issues and ethics.

Ramón Rojano is an experienced mental health, social services, and public health leader and practitioner specializing in developing effective strategies to improve the lives of underserved and vulnerable populations. A therapist and coach, he has worked as director of governmental and not-for-profit agencies and has taught in several universities. He created the Community Family Therapy approach and the Middle Class Express, a social mobility program. Currently, he is dedicated to teaching, writing, and private practice.

Jesse Tauriac, PhD, MA, BA, is the director of the Donahue Institute for Ethics, Diversity, and Inclusion and an associate professor of psychology at Lasell College. He received his PhD and MA in clinical psychology from the University of Massachusetts, Boston, and his BA in psychology from Boston University. He was a fellow of the American Psychological Association's Minority Fellowship Program. He has taught numerous undergraduate and graduate courses addressing racialization, cultural competence, and social justice.

John Tawa, PhD, is a member of the Psychology Department at Salve Regina University in Newport, Rhode Island. He also teaches Asian American Psychology as an adjunct at the University of Massachusetts, Boston, where he completed his doctorate in clinical psychology. John's research focuses on interminority relations, with a specific focus on black and Asian relations. He lives in Boston with his two daughters, Amaya Christine and Kalia Rain.

Julie Tilsen, PhD, is a white, cis, queer woman who has questioned everything for over half a century. She is the author of *Therapeutic Conversations with Queer Youth: Transcending Homonormativity and Constructing Preferred Identities,* and her work is featured in several counselor training videos. Julie teaches in Dulwich Centre's Narrative Therapy and Community Work Program and in the University of Minnesota's Youth Studies Department. She and her partner Lauri watch hockey and drink cold press in Minneapolis.

Acknowledgments

We are especially grateful for the patience and support of our authors during the extensive time it took to bring this work to fruition. To Monica McGoldrick, Nydia Garcia-Preto, and Ruth McRoy, who read parts of the manuscript and provided much-needed encouragement and support. To long-ago supporters and teachers of yore: Lucille Austin, Connie Lemon, Gaulda Edinburg, and those more recent: June Hopps, Monica McGoldrick, and Ann Hartman.

—Elaine Pinderhughes

To Ruth and George Jackson, for being my first models for right use of power. To Jack Kirkland, Elaine Pinderhughes, and Jean Caine, for nurturing, pushing, and always believing in me. To Patricia Romney, for her focus, calm, and fierce editing. To my power circle: Deborah Grayson, Kim Brundidge, Trystan Cotten, Leona Warner, Pamela Freeman, Sandy Stewart, Jean King, Cynthia Newbille, and Cherie Lyon, for keeping me clear and grounded throughout this process. A special thank-you to Dennis Streat, for your patience and love.

—Vanessa Jackson

To Elaine Pinderhughes and Vanessa Jackson, with deep gratitude for recentering my lens on the centrality of power in the helping process and for inviting me to join this important project. With gratitude to my sister/colleague Hye-Kyung Kang, who assisted us with syllabus development. And to my husband, Paul H. Wiley, whose love has enabled me powerfully and positively for more than three decades.

—Patricia Romney

Foreword

Monica McGoldrick

I have been waiting for this book for many years! The editors have far exceeded their hopes to provide helpful examples of how power operates and to share some novel ways clinicians, researchers, and consultants are thinking about power and working toward emancipatory practice. This is an amazing book in its exploration of how power operates in clinical practice. The need for this examination of the dynamics of power is obvious. As the editors point out, "In spite of all of the funding directed to so-called empowerment programs over the past few decades, few social workers have been trained to analyze power dynamics, and even fewer have been given the space to struggle with power—power to, power over, power within and power with—on a personal level and as part of their professional training." *Understanding Power* offers a candid exploration of the issues at stake in this crucial dimension of our clinical practice and of our lives.

I believe the editors (Elaine Pinderhughes, for certain!) have been preparing for this book their whole lives. Elaine has been thinking and talking to others about issues of power and how they fit into systemic thinking since she was a child.

Many years ago, Elaine mentioned to Murray Bowen that she had noticed that he had waited many years before publishing his ideas on societal regression. She wondered if this was because he knew the idea would be hard for people to digest because of the power issues embedded in this systems concept. His response was one of his wry, silent smiles. I believe Bowen's response reflected his realization that Elaine was on to him; she had recognized how controversial his ideas were. She took great advantage of his concept of the societal projection process in the evolution of her own thinking about how racial power operates in our society and how projection can explain the power dynamics involved in the way bias, myth, and stereotyping sustain this anxiety, reducing function in families and other systems (see Pinderhughes, chapter 1).

I first got to know Elaine while publishing her early paper on this subject in our book, *Ethnicity and Family Therapy*, in 1982. She has been challenging my thinking about systems theory and concepts of power ever since. I doubt we have ever had an outing together when we didn't sooner or later get onto the topic of how power operates.

In the half century that family systems theory has been developing, many have struggled to understand how to take power into account systemically. We have been mystified for many years in our society and in our field by the workings of power. Most family therapists have eschewed analyzing how power operates directly. Indeed, Gregory Bateson, one of the most brilliant of all systems thinkers, was deeply skeptical of the concept of power altogether (Guddemi, 2010). Some systems thinkers seemed to suggest that considering power makes systemic thinking impossible. This is, of course, not true at all. But we also cannot think of power as a simple equation that can be quantified with a formula. As Foucault (discussed by David Anderson Hooker in chapter 2) made so clear, power is a relational phenomenon, exercised only in relation to others. Bateson (1972), of course, said that all things exist only as relational phenomena. In any case, power is an essential component, constantly in operation in all systems.

The complexity of the subject of power and its centrality to systems thinking are the reasons this book is such an important contribution to our field. It is a great stimulus to our integration of the analysis of power into systems thinking.

The many arenas in which power operates at a societal level must be thought of together. Race, gender, social class, ethnicity, sexual orientation, body size, ability status, and many other dimensions must all be taken into account as we live our lives, assess clients' problems, and try to empower them. This book is a tremendous boon to us in pushing this thinking forward.

Almost half a century ago, Martin Luther King labeled the systemic issues of power in our society brilliantly in relation to racism. His insights on the relationship of power to systemic thought still hold true:

> One of the great problems of history is that the concepts of love and power have usually been contrasted as polar opposites. . . .We've had it wrong . . . and this has led Negro Americans in the past to seek their goals through love and moral suasion devoid of power, and white Americans to seek their goals through power devoid of love and conscience. . . . It is precisely this collision of immoral power with powerless morality which constitutes the major crisis of our times. (King, 1967)

King seemed to understand at the most profound level the complexities of the systemic intertwining of love and power. It is only by taking the complexities of the systemic intertwining of love and power into account and contending with them that we can maximally help ourselves and our clients to be demystified about how power is organizing their lives and our society. This complexity is, of course, embedded in the very contours of the health care and mental health care we deliver.

The dangerous aspect of power is when it refers to power over others, not when it pertains to power to collaborate with others or power to make one's dreams come true.

A crucial reason why we need to develop a good analysis of power is the way we are mystified by those who use power without love. This mystification is intentional. It is an essential aspect of how the powerful manipulate power. Their maneuvers are designed to conceal how they use power to maintain societal control.

The U.S. government built slavery into the Constitution, and it remained in place institutionally for almost 100 years without the word "slavery" ever being used. Women have been kept out of power and taught to obey and serve for generations on the basis of the mythology that this is the "natural" state of humanity or a structure that aligns with certain religious ideals. Our media mystify the way laws support extreme distortions of the social justice implied by the concept of "liberty and justice for all."

The mythology of individual will and agency in determining one's fate is perpetrated by those in power to hide the way power actually operates. We are meant to believe that everyone has an equal chance in our society when, in fact, power is kept in the hands of the few at the top of our society.

This is why learning to analyze power dynamics is so critical for clinical theory, research, and practice. Unless we unpack the systemic patterns of power abuse, our theories, media, and institutions will keep us from recognizing how power operates to keep some at the margins and others at the center of our society.

Like our constructions of gender, sexual orientation, and social class, whiteness is a social construct, not a reality. It has no biological basis whatsoever. It is meant to give power to one group at the expense of others and to maintain that power through institutional patterns of white supremacy, which have been kept in place generation after generation.

It is essential that the theory and practice of our educational, mental health, health care, and political systems shift to take account of these power patterns and that we rectify our situation, so we can truly experience "liberty and justice for all."

This book goes far toward unraveling the mystifications in which our lives are embedded. Those deprived of power must contend with adaptive behaviors that derive from powerlessness. For those with extra privileges afforded to the dominant groups of our society, the price of an unjust system is harder to see. It is difficult for those with unearned privileges of whiteness, maleness, heterosexuality, high socioeconomic status, and other assets to remain mindful of the disabilities of obliviousness to unearned power and the disadvantages of a lifetime of learning not to notice the inequities.

For me, coming from a primarily privileged social location in our society on most dimensions except gender, the hardest dimensions of power to understand and to own have been those of my white privilege, social class privilege, and sexual orientation privilege. I believe this is largely because society intentionally makes those with privilege feel comfortable with their superior status. What is much harder to notice is the deadening that such privileges lead to. As Peggy McIntosh (1988) described so well long ago, we carry an invisible knapsack of privilege, free checks, and credit cards to which others have no access. I have used McIntosh's own working paper on correspondences between race and gender to help me get more conscious of the areas of my privilege. I think about what I wish men would appreciate about gender inequities. I try to keep doing conscious translations to become more aware of what others require of those of us with white privilege, heterosexual privilege, and social class privilege.

Recently reading Eula Biss's (2015) essay on racial privilege, "White Debt: Reckoning with What Is Owed—and What Can Never Be Repaid—for Racial Privilege," I was shocked by her question of "whether white supremacists are any more dangerous than regular white people, who tend to enjoy supremacy without believing in it." What is so scary about whiteness is our complacency and failure to even realize the societal degeneracy of which we are a part.

Biss's (2015) conclusion is that "whiteness is not an identity but a moral problem," which seems obvious once you think about it. But how can we wake ourselves up? How can we not use our power to perpetuate the immorality of the system? Our denial involves an erasure, as Biss asserted, of both the past and the present—denial that the myths of "liberty and justice for all" has never been true and is not true today.

I think it is extremely difficult for those of us who are white to appreciate what the power of our whiteness, our unearned privilege, and our participation in the oppression of nonwhites does to us in subtle ways. There is a kind of blankness, coldness, superficiality, and a deadness that comes from never acknowledging our unearned advantages. The acknowledgment would cause us not only pain but tremendous cognitive dissonance to see ourselves as participants in the oppression of others, whether actively or by our silence about their disadvantage, which is really about our advantage at their expense.

But I find it very hard to get a clear hold on this idea. Biss (2015) compared it to living in a house so long we forget that it still has a big mortgage. Despite not paying it off, we've come to feel the house belongs to us anyway! Ta-Nehisi Coates (2014) compared it to having huge credit card bill, but, because we have decided not to charge any more, we "remain befuddled that the balance does not disappear, although we are not paying off the debt" (p. 27). How can we who are made to feel so comfortable and at home in our skin overcome our complacency and blindness to our actual place in the universe? We must challenge ourselves to understand how power has influenced our own blinders to do any real power analysis of the systems in which we participate.

Power determines which theories and clinical practices get accepted; what kind of evidence is considered relevant to diagnosis or treatment; and what research gets done by whom, with whom, and on what topic. Excellent challenges of this dominant research structure are provided by Davis in chapter 15 and Tilsen in chapter 16 of this book. Throughout U.S. history, most mental health interventions have been oriented toward a paradigm of individual adjustment to life circumstances, with almost no analysis of the organization of our nation that involved slavery, colonization of certain populations, marginalization, exploitation, and systematic demeaning of certain groups within the society (see Hye-Kyung Kang, chapter 8). Such perspectives mystify both mental health workers and consumers, operating on the assumption that adjusting consumers to the "American way of life" is a good thing, no matter what.

The authors of this book have explored the importance of power in therapy on many dimensions. Pinderhughes offers an excellent overview of the issues (chapter 1). Hooker explores in depth the multigenerational dimensions of trauma that make clinical attention to history essential for understanding our clients' experiences. Jackson (chapter 4) offers an excellent chapter on what empowering therapy entails. Other authors explore working with African Americans in therapy (McAdams-Mahmoud, chapter 3; Jones, chapter 6; and Akinyela, chapter 7), work with Native Americans (Robbins, Drabenstot, and Rischard, chapter 5), social work with immigrants (Hye-Kyung Kang, chapter 8), work in organizational consulting (Romney, chapter 9), and work in community family therapy (Rojano, chapter 10). In chapter 11, Mahoney and McGaffigan explore the renegotiations of power in client-designed and -controlled care services for aging and disabled consumers in programs called "Cash & Counseling," in which consumers get to decide how their service dollars are spent.

In chapter 12, Tawa and Tauriac take on the complex topic of teaching about power in racialized cultural contexts and describe methods to overcome students' resistance to accepting awareness of their own group's structural disadvantages within the dominant culture. As they point out, "the notion that some groups are favored challenges a deeply internalized view of the world as safe and just." This is a crucial point in teaching about power: attending to each person's experience of power and powerlessness and the impact that awareness of it may have on the person's sense of self and of the world around us.

Further dimensions of power in cultural training are illustrated by Mostow in chapter 13, which describes incorporating training on race and power in medical education and in chapter 14 by my own dear colleagues of the BICAP group, who relate how power intersects with race, gender, and social location for a group of committed and thoughtful trainers who explore their own personal and group processes.

The pernicious potential of power to destroy human lives—as still happens for all those groups oppressed by race, poverty, gender, and so on—is the reason we need a clear analysis of how power operates in our world. The editors and authors of this crucial and timely book have done us a great benefit in laying out a roadmap for our consideration on how to understand power in clinical practice.

REFERENCES

Biss, E. (2015, December 2). White debt: Reckoning with what is owed—and what can never be repaid—for racial privilege. *New York Times.* Retrieved from http//www.nytimes.com/2015/12/06/magazine/white-debt.html

Coates, T.-N. (2014, July). The case for reparations. *Atlantic Monthly.* Retrieved from http://www.theatlantic.com/magazine/archive/2014/06/the-case-for-reparations/361631/

Guddemi, P. (2010). A multi-party imaginary dialogue about power and cybernetics. *Integral Review: Toward Development of Politics and the Political, 6*(1), 197–207.

King, M. L., Jr. (1967, August 16). *Where do we go from here?* Annual report delivered at the 11th convention of the Southern Christian Leadership Conference, Atlanta. Retrieved from https://kinginstitute.stanford.edu/where-do-we-go-here

McIntosh, P. (1988). *Working paper: White privilege and male privilege: A personal account of coming to see correspondences through work in women's studies.* Wellesley, MA: Wellesley College Center for Research on Women.

Pinderhughes, E. B. (1982). Afro-American families and the victim system. In M. McGoldrick, J. K. Pearce, & J. Giordano (Eds.), *Ethnicity and family therapy* (pp. 108–122). New York: Guilford Press.

Preface

Elaine Pinderhughes

Understanding power is essential to the provision of human services. Human services providers (therapists, counselors, physicians/other health care personnel, teachers, and others such as judges and parole officers) are charged with helping people who are directly or indirectly affected by the way power has operated in their lives. As a result of how power operates, service users struggle with numerous challenges marked by ignorance, conflict, confusion, despair, and a sense of entrapment.

Human services providers are called to help service users transform their ignorance into knowledge, relieve the stress of their entrapment in powerless roles, and alleviate the conflicts within themselves or with others. To accomplish this, human services providers have the legitimate right—and thus the power—to impart knowledge and to evaluate, diagnose, treat, and dispense needed resources. Power therefore is implicated in the creation and maintenance of the problems and needs service users present; in the goals sought and strategies used to help them; and, very important, in the relationships they have with the providers who seek to help them.

To overcome feelings of powerlessness, people must find, discover, reclaim, or enhance their own power and liberate themselves from disempowering, entrapping social roles and behaviors. Once this has been achieved, they can use their power to solve their problems, reach their life goals, and meet their needs. When helping service users, practitioner effectiveness depends on an understanding of the forces that constrain or enhance the ability of people to use their power. This means understanding the following about power: (a) its purposes; (b) what it looks like and how it can be identified; (c) how and when it is acquired, maintained, and enhanced, and how it is constrained; (d) how and when it is abused and exploited; (e) its consequences for those who have it (that is, those who have leadership, privilege, high social status, and resources) and those who do not; and (f) how it is exercised effectively and justly.

Of critical importance is the understanding that *power is amoral*. As psychologist Kenneth Clark (1974) (whose research was used to validate the Supreme Court's landmark decision on *Brown v. Board of Education*) asserted, we are "caught in a continual struggle against the immoral exercise of power" (p. 12). Because power itself is amoral (due to its relative, dynamic shifting nature), it can be—and often is—exercised immorally. It is necessary that power be exercised so that, as Clark wrote, "the right of any group of human beings to impose their will upon other human beings must be restrained . . . by means consistent with morality, without resorting to methods that violate human respect, human dignity, and human life" (p. 12). This is a moral imperative, and it is the perspective of the editors and contributors of this book.

We offer this exploration of power as a step in the process of building a coherent and useful understanding of its operation. We believe that this meta-conceptualization will help human services providers to use the power of their professional roles to facilitate people's attempts to have power and exercise it effectively. It is intended to articulate the contradictions, paradoxes, and dilemmas that confront people as they seek to exercise their own power. Finally, although it does not present specific models of intervention, this writing is offered as a guide to the thinking needed for designing interventions. The concept of power presented here is not finished; it is open for revision and explicitly invites fuller explanation.

Although the focus of this book is primarily on the issue of power in service provision to individuals, groups, families, organizations, and small communities, we also look broadly at the operation of power on all levels, including large communities and nations, for insights into common and differing dynamics. It is our hope that this book will make the case that such information should be basic to the training of all human services practitioners and that it will spur the initiative to expand the knowledge needed for effectiveness and change.

In the first chapter, I present some basic concepts explaining the multilevel, bidirectional, and recursive operation of power; its effects; and the thinking needed for effective intervention. In subsequent chapters, practitioner/scholars from social work, psychology, medicine/psychiatry, nursing, and the ministry explore how they use their understanding of the operation of power in practice, research, teaching, training, and supervision. Our contributors describe how their understanding of power has shown up in their work, in their relationships with service users, and in how and where they intervened. They also describe the approaches they used and the approaches they feel are still needed. In the final chapter, the authors summarize the insights drawn from the preceding chapters, presenting newer ideas about shifting power usage. We have also included a syllabus for a graduate course or in-service training on power.

Our hope is that readers of this volume will come to see what my lifelong research has demonstrated: that power plays a primary role in human interactions and that understanding and making right use of power are the keys to efficacy in all helping relationships.

REFERENCE

Clark, K. B. (1974). *Pathos of power*. New York: Harper & Row.

1

Conceptualization of How Power Operates in Human Functioning

Elaine Pinderhughes

WHAT IS POWER?

Having power has commonly been defined as having sufficient control over forces affecting life to meet individual or group needs, secure necessary resources, and bring about desired goals. Control of one's destiny to some reasonable extent constitutes "the essential psychological component of all aspects of life" (Basch 1975, p. 513), which means that perceiving oneself as having such power is critical to one's health and mental health. Powerlessness—not having such power and control—is painful and will often be defended against by behavior that seeks to create some sense of power (McClelland, 1975; Pinderhughes, 1983, 1989, 1997). Power in the sense of some control of one's environment is critical to survival and constitutes the most fundamental of all human motives (Guinote & Vescio, 2010). Dynamic, systemic, often paradoxical, power, according to Foucault (1982), exists everywhere. Russell asserted that power is "the fundamental concept in social science in the same sense that energy is the fundamental concept in physics" (1938, p. 4). Power operates in all the levels of human functioning and is critical to all relationships: those between individuals, within families and groups, within communities, and within groups in the larger social system.

Visible on an individual level as personal ability or capacity, power exists on other levels of human functioning, as a component in all relationships, being shaped by people's interactions. Thus, power is also seen as a force in social systems, as a thing that is possessed by leaders and the privileged, and also as the quality of the relationship between the privileged and subordinates. Social activists Hunjan and Keophilavong

1

(2010) defined power as "dynamic, relational and multidimensional, changing according to context, circumstance and interest. Its expression and forms can range from domination and resistance to collaboration and transformation" (2010, p. 11). Institutions and social norms are sources of power, as are people's determination and will.

Jerry Tew (2006), clinician and activist, identified power as a "social relation" existing between people, a social relation that creates individual or social change. Dominating others in a "double edged, contradictory process," it limits and constrains under certain conditions and is productive or protective in others. It "may take form at various scales from the systemic patterning of the social whole, through the more local structuring of interpersonal interactions, to the construction and organization of personal identities (the internalization of power relations)." In creating change, power as a social relation can open up or close off opportunities for individuals or groups, and "may be anything from accessing resources and social or economic participation, through to developing personal identities and capabilities, expressing needs, thoughts and feelings, and renegotiating relationships" (2006, pp. 39–40). Power is, indeed, everywhere.

A Definition from Research

On the basis of findings from extensive research, social psychologists Guinote and Vescio (2010) defined social power as "a dynamic force negotiated in specific contexts on the basis of group needs, the self-serving biases of power holders, legitimating ideologies, and subordinates' tendencies to consent versus resist power" (p. 446). This means that the operation of power involves consideration of (a) whether, as a result of negotiation, the needs and goals being pursued by power holders reasonably encompass those of subordinate individuals and groups, including subgroups within the larger social system; (b) whether the belief systems that exist to justify the legitimacy of power distribution support the interests of both subordinates and power holders; (c) whether the power holders use self-serving biases (stereotyping) or are capable of perceiving and treating the lesser powered in accordance with who they really are and not according to myth or stereotype; and (d) whether subordinates consent or resist the power as exercised. Importantly, Guinote and Vescio stated that "Power is, therefore, relative rather than absolute and is a feature of situations rather than a force that resides solely within people" (p. 447). Power is, therefore, situational. This understanding embodies several of the most basic aspects of power, highlighting the primacy of the relationship between power holders and subordinates, the context or situation that influences that relationship, determining its origin in people's negotiation with their environment as they seek to meet their needs.

Power originates, then, from people's relationships as they negotiate with one another in pursuit of group goals. Influencing, controlling, and shaping interactions between individuals; within groups such as families, work groups, or communities; and between groups within a larger social system (communities and other groups based on class, race, or ethnic origin), power originates when "interpersonal control over valued outcomes creates interpersonal power (such that) asymmetrical possession over physical, social and economic capital creates power differences at the intergroup level" (Guinote & Vescio, 2010, p. 3).

The force that emerges functions as a necessary organizer and stabilizer, defining the norms, regulations, and guidelines for the different roles and positions people occupy, assigning and legitimating the level of influence (power) that exists in the relationships that develop between individuals and groups. In the process of negotiation, resources (money, material goods, influence, knowledge/wisdom, skills, will and determination, and so on) become the sources of influence in the system, and the persons with the most resources become the ones with the most power: the power holders, the privileged, and the leaders. Guinote and Vescio suggest that power holders get there because they have need for power and are also the most qualified. At the same time that power is critical as an organizer, stabilizer, legitimizer, regulator, and role assigner, whether or not it is reasonably stable is a key question.

How the power is exercised (justly or unjustly) is critical to the degree of stability in the system because power operates recursively, in a seemingly contradictory, paradoxical manner—like an elastic, being enhanced or constrained by a number of factors. Instability is determined by the degree of turmoil and conflict in the relationship between power holders and subordinates. The degree of conflict depends on whether or not subordinates accept or resist leaders' goals and activities. Subordinate resistance depends on (a) whether or not subordinates believe that leaders' pursuit of goals for the group includes their (subordinates') interests as they perceive them and (b) whether subordinates are able to resist. From this perspective, the stability and legitimacy of the power/leadership depend on the nonresistance of subordinates or the ineffectiveness of their resistance; and on their (apparent) acceptance of the status quo. When subordinates view the power as exercised to be illegitimate or unjust and feel power holders' actions are not directed toward goals that are in their (subordinates') interests, they may resist. If subordinates' resistance is strong enough, it undermines the stability of the system, jeopardizing the functions of power as stabilizer, legitimizer, regulator, and role assigner, and calling into question assigned roles and positions and the power holders' pursuit of goals and perspectives (Guinote & Vescio, 2010). This tendency of power to be jeopardized by the resistance of subordinates functions as an important constraint on the unjust exercise and abuse of power.

Subordinates, however, may not resist leader goals even when they consider such goals to be unjust. Their need to avoid anxiety and to have "order, structure, closure, stability, predictability, consistency and control" (Kay, Banfield, & Laurin, 2010, p. 327) prompts such reluctance to resist. This circumstance, indicative of a "symbiotic relationship" (Kay et al., 2010) between low- and high-status people, can reinforce the current unjust or unequal power distribution, enabling the privileged to keep their power.

Under certain circumstances, high-power people manipulate this dynamic to maintain their power (that is, they inspire fear and anxiety in subordinates, as has been seen recently in many political campaigns). Subordinates, on the other hand, may not resist leader goals that they consider unjust if they can see no benefit. As noted previously, whether or not the power holders see their subordinates and their needs as they really exist (as subordinates see them) is a factor in how power operates. Power holders are more vulnerable to using myths, bias, and stereotyping in their perceptions of subordinates when they have a personal need for power, when the system becomes unstable and their power is threatened, when power/privilege has existed over for a long period of time, or when stereotyping will forward leader goals.

Levels, Types, Sources, and Processes of Power

For our purposes, we identify the levels of power as individual, interpersonal or inter-actional, intragroup (within family/group/community), and intergroup (between sub-groups that exist within groups and communities and within the larger society).

Individual power, known also as personal power or power within, exists as ability or competence. Interpersonal power exists between two parties whereby one party has dominance or privilege stemming from role or resources or there is symmetry/shared power between the parties. Power in families, groups (also known as intragroup power), and communities exists internally as dominance, leadership/authority, and decision making and externally as privilege and high social status. Intergroup power exists as subgroups influence and achieve potency within the larger group.

The notions of "power over," "power to," "power with," and "power within" facilitate the understanding that power also exists across and between levels and is used by clinicians as well as community developers and activists (Baker-Miller, 1976; Fishbane, 2011; Nelson & Wright, 1995; Oxfam, 2009). *Power over* refers to domination/privilege over subordinates. *Power to* refers to the capability to decide actions and to carry them out. *Power with* refers to the force of influence and potency that emerges from people collaborating, having solidarity, and taking collective action. *Power within* refers to personal self-confidence and is often linked to culture, religion, or other aspects of identity that influence the thoughts and actions that appear legitimate or acceptable.

In couples therapy, clinicians use the formulation of power over, power to, and power with to explain and work to resolve couples' struggles over power and their entrapment in emotional reactivity (Fishbane, 2011; Knudsen-Martin & Huenergardt, 2010).

Illustrating how power operates across levels from the personal/individual to the institutional/structural, Nelson and Wright (1995), participatory development workers in poor communities, favor Hartsock's (1989) formulation: "The point is to develop an account of the world which treats our perspectives not as subjugated or disruptive knowledges, but as primary and constitutive of a different world" (p. 171). Nelson and Wright then go on to parse the relationship between developing personal "power to" and working with institutions and structures that have "power over":

> First, the personal level involves developing confidence and abilities (including undoing the effects of internalized oppression). Second, is the ability to negotiate and influence close relationships. The third involves working collectively to have greater impact than each could have alone. This is where 'power to' overlaps with the next model of power. (p. 8)

Moving to that next model of power, "power over," Nelson and Wright (1995) identified several key steps for work at this level. Gaining "treatment as equal partners in a process of development . . . so that they have long-term access to resources and decision-making" (p. 9) and working to "institutionalize processes whereby those with newly acquired 'power to' can negotiate with those with 'power over'" (p. 13) were key among the factors named.

This example of how power operates not only identifies the power relation that operates on and between different levels but also emphasizes the process of acquiring power that involves subjugated people changing internal restraints, developing skills and self-confidence in relating to others, working with others, developing the capacity to negotiate, and functioning as partners and decision makers.

Kinds of Power

There are many types of power. Each kind can be identified from its source.
Examples include:

- Authoritative power: power stemming from legitimate sources such as laws, organizational structure, and so on
- Ascribed power: nonlegitimate power attributed by others (for example, the view that Asians are innately more intelligent than other ethnic groups)
- Good power: "soft power" (Guinote & Vescio, 2010); power that is constructive, not oppressive, and does not exploit subordinates but facilitates use of their own power to have their needs met
- Bad power: dominating, exploitative power

Family therapist Marlene Watson (2014) also defines good and bad power in terms of the liberatory and oppressive aspects of each: Oppressive power may exist at the level of ideas (for example, white is better, or I, as an African American, am worthless), relationships (for example, domestic abuse, loyalty or work), social status (for example, racism, sexism). Liberatory power may emerge from knowledge (intellectual power), personal affect (emotional power), faith (religious/spiritual power), and/or connection (soul power) (personal communication). Specifying the kind of power under consideration is critical to understanding.

Tew's conceptual matrix (2006; see Table 1.1) adds the necessary specificity that also illuminates the shifting, recursive nature of power.

Oppressive power involves exploiting differences to enhance one's own position and resources at the expense of others. For example, the service provider exercises power to meet his own needs, not those of the service user. Sometime he is unaware of his vulnerability here. In the example below, the clinician struggles to recognize how he is exercising his professional power to meet his own needs:

I was working with a Black prisoner who was very manipulative and controlling. He tested me constantly, asking where I lived, did I have kids, what am I thinking and constantly bringing up the fact that I am white and he is Black. I

TABLE 1.1:   Conceptual Matrix

	Power over	**Power together**
Productive modes of power	*Protective power* Deploying power in order to safeguard vulnerable people and their possibilities for advancement	*Co-operative power* Collective action, sharing, mutual support and challenge—through valuing commonality *and* difference
Limiting modes of power	*Oppressive power* Exploiting differences to enhance own position and resources at the expense of others	*Collusive power* Banding together to exclude or suppress 'otherness' whether internal or external

Tew, J. (2006). Understanding power and powerlessness: Towards a framework for emancipatory practice in social work. *Journal of Social Work,* 6(1), 41. Reprinted with permission from Sage Publications.

focused on his toughness and his fear of dependency as narcissistic, but I wasn't looking at my part. I was battling with him over control. I was angry and upset at his assertive behavior, challenging my authority, but also not staying in his place—inferior and powerless. How dare he? (Pinderhughes, 1989, p. 138)

Cooperative power is using collective action, sharing, and mutual support. Differences are transcended in order to build alliances. Social movement groups are examples. In collusive power, differences are used to band together and exclude or suppress otherness, for example, white people's use of race to exclude people of color. Examples of protective power occur in child welfare and mental health where vulnerable clients and those around them must be safeguarded. However, intervention with them is always used with the goal that their possibilities for self-determination may eventually be realized, that they will eventually be able to mobilize her resources on their own behalf.

Tew uses this matrix to show the shifting nature of power: how cooperative, protective power can shift into being constraining and oppressive; and how collusive, oppressive power can be moderated or transformed. For example, cooperative power can shift to be oppressive when a group working together splits into cliques, with one subgroup becoming dominant and controlling.

Protective power can slip into being oppressive when the provider becomes patronizing, "takes over," "does for," or "works harder" than her client instead of working in partnership. Oppressive and collusive power becomes cooperative, productive power through the use of dialogue. In this process, when subordinates and dominant persons come together to find common ground, they may find new ways of interacting such that the privileged become free from the isolation that they are so vulnerable to being trapped in; subordinates develop hope and confidence to express needs and requirements, and new ways of exercising power open up for both the highly powered and subordinates. Invitations to cooperate and work alongside one another may potentially allow shifts from entrenched identities (such as expert or victim) and start to undermine divisive social constructions, thereby opening up opportunities for all participants to enter into a process of transformation (Fitzsimons & Fuller, 2002; Romney, 2005; Tew, 2006). A good example of this in organizations is diversity and inclusion committees, in which people of different ranks and organizational power work together to make decisions in the interest of the organization.

Tew (2006) wrote that to open up opportunities for "accessing resources and social and economic participation" (p. 40), individuals must develop power and see it not just as a "thing," but as a "social relation." This understanding of power correlates with what successful diversity and inclusion committees do. Individuals in these committees have to develop and build relationships with one another. Because the committee members are diverse in terms of gender, race, sexual orientation, nationality, ability, and organizational rank, they bring different experiences and perspectives to the table. They have different priorities for organizational change. Power in these committees is generated through the very fact of working together, dialoguing, and negotiating with one another to establish priorities and to empower themselves and the organizational members they represent. The dedication to missions that involve equity and fairness, respect, and transparency, which diversity and inclusion committees pursue and advance, is a perfect exemplification of power together that is productive and constructive.

Whenever the provider uses his power to meet his own needs, then the provider's power—which should be productive or protective—becomes oppressive. This is particularly true in work with people whose identity is culturally different from that of the provider wherein cultural bias and stereotyping may blind the provider, in his position of legitimate power, to many issues in the user's life and his own. Stereotyping is an anxiety-reducing mechanism (Pinderhughes, 1989) that can create emotional stability for the user. The following are examples: the teacher who holds low expectations for students who are poor or of color; the clinician who refuses to acknowledge the fear, guilt, and shame he feels in relation to his position of privilege and avoids this discomfort by failing to explore his client's painful realities or getting rid of the client; the physician who uses the excuse that his no-show patient has the right to withdraw without examining his oppressive behavior in his last encounter with the patient.

Gilbert Greene reminds social workers that, particularly in cross-cultural practice in which the practitioner belongs to the dominant majority and the client belongs to a minority group, the dynamic of power must be explicitly addressed. The practitioner must understand the client's unique experience as affected by the social, cultural, economic, and political context in which it has occurred; clients must fully participate in the process of change so that "they define their goals, construct their solutions, and control the pace of change" and "perceive themselves as causal agents in achieving solutions to their presenting problems" (Greene & Lee, 2010, p. 181).

Thus, operating as it does, dynamically, recursively, and paradoxically, having the capacity to enhance, heal, liberate, and transform and also to wound, injure, entrap, and immobilize, appearing as sometimes visible, sometimes not; operating on multiple levels; defining, regulating, coordinating, and legitimizing people's goal-driven actions and roles; determining the differential in the clout possessed by power holders and subordinates, power has serious consequences for each.

EFFECTS OF POWER

Power matters for those who have it and for those who lack it. Power matters because it affects one's ability to secure desired outcomes (including the satisfaction of basic human needs to control and to belong). Power affects the motivation to attend to others and social perception. Power determines self-regulatory focus and attention to rewards versus threats, experiences of positive versus negative affect, and the tendency toward action versus inaction. "Power affects the degree to which one is able to attend flexibly and effectively to important aspects of a situation and set goals" (Guinote & Vescio, 2010, p. 439).

As a result of its influence upon all of the functions listed above, power greatly influences people's health. Medical researchers have described the health effects of low social rank and entrapment in powerless roles: Lack of control and low social participation have a powerful influence on disease risk, and the stress of social subordination can increase mortality because of its effect on neurological, immunological, cardiovascular, and reproductive health. Researchers have:

> analyzed the physiology of power and noted a relationship between status rank . . . and two hormones—testosterone (T) and cortisol (CORT). When rank is stable, high (compared to low) social rank is associated with (1) higher T levels, which set the stage for maintaining positions of dominance, and (2) patterns of basal CORT and CORT reactivity that promote effective responses to acute stress . . . predictability and controllability are greater, and therefore, stress is lower, the higher one's rank. Interestingly when power is unstable, controllability decreases, and the effects of power reverse; powerful people come to exhibit maladaptive stress responses when faced with potential loss of power. (Vescio & Guinote, 2010, p. 429)

Power affects people's behavior in that powerful people act more, use more variable behavior, and, compared with powerless people, more readily prioritize and engage in effective goal pursuit. In contrast, subordinates have to spend time and energy trapped in distractions that prevent their purposeful pursuit of goals. "Lacking power also inspires feelings of anger in the face of perceived lack of control" (Guinote & Vescio, 2010, p. 431). Feelings of inferiority and low expectations of themselves, confused thinking, inhibited behavior, and withdrawal of effort result.

Table 1.2 focuses on people's feelings and behavioral responses to differences in power.

This table was originally compiled from diversity training sessions for graduate social work students, psychiatric trainees, social agency personnel, and conference attendees, in which participants sought to integrate an understanding of themselves and their work through examining their experiences of having and lacking power in relation to difference and cultural and social identity. The goal was to understand what happens when practitioners—through a structured, facilitated process—are able to examine themselves as beneficiaries and/or victims in our social system, to explore

TABLE 1.2: Frequently Described Feelings, Thoughts, and Behaviors Consequent to Differences in Power

FEELINGS	
More Powerful	**Less Powerful**
Having some comfort, more gratification	Having less comfort, less gratification
Feeling lucky, safe, and secure	Feeling insecure, anxious, frustrated, vulnerable
Experiencing more pleasure, less pain	Experiencing less pleasure, more pain
Having less tendency to depression	Having strong tendency toward depression
Feeling superior, masterful, entitled	Feeling inferior, incompetent, deprived
Feeling hopeful	Feeling exhausted, trapped, hopeless, helpless, with few choices
Having high esteem	Having low esteem
Feeling anger at resistance and noncompliance in the less powerful	Feeling anger at inconsiderate control of the powerful
Having fear of the loss of power	Feeling anger at feelings of powerlessness
Having fear of the anger of less powerful	Having fear of abandonment
Having fear of retaliation by the less powerful	Feeling alone
Having guilt over injustices that may result from having or acquiring power	Having fear of the anger of the powerful
Having fear of losing identity as a powerful person	Having fear of own anger at the powerful
Having a sense of burden from the responsibility	
Having fear of abusing power	
Experiencing conflict and confusion resulting from (a) a sense of injustice versus a need to hold onto the power and (b) a wish to share the power versus the fear of rejection by one's own ethnic group	
Having a need for a victim, someone to scapegoat and control	Striking out, becoming verbally or physically aggressive to ward off powerlessness

(Continued)

TABLE 1.2:   (*Continued*)

THOUGHTS

More Powerful	Less Powerful
Justifying aggression, and exertion of power or violence, dehumanizing behavior; pleasure in human suffering	Identifying with the aggressor, leading to self-hatred, dehumanizing behavior, self-devaluation, and pleasure in human suffering
Identifying with the less powerful, leading to a wish to repudiate power	Use of deceptions, secrets, half-truths, lies
Projecting on the less powerful unacceptable attributes, such as being lazy, dirty, evil, sexual, and irresponsible as justification for maintaining power and control	Projecting onto the power group acceptable attributes, such as being smart, competent, attractive
Projecting aggression outside the group onto the less powerful enhances group cohesiveness and unity (This behavior is assisted by a sense of entitlement.)	Projecting aggression outside the group onto the powerful enhances group cohesion (This behavior is assisted by a sense of justice.)

BEHAVIORS

More Powerful	Less Powerful
Adapt easily because have fewer distractions	Many distractions interfere with clear thinking
Having the opportunity to influence the external system for self	Lacking opportunity to influence the external system or self
Having ability to create opportunity	Lacking opportunity to create opportunity
Devaluing one's own pain and suffering	
Blaming the less powerful for assuming the projections	
Having distrust, being guarded and rigid due to vigilance needed to maintain power and control	Having distrust, being guarded and sensitive to microaggressions and macroaggressions, which seems paranoid to the privileged
Denying one's powerful position and its favorable effects on beneficiaries and unfavorable effects on victims	Denying the less powerful position and its effects
Displaying a paranoia resulting in delusions of and the assumption of arrogant behavior and tendency to distort reality with a consequent unreal assessment of the self and the less powerful	Risk of accommodating to stereotypes or assuming them in exaggerated ways, such as a physical or stud image, dumbness, delinquency, and addiction, with a consequent unreal assessment of oneself and the more powerful

(*Continued*)

TABLE 1.2:   (*Continued*)

More Powerful	Less Powerful
Isolating, avoiding, and distancing from the less powerful; taking comfort in sameness; becoming unable to tolerate differences in people; and lacking enriching cross-cultural experiences: RIGIDITY	Isolating, avoiding, and distancing from the more powerful
Displaying entitled, controlling, dominating behavior	Using autonomous, oppositional, manipulative, and passive–aggressive behavior as a defense against powerlessness
Displaying rigidity in behavior; have to keep the power	Displaying rigidity in behavior: to control sense of powerlessness
Having a strong need for control; need for a victim—someone to control	Striking out, becoming verbally or physically aggressive to ward off powerlessness
Blaming the less powerful for assuming the projections	Devaluing one's own pain and suffering
Having distrust, being guarded and rigid due to vigilance needed to maintain power and control	Having distrust, being guarded and sensitive to macroaggressions, which seems paranoid to the privileged
Denying one's powerful position and its favorable effects on beneficiaries and unfavorable effects on victims	Denying the less powerful position and its effects

EMANCIPATORY RESPONSES	
Sharing Power	**Turning Powerlessness into Power**
Developing a tolerance for conflict ambivalence, and contradiction, which, when mastered, leads to flexibility, resourcefulness, creativity, and high self-esteem	Developing a tolerance for conflict ambivalence, and contradiction, which, when mastered, leads to flexibility, resourcefulness, creativity, and high self-esteem
	Engaging in ways to change powerless roles
Working to overcome and heal narcissism and borderline symptoms	Engaging in ways to change powerless roles and perceptions of self as powerless
	Sublimating aggression in adaptive ways
Moderation	
Having opportunity to take responsibility, exert responsibility	Taking responsibility can create the risk of self-blame

their experiences of privilege and lack of privilege in relation to cultural/social identity and connectedness (see Pinderhughes, 1989; amended 1997 and 2013). The table shows the shifting, recursive nature of power through the behaviors used to defend against powerlessness and acquire a sense of power, behaviors that, while conveying some sense of power, are often destructive and costly to self and/or others. The paradoxical nature of power is manifest in its positive and negative effects on those who have privileged status, such as feeling and behaving not only as competent, privileged, and entitled but also as fearful, anxious, and threatened about losing their power and its benefits. Loss of power, even though small in degree, can become an experience in powerlessness with its attendant discomfort.

The coping responses of subordinate populations or individuals, while conveying some sense of power, can under certain circumstances also be disempowering. These coping responses may be as follows: In families, coping behaviors such as isolation, overfunctioning, or underfunctioning, and in individuals, such behaviors as dependency, manipulation, or violence, which may be used to gain some sense of power, create further stress within the family or community. Moreover, such reactions are often seen by others, particularly power holders, as foolish, bizarre, criminal, or crazy.

Other examples include subordinates' assuming in an exaggerated way the stereotypical attributions of those who are dominant, using behaviors such as being aggressively passive, violent, supersexual, superdumb, superdependent, and superdisorganized. Likewise, the responses of high-status people to their own relative privilege (behavior such as arrogance, entitlement, use of bias, and stereotyping) can also create a sense of nonpower. Although many of their responses enhance their power, there are also fears of having to share it, of losing it, feeling a sense of burden, having guilt and shame regarding exploitation, distrust, and—although they may be unaware of it—vulnerability to dehumanizing persons of lower status. The responses of both the subordinates and the privileged demonstrate the recursive nature of how power operates. The risk for subordinates is that behaviors they use to empower themselves can compound their sense of powerlessness, whereas behaviors that power holders use to maintain their power may set in motion processes that actually constrain their power.

POWER AND CULTURE

Persons occupying powerless roles must learn to survive and deal with stress, conflict, and contradiction that those from privileged groups are not required to cope with. They must find ways to cope with effects of their lesser power roles, with the sense of powerlessness that is mobilized, and they must seek some sense of power for themselves. Coping responses to powerless roles and sense of nonpower vary from time to time and from community to community but can become the essence of the culture developed by a group. Culture represents people's response to the political, economic, and social realities they face (Navarro, 1980). For subordinate populations, the realities they face are intricately connected with their entrapment in systems of oppression such as racism, classism, and sexism. The values, beliefs, social roles, norms, family styles, and community practices that evolve from their efforts to cope and achieve some sense of power and control over their environment can take on a cultural meaning. Understanding how power operate in terms of social status assignment promotes appreciation of the subtleties that characterize cultural differences and of the creativity and complexity involved in people's cultural responses, which embody often unrecognized strengths, but also can involve disempowering consequences as noted earlier.

The following example illustrates the complex, systemic, recursive, paradoxical nature of power along with some of its multilevel, interactive aspects as manifest in the entrapment, confusion, contradiction, and stress of low-social-status populations: As many African Americans live with chronic anxiety, fear, and high levels of tension, and have done so for generations, their oppression and entrapment in lesser power roles undermines physical and mental health. Families and relationships become threatened and are prone to misunderstanding, tension, and conflict. The greatest danger lies not only in the inflexibility and rigidity of functioning that can occur in the attempt to control the consequent stress, anxiety, and affect but also in the paradox they face. The strength and determination they must summon (and the behaviors they use) to manage these stresses can push the flexibility, mutuality, and adaptive compensation so necessary to healthy functioning to exaggerated and destructive levels.

Under the stresses endemic to their societal roles, the coping mechanisms of hard work, determination, and persistence can result in rigidity or driven dedication; being strong and tough can become domination and abuse of power; flexibility can lead to disorganization and inconsistency; and caution can slip into immobilization, passivity, or withdrawal. Thus, African Americans and others of low social status are confronted with this dilemma: To maintain healthy family and couple functioning, they must manage the anger and frustration stemming from their struggles with their societal role so that the vulnerability and mutuality that are so necessary for intimacy are not destroyed by the invincible stance and the readiness to struggle (power stance) that are needed to cope with that role. Maintaining satisfying intimate relationships in the face of ongoing disruptive circumstances that demand very different behaviors means they cannot afford to channel their anger and frustration into their bodies or discharge their feelings onto mates or children. Males from subordinate populations especially have to guard against using domination as compensation in their relationships. All must guard against becoming rigidly committed to defensive, power-over, conflict, and violence-prone behavior. This requires a state of carefully regulated flexibility and vigilance. Such functioning requires energy, effort, and discipline, all of which are likely to be severely compromised and in short supply given the transgenerational vulnerability embedded in their entrapment. The current condition of male–female relationships in these cultural groups indicates the herculean nature of this task. Any solutions to marriage decline for these populations must take into account this stressful dilemma (Pinderhughes, 2002). This example of coping mechanisms that can compound people's stress and sense of powerlessness illustrates the situational nature of power operation for African Americans and its dynamic, recursive nature, whereby role entrapment as a result of social status assignment threatens the stability of family functioning and places relationships at risk. Effective coping with the constraints to the use of one's power depends on a number of factors: having a certain degree of emotional and behavioral flexibility—not too much (danger of chaos) and not too little (danger of rigidity)—and having the time and energy in the face of multiple distractions and exhausting demands. As noted earlier, biased and stereotyping perceptions about subordinates are used when they can facilitate power holders' goal pursuit (Guinote & Vescio, 2010). When bias and stereotyping become part of a belief system within the community that influences the structure of the social system through assigning value to people according to identifiable characteristics, creating social structures that exclude and marginalize them, a status system is then created.

Status systems serve to create stability and reduce anxiety for power holders, while creating vulnerability to stress for the less powerful. I use Murray Bowen's (1978) concept of the societal projection process to explain the power dynamics involved in the way that bias, myth, and stereotyping are implicated in sustaining this anxiety-reducing function in families and other systems. An elevation of his family projection process concept to the societal level illuminates the purpose that oppression has served in our social system and points the way for focus on its effects upon both victims and beneficiaries. Just as the family scapegoats a member in order to reduce anxiety, conflict, and tension and stabilize itself, so also does the dominant group in a societal system relieve anxiety and reduce tension for itself through attributions upon a less powerful group, thereby improving its own functioning. Bowen identified lesser powered people such as minorities, delinquents, the poor, and the mentally ill as victims of this projection process.

Bowen wrote:

> These groups fit the best criteria for long-term, anxiety relieving projection. They are vulnerable to become the pitiful objects of the benevolent, over sympathetic segment of society that improves its functioning at the expense of the pitiful. Just as the least adequate child in a family can become more impaired when he becomes an object of pity and sympathetic help from the family, so can the lowest segment of society be chronically impaired by the very attention designed to help. No matter how good the principle behind such programs (to help subordinates), it is essentially impossible to implement them without the built-in complications of the projection process. Such programs automatically put the recipient in a "one down", inferior position and they either keep them there or get angry at them. (1968, p. 445)

Expanding this concept, I have suggested that persons who are holders of high-status positions become beneficiaries whose positions allow them to use their privileged roles and behaviors to stabilize themselves. These roles and behaviors allow beneficiaries to keep victims excluded and separate so that much of the tension, contradiction, and confusion that belong in the larger social system remains confined to victims and their communities. This is illustrated in (1) the negative stereotypical views held about less powerful groups, stereotyping being understood as a tension-relieving mechanism; (2) the creation of ghettos, reservations, and barrios where large numbers of the lesser powered live amidst noise, expressways, halfway houses, inadequate schools, drug abuse, and violence, in contrast to suburbs where a majority of beneficiaries live in relative tranquility, stability, and security.

Oppression functions as a stabilizer of the social system and a benefit to the higher powered for whom it promotes comfort, a sense of competence, superiority, and entitlement, thus reinforcing their power status. Power holders in the system benefit from perceiving and treating subordinates as societal problems, as inferior, incompetent, and weak (Pinderhughes, 1989, 1997).

Hunjan and Petit (2011) sum up this issue of bias, stereotyping, and social structure in the way that power operates:

> Power can also be understood not as a resource or ability, but as the prevailing social, political and economic norms and structures that create hierarchies within society, as well as the attitudes and behaviour leading to marginalisation. Discrimination on the basis of gender, ethnicity, disability, sexuality and other identities is often caused by such norms and structures of power, making it more challenging to address discrimination. These norms and structures are often 'internalised', becoming part of the unconscious social patterns to which people conform—whether 'powerful' or "powerless." Challenging power then becomes a question of recognizing, naming and shifting these socialized boundaries. (p. 11)

The operation of power thus is implicated in this entrapment on individual, group, and intergroup levels. Opportunities for these populations (non-white, female, gay/lesbian/bisexual/transgendered, handicapped, immigrant) to use their power to meet their needs are blocked by the prejudice, stereotyping, and exclusion that mark their experience. People's specific behavioral responses to such entrapment are often intricately connected with the problems they bring to practitioners in terms of their health, mental health, thinking, behavior, and quality of life. For low-status populations, many of these behaviors represent attempts to cope, to get a sense of power, or to turn their sense of powerlessness into a sense of power. Many of the responses of higher status populations trapped in the societal projection process constitute attempts to acquire, hold on to, exploit, or benefit from their power. Responses are positive but also may be negative (see Table 1.2).

To summarize, we have examined the significance of power relations and group status in the operation of power; how power emerges from the negotiations between people relative to having or not having access to resources. "[A]symmetrical possession of physical, social, and economic capital" (Guinote & Vescio, 2010, p. 3) leads to the establishment of power differentials between the parties involved, the formation of high-status/privileged and low-status/subordinate individuals and groups, and eventually to systems of oppression.

Power holders are vulnerable to using bias and stereotyping in their perceptions of subordinates when it would facilitate the goals they pursue and not when it would interfere with their goal strivings. Power is dynamic and bidirectional (and sometimes paradoxical) so that the beneficial effect of power on power holders is moderated by the degree to which the power remains stable. The stability of the power hierarchy is a key factor in determining these primarily positive effects for high-ranking groups and negative effects for low-ranking groups. When power is stable, its right to exist is endorsed not only by the powerful but also by the lesser powered through their consent. The legitimacy of this function can become jeopardized when low-status persons view it as illegitimate or unjust and attempt to change the power differential. Then, the effects of power can reverse. Faced with potential loss of power, high-ranking individuals experience a decrease in their controllability and "come to exhibit the sorts of maladaptive stress responses typical of low-rank (low-power) people who live with chronic stress" (Guinote & Vescio, 2010, p. 446).

Social status rank, group identity, and connectedness affect people's feelings, thoughts, beliefs, behaviors, relationships, values, expectations and sense of possibilities, determining people's quality of life, life chances, health, longevity, and mortality. The difference in the degree of power between the parties involved makes the relationship between them as important in how power operates as is a sense of individual control. Thus, control of forces affecting the people's situation and the relationship between the lesser powered and the privileged—whether the power relation is exploitative, oppressive, and constraining or nonexploitative, productive, protective, "soft power"—is key (Guinote & Vescio, 2010; Tew, 2006). Soft power, moral power, is exercised so that it does not exploit subordinates but facilitates subordinates' use of their own power to meet needs and reach goals.

Although we do not yet have the language or the research to adequately track in detail the intricate ways that power works, this discourse takes further steps on the journey undertaken by Bowen (1978), Tew (2006), Clark (1974), Guinote and Vescio (2010), Foucault (1982), and many others. Definitions of power are debated and ever emerging, and we may never understand this complex and robust concept fully. We still must work to translate current knowledge of these complexities to provide effective assistance to people whose problems bring them to service providers.

SOME QUESTIONS TO GUIDE OUR THINKING

Where do we begin? Where should we, given our present state of knowledge, intervene? What does this conceptualization of power tell us about our current models of service delivery, the current theories and concepts that guide our practice, and the relationship between the service providers and the service users? Although much of this conceptualization may seem to apply specifically to social workers, psychologists, and social activists, what is its implication for teachers, physicians, spiritual leaders, lawyers, and other service providers? Can intervention at one level (for example, the individual), whereby some needed sense of power is attained, affect the constraining effect of powerlessness at the social status level?

In a given situation, can an intervention executed in a single nodal place be sufficient to address all the power constraints, or will a set of more comprehensive strategies be necessary? Can we encourage a sense of "power to" in our clients without rescuing them? Can service providers' use of protective power (as in child placement, institutionalization in mental health) ever reach the goal of client setting their own agenda?

INTERVENTIONS

Solomon (1976) advised that the goal of empowerment for social workers working with lesser powered populations such as poor people and people of color should be to focus on removing the blocks to people's power, the constraints to people's use of their power. Our conceptualization suggests that the goals of service providers should be to assist people in locating, reclaiming, and enhancing their sense of power (power to); to help them strengthen their ability to use power with; and, when required, to use productive, soft power over to help them meet goals and needs.

According to Tew (2006), "[t]he versions of empowerment we have are not actually about service users setting their agenda" (p. 35). Helping service users to set their own agenda would require their being able to identify the constraints to their effective exercise of power and the many ways that power operates to produce these constraints and removing them. Constraints may be identified as whatever forces create the sense of not having enough power to pursue goals and obtain needed resources. Examples include poor physical and mental health status, lack of information (knowledge/education), and lack of access to resources (decent housing, education, employment, and so on). Some constraints can be removed by the provision of information or the educational process, whereas others require attention to whatever is blocking people's effective use of that information or education. Examples include barriers to access erected by structures within the social systems, such as laws, customs, values, belief systems, and institutions.

As noted earlier, other barriers can be seen in people's own constraining responses to their entrapment in social roles, responses that compound their entrapment and prevent their use of access should it exist. These responses include self-perceptions of inferiority, giving up, using uncontrolled anger, unregulated aggression, and so on. These responses have been adopted to bring some sense of power and control, but they become maladaptive. In a stable, organized society, the cost is high, resulting in constraints upon such behavior that range from disapproval and marginalization to punishment. An example of this is the large numbers of people of color trapped in our prison system.

These responses, however, may not constitute the primary force constraining the power of subordinate persons. That force is the exercise of immoral oppressive power by the high powered, so that the lesser powered are blocked from reaching their goals. Unfortunately, much of intervention does not focus on this primary cause—which remains largely hidden—but on the secondary cause: people's responses to the oppressive power embodied in their subordinate status, which is more visible and for which subordinates are often blamed.

Using this conceptualization, here are some logical approaches to work with subordinates that address some power constraints: Provide an experience of subordinates being treated with respect, their voices being heard, being seen as knowledgeable about self, and having an experience in (a) becoming hopeful; (b) being educated about the ways that oppressive power contributes to a sense of powerlessness; (c) recognizing that one has a choice about how to view one's sense of powerlessness and how to view the constraint, having a vision of the possibility of a change in the power constraint and in the oppressive power relations that maintain the constraint, and believing there can be a change in the oppressive power; (d) identifying ways in which the service user has exerted power and is competent (strengths and successes are identified); (e) having a successful experience in working with others to change a constraint to one's power, such as removing blocks to opportunities, and developing the ability to use opened opportunities; (f) success in social participation and leadership to shift oppressive power, to fight back when needed. Clark warned that when the nondominant person seeks real power, power conflicts emerge.

How should power conflicts be managed toward the goal of justice, of people's opportunity to set their own goals and meet their own needs? Here are some logical approaches in work with high-powered/privileged individuals and groups, including oppressive power holders such as abusers: Being held accountable and then accepting responsibility for exercising oppressive, constraining power; having information about the costs to power holders of oppressive power in terms of vulnerability to stress, isolation, fear (fear of subordinates, fear of losing power); vulnerability to use of stereotypes and myths about subordinates; use of dehumanizing behavior; having guilt, etc. (see table). Focus should also be on acquiring information about the benefit of power sharing, of using "soft" power, of shifting the exercise of oppressive power to learning skills in sharing power, using power non-exploitatively, using productive, cooperative power. Can using these approaches enable service providers to help service users to use their own power and set their own agenda?

Activists, community developers, clinicians, and other service providers use varying language to describe needed changes in the power relation that produces oppressive, constraining power. Some experts identify the needed change as power sharing; others speak of power shifts. Still others call it transformation of the power relation. There is no clarity on whether the goal should be to moderate the degree of power difference (that is, the degree of oppression) or to seek equity in the power relation. Those who use the language of equity advocate that both parties participate in the process of the power change: a sharing of power. Clinicians using this approach suggest that both parties develop an expanded vision, a new perspective of "knowing and being known by the other" (Weingarten, 1991, p. 295), using shared understanding, mutuality, mutual attunement, mutual empathy, mutual support, power sharing, shared goals, power-with approach, cooperation, alliance, working together, looking together at, co-construction of reality, equal commitment, and co-responsibility to the goal and the relationship.

In any model of making alliances and working together, the skill of dialogue and engagement becomes key, as do the principles of including subordinates and having their voices heard. It also involves their becoming able to see themselves as equals, becoming skilled in dialogue, verbalizing their needs, and being involved in every step in the process needed to achieve change (Tew, 2006). The privileged must acknowledge their responsibility for the way they have exercised power and become accountable for their privilege (Almeida & Bogard, 1991). Almeida's model of working with abusers involves placing them in a group with other abusers who have already learned to take responsibility for their abusive power. Involving recovered abusers with current abusers in a dialogue about the cost of abusive power and the benefit of sharing power, the latter find space and support for change.

In couples' therapy, family therapists use what they call "social intervention" as they work with individuals and couples to counteract social inequalities. They do this through attention to power inequities in couple relationships, examining how these are reflective of customs and behavioral expectations embodied in cultural roles (Knudsen-Martin & Huenergardt, 2010). Therapists work with power struggles and imbalances of power to facilitate equality, mutual respect, and "relational empowerment." They explain, demonstrate, and have the couples rehearse power-to and power-with perspectives and behaviors that ameliorate some power-over dynamics between partners.

Since power is not static, and often cuts across different forms, spaces, and levels, activists call for transforming the power relation by using a multilevel lens, looking within and across the systems of human functioning to map the many ways that power is manifest, and intervening with more than one action at a time in more than one location at a time. Mapping the operation of power requires language that can specify the kind of power and the complex processes involved (Hunjan & Keophilavong, 2010; Miller, VeneKlasen, Reilly, & Clark, 2006; Oxfam, 2009).

Clinicians also remind us that identifying appropriate strategies requires having a more complete understanding of the power relations at play; that there is no single solution, no one size fits all; and that for lasting change, intervention should address more than one dimension at a time with action on more than one level. Gains from work confined to the individual or family are maintained only when power sources in social, economic, and institutional structures are opened. Work at the societal level is effective only when subordinates develop the ability to take advantage of opportunities that offer inclusion and participation, which then allows them to acquire resources. Such work requires taking actions that link personal, interpersonal, and sociopolitical dimensions of power (O'Melia & Miley, 2002).

Madsen (1999) described the power shift in terms of providers becoming "appreciative allies standing in solidarity with people as they resist the influence of problems in their lives" (pp. 15–16), developing partnerships and mentorships, becoming allies with colleagues, and developing agency-to-agency relationships geared toward opening opportunities (O'Melia & Miley, 2002).

All insist that strategies must involve people considered as subordinates, who must have equal voice in the process and interaction that is working toward that shift. The privileged take responsibility for the consequences of their privilege; the underprivileged develop voice and power. While opposing oppressive power is a recommendation by all, the manner of opposition varies. "Fight-back" strategies and outright conflict are not preferred by clinicians. While constraints are identified, major focus is on sources of strength and how they can be used to transcend constraining power. Rather than a "head-on" approach, Tew advocates creating a shift from oppressive to cooperative modes of power through dialogue and engagement, as in the aforementioned example of working with abusing men. However, new models are emerging that offer promise that providers can work in ways that do help people to set their own power agendas. Recently, the Carnegie UK Trust developed an action-oriented program based on a process called "power analysis" that has sustained significant success in helping disadvantaged groups and communities facing issues of power inequalities in their work to understand the operation of power and use their understanding to achieve their goals. The primary focus of this process is on identifying the people's own power and figuring out how to use it effectively. This means helping people to understand their power as individuals and the power they have when they work together with others in their communities. It is also about helping people to understand how other systems and institutions, such as business and banking, may exercise their own power in less transparent ways to achieve the change they want and the impact of this on the change people are seeking.

Reports of the process called "power analysis" (Hunjan & Petit, 2011) and of the project itself (Hunjan & Pettit, 2011) describe how power analysis allows groups, organizations, and communities to explore different dimensions of power, the way it operates, and the best strategic options to achieve the required change. It brings people together and helps them to analyze the bases of power they possess and decide on the best courses of action and channels to create or pursue, enabling individuals and groups to exercise their own power in the most effective ways. Tried and tested on a variety of organizations facing issues of power inequalities in their work, this report brings power squarely onto the table and provides a potent tool to effect positive change beyond traditional analysis and change management processes.

Power: A Practical Guide for Facilitating Social Change (Hunjan & Petit, 2011) describes how the power analysis process works: Facilitators help people explore issues of power in terms of its operation in their lives (work, home, community, larger system institutions, and so on) over a sustained period of time through workshops, one-on-one mentoring, and self-reflection. The guide describes the frameworks, theories, conceptualizations of power dynamics, and tools that facilitators use to help participants engage in the analysis. Tools such as experiential exercises, creative writing, storytelling, drawing, diagrams, drama, films, or games are made relevant to the situations under analysis and to the people working within communities to achieve change. Combined with the structured process, these tools enable participants to identify the power they have, the sources of that power, and ways they can use it to achieve the goals they seek. The authors and publishers believe this project and its report prove that when people can examine their own power from a variety of perspectives, using structured frameworks in facilitated groups of others who also have need for such understanding, they can come to see how they can exercise their own power in the most effective ways.

My work to develop a diversity training model (Pinderhughes, 1989) grew out of a similar—though much less complex—process whereby participants used self-reflection to examine the operation of power in their lives. Structured to examine experiences with having and lacking power in relation to culture (ethnicity, race, gender, and other social identities affected by the operation of power) and difference, my model limited the examination to experiences within the family, workplace, and community and did not extend, as does the UK model, to other systems such as banking institutions. The field of examination expands widely in the UK model to include other institutions, laws, social policies, belief systems, and so on as the lens through which power is viewed extends from individual, family, and community levels to national, regional, and even global levels. Participants may consider how they and their experiences are linked to power operation in all of these areas. There is a major focus on the ways they have experienced the operation of power in their lives, how they have used power successfully and unsuccessfully, and the ways they can now plan to use power more effectively. This UK model appears to be a promising tool for enabling people to use their own power to meet their own needs and reach their life goals.

Tiziana Dearing, a professor at Boston College, is calling for the development of "New Economy Neighborhoods" that will bring innovation and micro-economic development to Boston's inner city, where many poor and people of color are trapped and economically powerless. Innovation clusters "right where people live" could turn these disenfranchised communities into "small-scale engines of tomorrow." Dearing offers several examples. For instance, in a public housing development, small groups using "3-D printing could produce component parts for manufacturing elsewhere" (Dearing, 2013); an urban grower's association could be formed using apartment gardening equipment to supply local food to restaurants and markets. Listening to leaders in these neighborhoods, who are already aware of such possibilities and whose voices must be heard, City Hall should "identify opportunities, and then coordinate the human and geographical potential of these areas with the companies and research efforts that could use them" (Dearing, 2013). As Deering (2013) said, "Cities help smooth these connections for big industry all the time. Why not for communities of color?". This is some of the latest thinking on power.

The following chapters illustrate how some service providers have used and can use their understanding of the operation of power in their work considering the present level of understanding of how power operates. Our concluding chapter will summarize the approaches in terms of the conceptualization presented here. As you peruse these chapters, we ask that you ask yourself what you, the reader, can add. Each practitioner may have to evolve his or her own perspective on how to fit the perplexities into a coherent guideline for considering practice intervention in particular situations. Conceivably, perspective is as important as—or more important than—strategies, goals, or interventions. Our perspective is one centered on emancipatory practice achieved by means of the service provider's and service user's shared emancipatory aims. What are yours?

REFERENCES

Almeida, R. V., & Bogard, M. (1991). Sponsorship. *Journal of Feminist Family Therapy,* 2(3–4), 243–259.

Baker-Miller, J. (1976). *Toward a new psychology of women.* Boston: Beacon Press.

Basch, M. (1975). Toward a theory that encompasses depression: A revision of existing causal hypotheses in psychoanalysis. In E. J. Anthony & T. Benedek (Eds.), *Depression and human existence* (pp. 485–534). Boston: Little, Brown.

Bateson, G. (1972). *Steps to an ecology of the mind.* Chicago: University of Chicago Press.

Bowen, M. (1978). *Family therapy in clinical practice.* New York: Jason Aronson.

Clark, K. (1974). *Pathos of power.* New York: Harper & Row.

Dearing, T. (2013, November 10). A whole city of innovators. *Boston Globe.* Retrieved from https://www.bostonglobe.com/ideas/2013/11/10/whole-city-innovators/mbabzARjFiLt48IceKRQnI/story.html

Fishbane, M. (2011). Relational empowerment. *Family Process, 50,* 337–352.

Fitzsimons, S., & Fuller, R. (2002). Empowerment and its implications for clinical practice in mental health: A review. *Journal of Mental Health, 11,* 481–499.

Foucault, M. (1982). The subject and power. In H. L. Dreyfus & P. Rabinow (Eds.), *Michel Foucault: Beyond structuralism and hermeneutics* (pp. 208–226). Brighton, UK: Harvester.

Greene, G., & Lee, M. Y. (2010). *Solution-oriented social work practice: An integrative approach to working with client strengths.* New York: Oxford University Press.

Guinote, A., & Vescio, T. K. (2010). *The social psychology of power.* New York: Guilford Press.

Hartsock, N. (1989). Foucault on power: A theory for women? In L. Nicholson (Ed.), *Feminism/postmodernism* (pp. 157–175). New York: Routledge.

Hunjan, R., & Keophilavong, S. (2010). *Power and making change happen.* Dunfemine, Scotland: Carnegie UK Trust.

Hunjan, R., & Petit, J. (2011). *Power: A practical guide for facilitating social change.* Dunfemine, Scotland: Carnegie UK Trust.

Kay, A. C., Banfield, J. C., & Laurin, K. (2010). The system justification motive and the maintenance of social power. In A. Guinote & T. K. Vescio (Eds.), *The social psychology of power* (pp. 313–340). New York: Guilford Press.

Knudsen-Martin, C., & Huenergardt, D. (2010). A socio-emotional approach to couple therapy: Linking social context and couple interaction. *Family Process, 49,* 369–384.

Madsen, W. (1999). *Collaborative therapy with multi-stressed families: From old problems to new futures.* New York: Guilford Press.

McClelland, D. C. (1975). *Power: The inner experience.* Oxford, UK: Irvington.

Miller, V., VeneKlasen, L., Reilly, M., & Clark, C. (2006). *Making change happen: Power. Concepts for revisioning power for justice, equality and peace.* Retrieved from http://www.justassociates.org/en/resources/mch3-power-concepts-revisioning-power-justice-equality-and-peace

Nelson, N., & Wright, S. (1995). *Power and participatory development: Theory and practice.* London: Intermediate Technology Publications.

O'Melia, M., & Miley, K. K. (2002). *Pathways to power: Readings in contextual social work practice.* Boston: Allyn & Bacon.

Oxfam. (2009). *A quick guide to power analysis.* Retrieved from http://www.powercube.net/wp-content/uploads/2009/11/quick_guide_to_power_analysis_external_final.pdf

Pinderhughes, E. B. (1983). Empowerment for our clients and for ourselves. *Social Casework, 64,* 331–338.

Pinderhughes, E. (1989). *Understanding race, ethnicity, and power: The key to efficacy in clinical practice.* New York: Free Press.

Pinderhughes, E. (1997). The interaction of difference and power as a basic framework for understanding work with African Americans: Family theory, empowerment and educational approaches. *Smith College Studies in Social Work, 67*(3), 322–347.

Pinderhughes, E. (2002). African American marriage in the 20th century. *Family Process, 41*(2), 269–282.

Romney, P. (2005). The art of dialogue. In P. Korza, B. Schaffer Bacon, & A. Assaf (Eds.), *Civic dialogue, arts & culture: Findings from animating democracy* (pp. 57–79). Washington, DC: Americans for the Arts Press.

Russell, B. (1938). *Power: A new social analysis.* London: Routledge Classics.

Tew, J. (2006). Understanding power and powerlessness: Towards a framework for emancipatory practice in social work. *Journal of Social Work, 6*(1), 33–51.

Watson, M. (2014). *Power is a word: Self-empowerment for African Americans.* Unpublished manuscript.

Weingarten, K. (1991). The discourses of intimacy: Adding a social constructionist and feminist view. *Family Process, 30*(3), 285–305.

2

Legacy and Aftermath: The Mechanisms of Power in the Multigenerational Transmission of Trauma

David Anderson Hooker

This chapter presents the mechanisms by which the effects of and reactions to historically injurious conditions are transmitted through multiple generations, specifically, in the absence of or substantial modification to the originally harmful conditions. After the introduction, the chapter is presented in three segments: First, I briefly present the foundational concepts of *trauma*, *historical trauma*, and a *Foucauldian construction* of *power*. The second section presents the constructs of *legacy* and *aftermath*, which are proposed as the mechanisms of power through which traumatic responses are transmitted between and among people and across generations. Finally, I offer a framework for individual and collective engagement that minimizes or eliminates the continuing transmission of trauma-based behaviors.

INTRODUCTION

History is replete with examples of societies in which certain groups are isolated, oppressed, violently repressed, or, in extreme cases, targeted for genocide, eradication, or cultural elimination; what I call "organized lovelessness."[1] This is often based on

---

[1] There is not space in this chapter to fully present this concept, yet I submit that this is an important concept and would be a very powerful discussion. The discussion would be centered around the following questions: What is love? How can it be more consciously used as an intervention? How can the received narrative/discourse that constructs the "other" be re-storied through sharing/witnessing narratives to mitigate the transmission of trauma and allow all to regain the lost power?

ethnocentrism, cultural imperialism, or the labor imperatives of a dominating culture. In most instances, the nature of the discrimination, repression, or genocide affects every aspect of life and culture: personal relationships, family and societal structures, institutions, policies, laws, and values. Often, there are also legal and cultural constraints on whether and in what ways oppressed and dominant groups can relate to one another (for example, segregation). All of these forms of state-sponsored or sanctioned violence tend to be traumagenic for all who are exposed (victim, victimizer, and bystander). To reflect the understanding that certain events or circumstances can be the genesis of trauma for some and not others, I coined the term "traumagenic." Individuals and communities have different capacities to bear hardship and respond to events and circumstances. Therefore, it is not accurate to say that an event or circumstance is either "trauma" or "traumatic." The event may produce trauma reactions for some but not others, which means it is potentially traumagenic; the emotional, physical, spiritual, and relational reactions to traumagenic moments are properly described as trauma.

The conditions that produce and reproduce oppression and traumagenic conditions have their rationale inside of particular relations of power. For those seeking to transform societal inequities, the analysis and strategy must consider the relations of power and not any particular institutional arrangement. On the basis of this understanding, this chapter specifically describes the role of power in the process for the multigenerational transmission of trauma. The constructs of "legacy" and "aftermath" offered are models for understanding relations of power established in response to traumagenic conditions and how they are perpetuated across multiple generations.

Why Don't We Just Get Over It?

When experiences and conditions that produce collective harm and social injury occurred in an earlier historical period, people who experienced those injuries and often their descendants are asked: "Why can't you just let it go, get over it and move on?" Similarly, when the political and societal conditions that produced the initial harms are no longer present, but the descendant communities still exhibit behaviors, emotions, patterns of thought, and interactions that might be better associated with those earlier traumagenic conditions, the question again is raised: "That was so long ago, what does that have to do with you people today?" Although the continuing injuries are usually more visible among the descendants of those who were oppressed, the descendants of the oppressors are also injured, and the performative aspects of those injuries often persist unwittingly in them. In seeking to explain the persistence of such traumagenic experiences in regard to the experience of African Americans, Sharifa Rhodes-Pitts (2014) wrote,

> A path can be traced from slavery to the killing of Michael Brown. The sociologist Loïc Wacquant asserts that racialized slavery was only the first in a series of "peculiar institutions" (as went the 19th-century euphemism gilding the nation's founding contradiction) to enforce caste and class in the United States. The most recent is the "hyperghetto" and "hyperincarceration" that presides today, wherein there's little hope of mobility and uniformly dire possibilities.

The presence of trauma—the responses to traumagenic conditions and the systemic ways in which it is enforced and reinforced—becomes woven into the societal fabric and the cultural milieu in such ways that even when the traumagenic policies and practices are officially eliminated or outlawed (emancipation, liberation, transitional justice), the residual performances of trauma persist, often for several generations that did not directly experience the traumagenic source. When trauma effects and affects are present in generations of persons who did not directly experience the traumagenic policies and practices, or at least did not experience them at the peak intensity, this is called either intergenerational (one generation) or transgenerational (across at least two, often several, generations) transmission of trauma. I use the term "multigenerational transmission of trauma" when speaking of inter- and trans-generational together, not distinguishing the number of generations as much as acknowledging the fact of the transmission. In the next section, I describe three constructs—*trauma*, *historical trauma*, and *power*—that are foundational to understanding the phenomenon of multigenerational transmission of trauma.

TRAUMA, HISTORICAL TRAUMA, AND POWER

Trauma, according to Levine and Frederick (1997), is not a particular event or situation. Rather, "trauma" describes the set of reactions and responses to an event or set of circumstances that are perceived to be threatening and that overwhelm an individual's or a community's collective capacity to respond. There are four typical trauma reactions, which may be instinctually encoded and psychobiologically determined: fight, flight, freeze, or nurture. The overwhelming circumstances can be large and sudden, small and cumulative, chronic, persistent, and even normalized. As response to events, trauma is both performance and performative. It is *performance* in the various ways that people and societies act in response to the experience of overwhelm. In this regard, thoughts and feelings can be considered actions as well. Trauma is also *performative* in the sense that the actions themselves produce certain affects and effects (Austin, 1962; Bruner, 1987; Butler, 1997).

Traumagenic conditions can have differential effects on individuals and communities, and similarly, trauma responses can also vary widely. Some individuals and communities will respond with actions that are destructive to self and others or through isolation, marginalization, and repression. Others will develop courage, compassion, wisdom, and spiritual strength and create systems that strive for equity and inclusion.

Historical trauma is reflective of the responses to traumagenic conditions when those conditions were specifically directed at a particular group. In considering the experiences of entire societies under extreme conditions like genocide, colonization, enslavement, and holocaust, several psychologists (Brave Heart, 2001), psychiatrists (Cabrera, 2001; Danieli, 1998; Mehl-Madrona, 2007), sociologists (Alexander, 2012; Atkinson, 2002), and even public health specialists (Jones, 2000) have explained the reactions and results of these circumstances within the framework of "gross societal trauma." Dr. Maria Yellow Horse Brave Heart (2001) conceptualized historical trauma in the 1980s as a way to better understand why life for many First Nations people living in North America was not fulfilling the "American Dream." Historical trauma is characterized as having cumulative emotional and psychological effects across generations, especially when sourced from traumagenic experiences that affect the masses. Similarly, Cabrera (2001) coined the description "multiply wounded societies." She recognized that in many societies, the wounds and losses have occurred in such rapid succession over such an extended period that there has never been time to properly process any one of the losses. Historical trauma occurs when a people or community is assaulted or their very existence (physical, cultural, spiritual) is threatened in ways that overwhelm their individual, collective, and systemic capacity to respond. In the face of broad-scale traumagenic conditions, individual and community responses are fashioned that are reasonable and appropriate under the circumstances. If the traumagenic conditions extend over a long period, the reactions and trauma responses become normative, systematic, reflexive, and unconscious.

What Cabrera (2001) describes is an unbroken chain of traumas in which people experience traumagenic conditions for multiple generations. The legacy and aftermath mechanism described in the next section are similar and yet have an important distinction. Humans are meaning-making beings who pass meanings between themselves through stories, signs, and symbols. Humans are socialized to perform, talk, feel, and think in ways that are often constructed and reshaped to make sense or regain control in response to threatening and overwhelming circumstances. Through these socializing patterns, succeeding generations may learn to perpetuate the behaviors and ways of thinking that were appropriate responses to traumagenic circumstances, even when those circumstances have altered dramatically or no longer exist. This transmission occurs, unlike the Braveheart formulation, even if there are no currently traumagenic acts or circumstances. To understand how this transmission occurs, it is also essential to understand the role of power in both trauma's formation and its mitigation. Among the many approaches to power, I find Michel Foucault's framing to be essential to understanding the legacy and aftermath mechanisms.

Foucault on Power

In Foucault's (1980, 1994, 2001) formulation, power is not an entity possessed by some and not others. Rather, power is a relational phenomenon that exists only as exercised in relationship to others (Foucault, 1994). Foucault distinguishes relationships of power from force, in that power does not act directly and immediately on others. Instead, power acts upon their actions. Power directly or indirectly influences, shapes, or, in the case of total domination, determines the present and future actions of others. Power has its effect not as a matter of consent, a renunciation of freedom, or a transfer of rights, but in a person's exercise of what occurs as their own choice or will. Power shapes what people see as the range of possibilities in a given circumstance. People presume to exercise their own agency in a given circumstance, but power determines what even seems possible (Foucault, 1994).

A poignant example of the operation of the Foucauldian construct of power can be witnessed during this period of deep tension and conflict between local police forces and black- and brown-bodied (African American, Latino/Hispanic, Muslim/Arab/south Asian) people in the United States in what is known colloquially as "the talk." It has become an accepted description of reality that black- and brown-bodied people living in the United States will experience differential and unfavorable treatment at the hands of law enforcement. In preparing young people for this reality, parents are often said to have "the talk" with their children. The talk describes ways that children should constrain or curtail their behaviors and their expectations for affirmation of dignity when interacting with police officers. The patterns of behavior and thought that are taught are based on historical experiences of fear and assaults on both body and dignity. The effect of the talk is the operation of relations of power. People of color would undoubtedly want their children to experience fundamental fairness in society. However, having the talk shapes the future behaviors of children, the way they view relationships and interactions with police, and the expectations that they have for themselves and their futures. In essence, their identities are shaped by the operations of power that they seek to overcome. Similarly, when some people of color are seen by others as acting in ways that do not reflect an acceptance of the so-called reality of their status, their actions and speech are somehow perceived as naïve and unrealistic. This is not to say that the patterns of interactions between the police and people of color do not sometimes have a negatively racialized tone; however, it is perceived to be by free will and self-agency that parents of color constrain the possibility horizons for their children. This is power in full view.

Many operations of power are productive; they do not stop people from acting but rather encourage people to act in certain ways. Some of the ways that people act in response to relations of power enhance their agency, yet others produce, reproduce, or reinforce the specific relationships of power that serve as limits on their actions. In a cyclical manner, one of the productive results of power is that people sometimes give their consent to allowing the mechanism to have power in their context. When subjected to relations of power, people sometimes act in ways that are against their own interest, and they do so believing that they are choosing to act this way.

Foucault (1994) also believed that one must analyze institutions from the standpoint of relations of power, rather than vice versa, and that the fundamental point of anchorage of the relationships, even if they are embodied in an institution, is to be found outside of the institution. Trying to analyze power and its effects from within the operations of any particular institution or network of institutions will hide the workings of discursive power. Although the institutions seem to possess and wield power, in fact, it is the relations of power embedded in broader societal narratives that allow the institutions to make sense. The institutions themselves are simply vehicles for the affirmation of the relations of power established in discourse and embedded in those institutional arrangements.

For example, in the wake of the tragic deaths of Eric Garner, Michael Brown, John Crawford, Tamir Rice, Freddie Gray, Walter Scott, and so many other African Americans in the United States at the hands of police officers, activists all across the country are demanding changes in the system of policing. The calls for change are based on the internal analysis of policing systems. The solutions proposed include such things as anti-racism and implicit bias training, accountability and citizen oversight, independent prosecutors, and increased diversity on the police force. None of these solutions are based on an external understanding of relations of power that undergird the police and other socializing systems. Rather, they seek to make changes from within the system. Although these are all valuable short-term propositions, the change that activists seek can come only from changes of the discursive relations of power within which policing is conducted.

An analysis of the relations of power and the discourses that establish the role of police in society would reveal that policing is part of a network of institutions put in place to contain the existential threats of the "other" that are present in society. These same discourses inform the work of schools, popular art and media studios, social workers, mental health practitioners, and many mainstream religious workers. The roles and actions of socializing actors and institutions in the repression of African Americans will change only with the shift away from the discourse of African Americans as imminent threats.

In the Foucauldian sense, socializing institutions and historical narratives are structured to reflect and affirm the relations of power. By consciously or unwittingly passing on not only the historical narratives but also, more importantly, the appropriate modes of action (including forms of logic, range of emotions, and forms of relations), the relations of power established in response to traumagenic conditions are transmitted from one generation to the next. I propose that the discourse and narratives and the systems and institutions formed to affirm those narratives—legacy and aftermath—are the mechanism by which trauma-sourced behaviors, emotions, logics, and relational patterns are reproduced across generations and contexts. The next section describes these mechanisms.

LEGACY, AFTERMATH, AND THE PLACE OF POWER IN THE MULTIGENERATIONAL TRANSMISSION OF TRAUMA

The legacy and aftermath of historical trauma are the mechanisms of power that act as invisible and unconscious limits on individual and collective ability to exercise agency when seeking self-definition and self-determination. The mechanisms also act to limit the capacities of communities of victimizers and bystanders (and their descendants) by providing them with them a trauma-based logic that is reproduced when they unconsciously rehearse narratives and maintain systems that constrain their available range of emotional expression and fail to produce the systems of justice and equity that many of them claim to seek.

Legacy is the collection of beliefs, ideas, myths, prejudices, and biases that are embedded in discourse, expressed in stock narratives, and subsequently disseminated and inherited by and/or about differing groups. Legacies are often contained in the official "history," folklore, language, and symbols of a people in ways that subtly or blatantly pass on trauma-sourced logic as truth.

Aftermath refers to the institutions, laws, political structures, and other systems that were formed to enforce or reinforce particular aspects of a legacy and that remain long after the overt traumagenic policies and practices have been stopped or reconsidered. When thinking of aftermath, the picture that often comes to mind is the structural remains of a natural disaster or war. Torn-down buildings, broken levees, and bomb craters are all examples of aftermath: the broken and tattered infrastructure and material that remain after a society has experienced great destruction. This same imagery depicts a society after a historical trauma. In efforts to rebuild the society, rubble is simply buried or pulverized. However, the recycled materials are still very present in the environment. This is the case for the aftermath of historic trauma as well. Aftermath is usually still present even when the legacy (that is, myths, prejudices, and biases) has been officially discredited.

Legacy and aftermath collectively operate to transmit and reproduce the limitations on action that were first established or perceived in response to a traumagenic circumstance. Atkinson (2002) noted that "trauma victims adapt their behaviors and belief systems to compensate for their traumatization, compounding their traumatization [as a mechanism for survival]." This adaptive behavior and the beliefs and moral code associated with it become the new normal in subsequent generations, who then perform the trauma without having the direct experience of the traumagenic circumstances. This new normal is transmitted from one generation to the next through history, folklore, myth, and socializing rituals. The trauma transmitting narratives are contained and affirmed in the symbols, signs, and institutional patterns and practices of a society. The strongest carriers for both legacy and aftermath, therefore, are family (Danieli, 1998) and what is described as culture (Atkinson, 2002). *Culture* is:

> the set of beliefs, values and rules for living that is distinctive to a particular human group. Culture is passed down the generations in a complex set of relationships, knowledges, languages, social organizations and life experiences that bind diverse individuals and groups together. Culture is a living process. It changes over time to reflect the changed environments and social interactions of people living together. (p. 111)

Aftermath is similar to what Jones (2000) described as the institutional or systemic/structural level of discrimination. At this level, the discrimination is built into structures, rules, traditions, and practices so that personal action is not required to maintain marginalizing and traumagenic effects. However, following the Foucauldian construct of power, it does not make sense to try to understand the nature of power that perpetuates trauma from inside those systems. Rather, the systemic and institutional arrangements are merely operationalized power otherwise contained in the legacy. Connecting the systemic and institutional arrangements to the unveiled legacies will allow people to consciously make changes that reflect their preferred narratives. The constraining and productive power of these preferred narratives is often thwarted by the lack of awareness of the legacy narratives, which represent either the basis for the traumagenic conditions or the meaning that was made from the resulting trauma responses.

One obvious but usually uninvestigated component of aftermath in the United States is the continuing categorization of people into various races. Race, as a physiological construct that has been discredited and fully established to be a fiction, is no more worthy of belief than any children's fairy tale (Smedley & Smedley, 2005). Racial categorizations are a structural artifice (aftermath) that accompanied racism. They were offered as foundational logic for the hierarchical arrangements of power and as an indispensable pillar of the narratives (legacies) of inequality designed to justify the racialized distinction of access to power, privilege, and a sense of place. This is true in the United States and in most every other society that experienced some degree of European and Arab colonization. Race is now simply accepted as an objective reality. Race is both aftermath and a unifying construct for much discursive legacy that perpetuates the disparate lived experiences.

For community practitioners, any combination of practices, theories, and skills that seeks to minimize and eventually eliminate the multigenerational transmission of trauma must account for several dimensions of traumatic impact, including mind, body, spirit, emotion, and each level of societal organization: individual, family, organization, community, nation, and global; and must also account for the short-, medium-, and long-term impacts of traumagenic circumstances. Although it is difficult, if not impossible, to address all these dimensions in any singular intervention approach, it is vital to be aware of each level and dimension in the activities' design. The value of the legacy and aftermath framework is that present-day behavior, thought, emotion, and action, as well as systemic and institutional arrangements, can be connected with deep historical patterns and future practices and understood at every level of societal organization through the same analysis. In seeking to address each of these dimensions and time frames, I think the most versatile practices are emerging from the narrative turn reflected by White and Epston (1991) and others (Freedman & Combs, 1996; Monk, Winslade, Crockett, & Epston, 1997).

Without identifying the legacy and aftermath that perpetuate these beliefs, feelings, and experiences, it is all too likely that they will persist for multiple generations going forward. What makes legacy and aftermath difficult to address, diminish, or remove is that over several generations, the beliefs, values, and the associated logic, relational practices, and institutions become the "new normal." As a result, they fade into the background for inquiry for societal change. Over a period of several generations, children learn by observation and determine what is normal and, therefore, probably "right" by what is most visible. Relationships and the emotions associated with those relationships become fixed and regularized through the discourse and narratives that explain them. If the traumagenic circumstances persist over multiple generations, it is often the case that there is no one alive who remembers the pretraumagenic standards. The original traumagenic conditions are rarely discussed in ways that could support reconsideration or change of behavior or thinking. In fact, traumagenic circumstances and the explanations for the conspiracy of silence are all woven into the complex legacy, which transmits the trauma from one generation to subsequent ones. In order to maintain this legacy, children would:

- not be able to fully explore their own history;
- learn to ignore the injustice experienced by others;
- watch adults and learn from them how to suppress, ignore, or deny their own emotions; and
- fail to acknowledge any level of sympathy/empathy for others.

In their extreme expression, each of these traits is symptomatic of significant mental and emotional illness. When, however, the attributes of illness become the new norm and are reinforced societywide, then it is much more difficult to heal the historical harm.

The content of the legacy is transmitted in stories and ritual narrative forms. Psychiatrist Lewis Mehl-Madrona (2010) states that "over time we rehearse (perform) certain stories so many times that they become virtually automatic responses—what we call 'second nature'." These stories are so ingrained that there is no longer a conscious awareness of their presence or how they control what is seen as a possible landscape for action. Once the stories have become automatic, then all the institutions of society necessarily align with them in order to avoid the conflict that would require regular examination (why do we do it that way?). The institutions that support or align with the beliefs become embedded in societies in ways that render both the stories and the purpose and values of the institutions unconscious. The unconscious values of the institution become the aftermath that continues to perpetuate the trauma responses across the institutions.

Many efforts in communities to overcome a history of historical trauma will focus on strategies of prejudice reduction or making connections and sharing history (legacy interruption). Alternatively, the strategies might consider structural, institutional, or policy change (aftermath dismantling). Less often is it the case that the same effort works on both legacies and aftermath simultaneously. Even more rarely, a particular aspect of aftermath is identified and connected directly to a particular legacy in ways that unveil the relations of power outside the institution that give the institutional arrangements their internal logic.

If awareness is not raised about the connections and if both aspects are not addressed simultaneously, the manifestations of the legacy or aftermath will likely re-emerge. When a legacy (myth, value, stereotype, belief) is prevalent in society, there are many structural (relational, policy, and institutional) arrangements that are put in place to demonstrate, reinforce, or manifest the legacy. If the institutions and policies are undone or reformed and the beliefs and narratives remain, people will inevitably recreate new structural arrangements to reinforce the continuing belief. If, on the other hand, the legacy is addressed—the myth debunked or the prejudice reduced (never completely eradicated)—but the institutional and policy arrangements that were constructed to support that legacy are not at the same time undone, then the self-vindicating apparatus of the structural arrangements will invariably cause the legacy belief to resurface. This will require long-term, concerted, and coordinated efforts.

Identifying the Connections between Legacy and Aftermath

How would a group go about identifying a connected pattern of legacy and aftermath that they might work on in an effort to heal historic harms? (See Table 2.1.) The following is a proposed set of questions that might support the inquiry.

Is there hope for mitigating these impacts, or must our history continue to control us? If trauma-based stories that act as limitations on the perceived range of action and

TABLE 2.1:   Identifying the Connection between Legacy and Aftermath

- **Step 1:** Identify an area of community experience that differs by group (that is, land ownership, wealth, justice/law enforcement, health indicators, child-rearing practices, and so on). Equity is an important concept in this exploration: Are there aspects of community life for which identity is a predictor of success or failure?

- **Step 2:** Ask whether there are cultural/biological characteristics of either (or both) group(s) to explain differential experiences.

  What, if any, "naturally occurring" aspect of each group explains the differential experience?

  With regard to the "cultural" differences, are these adaptations to multiple wounding or authentic cultural transcendences? (Although this is virtually impossible to determine, allow both imagination and reason based on historical circumstances to guide this exploration.)
  Are those characteristic differences based on myth/prejudice/environmental factors/value differences?

- **Step 3:** Ask why this differential experience has come to be the case—"three why's back".

Consider as an example the rate of suspension and expulsion for black and brown children. The level of suspension for black and brown children has been more than 3.5 times the rates for similarly situated white children for more than 40 years (Children's Defense Fund, 1975; Losen & Skiba, 2010). I am drawing on national statistics, but the same analysis could be done at the local level.

This is, of course, a complicated analysis. It may be the case that there are behaviors in many urban school settings that are culturally specific that result in increased suspensions. Are these behaviors the cause, the result, or both? In any instance, it would not be possible to say that these are "naturally occurring" cultural differences; rather, the behaviors and the interpretation of the behaviors, which is the basis for the sanction.

Why is that? The placement of police and law enforcement officers in schools has increased the likelihood that traditional and predictable behaviors of school-age children will be criminalized.

Why is that (asked about the answer to the previous "why")? Why were officers placed in school in the first place? This was a structural support (aftermath) for the political story (legacy) that urban youths are dangerous. This was narrative embedded inside the "war on drugs" and the "war on crime." Police were also placed in schools because urban parents believed the reports (relation of power) that urban youths were inherently more dangerous. This is reflective of an infiltrated consciousness and the mentacidal delusion that the law enforcement apparatus that was primarily organized for the repression of the black community would, at some point, act to protect their children.

(Continued)

TABLE 2.1:   *(Continued)*

Why is that (asked about the answer to the previous "why")? Why were the war on drugs and the war on crime ever initiated? These were political strategies that constructed counternarratives to push back against the prevailing counternarrative of racial equality that was developing as a result of civil-rights-era advances. The narratives themselves drew on latent discourse (legacy) about the threatening nature of the "free black." These narratives precede emancipation. This is an example of where the structural issues were addressed (emancipation and civil rights), but because the legacy issues were not dealt with, new structures are now emerging to reproduce the old beliefs. This confirms the Foucaldian notion that you cannot understand the systems by analyzing the systems themselves; rather; we must understand the relations of power that are the basis of the systemic structure.

Certainly, this analysis is much more complex, yet this is an example of how to begin the analysis for purposes of societal transformation.

• **Step 4:** If the difference is not naturally occurring but culturally predictable, how is the difference maintained? An excellent resource to help think about this is Jones (2000).

Institutionalized—Are there policies, practices, and systems that maintain the disparate experience?

Institutional—The zero tolerance policies for violence give teachers and administrators the discretion to interpret behaviors, and based on the interpretation students can be suspended or expelled for "violent" acts. Interpretations such as "defiance," "disrespect," "failure to comply" are not able to be challenged even though they are not facts but rather interpretations.

Personally mediated—Are there beliefs, biases, prejudices, or myths contained in certain relations of power that perpetuate the disparate experiences?

Personally mediated—The interpretations that are the basis for discretionary suspensions are embedded in the teachers' and administrators' mental map through the larger societal discourse of urban youths of color as threatening, disrespectful, and "super-predatory."

(Continued)

TABLE 2.1:   *(Continued)*

Internalized—Are there beliefs, biases, prejudices, and myths (internalized oppressions and powerlessness) held by those who are negatively affected by systems that result in either acquiescence to the disparity or even perpetuation, support, and justification of the disparity-producing systems? What were the experiences/conditions that existed that made these reasonable responses? What aspects of those conditions are still present? Are there alternative narratives that could be used to respond in the same circumstances?	**Internalized (Infiltrated Consciousness)**—Many youths of color have embraced the societal images and act in ways that reinforce the narrative of urban youths as violent, unconcerned about education, and disregarding of authority, especially in systems like school and church that have seemingly abandoned the cause of urban youths of color.
Considering the beliefs and values that are embedded in the legacy/myth/prejudice, where else are those beliefs and values systematically and institutionally reinforced (look for interrelated systems and practices)?	
Strategy—To establish strategies to transform this circumstance, there must be structural changes that are connected to the process of creating a counternarrative to address the relations of power that give the system a sense of logic.	For instance, a campaign that claims "uneducated children are our greatest danger" would support structural changes that resist suspension and expulsion and directly take on the narrative of the dangerous and defiant child.

agency are learned, rehearsed, and performed mostly in the early youth and formative years before we are even verbally communicative; if the process of becoming a competent adult includes knowing, reciting, accepting, and acting in accordance with the stories (Mehl-Madrona, 2010, pp. 76–77); and if the institutions that we confront as members of a society include the embedded values and principles of the stories that have become second nature, is there any real hope of counteracting or impeding the impact? To further complicate the question, if the stories were crafted in support of or in response to traumagenic conditions, and if they have been in circulation for so long that there are few, if any, people still alive who remember the pretrauma values and beliefs were, how is trauma interrupted? The answer is in the creation of counternarratives and the telling of stories that invoke a competing (and more desirable) value set.

To fully resolve the individual and the collective impacts that historical traumas have had on the physical, mental, emotional, economic, communal, and organizational lives of victims and their descendants, perpetrators and their descendants, and bystanders and their descendants, it is essential that history be told in all of its dimensions; that unresolved emotional and psychological wounding be unveiled and healed; that connections be drawn between the individual lives and collective experiences of each group (victim, perpetrator, and bystander); and that collective action be taken to undo the lingering vestiges of systems designed to perpetuate the trauma (Hooker & Czjai-kowski, 2012).

What indigenous healers have known for generations, what Pinderhughes (1989) argued, and what mainstream Western mental health professionals and political activists are discovering, is that there is nothing but the story. So-called bad people are living out and rehearsing stories, and their actions are being interpreted and given meaning within the framework of narratives about that "type" of people. Institutions are the systematic carriers of societies' stories, good and bad. In order to get people to question the appropriateness of institutional arrangements and to unveil the hidden values in stories, people need to be presented with counternarratives. Mehl-Madrona (2010) described the potential operation of counternarratives by stating that "within society, counter-narratives that rebel against destructive conventional concepts like racism or the oppression of women . . . are agents of social evolution" (p. 67).

The development of a healing counternarrative is a community-building model, not an individual therapeutic practice. In a subsequent article, I delineate a community empowerment/engagement and training strategy to incorporate the model as presented in this framework. The proposed strategy incorporates conversation, somatic engagement, ritual practices, and social justice practices and principles. There are also specific methods of inquiry to identify and connect the interconnected network of legacy and aftermath that operate in a particular community and serve as the invisible and unconscious power constraints in relationships among various people, particularly mainstream and marginalized populations of all stripes. In a later chapter in this volume, Vanessa Jackson counsels that the first question to ask in any community when applying these strategies is this: "Are you (is your community) ready to be healed?" If the answer for even a small number, "a critical yeast" (Lederach & Lederach, 2010), is "yes," then the difficult and long-term work is worth pursuing.

CONCLUSION

In traumagenic circumstances, where individual and community capacities to respond to threatening and injurious conditions have been overwhelmed, it is often the case that the range of action options is perceived as limited. Power is manifest in the resulting relationships and societal arrangements. The limitations established as the trauma-based range of available options for action get transmitted from one generation to the next through legacy and aftermath. Over time, the societal arrangements produced and reproduced by legacy and aftermath are seen as normal, natural, and even appropriate. As a result, generations of people who never directly experienced the traumagenic conditions perpetuate the trauma simply by acting within the range of options presented to them by the earlier generations. The signs, symbols, and structures in society as well as the background discourse will continue to perpetuate the trauma-based beliefs and behaviors unless they can be investigated, deconstructed, and challenged through the creation of powerful counternarratives. With this understanding, practitioners and scholars can conduct "re-story-action." Deconstructing legacy and dismantling the related aftermath in favor of equity and justice shifts relations of power in ways that transform the mechanisms of power that have transmitted trauma for multiple generations.

REFERENCES

Alexander, J. C. (2012). *Trauma: A social theory.* Malden, MA: Polity Press.

Atkinson, J. (2002). *Trauma trails: Recreating song lines: The transsgenerational effects of trauma in indigenous Australia.* North Melbourne, Australia: Spinifex Press.

Austin, J. L. (1962). *How to do things with words* (2nd ed.). Cambridge, MA: Harvard University Press.

Brave Heart, M.Y.H. (2001). *Welcome to Takini's historical trauma.* Retrieved from http://www.historicaltrauma.com/

Bruner, J. (1987). Life as narrative. *Social Research, 54*(1), 11–32.

Butler, J. (1997). *The psychic life of power: Theories in subjection.* Stanford, CA: Stanford University Press.

Cabrera, M. (2001). *Living and surviving in a multiply wounded country.* Retrieved from http://www.medico.de/download/report26/ps_cabrera_en.pdf

Children's Defense Fund. (1975). *School suspensions: Are they helping children?* Cambridge, MA: Washington Research Project.

Danieli, Y. (Ed.). (1998). Introduction. In *The international handbook of multigenerational legacies of trauma* (pp. 1–18). New York: Plenum Press.

Foucault, M. (1980). Power/knowledge. New York: Pantheon Books.

Foucault, M. (1994). *Power* (J. D. Faubion, Ed., & R. Hurley, Trans.). New York: New Press.

Foucault, M. (2001). *Power: The essential works of Michel Foucault 1954–1984* (Vol. 3). New York: New Press.

Freedman, J., & Combs, G. (1996). *Narrative therapy: The social construction of preferred realities.* New York: W. W. Norton.

Hooker, D. A., & Czjaikowski, A. P. (2012). *Transforming historical harms.* Harrisonburg, PA: Eastern Menoninte University.

Jones, C. P. (2000). Levels of racism: A theoretical framework and a gardener's tale. *American Journal of Public Health, 90,* 1212–1215.

Lederach, J. P., & Lederach, J. (2010). *When blood and bones cry out: Journey through the soundscape of healing and reconciliation.* Oxford, UK: Oxford University Press.

Levine, P. A., & Frederick, A. (1997). *Waking the tiger: Healing trauma.* Berkeley, CA: North Atlantic Books.

Losen, D., & Skiba, R. (2010). *Suspended education: Urban middle schools in crisis.* Montgomery, AL: Southern Poverty Law Center.

Mehl-Madrona, L. (2007). *Narrative medicine: The use of history and story in the healing process.* Rochester, VT: Bear & Company.

Mehl-Madrona, L. (2010). *Healing the mind through the power of story: The promise of narrative psychiatry.* Rochester, VT: Bear & Company.

Monk, G., Winslade, J., Crocket, K., & Epston, D. (Eds.). (1997). *Narrative therapy in practice: The archeology of hope.* San Francisco: Jossey-Bass.

Pinderhughes, E. (1989). *Understanding race, ethnicity and power: The key to efficacy in clinical practice.* New York: Free Press.

Rhodes-Pitts, S. (2014, October 9). *The worth of black men, from slavery to Ferguson.* Retrieved from http://www.nytimes.com/2014/10/12/magazine/the-worth-of-black-men-from-slavery-to-ferguson.html?module=Search&mabReward=relbias%3Ar%2C%7B%222%22%3A%22RI%3A13%22%7D&_r=0

Smedley, A., & Smedley, B. D. (2005). Race as biology is fiction, racism as a social problem is real: Anthropological and historical perspectives on the social construction of race. *American Psychologist, 60,* 16–26.

White, M., & Epston, D. (1991). *Narrative means to therapeutic ends.* New York: W. W. Norton.

3

Racial Shaming and Humiliation: Tools of Oppressive Power

Vanessa McAdams-Mahmoud

When a therapist treats people who have a history of being oppressed, the therapist should understand how methods of cultural or racial shaming and humiliation act as oppressive psychological tools. People in power who wish to hold on to power may use these psychological tools to control and manipulate others. This is as true in the dyads of personal relationships as it is between large groups of people. When an abuser seeks to control a victim, he or she will often shame the victim through verbal abuse (name calling, swearing, yelling), emotional abuse, and actions that which disrespect and devalue, before proceeding to violence. This is also true in large groups. Propaganda campaigns that dehumanize a targeted other via name calling, stereotyping, vilification, and increasingly aggressive acts, precede violence and war, and in particular, wars of genocide. The way in which the targeted other is perceived can become a matter of life and death and not simply a matter of spoken petty prejudices or bigotry.

Our human struggle for dignity and a sense of personal power over our lives correlates with our feelings of self-worth and meaningful living. Therapists are aware of how feelings of shame can anchor and exacerbate traumatic experiences in painful, persistent ways. Therapy with people who are survivors of deliberate and persistent physical, sexual, and emotional abuse, involves assisting the individual to tolerate and eventually reduce lower the distress that is triggered by the memories of abuse. These memories are so unpleasant that people will strongly avoid and suppress them. This avoidance, typical of those who have been traumatized, may also mute or suppress verbalization of the experience.

One of the primary feelings associated with abuse is shame. Repression, denial, and avoidance are common defense mechanisms used to avoid unpleasant, traumatic memories. These defense mechanisms are largely unconscious. Often, the shame a person feels is invisible to others and may remain unnamed. Consciously, the individual will sometimes behave as if nothing is wrong and that he or she is not bothered by the shaming event. Some people block the memories of the event. The more shame provoking the event, the less the person wants to discuss it.

Shame has the ability to silence, diminish, and inhibit speech about the triggering event. Fossum and Mason (1986) stated that "people are reluctant to speak directly of feeling ashamed, since to acknowledge shame is (in their eyes) to admit that there is something of which to be ashamed" (p. 5). In addition, ego psychology theorizes that because shame is first felt at a preverbal developmental age, memories associated with feelings of shame are more likely to remain unspoken, unaddressed, and unhealed.

When working with survivors of trauma, therapists may find that a survivor may more easily discuss feelings of guilt. Developmentally, guilt is an older feeling. Shame involves a feeling of helplessness, and an inability to act, in the face of victimization, oppression, or persecution. Unconsciously, the therapist may be tempted to collude with the survivor and talk only about guilt, without listening for and facilitating exploration of feelings of shame. Discussions of shaming events can elicit feelings of mutual embarrassment in the therapeutic dyad. This is akin to watching people embarrass themselves in public, or witnessing someone being embarrassed and humiliated, and wanting to avert one's eyes in order to avoid the display.

We all need a healthy sense of shame, at least enough to understand and appreciate the value of humility. Shame assists us with keeping a realistic check on our egos and prompts us to empathize with others who may be suffering. However, an overabundance of shame is emotionally crippling and toxic to an individual's healthy sense of self-worth.

CULTURAL AND RACIAL SHAMING

The systematic cultural and racial shaming of a group of people is never an accident. Deliberate distortion, dehumanization, and debasement of other human groups are patterned tactics of abusive power. Name calling; distorting history; exaggerating cultural or racial flaws; or lying about the group's history, beliefs, and values are all in service of justifying abuse, ignoring human rights, and depriving the targeted group of property and life. These microaggressions and overt abuses are experienced by members of the targeted group in disparate ways. Some individuals are used as examples and publicly shamed and abused as object lessons to other members. Others may be favored, but only if they betray members of their own group, and others may be privileged to experience little discrimination. The side effect of persistent, long-lasting exposure to patterned racial or cultural shaming is the creation of a defensive culture that may be shame bound. As Fossum and Mason (1986) wrote,

> A shame-bound [culture] is a [culture] with a self-sustaining, multigenerational system of interaction with powerful others who are loyal to a set of rules and

world views that demanded control, absolute obedience, that emphasized blame and denial. This pattern over time inhibits or defeats the development of authentic intimate relationships, promotes secrets and vague personal boundaries, unconsciously instills shame in family members, as well as chaos in their lives and binds them to perpetuate the shame in themselves and their kin. It does so regardless of the good intentions, wishes and love which may also be part of the system. (p. 8)

The desired result of the deliberate practice of cultural and racial shaming is to induce in members of the targeted group what Fossum and Mason (1986) have called the toxic effects of chronic shame, or "an inner sense of being completely diminished or insufficient as a person . . . Self-judging the self . . . A pervasive sense of shame . . . the ongoing premise that one is fundamentally bad, inadequate, defective, unworthy or not fully valid as a human being" (p. 49).

In societies where there is widespread negative racial or ethnic stereotyping, discrimination, and prejudice, feelings of persecution, resentment, and memories of humiliation permeate members of the targeted group. These feelings will also foment a desire to exact revenge on the persecutors through rebellion and social revolution.

Harrell (2000) suggested that there were at least six types of racism-related stress that have the potential to affect the well-being of the individual.

- Racism-related life events (discrimination, racist taunts)
- Vicarious racism experiences (observing another become the victim of racism)
- Daily racism microstressors (for example, being followed around in a store)
- Chronic contextual stress from racism (being the only person of color in a racially charged social environment)
- Collective experiences of racism (the knowledge of the experiences of friends and colleagues)
- Transgenerational transmitted stress from racism (familial and historical experiences of racism) (pp. 46–47)

Systems and cultures that enslave or oppress other human beings often keep targeted individuals naked, cold, hungry, thirsty, dirty, ignorant, disoriented, or separated from familiar people. Laws or cultural shaming may be used to restrict language. Rebellion in even subtle forms is severely punished. Ethnic names may be taken away or changed, and numbers or nicknames substituted. These techniques are designed to induce shame and humiliation and to minimize personhood. The goal of these tactics is to make the person feel like a thing rather than a human being.

Racist abuse can include acts of discrimination and scapegoating. It can also consist of race baiting and provocative acts by people in power. It can consist of shunning and ostracizing, racial segregation/apartheid, and social isolation. Racist abuse can also consist of poisoning, abduction, drowning, murder, rape, lynching, and beatings. It can also include entrapment, tricking, or betrayal. At its worst, cultural and racial abuse can become genocidal.

The dynamics of large-group cultural and racial shaming have another component. This component enlists as many people in the favored group as possible and induces them to believe in the targeted groups' inferiority. The most extreme form of this is pre-genocidal propaganda. Pre-genocidal beliefs include notions of the others' debased humanity; falsified and distorted history; and the belief that the targeted group is unworthy of justice, respect, or dignified treatment. At the height of genocide, those in power believe that the victim deserves any negative treatment they receive, including the loss of their lives.

Dr. Gregory Stanton (2013) suggested that there are 10 stages of genocide. His paper is used by human rights groups internationally and as the basis of the group, The International Alliance to End Genocide. The stages are:

1. Classification: Society is divided into us versus them.
2. Symbolization: Symbols may be forced onto groups to further target them.
3. Discrimination: Law, custom, and political power are used to deny the rights of other groups.
4. Dehumanization: Overcomes the normal revulsion against murder.
5. Organization: Genocide is always organized, usually by the state, often using independent militias to provide deniability of state responsibility.
6. Polarization: Extremists drive the groups apart.
7. Preparation: The populace is indoctrinated with fear of the victim group. Leaders often claim that "if we don't kill them, they will kill us." Special army units or militias are often trained and armed.
8. Persecution: Victims are identified and separated out because of their ethnic or religious identity. Death lists are drawn up.
9. Extermination: The mass killing legally called "genocide." It is "extermination" to the killers because they do not believe their victims to be fully human.
10. Denial: The killers deny that they committed any crimes and often blame what happened on the victims.

What is the role of the therapist when treating a person who has been targeted for such treatment? Some may say that this is a rather academic question, because we no longer are in the era of the Nazis or Fascists. How often would we encounter such individuals, either those in the favored group that has swallowed such propaganda whole or those who have survived dehumanizing treatment at the hands of the state—or powerful other—in our daily therapeutic practice?

In the course of my own practice, over the years, I have encountered such individuals with increasing frequency. These individuals include men and women of color who are felons, convicted unfairly and imprisoned unjustly; refugees who have survived state-sponsored torture from countries like Burundi, Somalia, Liberia, Iraq, and Afghanistan; veterans who helped to build prisons that were used to torture human beings; members of militia groups who believe that a race war is imminent, and long for its beginning; and women who escaped abuse, poverty, and racism and joined the military, only to be sexually victimized by powerful others, who were too often protected from prosecution.

Other potential targets of systematic shaming are men and women of color who have been targeted for workplace discrimination and unfair treatment as a result of corporate raiding or politically based downsizing, women who have been sexually harassed for being in jobs that have traditionally been held by men, people who have been misinformed about the environmental dangers of their jobs and have contracted chronic illnesses, and union members who have been targeted for persecution in attempts to break their union and their resistance to oppression.

When we begin to cross into the public practices of discrimination, we also cross into the realm of humiliation.

HUMILIATION AS A TOOL OF OPPRESSION

Hartling, Rosen, Walker, and Jordan (2000) have closely examined shame and humiliation in an attempt to understand the differences and similarities between the two feelings. They consider both of these to belong to the domain of self-conscious emotions. They state that "shame is a felt sense of *being* unworthy of connection, and humiliation might be thought of as a feeling associated with being *made to feel* unworthy of connection" (p. 3). Humiliation describes an intensification of shame due to conscious awareness of the fact that someone else has actually witnessed one's public shaming. In a similar vein, Trumbull (2003) conceptualized shame as a stressful reaction to a disavowed image of oneself as seen through the gaze of another. Shame is a feeling that is triggered when one imagines oneself as compromised in another person's eyes. This subtle nuance is important to understand because it informs us how victims of torture and racist discrimination and abuse internalize the humiliating treatment to which they are subjected by the perpetrator.

Humiliation is felt because one has been shamed and others have witnessed the shaming act. It has a public stage. It is damage viewed as being unjustly inflicted on us by others. In families that have high levels of shame-based behaviors, the practice of scapegoating a family member, targeting them for ridicule, rejection, and humiliating treatment is a way of deflecting onto one individual the fault and blame for family dysfunction. It is always to the advantage of "the dominant group to attempt to persuade the subordinate group that they are deserving of shame, that they are responsible for the damage they have brought upon themselves [and] to blame them for some deficiency or supposed inferiority" (Hartling et al., 2000, p. 3).

The public practice of targeting groups for culturally based or racial humiliation is exemplified by the stage in pre-genocidal societies described by Stanton (2013) as persecution:

> Victims are identified and separated out because of their ethnic or religious identity. Death lists are drawn up. In state sponsored genocide, members of victim groups may be forced to wear identifying symbols. Their property is often expropriated. Sometimes they are even segregated into ghettoes, deported into concentration camps, or confined to a famine-struck region and starved. They

are deliberately deprived of resources such as water or food in order to slowly destroy them. Programs are implemented to prevent procreation through forced sterilization or abortions. Children are forcibly taken from their parents. The victim group's basic human rights become systematically abused through extra-judicial killings, torture and forced displacement. Genocidal massacres begin. . . . They realize that the international community will again be bystanders and permit another genocide. (p. 1)

Du Bois (1903) talked about the experience of racial humiliation and the double-consciousness it engendered in the African American. He described the experience of double-consciousness in this way. A black man sees himself in:

a world which yields him no true self-consciousness, but only lets him see him-self through the revelation of the other world. It is a peculiar sensation, this double-consciousness, this sense of always looking at one's self through the eyes of others, of measuring one's soul by the tape of a world that looks on in amused contempt and pity. One ever feels his two-ness,—an American, a Negro; two souls, two thoughts, two unreconciled strivings; two warring ideals in one dark body, whose dogged strength alone keeps it from being torn asunder. (p. 3)

During the enslavement of Africans in the Americas, the public whipping and physi-cal humiliation of a targeted person, witnessed by other enslaved people, was a way of con-trolling and subduing the oppressed population. Later, during Reconstruction, the public exercise of white supremacist terrorism was expressed by public lynchings and castration.

When someone is punished as an example or made an example, it is to inhibit the behavior of others who are seen as belonging to the same group as the person being humil-iated. Thus, it is not only the selected individual who is punished but also, by proxy, the larger group. Torture techniques tend to work because they convert the acts perpetrated by the torturer into a deep internally held sense of humiliation and loss of self within the tortured. The feelings of shame and humiliation that are invoked produce a silencing, so that often victims of torture are unable to verbally describe their experiences. Shapiro (2003) has also noted, "Shame is a major psychological issue for survivors of torture." He described a picture of a soldier involved in the torture of prisoners in Abu Ghraib:

Lynndie England's eyes seem sicklied o'er with indifference and ignorance. Lynndie and other American soldiers piled up Iraqi prisoners, nude and played games with them. Lynndie posed, smiling, beside the stacked up humiliated prisoners. . . . Imagine standing in the presence of someone whose eyes refuse to soften toward you, whose eyes refuse to sympathize or to recognize your humanity. And you are humiliated not just by the physical injuries committed against you, or the deprivations; you are humiliated by the refusal, evident in the aggressor's eyes, to see you as sympathetic, to see you as a worthy, equal subject. These eyes disenfranchise and eject the other from a sanctuary or estate—a birthright—that some people call 'the kingdom of God' Such contempt is an intensely negative emotion, regarding a person or group of people as inferior, base, or worthless—it is similar to scorn. It is also used when people are being sarcastic. Contempt is also defined as the state of being despised or dishonored. (p. 1133)

In the book *Contempt and Pity*, Scott (1997) said,

I call it the "Jim Crow gaze." The eyes of a white person, a white supremacist, a bigot, living in a state of apartheid, looking at a black person . . . this intolerant gaze contains coldness, deadness, and non-recognition. This gaze doesn't see a person; it sees a scab, an offense, a spot of absence. Nothing in the face giving a Jim Crow gaze will acknowledge the humanity, likeability or forgiveablity of what it sees. (p. 33)

Public humiliation and character assassination have been used in recent years in the media, in the service of particular political agendas. They have been used against prominent men and women in politics and entertainment. Cyberbullying is the most recent form of using media to humiliate. Public humiliation of certain celebrities has been used to persecute those who seem to have gained too much popular attention in the broader society.

Lynching is a practice that exemplified this method. Lynching was not an aberration in American race relations. Rather, it served as an extreme reminder of the unreasoning power the basest passions, fears, and hatreds of white Americans could exercise over the lives and humanity of black Americans. For "the ultimate goal of lynchers," as Ralph Ellison reflected in *Going to the Territory* (1986), "is that of achieving ritual purification through destroying the lynchers' identification with the basic humanity of their victims. Hence their deafness to cries of pain, their stoniness before the sight and stench of burning flesh" (p. 178). At issue, then, in historical terms and the imaginative terms of African American literature, is lynching's ritual capacity to define and annihilate the humanity of the black victim and that of every last member of his or her race, symbolically or, if necessary, literally (Zangrando, 1980).

When this cultural or racial humiliation is patterned and persistent, resentment and rage will permeate members of the targeted group. These feelings foment the desire to exact revenge on the persecutors through rebellion and social revolution.

Lindner, one of the leading scholars interested in human dignity and humiliation studies defined humiliation as "the enforced lowering of a person or group, a process of subjugation that damages or strips away their pride, honor or dignity" (Lindner, 2007, p. 5). She further explained the experience of being humiliated as "being placed against your will in a situation that is greatly inferior to what you feel you should expect. It involves demeaning treatment that transgresses established expectations. You are forced, pinned into a position of helplessness and passivity" (Lindner, 2007, p. 5). Cultural and racial humiliation often involves police, the military, unauthorized militia, or mobs. Individuals who have had more police contact also report more trauma and anxiety in direct proportion to the number of encounters, their intrusiveness, and the level of fair treatment (Geller, Fagan, Tyler, & Link, 2014). Lindner (2007) asserted that humiliation is not ahistorical but rather is a "historical-cultural-social emotional construct that changes over time" (p. 5).

THERAPEUTIC INTERVENTIONS

People who come from societies that perpetrate systemic oppression may have suffered physical, verbal, sexual abuse, physical torture, maltreatment, imprisonment, forced labor, and sexual trafficking. In my practice, I have worked with people who have suffered some of these experiences. They have come from India, Malaysia, Pakistan, Rwanda, Mexico, Somalia, Afghanistan, Sudan, and Liberia. They also have come from Mississippi, Georgia, South Carolina, California, and Washington, DC.

Experiencing empowerment and dignity is opposite to experiencing shaming and humiliation. Our human struggle for dignity and a sense of personal power over our lives correlate with our feelings of self-worth and meaningful living.

If pride is the opposite of shame, then human dignity is the opposite of humiliation. When working with survivors of racial discrimination, shaming, abuse, and humiliation, the therapist must help the individual move toward healthy, realistic pride in self, strategic rebellion against oppression, and the reclamation of human dignity.

Elaine Pinderhughes (1989) has said that:

> this necessary shift in power that must occur in successful intervention means that there is a change in clients' perceptions of themselves as victims and without power. They no longer feel powerless nor do they collude in their own victimization or the denigration of their cultural group by aggrandizing the helper and/ or the helper's cultural group. Successful intervention means that clients can now see themselves as persons of power who belong to a group that has value and can behave in ways that aim to change their powerless status, including acquiring the resources necessary to cope with this reality. For practitioners this means their powerful role as experts, teachers, therapists has changed as has their dominant cultural group status. (p. 138)

As most therapists know, in working with survivors of trauma, the therapist must help to create a safe "holding environment" that has clear boundaries and is respectful of the individual's pacing and level of desire for healing. No matter how threatening or painful the therapist finds the individual's story of racial bias, discrimination, harassment, or abuse, the therapist must be willing to believe and understand the individual's point of view and to stand with them in facing humiliating and shame-provoking memories. A therapist who minimizes the role of racism in the individual's life, discounts it, or does not carefully address it as it appears, risks the danger of humiliating the individual further. Colluding with the patient's denial of racism's effect on their daily life does not assist the individual in personal growth.

Pinderhughes (1989) told therapists that "empowering behaviors and non-exploitative stances are more likely to characterize their work when practitioners can explore their reactions and look honestly at themselves and the vulnerabilities they must learn to control" (p. 136). This means that therapists, whether they belong to an oppressed group or a more powerful group, must be aware of what they bring to the psychotherapeutic encounter. They need to have a realistic sense of how they might be perceived because of their ethnic or racial group identification, personal biases, and blind spots.

Although existential freedom and psychic liberation are of primal importance in healing, a therapist should also be able and willing to stand with the struggling individual in their quest for economic and social justice. Helping a person wage practical fights to restore individual civil rights, assisting through court cases, strategizing and role playing new assertiveness skills, and exploring new neighborhoods and careers are part of healing, transformation, and empowerment.

Psychological liberation from systemic oppression and discrimination cannot be accomplished by a single set of interventions with a psychotherapist. On the macrosystemic level, the phenomena of the Truth and Reconciliation Hearings of South Africa (1996), in a court-like setting that was televised throughout the country, allowed perpetrators of violence and torture to admit to and begin to make amends for their participation in violent acts of oppression in exchange for amnesty. Although the hearings did not heal all of the dramatic systemic racial disparities within that country, they contributed to the peaceful transition of the government to a postapartheid status.

People who have been subject to humiliating multiple acts of racist behavior, subtle or gross, are often left with the feelings of a loss of self. They doubt their perceptions of themselves and are sometimes wounded deeply in their sense of self. Healing in the psychotherapist's office must be paired with practical life successes and positive experiences while facing personal fears in everyday life.

Although groups may be targeted for humiliation and oppression, the suffering brought about by this treatment is felt individually and is usually healed in individual ways. We should be able to recognize healing as it progresses.

It is a sign of health when the individual resists oppression and dehumanizing treatment. The individual can risk becoming like the oppressor when they go beyond gaining freedom and seek pleasure only in exacting revenge rather than seeking justice. Resisting destructive revenge involves the true maturation of the personality and is the very thin line between barbarism and civilization. A rare example of deliberate planning for large-group healing and empowerment is the example of South Africa.

The truth and reconciliation process is a type of deliberate, reparative justice on the macrosystemic level. Psychotherapy may be used to assist the healing of a survivor of racial abuse by facilitating the process of addressing the humiliation and pain suffered at the hands of a tyrant or predatory process. It involves truth telling about the humiliating experiences to self and to at least one other. The individual is helped to gradually articulate and acknowledge awareness of the evil done; the nature of the predator; and the extent of the psychic, emotional, and physical damage. The conversations about the meaning of the abuse are the most important the therapist will have with the client. How the individual makes meaning of trauma is not always logical, rational, or functional. However, the articulation of personal meaning helps to crystallize and focus the therapeutic process.

It may be helpful for therapists to review the list of therapeutic stances and interventions I have found helpful to use with those who are attempting to heal from racial humiliation and shaming.

1. Through rage, grief, and suffering, the individual tells their truth in therapy, with the skilled therapist as witness and ally.
2. As therapists, we affirm our belief in the experience of the oppressed.
3. We collaborate and act as allies in the mutual exploration of the historical, cultural, social, and emotional context that surrounded the shaming and humiliating experiences.
4. We help the individual to discuss their rage in detail, including their fantasies of revenge.
5. We help the individual to describe and cognitively process what has happened to them in detail, until it begins to lose some of its traumatizing power (that is, eye movement desensitization and reprocessing, prolonged exposure therapy, cognitive processing therapy, image rehearsal therapy, and forms of gestalt dream interpretation or guided imagery).
6. We help the individual to tell their experience to at least one loving significant other in detail and with meaning.
7. We assist the individual in identifying what shames them the most, what they feel guilty about, and what makes them proud about surviving their experience.
8. We assist the individual in the retelling of their experience in a way that reinforces their strengths, creative powers, intelligence, endurance, stubbornness, integrity, wisdom, and determination. We help the individual formulate a statement that encapsulates and gives positive meaning to their survival (I never gave in, I fought as hard as I could for what was right, I stood up and told the truth, and so on).
9. When working with a group, we might incorporate culturally normative behaviors as part of the rituals for healing (for example, having tea, handcrafts, homemade snacks, music, storytelling). This practice can serve as a bridge from humiliation back to dignity.
10. We encourage and strategize active resistance and positive social activism against conditions that led to the oppressive acts, if the individual wishes to engage in such work.
11. We might have the individual record, write or draw, compose music, and so on, helping them to create a positive product based on what they have learned from their worst experiences.

At the end of this process, I have found that the result is a sense of healing, wholeness, and completeness that the individual did not experience before.

THERAPY STORY

Sara was the darkest skinned child born to a Puerto Rican woman and African American man. Her father, who had been in the military, was killed in a motorcycle accident when she was a baby. Sara was told that because her father had no insurance, his care was delayed at a local hospital. Her mother believed that he would have lived if he had received timely care. After his death, Sara's mother, Grace, moved back to her mother's home. In her grief, Grace slipped deeper into depression and alcohol abuse. She eventually was told to leave her mother's home because of her behavior and her inability to contribute to the household. Grace left Sara in her family's care and left the home to seek work. She would hold odd jobs from time to time but never successfully recovered from her depression. She died from pneumonia early in Sara's sixth year.

Sara remained in her grandparent's home. There were six other children in the home, most of whom were her first cousins. She was the only girl. She was darker than any of her cousins, and she was often teased and called names. She was beaten and locked in a closet. She was kept from going to school and made to do housework instead. Later, she became the object of sexual abuse at the hands of her cousins, who continued to call her "nigger" and intimidate her. She told her grandmother, who beat her and told her never to make such accusations again.

Sara left home as soon as she could and married an older Irish American man. She got a job at an electric power company as one of the first female linemen. The white men resented her on her job. They promptly began to haze her and set her up for failure. She was sexually harassed and taunted and given some of the most dangerous jobs. She became pregnant and worked well into her eighth month of pregnancy. At one point, her coworkers attempted to bury her in dirt when she was sent down in a hole dug for a task they needed to complete. They left her anonymous notes that threatened her or pornographic pictures that depicted black women in sexual positions. At one point, she woke up at her home and saw them rearranging the furniture on her patio in bizarre ways, in their campaign to make her feel unhinged. During this period, her husband quit his job and became very comfortable with her supporting them. He would not do housework. She remembers that, during a time when she was supposed to be on bed rest, he refused to help her, and she had to sit in a chair to cook dinner for him.

The stress from the job and the marriage contributed to the premature birth of her baby. She returned to work but could not tolerate the harassment that began again on her return. Her depression deepened postpartum, and eventually she spent time in an inpatient psychiatric facility.

She had made an ally of a woman who used to work in the office of her current employer and was suing them for sexual harassment. Sara was in awe of this woman and her strength. Her friend, Diana, encouraged her to go talk to someone, to get into counseling. It was at this point that she came into therapy.

If we examine and analyze Sara's story looking for acts of shaming and humiliation, we see multiple occurrences. By the time she entered therapy, she found it difficult to talk, to concentrate. She demonstrated the classic symptoms of posttraumatic stress: hypervigilance, exaggerated startle reflex, avoidance, nightmares, irritability, anxiety, and dysphoria.

Over the course of the next two years, we collaborated to assist her to:

- Tell her story in great detail (recording her most traumatic events via digital recorder and in writing); revisit the most traumatic events multiple times via

> prolonged imaginal exposure; and decrease level of distress, shame, and humiliation triggered by memories.

- Discuss the events for which she felt the most shame, guilt, and humiliation. Discuss the conclusions she has made about why these traumatic events happened to her. What does it mean to her that these events have occurred? What does she think about herself since she experienced these events?
- Discuss the events that gave her pride and times when she kept her dignity as intact as she could manage.
- Plot resistance. Assist her to fight back in assertive, effective ways (legal, verbal, research, alliance, self-advocacy). Assist her in making decisions about whether to sue and seek redress for her grievances and whether to divorce.
- Frame her struggle as an exercise in empowerment to understand some of the themes and realities she was fighting against; for example, racism, internalized racism, sexism, poverty, abuse, the role of history, culture and ethnic differences.
- Engage in acts of political activism, protest, and citizenship.
- Use cultural strengths in the service of healing (belief system, place of worship, spirituality, music, dance, cooking, and so on).

For many survivors of systemic oppression, their experiences are nested in families where there is internalized oppression and abuse. I think of this dynamic as "nested oppression." This fact complicates and slows the process of healing. The challenge for the therapist is often to help the client to see the interlocking nature of the types of oppression that are present in her life by encouraging greater awareness and self-analysis in both intrapsychic and politico-historical ways. However, the search for the meaning of the experiences to the individual is at first tentative or nonexistent. As therapy progresses, the meaning of those experiences should become richer and more fully describable to the individual.

The end of therapy results in a greater sense of pride in self for overcoming, struggling with, and resisting those internal and external forces that seek to engender a poisoned, atrophied sense of self-esteem and self-worth. Human dignity and self-respect can grow as a result of this struggle. As a therapist, there is no higher honor than to be a participant–observer in this process.

REFERENCES

Du Bois, W. E. (1903). *The souls of black folk.* Chicago: A. C. McClurg.

Ellison, R. (1986). *Going to the territory.* New York: Random House.

Fossum, M. A., & Mason, M. J. (1986). *Facing shame: Families in recovery.* New York: W. W. Norton.

Geller, A., Fagan, J., Tyler, T., & Link, B. (2014, December). Aggressive policing and the mental health of young urban men. *American Journal of Public Health, 104,* 2321–2327.

Harrell, S. P. (2000). A multidimensional conceptualization of racism-related stress: Implications for the well-being of people of color. *American Journal of Orthopsychiatry, 70*, 42–57.

Hartling, L. M., Rosen, W., Walker, M., & Jordan, J. V. (2000). *Shame and humiliation: From isolation to relational transformation.* Wellesley, MA: Wellesley Centers for Women.

Lindner, E. (2007, March). In times of globalization and human rights: Does humiliation become the most disruptive source. *Journal of Human Dignity and Humiliation Studies, 1*(1). Retrieved from http://www.humiliationstudies.org/documents/evelin/HumiliationandFearinGlobalizingWorldHumanDHSJournal.pdf

Pinderhughes, E. (1989). *Understanding race, ethnicity and power: The key to efficacy in clinical practice.* New York: Free Press.

Scott, D. M. (1997). *Contempt and pity: Social policy and the image of the damaged black psyche.* Chapel Hill: University of North Carolina Press.

Shapiro, D. (2003). The tortured, not the torturers, are ashamed. *Social Research, 70*, 1131–1148.

Stanton, G. (2013). *The 10 stages of genocide.* Retrieved from Genocide Watch Web site: http://genocidewatch.net

Trumbull, D. (2003). Shame: An acute stress response to interpersonal traumatization. *Psychiatry, 63*, 53–64.

Zangrando, R. (1980). *About lynching.* Retrieved from http://www.english.illinois.edu/maps/poets/g_l/lynching/lynching.htm

4

Power-Based Therapy: Transforming Powerlessness into Power

Vanessa Jackson

This chapter examines a model for transforming powerlessness into power in clinical and community work. It explains the dynamics of power as they operate on all levels of human functioning. The multilevel operation of power can create emotional distress and is implicated in power constriction or power wounding for individuals and communities. These dynamics complicate the traditional therapeutic and community processes of diagnoses, problem assessment, and problem solving. The model explains how healing can occur and effective power assumption restored.

This model builds on the work of Pinderhughes (1989), which has guided my clinical practice for over two decades. It was in an Intervention Approaches with Minority Families course where I was first exposed to Pinderhughes's work on power and powerlessness. The course required that I examine my experiences with having and lacking power and expose my own stories about powerlessness and power. I walked away with an understanding of the necessity of engaging individuals in an exploration of power as a tool for understanding dynamics within their selves; their relationships; and their larger social, economic, and political environments. I understood the importance of these conversations in facilitating connections to others as people begin to understand and acknowledge how they have been affected by power and powerlessness. We can become truly visible to each other if we are willing to risk being honest and vulnerable in our discussions of power and how it affects us individually and as communities. In fact, it is my belief that understanding and shifting power dynamics is the only way that we can heal as individuals and as a society.

THE LANGUAGE OF POWER

We are constantly affected by power dynamics as we move through our daily lives, but we are rarely given the language or context to negotiate these dynamics in a conscious manner. Heller (1985) defined power as "the capacity to have some control over the forces that affect one's life, the capacity to produce desired effects in others, and to demonstrate mastery over self as well as nature and other people" (p. 30). Hopps, Pinderhughes, and Shankar (1995) noted that "a sense of power is critical to mental health. Everyone needs it, and everyone strives to acquire it in some way. Powerlessness is painful, and people defend against powerlessness by behavior that can bring them a sense of power" (p. 2). Martín-Baró (1994), reflecting on the work of Max Weber, offered a definition of power as "the disparity of resources that occurs in human relationships and that allows one of the actors to make his or her objectives and social interests prevail over those of other" (p. 61). Starhawk (1987) identified three types of power: power-over, power-from-within, and power-with.

1. Power-over: This is linked to domination and force, which includes the ability to withhold required resources.
2. Power-from-within: This is personal power that celebrates our mastery of tasks and unfolding of abilities. Power-from-within does not even need to be manifested in actions; some of the most amazing examples of power-from-within are attitudes and beliefs that guide an individual.
3. Power-with: This is the power of a strong individual in a group of equals and is manifested in influence. This is the power of collaboration, cooperation, and shared vision. Power-with is premised on trust and mutual support.

Clinical and community work require an understanding of (1) the interactional nature of power and the way it can change dramatically when an individual or group shifts contexts, (2) its various components (over, within, and with), and (3) the importance of a sense of power to the emotional well-being of individuals and communities. Lerner (1986) suggested:

> People are powerless to the extent that they are prevented, either on an individual basis or social basis, from actualizing their human capacities. Real powerlessness refers to the fact that economic, political and social arrangements prevent this actualization from occurring. (p. 23)

Lerner further described "surplus powerlessness," a condition in which:

> human beings contribute to this powerlessness to the extent that their own emotional, intellectual, spiritual makeup prevents them from actualizing possibilities which exist within the context of real powerlessness in ways that might potentially yield more possibilities for them to actualize their Human Essence. (p. 23)

Using the concept of surplus powerlessness in clinical and community work requires caution and must always be used in the context of a clear analysis of the social, economic, and political barriers for an individual or community. Out of context, surplus powerless can result in victim blaming, which creates more psychological wounding. Complicating matters is that "real powerlessness"—as a result of economic, political, or social arrangements—may damage an individual or community's sense of its own efficacy. This results in a stance of surplus powerlessness. In that situation, guiding the client through an exploration of their wounding/constriction—how it happened and how it affects them in the present—can allow for identification of previously obscured areas of power along with functional and liberating strategies for resistance.

A therapeutic or community practice that is grounded in an analysis of power dynamics needs a language to explain the impact of limitations or constriction of power on individuals and communities. This helps inform strategies that restore the sense and expression of power. Explicitly engaging power dynamics creates an opening for therapists to ground their work within a social justice framework, which facilitates an ongoing examination of how larger social, economic, and political forces negatively affect the lives of individuals, families, and communities. The personal is political, and the political—the actions and values of large systems that control necessary resources—is profoundly personal, especially to marginalized populations. Waldegrave (Waldegrave, Tamasese, Tuhaka, & Campbell, 2003) stated, "therapy can be a vehicle for addressing some of the injustices that occur in society. It could be argued that in not choosing to address these issues, therapist may be inadvertently replicating, maintaining, and even furthering, existing injustices" (p. 4). This chapter describes the process I developed for engaging clients around their experiences of power and powerlessness, with a focus on the wounds created by the operation of power in their lives and on strategies for healing.

POWER WOUNDING

As I committed to more explicitly exploring power within my practice, I began to talk with clients about how traumatic events have created a "power wound" that has left them feeling traumatized and compelled to shift vast amounts of their emotional energy to coping with anxiety, depression, hypervigilance, and other symptoms that are consequent to the traumatic experience. I define *power wounding* as an experience (which can be emotional, physical, spiritual, financial, or sexual) and its aftermath that result in significant compromising of an individual, community, or society's ability to function, and specifically to take action, in one's preferred manner. The severity, intensity, or chronic nature of the wounding has a significant impact on the individual's or community's ability to function and heal.

I began to talk with clients about strategies for shifting their energy and their sense of power back to the issues and experiences that formerly had allowed them to experience a feeling of agency and a positive perception of themselves. Use of the term "power wounding" supports such a shift, because it facilitates a perception of and way of talking about the experience that becomes an ongoing process, in contrast to the paralysis, entrapment, and sense of powerlessness that is often set in motion by the notion of trauma. Clients do not view their predicament as fixed and unchangeable. In her book, *Medicine Stories: History, Culture and the Politics of Integrity*, activist and historian Aurora Levins Morales (1998) described this shift in her identification of the challenges involved in recovering from emotional injuries:

> The heart of the challenge is to assimilate the terrible, the unbearable, transforming it into something that can be integrated; something that can nourish us and leaves us with a vision of the world, ourselves, of humanity, that is bigger than the horror. (p. 19)

In contrast to the notion of power wounding, I found that the diagnosis of posttraumatic stress disorder seemed to trap clients into an unchanging identity and rigid stance of passivity, hopelessness, and powerlessness. The focus on trauma also seemed to ignore the external forces, whether it was individual perpetrators or larger systems that colluded in creating the power wound. Perpetuation of low-wage employment, barriers to adequate housing and health care, or oppressive and racist immigration policies are examples of external forces that have a profound impact on individual functioning. Focus on the individual trauma without a simultaneous acknowledgement of the continually victimizing social, economic, and political forces at work can contribute to a condition of surplus powerlessness. This combination can impede the ability to identify and implement collective strategies to change the situations or at least highlight the injurious nature of policies and practices.

Using the language of power wounding invites clients (individuals or communities), along with the clinician or consultant, to begin a dialogue designed to identify how the emotional injury or wound occurred and what keeps it active, while also providing opportunities to imagine and take action on possibilities for healing. Power wounding challenges us to simultaneously attend to the actions or actors that caused the wounding and our responses to the wound. This facilitates a dynamic widening of the clinical lens to include environmental as well as relational triggers to problem behaviors and emotional expression. For example, the use of explicit power language and analysis allowed an African American lesbian client to (1) clearly link her depression and anxiety to the toxic, homophobic workplace environment she felt unable to leave due to economic necessity and (2) to examine her internalization of homophobic attitudes. Such a dilemma constitutes a form of power constriction, externally imposed but internally accepted and acted on.

The term "power constriction" can be used interchangeably with power wounding and may be more acceptable to individuals who find the notion of power wounding threatening. The term "constriction" conjures up a metaphor of a valve that can be adjusted, and it invites individuals and communities to explore the conditions under which the valve allows for maximum flow and expression of power along with the circumstance under which power is severely limited. There is an aspect of externalization (or maybe just visibility) in the discussion of power dynamics that create distance and emotional space, providing opportunity for evaluating the nature of our power interactions and the impact of those interactions on our own functioning and the functioning of others. I will continue to use "power wounding" as the primary term because it does convey the sense of injury and devastation described by many of my clients and the marginalized, enabling individuals and communities who have frequently experienced minimization of their pain and sense of powerlessness. Naming the harm they have experienced in a clear and direct manner is liberating and motivating.

The key to liberation is the ability to have choice. Even if the choice is only in how one views the situation, this can increase the capacity for emotional flexibility. Increased emotional flexibility allows one to consider new options and practice these behaviors, despite the fear and notwithstanding either the internal or the external resistance. Exploration of power constrictions and abuses creates opportunities to break down isolation and shame—which are common experiences when people are locked in an individual and limited view of a problem—and identify collective change strategies that can interrupt their experience of abusive power-over behaviors by others.

The Art of Healing

My knowledge of power and my commitment to social justice, which guide my clinical practice and community work, have led me to embrace the concept of healing as the goal of my work. The Oxford Dictionary (10th ed.; Pearsall, 2002) defines *heal* as: "v. 1. To make healthy or sound again. 2. To correct or put right (an undesirable situation)."

I am struck with how frequently the term "healing" is overshadowed by concepts like assessment, intervention, treatment, and community development. These terms connote things that are done to someone. This language immediately shifts the power to the individual or institution that has been socially or politically sanctioned to engage in these activities. My practice focuses on a relational view of healing as described by Fett (2002), which emerged out of her exploration of healing within the context of enslavement and extended beyond the slaveholders' concept of "soundness" as a standard of health. This relational view emphasizes the importance of community to individual well-being. Individual healing was not possible without the consideration of extended social relationships (such as families or church communities). Traditionally, Black healers have grounded their work in notions of spiritual power, human relationships, and community resourcefulness, thus addressing a wider range of healing needs than slaveholders considered legitimate in the physical healing process. In my work, this requires that I attend to and explicitly invite my clients to examine the health or illness—and, by extension, the sense of power or powerlessness of their social context—and its impact on their gender, ethnicity, race, sexual orientation, and class identities.

My definition of *healed* includes the development of knowledge and skills that allow one to feel that an emotional injury or wound has been resolved and that he or she could reasonably deal with future life challenges with a sense of optimism. Healing indicates that flexibility, hopefulness, a sense of agency, and competency have been restored or established.

THE HEALING QUESTIONS

The three initial Healing Questions were offered to me by Pemina Yellow Bird, an indigenous rights activist, during a discussion of African American and First Nations' communities' experiences in American mental health systems. We were both involved in researching the psychiatric experiences of our respective communities and were enraged and saddened by the horrific abuses experienced by our communities under the guise of treatment. As we discussed the limitations of the medical model of mental health, we wondered about how services grounded in the social, political, economic, and spiritual realities of people of color might affect their recovery from emotional crisis. Yellow Bird shared with me what her tribe referred to as the Magic Questions. Over the years, and in consultation with Yellow Bird, I have expanded the Magic Questions to create the Healing Questions: (1) What happened to you? (2) How does what happened to you affect you now? (3) What do you need to heal?

My immediate thought was, "How different my journey through depression would have been if I had been asked those questions at my initial assessment." It would have allowed for me to explore how I was feeling and identify the experiences that I felt were contributing to my emotional distress. If I had also been asked, "Where do you feel powerless and where do you feel like you still have power?" that would have immediately made me feel more hopeful and would have pointed me firmly in the direction of resolution. My personal experience as a recipient of a psychiatric label and my own use of these diagnostic categories as a guide for treatment pushed me to find a new way of looking at the emotional injuries and pain at the core of emotional distress.

During my research on African American psychiatric history, I encountered many people who had been labeled with inaccurate diagnoses and unsuccessfully treated for years. In addition, they frequently described being silenced or forcibly medicated when they attempted to describe the experiences, such as abuse, poverty, or homophobia, that contributed to their emotional distress. I witnessed many misdiagnoses and episodes of abusive treatment during my work as a mental health legal advocate in a state protection and advocacy program. I wanted to develop a more humane and collaborative process for identifying the cause of emotional distress, which was frequently disabling, and create empowering strategies for supporting clients in living with minimal emotional distress and maximum ability to cope with emotional challenges.

The ideas of powerlessness, healing, and the creation of empowered individuals move beyond the knowledge of social work and psychology to include political science, literature, spirituality, and economics to create a more holistic view of the impact of powerlessness and power in the lives of individuals and communities. At the center of my work is the belief in the power and necessity of storytelling as a tool for data collection, assessment, and, most critically, connection. Powerlessness thrives in environments of isolation, silence, shame, and confusion. I explain to clients that a priority in therapy and community consultations is to identify where the power wounding experience has resulted in a sense of shame. Brown (2004), in her research on women and shame, offers the following definition: "Shame is the intensely painful feeling or experience of believing we are flawed and therefore unworthy of acceptance and belonging" (p. 15).

Although Brown's work focused on women's experiences of shame, I believe that the same dynamics affect men, and possibly more intensely, as patriarchal values and the rigid ideas of masculinity offer little permission for men to express feelings of isolation, vulnerability, or powerlessness. Breaking down the sense of isolation and the view of the problem of being somehow unspeakable allows for the possibility of healing. I was drawn to the work of narrative therapists such as White and Epston (1990), Freedman and Combs (1996), Wingard and Lester (2001), and Waldegrave (Waldegrave et al., 2003) and storytelling traditions reflected in the work of Stone (1996) and Mehl-Madrona (2010) because they privilege the voices and experiences of the people or communities experiencing distress. The power of the clinician or community consultant is in his or her ability to compassionately witness, to be curious, and to invite out new levels of understanding. The client remains in charge of the narrative-sharing the pieces that he or she feels are most central. Over the course of the exchange and with the use of the healing questions, new areas of challenge and possibilities can be identified and addressed.

Underlying the healing questions as a tool for transforming powerlessness into power is the critical need to accurately name the problem, including the external social, political, and economic factors that result in wounding and serve as barriers to healing. The next step is to assess the impact of the wounding experience and to identify the often multiple levels of wounding and impact. This immediately opens up possibilities for healing and resolution as clients are invited to name, explore, express, and be witnessed in the context of supportive relationships (clinical and/or community).

THE POWER OF NAMING

These first four Healing Questions support clients and clinicians in naming their experiences: (1) What happened to you? (2) How does what happened affect you now? (3) What are the external factors (for example, racism, classism, poverty) that create or maintain power wounds in your life? (4) What needs to be healed?

The first step in challenging powerlessness is to name it, to determine how it is affecting individuals and communities, and to identify its vulnerabilities. What are the conditions that undermine a sense of powerlessness, and what are the conditions under which a sense of power is restored?

I expanded Yellow Bird's Magic Questions into the Seven Healing Questions, which serve as the framework for how I understand power wounding and how clients and communities can heal from wounding experiences and prevent or minimize future wounding. The questions guide the naming process and invite clients to name their own experience including the impact of those experiences on current and future functioning (spiritual, emotional, political, and so on). I feel that honoring and expanding the power and the responsibility of the client to name his or her reality is central to the healing process. Limiting the authority of the clinician creates space for clients to learn to value their own wisdom and abilities and increases the likelihood that they will transfer the knowledge gained through the healing of the presenting power constriction to other areas of constriction in their lives. The clinical interaction is viewed primarily as a laboratory for change, practice, and skill building. Throughout my engagement with clients, I remind them of their responsibility for staying in their power and constantly monitor my assumptions and language. I will frequently check to see if an observation fits for the clients and ask them to identify descriptions of problems and solutions that resonate for them.

CASE PRESENTATION

At the beginning of each consultation, I provide clients with the list of the Healing Questions and share with them that these questions will guide how we will engage their presenting concerns. Clients are invited to use the questions in journal writing but are reminded that the answer may evolve over time and that they are not expected to be answered in a single session. I will demonstrate the Healing Questions process through the case of "Serena," who began therapy with me in the early days of my work with the Healing Questions and was, in many ways, a co-creator of the process, along with all of my clients, as I struggled to create equal partnerships and empowering strategies for healing emotional wounds.

Healing from Multiple Wounds

Serena is a 44-year-old heterosexual African American woman living in a large metropolitan community. She is married (second marriage for both Serena and her husband) and raising two late adolescent children from previous relationships. She initially presented with concerns about work-related stress, posttraumatic stress disorder due to prolonged sexual abuse by her male siblings throughout her childhood and adolescence, and emotional and physical abuse by her alcoholic mother. Serena had experienced a psychiatric hospitalization five years before coming to see me and had been given a diagnosis of bipolar disorder. She was on a number of powerful antipsychotic medications, and her life was reduced to sleeping and mustering up enough energy to raise her children and perform her job. She noted that at no time in her previous treatment had the abuse issues been clinically addressed. She was also experiencing hazing and sexual harassment on her job. Serena was very concerned that her psychiatric history would be exposed and that she could lose her job and jeopardize her ability to provide for her children. It was important for her to identify this external constraint on her ability to seek treatment and request any accommodations in the workplace for fear of being discriminated against on the basis of a psychiatric disability.

As we began to explore what happened to Serena, she began to tell her story of being the eldest daughter of an alcoholic mother who verbally and physically abused her and failed to protect Serena from her sexually abusive older brothers. Through our conversations about power and boundary violations, Serena began to see that the harassment and hazing on the job was re-stimulating her childhood wounds and draining her of the energy to focus on healing from her abuse. However, she was very concerned about the economic ramifications of quitting her job and attempted to hang in for an additional five years until she could become vested in the retirement fund. Serena identified the multiple abuses throughout her childhood, continuing hypervigilance, tactile and auditory hallucinations, and a toxic work environment as her primary "wounds."

Serena reported that the abuse continued to affect her by creating a profound sense of shame and rage, an inability to talk with her husband about what happened to her, and difficulty trusting others. It was important to her healing process to clearly identify the external factors of childhood poverty, workplace sexism, discriminatory attitudes toward people labeled with mental illness, and the misdiagnosis of her condition by the mental health system as barriers to her healing. The initial focus of our work together (What needs to heal?) was on reducing the negative impact of the toxic work environment on her emotional function (including exploration of whether remaining in the position was a viable option), releasing the bipolar label, engaging the wounding from the abuse, and increasing her ability to openly share her wounding and healing process with her partner.

The Power of Resistance and Resilience

The final three Healing Questions support the creation of meaning in the face of power wounding: (5) How, in spite of what happened, have you been able to triumph? (6) What gifts have you received out of this wounding experience? (7) What lessons/wisdom can you share with others based on your experience with power wounding and healing?

Although it is an essential part of the healing process, naming is not sufficient for resolution of a wound. We must shift to engaging resistance and resilience strategies that open up the possibility of a restoration of power, especially power-within and power-with. In a world focused on power-over, it is important for these marginalized aspects of power to be validated, as they are typically the most easily recovered aspects of power and can be a springboard to resisting power over.

An essential step in the healing process is to identify, where possible, how to increase functional survival skills. I referred to these as thriving strategies that create the opportunity for celebration and connection and that lead to the creation of positive meanings connected with the wounding experience. Answering the resilience questions was key to Serena's reclamation of a sense of personal power. Failure to identify thriving/triumph experiences and skills traps clients and communities in a helpless and hopeless position of powerlessness or defeat. From the very beginning, I asked Serena to identify ways in which she has been able to survive and even triumph in her childhood home and in a toxic work environment. She reflected on an episode when she was four or five years old and being shoved by her brothers down a long flight of stairs. She said, "I knew in that moment that there was something wrong with *them* and that if I could just survive to adulthood I would be okay." I began to think of that knowledge as her "power spark." As I began to talk with other clients about power wounding and resistance, they offered up their own "power spark" moments that allowed them to hold onto the hope that things could get better.

Serena and I also used humor to strengthen her attachment to her resistance strategies. We began to refer to her experience as the Marilyn Munster syndrome (based on the experiences of a human in a household of monsters who was viewed as unattractive and "other" by her family). This language allowed her to name the crazy-making experience of trying to operate with concern and compassion in an abusive family. Serena was able to point to her ability to provide her own children with emotional and economic security as a key triumph experience. Serena experienced triumph regarding the work situation by documenting the abuses and refusing to engage in departmental cover-ups. Ultimately, she did quit her job in spite of the profound economic impact of that decision. Often, it is necessary to engage the triumph questions or questions of an alternative vision for self or community before there can be a full naming or assessment of the power wound or constriction in order to instill and nurture hope.

When dealing with powerlessness, it is essential to begin to develop a vision of what restoration of power would look and feel like to the individual and/or community. There is an aspect of conjuring power into existence by searching for places where it currently exists, even if in a muted form, and working to expand how that belief or strategy can facilitate healing and contribute to a sense of power.

In Serena's case, taking a stand for self-preservation and leaving her job allowed her more physical and emotional energy to begin to re-assess her need for medication. One thing she immediately noticed once she quit the job was that she stopped having visual and tactile hallucinations, which consisted of two large black dogs menacing her when she was in bed. We had been engaging in discussions about the meaning of the dogs and noticed that the hallucinations tended to occur when she was experiencing stressors in her day-to-day world. She also connected the panic and threat she felt during the hallucinations to the feelings she experienced when her brothers would come into her bed at night to abuse her. She decided to reframe her view of the dogs as less about threatening her and more about protecting her, because they showed up whenever she felt threatened. This understanding, coupled with the elimination of the workplace stressors, encouraged Serena to stop the psychotropic medications. I provided her with information from several psychiatric liberation organizations related to medication withdrawal and assisted her in locating a psychiatrist who would medically supervise her withdrawal.

As the person begins to heal the wounded spaces and to interrupt and block ongoing wounding, there is a shift to explore the meaning of the wounding and the lesson, and even gifts that can result from painful experience. This allows an individual to create an expanded version of herself or her community beyond the wounding or powerlessness experience. There is the invitation to expand beyond her personal benefits to examine how her survival and quest to thrive in spite of the wound has been beneficial to her community (which can be defined as family, affinity groups, geographic region, and so on) The healing of the wound then allows for contributions to the community that are generally experienced as validating and engendering a sense of power.

One example of transforming a wound into a community gift is reflected in the work of a client who had already written a book and created a workshop for women dealing with abuse out of her need to share her healing process with other women. In therapy, we continued to identify other writing and community projects that would allow her to share the wisdom gained through her own healing process. This "bring something back to the tribe" is part of the Hero/Heroine's journey. Campbell and Moyers (1988) described this as a spiritual deed "in which the hero learns to experience the supernormal range of human spiritual life and then comes back with a message" (p. 123). There is a healing power in breaking through isolation and creating a sense of belonging. There is a restoration of power in transforming one's individual wound into a pathway of healing for others.

GUIDING PRINCIPLES FOR USING THE HEALING QUESTIONS

I feel that it is important to explicitly state the values and principles that shape my work. I do so, in part, to be transparent in my interactions and create space for challenges and modifications to these principles. Clarifying my own guiding principles has given me a new tool to use with my clients in their healing process. I have begun to more systematically invite clinical clients (I had been doing this for some time with organizational and community clients) to articulate their own philosophy of change and healing. When positive—meaning successfully moving me toward my desired goals and able to use my power with minimal constrictions—these principles provide me with a roadmap through the change process. However, guiding principles can also highlight places where we are stuck in patterns of power-over or surplus powerlessness. The core principles that guide my work are as follows:

1. All wounds can be healed. The first question I ask is, "Are you ready to be healed?" This is a powerful statement because it begins to identify the individual's readiness to enter back into the pain of the wounding and unpack the story for the purpose of healing and resolution. The question also reminds us that there are roles, beliefs, and feelings that resulted from the wound that will need to be released for healing to occur. Often, these adaptations to the wound are hard to distinguish from one's core identity, and there may be resistance, conscious or unconscious, to releasing the adaptations in the service of healing for fear of losing all sense of self.
2. The clinician/community organizer and the clinical client(s)/community must develop a vision of healing. This vision of healing, which may be related to wholeness or restoration, will be the focus of all discussions and activities. The standard of what it means to be healed may shift and expand throughout the recovery/restoration process.
3. The process of naming and acknowledging the wound is fundamental in the healing process. It is impossible to heal a wound that has not been identified. A key goal of the clinical or organizing work is to create an accurate description

of the power wound and how it currently affects the functioning of individual/ family/community.

4. The creation of "safe-enough space" within the clinical interface, the family system, the wider community, and ultimately at the societal level to allow for a naming of the wound and the emotional vulnerability required to engage in an authentic naming and healing process. This requires releasing any illusions that there is an absolute safe space. Authentic healing and change require a willingness to take a calculated risk to be vulnerable and possibly risk further wounding.

5. It is important to create a container to hold and protect individuals during any process that uncovers shame and vulnerability. The container may be the shared understandings (confidentiality, mutual respect, equalization of power, and so on) that are created at the beginning of a process. The container is also the hope that can be generated through the healing relationship. One of my clients described me as a temporary "holder of hope" until she reached a point where she could consistently carry hope for herself. The consistency of the connection is an important container—trusting that the time and place to process the wounding and transform the experience will be there for as long as it is needed. When there are time limitations, the limits to what issues can be reasonably addressed within the parameters of the clinical or community con-sultations should be clearly stated and agreed on. Boundaries, clearly defined and consistently respected, are crucial to the development of a "safe-enough" container for healing work.

6. The identification of resiliency skills and unwounded spaces in the self/ community early in the healing process is crucial to sustain and build hope for resolution and restoration to wholeness. There is a profound power in hope throughout the healing process, and it is central to the healing process to iden-tify these "footholds" of hope. This is the belief in the possibility of healing that is grounded in awareness that one has been able to triumph in some aspects of one's life or that the community has been able to preserve some sense of power and/or agency.

ROLE OF THE THERAPIST IN TRANSFORMING POWERLESSNESS INTO POWER

One role of the therapist or community consultant is to invite richer, thicker descriptions of the desired state of power. Freedman and Combs (1996) state that:

> Narrative therapists are interested in working with people to bring forth and thicken stories that do not support or sustain problems. As people begin to inhabit and live out alternative stories, the results are beyond solving problems. Within the new stories, people live out new self-images, new possibilities for relationships and new futures. (p. 16)

One of the ways in which I invite clients to thicken their descriptions of alternative stories is to have them describe in detail what their lives would look and feel like if the wound were healed. One severely depressed client struggled to tap into her vision but was eventually able to vividly describe her desired workplace, living situation, and healthier relationships. A year later, we reflected on that process, and she noted that she thought that I was out of my mind to ask her to create a healing vision when she was in so much pain but that she had accomplished most of the goals that she had identified in her emotionally compromised state.

In my office is a flip chart with markers that I use to document some of the comments that clients share during session. This technique emerged out of my observation that one client was regularly attributing to me the comments and wisdom that she shared in session. I noted to her that it minimized her own wisdom and overvalued mine (which was something she frequently did in relationships). So, I began to write down her "power statements" and transcribe them so that she could retain a copy of her truth. Our process evolved to a point where she began to direct me to "flip chart" what she was saying so that she had a record of new understandings and commitment to action. I began to routinely use the flip chart summaries in my work with clients, because it seemed clear to me that many of the women who came to me for therapy had lost connection with their own voice and authority and that there was something very powerful for them about seeing their truths in writing. I found flip charting especially useful in helping women to track wounding experiences, because the visual seem to help them understand the energy drain associated with multiple wounds. In fact, we could celebrate that they were still standing and resisting in spite of the severity of the power wounds.

QUESTIONING COMMUNITY: APPLYING THE HEALING QUESTIONS TO COMMUNITY CHANGE

Mindy Thompson Fullilove's book, *Root Shock* (2004) helped me to understand that my community was one of many communities wounded through urban renewal. As yet another wave of gentrification menaces poor and working-class neighborhoods, the Healing Questions can be used by communities to assist in resisting what Fullilove refers to as "development-induced displacement." We can create community consciousness and action that can result in the revitalization of communities.

Jack Kirkland conducts a tour of metropolitan St. Louis every year as part of his Revitalizing Depressed Communities course. He challenges students to understand the history of communities and the impact of racial policies, loss of industries, limited political clout, and underinvestment in infrastructure and basic services on community functioning. He also works to inspire them regarding the possibility of healing and ways in which social work, business, and law students can use their skills in support of wounded communities. Central to Kirkland's work is engagement of the community and a respect for the leadership within that community. He offers an analysis of power dynamics that negatively affect a community's ability to recover. He noted that many inner-city neighborhoods are colonies, not communities. People who have the least are at the disposal of people with resources, and that will continue to be the case unless communities develop thrust, clout, and power (Kirkland personal communication, March 1, 2011). Fullilove (Fullilove & Booth, 2005) has effectively used community gatherings and the creation of documentary films to increase community awareness and develop community resistance strategies for neighborhoods struggling with development-induced displacement.

McKnight and Block (2010) offer the vision of the "abundant community," which is a call to empower communities to reclaim functions (caregiving, recreation, mutual aid, and so on) that have been usurped by the professionalization of human services. This can occur at all economic levels but is especially dangerous to communities already marginalized as a result of race, ethnicity, or class. Communities cannot create and maintain power when residents believe that they are incapable of performing basic functions without the intervention of professionals or government funding.

In my presentation, "Bulldozed: The Mental Health Consequences of Development Induced Displacement," I attempt to build on Fullilove's and Kirkland's work and explore community wounding and recovery through the Healing Questions. The presentation includes photographic documentation and reflections from community members in two communities affected by urban renewal. It is very important to obtain historical background on communities targeted for so-called revitalization, because developers and politicians rely on lack of communal memory when spinning the story that they are simply responding to community concerns and removing blighted public housing. Asking what happened and how it affects communities creates space to widen the lens and see the impact of economic shifts, lack of political clout, and the deliberate underdevelopment of communities. It is important for clinicians to understand these processes because their clients are frequently casualties of these development efforts. It is important for us to understand the grief, anxiety, anger, fear, and uncertainty that come from loss of place. These feelings reflect the power wounding experienced by a community and trickle down into the lives of individuals and families. One community member noted, as she discussed the displacement of elders in a senior complex slated for demolition, "we have lost our wisdom." Although she also wanted a safe and attractive environment in which to raise her family, she needed to honor the gift of the community—the relationships and history that were sacrificed for progress.

CONCLUSION

In this chapter, I put forth a process that can serve as a series of guideposts to therapists and community organizers who accept the challenge of walking with individuals, families, and communities through their greatest pains and helping them transform their wounds into a sense and source of power.

REFERENCES

Brown, B. (2004). *Women and shame: Reaching out, speaking truths and building connection.* Austin, TX: 3C Press.

Campbell, J., & Moyers, B. (1988). *The power of myth.* New York: Doubleday.

Fett, S. (2002). *Working cures: Healing, health and power on southern slave plantations.* Chapel Hill, NC: University of North Carolina Press.

Freedman, J., & Combs, G. (1996). *Narrative therapy: The social construction of preferred realities.* New York: W. W. Norton.

Fullilove, M. T. (2004). *Root shock: How tearing up city neighborhoods hurts America, and what we can do about it.* New York: One World/Ballantine.

Fullilove, M. T. (Producer), & Booth, S. (Director). (2005). *Urban renewal is people removal* [Motion picture]. USA: LaBooth Production.

Heller, D. (1985). *Power in psychotherapeutic practice.* New York: Human Services Press.

Hopps, J., Pinderhughes, E., & Shankar, R. (1995). *The power to care: Clinical practice effectiveness with overwhelmed clients.* New York: Free Press.

Lerner, M. (1986). *Surplus powerlessness: The psychodynamics of everyday life and the psychology of individual and social transformation.* Atlantic Highlands, NJ: Humanities Press International.

Levins Morales, A. (1998). *Medicine stories: History, culture and the politics of integrity.* Cambridge, MA: South End Press.

Martín-Baró, I. (1994). *Writings for a liberation psychology.* Cambridge, MA: Harvard University Press.

McKnight, J. M., & Block, P. (2010). *The abundant community: Awakening the power of families and neighborhoods.* San Francisco: Berrett-Koehler.

Mehl-Madrona, L. (2010). *Healing the mind through the power of story: The promise of narrative psychiatry.* Rochester, VT: Bear & Company.

Pearsall, J. (Ed.). (2002). *Concise Oxford English dictionary* (10th ed., rev.). Oxford, UK: Oxford University Press.

Pinderhughes, E. (1989). *Understanding race, ethnicity and power: The key to efficacy in clinical practice.* New York: Free Press.

Starhawk. (1987). *Truth or dare: Encounters with power, authority and mystery.* San Francisco: Harper & Row.

Stone, R. (1996). *The healing art of storytelling: A sacred journey of personal discovery.* New York: Hyperion.

Waldegrave, C., Tamasese, K., Tuhaka, F., & Campbell, W. (2003). *Just therapy—A journey: A collection of papers from the Just Therapy Team, New Zealand.* Adelaide, Australia: Dulwich Centre Publications.

White, M., & Epston, D. (1990). *Narrative means to therapeutic ends.* New York: W. W. Norton.

Wingard, B., & Lester, J. (2001). *Telling our stories in ways that make us stronger.* Adelaide, Australia: Dulwich Centre Publications.

5

Tsalagi Spiral Conjurations in Ghost Country: Exploring Emergent Power Differentials with a Native American Client

Rockey Robbins, Scott Drabenstot, and Mollie Rischard

There is little evidence to support the efficacy of Western psychological counseling with Native American clients (Gone & Trimble, 2012). Sue, Zane, Hall, and Berger (2009) contend that there is an apparent incompatibility between conventional psychotherapeutic approaches and the cultural practices of Native Americans. Many Native Americans are not willing to forsake traditional healing approaches for Western psychological approaches. Beals, Manson, Whitesell, Spicer, and Novins (2005) reported that 40.1 percent of Northern Plains Native Americans with lifetime depression and/or anxiety disorders sought help from mental health professionals compared with 33.7 percent who sought help from traditional Native American healers. Thirty-six percent of Southwestern Native American people with lifetime depression or anxiety disorders sought help from mental health professionals compared with 48.9 percent who sought help from traditional Native American healers.

Counseling and clinical psychology researchers advocate the use of culturally adapted interventions, which typically make use of existing evidence-based interventions adapted to make them more culturally or tribally relevant (Bigfoot & Schmidt, 2010; Trimble & Gonzalez, 2008). Other researchers encourage therapists to collaborate with traditional native healers for effective treatment with Native American clients. Wendt and Gone (2012) described a shift and emphasis in the psychological literature from the production of culturally competent therapists to the development of culturally commensurate therapies. Robbins, Hill, and McWhirter (2008) argued that perspectives about Native American clients regarding psychological mechanisms, actions, and change processes should be derived from specific tribal and community epistemologies.

The therapist in this study specifically integrated Tsalagi tribal assumptions and healing practices with psychoanalytic theory when working with a Tsalagi client. The therapist had to face his own unacknowledged power position as a therapist, power issues inherent in his theoretical orientation and epistemological assumptions, as well as power issues related to overt oppression and prejudices in American society and history. Addressing unique Native American client needs in regard to acculturation level, traditional and historical predicament, tribal and community level of support, and tribal ideas regarding healing led to more appropriate interventions and therapeutic successes.

THEORETICAL APPROACHES USED IN THE CASE STUDY

Western psychology theories, for the most part, fail to offer Native Americans relevant outlooks that deal with the larger issues that Native Americans struggle with on a daily basis, such as contemporary prejudicial practices, community pressures, tribal histories, assaults on tribal identities, homeland issues, and epistemological conflicts. Sande Grande (2004) contended that Native Americans have been hesitant about creating their own theoretical models because the very notion of abstract theory is seen by many Native Americans as an indulgent privilege of the academic elite. Native Americans are embroiled in real-world struggles. Still, she worried that until Native Americans "theorize the inherent complexity of Indian-ness" (p. 3), their issues will continue to be examined through incongruous Western epistemic frames. She argued that Native Americans have valuable perspectives as a result of epistemological differences, indigenous diasporas and contemporary oppressions, and unique tribal philosophies related to their relationships with the earth. We begin by briefly foregrounding these three Native American perspectives before offering a cursory description of psychoanalytic theory, all of which will be addressed during the case study.

NATIVE AMERICAN THEORETICAL PERSPECTIVES

Power Relations

Native Americans suffer from current challenges related to their socioeconomic predicaments. They continue to suffer from economic hardship, poverty, unemployment, and a lack of education (BigFoot & Schmidt, 2010). Native Americans' income level is only 62 percent of the U.S. average, and their poverty rate is twice as high (U.S. Census Bureau, 2006). These factors contribute to increasing Native American mental health problems such as stress and trauma, which can often lead to more serious problems such as suicidal ideation. Native American adults are 70 percent more likely to attempt suicide than the general population (U.S. Bureau of Justice Statistics, 2006). Surveying Native Americans in regard to their experience of depression, The American Indian Service Utilization, Psychiatric Epidemiology, Risk and Protective Projects found that 7.8 percent of Northern Plains Native Americans and 10.7 percent of Southwestern Native Americans reported experiencing at least one major depressive episode during the course of their lives (Beals, Manson, Mitchell, Spicer, & AI-SUPERPFP Team, 2003). Therapists who work with Native Americans should consider the connection that may exist between the depression Native Americans frequently experience and their often dire economic predicaments.

Relationships between Western therapists and Native American clients may often implicitly reflect the power differences cited in the above paragraph. Power differences between Native American clients and professional caregivers can take on potentially menacing attributes. Therapists who are unaware of economic disparities and cultural dissonances and who continue to pursue Western treatments that do not take into account the societal oppression experienced by Native Americans may offer ineffective therapy. Helping Native American clients question internalized dominant cultural ideas and perspectives about the causes for their socioeconomic circumstances may help them to move into a position to reject these ideals and to embrace themselves as competent and worthy human beings.

It is crucial to be aware of the dangers of integrating and interfacing Western notions of equality and identity with Native American beliefs. Although hierarchies exist in every interaction, they may become oppressive when power is exerted without wisdom. Therapists must acknowledge they are always in a position of power and knowledge in relation to their clients. Even the most egalitarian therapists play the role of expert when they decide to question, interpret, or offer information. It is essential to be culturally informed and have the awareness to question the power dynamics in the treatment approaches that influence one's work.

It is vital to remember that historically Native American tribes were, for the most part, hierarchical communal societies led by elders (male and female) who were never viewed as distinct from their people. In many Native American communities today, elders continue to work with their tribal people in co-intentional ways. However, their extensive life experience gives them a special place of power, and their opinions are shown profound respect. The Native American client and therapist become partners in therapy, though they are not necessarily always equal. The Native American client's tribal knowledge may guide the therapy for a time, whereas the therapist's specialized knowledge may take the lead at other times. In some instances, they may work together as equals.

Historical Trauma

Over the past 15 years, historical trauma has dominated discourse among Native American mental health professionals (Gone & Trimble, 2011). *Historical trauma* involves exposure of an earlier generation to a traumatic event that, through lingering symptoms related to unresolved grief, continues to affect subsequent generations (Whitbeck,

Adams, Hoyt, & Chen, 2004). Brave Heart and De Buyn (1998) maintained that cumulative trauma related to forced removal, racism, betrayal, massacres, loss of tribal language, changes in diet, and denial of traditional spiritual expression has contributed to the current high levels of depression, negative career ideation, drug and alcohol abuse, and broken families among Native Americans. Evans-Campbell (2008) also argued that there is a critical connection between historical traumatic events and contemporary stressors among Native Americans. Whitbeck et al. (2004) reported comorbidity of historical trauma with anxiety disorders, depression, anger, and substance abuse.

In working to alleviate the emotional suffering of Native American clients, it is crucial for the therapist to validate the existence of not only this traumatic history, but also the continuing oppression. The only researched intervention reported in the literature that specifically focuses on historical trauma among Native American populations is the Historical Trauma and Unresolved Grief Intervention, which is characterized by the incorporation of traditional healing approaches (Brave Heart, 1999). Historical Trauma and Unresolved Grief Intervention is a supplementary intervention to facilitate more profound explorations regarding the forms and influences that oppressive powers may play in a client's life. In the present study, it is an approach that focuses on helping the client to understand the forces of oppression and coercive domination that affect his life in the domains of race, gender, ethnicity, history, spirituality, and tribe. Such therapy involves discourses about processes of decolonialization, helping the client to recognize internalized beliefs, ideologies, and/or stereotypes. For Native Americans, a vital element of this process involves recovering tribal histories that have been hijacked by dominant society. Such remembering entails not only cognitive re-inscription but also congruent emotional ventilation.

Nature and Place

Native Americans acknowledge land as being a nurturing female dimension, remembering the umbilical connection to certain places regularly during ceremonies. Native Americans have deep connections to locale, especially with their traditional homelands, the source of their cultural traditions and knowledge (Cajete, 2000). Embedded within Native cultures across North America is a strong sense of place that is both culturally constructed and highly localized (Cajete, 2000; Doering & Veletsianos, 2008). Considering themselves as part of nature and their local environment, rather than separate from it, they interpret their histories, culture, and natural events accordingly (Cajete, 2000). Place-focused therapy may facilitate Native American clients to reconnect with long-standing aspects of their tribal identities and to tap into a source of spiritual power.

PSYCHOANALYTIC THEORY

Psychoanalytic theory has undergone significant changes in its development, morphing into object relations and psychodynamic theories. This brief synopsis focuses on only a few of its elements that are directly relevant to the case study. The central premise of psychoanalysis is that a person's psychological conflicts emerge out of an oedipal complex (Freud, 1913/1955). For instance, clients may engage in acts that suggest a fixation on their mother or father. A psychoanalytic therapist may interpret a client's symptom as a secret, infantile, forbidden wish lodged in his or her unconscious. Primarily, psychoanalytic therapists aim to help their clients to uncover and verbalize what they repress (Freud, 1922/2010). The psychoanalytic therapist is alert to transference occurring during therapy sessions, carefully noting client emotions that may be associated with early caretakers, hoping to learn who might be the source of the transference. The psychoanalytic therapist also provides interpretations to facilitate the client's understanding and reformation of the self (McWilliams, 2011). However, power differences between a Native American client and therapist may be inherently established and ignored, with the therapist taking the dominant "expert" role in interpretation, which may be grounded in mainstream Western perspectives.

CASE PRESENTATION

Saloli, a 25-year-old self-identified Oklahoma Tsalagi man, went to college for one year, worked as a commercial artist for one year, then moved in with his uncle. He had not worked for pay for three years. He wrote on the perfunctory counseling form that his presenting problem was a need to talk about the loss of his father and mother and his "disturbing visions of his deceased mother." Because Saloli is a tribal person, it is necessary to describe his tribe first.

Tribal History

Tsalagi tribal people (Woodland tribe) have historically defined themselves not only as individuals, but also in terms of their participation in their family, clan, and tribe. Saloli is part of the Long Hair clan. The Tsalagi tribe represented here consists of a membership of approximately 280,000 (U.S. Census Bureau, 2000). In the 18th century, fur traders came, taking tribal wives and becoming members of the tribe. They brought Christianity, the English language, and European houses and guns, as well as a way of life that promoted the inequalities of wealth. Despite accommodations to the U.S. government, beginning in the 1830s, armies drove most Tsalagi from their lands in the Southeast, with over half dying en route to Oklahoma (Pace, Robbins, Hill, Blair, & Lacy, 2006). In 1898, the Dawes Commission abolished communal land and forced individual tribal families onto allotments of 160 acres of private property, disrupting the tribal people's relationship to the land. Many Tsalagi still reside on allotments granted to their families. In the early 20th century, unscrupulous businessmen cooperated with judicial systems to declare many Tsalagi insane, clearing the way for them to be appointed guardians of Tsalagi children and thus justifying their taking possession of Tsalagi lands (Debo, 1940). Though the Oklahoma Tsalagi tribal members have no reservation and many have become Christians, there is still a solid but small percentage who continue to honor their traditional lands, hold traditional beliefs and customs, speak their native language, and participate in stomp dance rituals. Stomp dances are Southeastern Indian dances in which participants dance spirally around a fire while repeating the words of a chanter and stomping the ground. It is used both as a sacred and social dance. A few women dance shaking turtle shells tied to their legs just next to the fire and the chanter. (*First Nation Histories*, 2002).

Presenting Complaints and Personal History

During the first session, Saloli reported the following: "living a dismal life," suffering from an unwillingness to work (he had never held a job more than six months and was currently unemployed), having problems in romantic relationships, having low self-esteem, and experiencing anxiety about his future. He said he had tried repeatedly to ignore his sadness over the past several months and lead a normal life but had never been successful.

He and his mother lived together for four years after his father died, nine years previously. When his mother died five years ago, he moved in with his uncle. He did not feel sadness regarding the loss of his father until the past year, at which time he also began experiencing headaches, backaches, and stomach cramps. In regard to his mother, he said he "deeply mourned" her death for a year, felt he worked through it, but was currently "feeling sad about it again." In the sixth session, he reported that over the past six months he had seen his mother's ghost two times, "wearing a red bandana and planting where she previously had a vegetable garden."

Saloli described his father as a "white moral Christian, a leader, and a smart executive," and admired him greatly for his monetary success. He had a picture of his father—his Pee Wee league baseball coach—and himself in baseball uniforms on his bedroom wall. He had the fleeting memory of his father giving him a sour candy that Saloli pretended was tobacco to better imagine himself being a "pro." He recalled having lots of fun playing baseball. He quit baseball when he was 12 and devoted his time to drawing, much to his father's dismay. He remembered feeling intense anger at his father for having "pushed baseball too hard." His father died the next summer after six months of fighting cancer. Saloli continued to draw. At age 21, after a year of college, he was hired to draw for a large company and at first enjoyed his work. But after four months, he found himself incapable of drawing due to his depression and feelings of sickness. He reported that he felt depressed for having failed at making money.

Upon inquiry about his mother, Saloli said, "She was a full-blooded Tsalagi, and she took care of me, and I knew she loved me, though she never said so." When asked to describe her, he said she was "unassuming, even invisible." Unlike his father, she was always at their house when he was growing up. She was, in his estimation, uneducated. "She cooked and watched over me, the only child, but never really made anything of herself." He said he "looked and was quiet" like her. She had been a shell shaker in stomp dances. She and he, without his father, went to all-night stomp dances through his grade school years and went to church with his father on Sundays. By the time he was about 10 or 11, much to his father's appreciation, they stopped going to stomp dances. The Christian church became their only spiritual outlet. He said he had enjoyed stomp dances and hated church. By 18, he no longer went to church and felt embarrassed about going back to stomp dances because "the Tsalagi" thought of him as having "gone white." He said he did not "feel white" but "felt separated from the Tsalagi world." He said he respected his father more than his mother because "he did something with his life."

When asked about his relationships over the past few years, he reported having problems in romantic relationships. He reported that as soon as relationships became intimate, he withdrew and offered odd explanations, yet he yearned for a close romantic relationship. He claimed that he used women and never allowed himself to sense their experiences. He was not sure whether he had the capacity to love. In fact, his last girlfriend told him he was "disagreeable and argued constantly over petty things," which kept her at a distance, though he claimed she exaggerated. She also told him that she believed he "used depression to make her obsessed about making him feel better." He claimed some of these patterns were repeating themselves with his current girlfriend.

Over the past three years, Saloli reported he became a casual friend with a "drug king" and had "slung" or sold drugs on a limited basis for a year after their initial acquaintance. He insisted that he never used drugs. He said that the drug king was "fairly wealthy" and was wise about life. The drug king said that most people lived lives of "quiet desperation," doing things they hated. Men made love to one woman when they wanted many women, suppressed all sorts of other enjoyments in the name of phony morality, and suppressed their own desires and needs to make things equal when people are really unequal. The drug king never took drugs and taught Saloli to never take drugs but said it was alright to sell drugs to "idiots who were dead already."

It bothered Saloli that the drug king sold drugs to adolescents. The drug king promised him that he would set him up as the operator of a clean cock-fighting barn within a few years, but Saloli chose not to continue "to sling." At first, he feared the drug king would kill him, but not only did he not kill him, they remained casual acquaintances. Saloli said he was terrified of the man but "kind of liked him, too."

Psychoanalytic Conceptualization

Therapist interpretations and guidance offered from Western theoretical frameworks may be irrelevant to Native Americans whose belief system is embedded in a complex tribal belief system and whose lives are embedded in tribal and community interrelationships. But in this case, Saloli presented as a very assimilated Native American, immersed in Euro-American worldviews, even about therapy. After an initial discussion about what he wanted from therapy, he chose to lie on the couch and engage in free association about his feelings about his mother and father. For 31 sessions, two per week, Saloli and I engaged in a short version of traditional psychoanalytic therapy, establishing the relationship, exploring crises and trauma in his life regressively, and working on transference issues. Starting with the 32nd session, I began to offer interpretations, which we discussed over the next 10 sessions.

The initial phase of therapy consisted almost entirely of talking about his father, with him making only occasional dismissive remarks about his mother. Saloli was 12 when his father died. Like many early adolescents, he described having experienced "stress and storm." He described having had, and continuing to have, ambivalent feelings toward his father. In his striving toward independence, he viewed his father as an oppressive devil one moment and a protective god the next (Freud, 1913/1955). He said that he both loved his father intensely and hated him and that his father's love for him had been "inconsistent." I wondered whether his current disabling hypochondria and depression were associated with the loss of his father, to whom he was deeply attached to the point of obsession (McDougal, 1989).

I also wondered whether his depression, hypochondria, and incapacity to work as an artist were self-punishment and obedience to his father. He had yet to work through the guilt he experienced for hating his father. He probably felt responsible on an unconscious level for his father's death. Unable to gain clarity on these underlying issues, he remained stuck in a repetitive cycle of sorrow and inadequacy.

On the other hand, we discussed whether his continued inability to work and his dependence on his uncle was another unconscious attempt to bind his father, that is to say, to indirectly regain his father's protective care by creating a child's world where he was guarded from work and other cares of adult life. Nonetheless, he was now cognizant of experiencing a "souring" of his innocent predicament.

His depression, apprehensions, and hypochondriasis used up energies that he could have used toward adult concerns and creative expressions (Horney, 1950). After all, he had even given up the art he claimed for his own as a result of experiencing alienation from his father. Now, he held fast to an uncle (father figure) on his maternal side who loved stickball (Woodland Indian game) and who provided for his nourishment and safekeeping. It is possible that Saloli's recent inability to draw or paint and to work was an example of deferred obedience, because the father preferred that his son play baseball instead of drawing. McWilliams (2011) argued that individuals may unconsciously "do their duty" for a father figure, sabotaging their own self-expression to assuage their guilt for not living up to their father's expectations (p. 124).

Saloli also regressed when engaging in romantic relationships. Possibly, fixated on his father and his mother to a certain extent, his libido was blocked. His inability to love might be interpreted as a paradoxical self-injurious form of self-preservation (Horney, 1950; McWilliams, 2011). His contradictory interactions with romantic partners were characterized by a form of dependence and sadomasochistic interaction. Instead of directing his energies toward a mature, loving relationship, he used his energies to wallow in his unresolved emotional issues. He punished his authoritative father and his "somewhat distant" mother through his girlfriends by never yielding to a love that may, after all, abandon him again. Bernstein's (2005) empirical study of dependency demonstrated that children of authoritarian parents have fears of abandonment that may lead to their vigilant attempts to avoid the negative effect they associate with intimacy.

Further, the drug king may be a displacement of his father. The possible ambivalence toward his father may be represented in the drug king, who is described as a respectable mentor and businessman sometimes and as a dangerous figure at other times. In some ways, the drug king is a caricature of his father. His father was a regular churchgoer and a successful and upstanding businessman who had even served as mayor in the small town where they lived. The drug king functions as a means for rebelling against his father, yet Saloli is able to remain in contact with him.

The last issue we worked on from a psychoanalytical perspective was his experience with ghosts. About the realm of the uncanny such as seeing a ghost, Freud (1919/1963) explained, "It is something that is secretly familiar, which has undergone repression and then returned from it" (p. 7). After being probed about what Saloli felt was the meaning of such sightings, he interpreted them as representing the distance he felt from his mother and his awareness of her provision of his food needs. I wondered whether he might himself have contributed to the distance he experienced with his mother because of his absent father, which may have put him in the position of surrogate husband. Could he have unconsciously maintained a distance from his taboo, fertile "garden" mother for fear of too great an intimacy? He said that such an interpretation "felt true."

Although Saloli was open to many of my interpretations, I experienced an objective distance during the interpretive sessions. I interpreted this distancing as transference. He told me that he did not agree with my interpretation that he was engaging in transference and that he would discontinue therapy if we continued to pursue this avenue. Yet if we could pursue other issues, he would "very much want to continue therapy." I told him I would consider his proposal. We reconvened therapy in two weeks, after I had come to believe I had assumed a disproportionate amount of power in making my interpretations.

I believe that Saloli was able, to a large extent, to recognize the repetitive patterns he engaged in, interpret how they might be related to his unresolved inner emotional conflicts with his parents, and ventilate the repressed emotions associated with early traumatic events. Now, therapy shifted to deconstruction of broader internalized social influences.

Exploring Power Differences

I ceased to offer interpretations from this point forward. Nonetheless, I did guide the conversations in the direction of helping him to consider the validity of some of the values he had assumed. The first value I asked him to explore was embedded in a comment his father had made: "Money isn't what life is all about, but it is the indicator of how well you are doing in life." We discussed the effectiveness of this "measuring stick" for assessing the ultimate value of people. He quickly determined that there were many individuals he highly respected who fell outside his father's descriptor. Next, we considered the larger social ramifications within a world where a great many people might justify their behaviors based on such a value. He considered the destructive consequences of the drug dealer selling drugs to minors within this framework. After a few sessions, he determined not to "repossess" this value. We also critiqued his father's idea that drawing was a lesser form of expression than sports and the drug king's views about "phony morality." With regard to both, he developed what he felt were effective "counterarguments."

Native American Themes and Interventions

Saloli and I agreed that our sessions might now focus more on topics such as historical trauma, balance, and harmony in his life. I was convinced that no matter how outstanding a therapist may be in using psychoanalytic techniques with a Native American client, it is unlikely they will be able to effectively address the ameliorating effects of Western patriarchal colonialism. And, even though I was involved in traditional Native American ways and ceremonies and knowledgeable of neocolonial schools of thought, I was lacking as a healing source to help Saloli in his cultural depths. I relinquished some of my control and power. Saloli and I called on a Tsalagi spiritual healer for consultation to provide counsel about sacred tribal ways.

The spiritual healer was an elderly man who had worked with other therapists and me at our Indian Behavioral Health Clinic. After telling him about our therapeutic work together, we listened to the traditional healer. He commented that he believed there were "forgotten branded marks" on all people, many acquired from our caretakers, but many also accumulated from generations of mistreatment. He then talked of a healing plant whose flower was a spiral shape. He said that he would eat it on behalf of us as he chanted. We were to perform the chant each day. He told Saloli to dance at a specific stomp grounds that summer. While dancing the spiral dance, Saloli was to consider the forgotten "branded marks" of the past. He explained that Saloli should pay special attention to the sacred fire and that he should "give up" his worries to it. The spiritual healer added that we should consider the ghost as an entity in itself, rather than just a psychological experience, and he would offer Saloli "protection" the next time they met.

Over the next several sessions, Saloli considered the devastation wrought on his tribe as well as on Native American people in general. At first, he blamed his father for his own sense of alienation from tribal ways because of the power of his degradations of Native Americans and their ways. Gradually, he came to perceive that his father was simply a part of a much greater political and social network that did not value Native Americans. We discussed how his internalization of such perspectives had contributed to his own self-loathing and possibly even his physical symptoms. We agreed that Saloli's healing was dependent on his understanding of the legacy of colonialization and his reconnection with Tsalagi ways.

When beginning our talk about the oppression of the Tsalagi, Saloli became unusually anxious. He said his father had told him once that he "despised Indian pity parties." His distress level having exponentially increased, he asked that we stop talking about "Tsalagi oppression." But two sessions later, he demanded, "we must talk about it." He argued that he had repeatedly heard people preach that Native Americans should "move on" and "leave it behind," and he added that many Native Americans try to do exactly that. Yet, he argued, by forgetting, we eventually lose our identities. To forget our past would amount to participating in efforts to annihilate our identities.

I realized that communicating about historical trauma was paradoxical and problematic. I was faced with the task of helping Saloli communicate about his tribal and personal traumas without his being destroyed by it. I knew I must help him talk about it without inadvertently opening the door to perpetual mourning. There was not a set way to deal with this problematic situation, except by being present and nonjudgmental with Saloli and being open to what might present itself.

After about a month and half, the spiritual healer called me and said that Saloli and I were to meet him at a recreational area about 20 miles away from our clinic. At first, I explained I had other clients and could not attend, but he was adamant. I reluctantly agreed.

He was there under a pavilion, waiting on us when we arrived. Instead of greeting us, he told us to sit with him and listen to the wind. We sat in silence for probably 10 minutes. He whispered, "This is a holy place. Our ancestors made this a new sacred site when they were driven here. When I was young, I danced here. I sat under a thatched arbor about right here." He said he could feel spirits in this location. Then he took out black and white photographs of Tsalagi people eating at a long table and others simply standing around talking. He said that after the grounds were abandoned, Tsalagi families still came here for community gatherings. He took out a Mason jar filled with a dark liquid, dipped a tobacco leaf in it, and smudged Saloli and then myself. He explained this would provide Saloli protection. He then told Saloli to come back to this place periodically to commune with spirits, not ghosts. Lastly, he told him it was time for Saloli to dance at a stomp dance ceremony.

Saloli was concerned that traditional Tsalagi people might not receive him warmly into their ceremonies. He was pleasantly surprised when some distant relatives were overjoyed that he might attend a stomp dance with them. The problem was that their families' ceremonial grounds did not have a stomp dance scheduled for two months. There was another family that had a stomp dance within two weeks, but some of Saloli's family felt that that group did not conduct stomp dances properly. Consequently, he had to wait almost two months for his families' scratching and stomp dance ceremony.

When he returned after the ceremony, he described a scratching ceremony in which he had participated in the Green Corn Ceremony. He showed me the scabs on his chest that were a result of what he endured during the ceremony. I asked him how those wounds were in any way similar to the historical trauma we had discussed. He speculated whether wounds endured and survived could be viewed as a source of strength, even a gift, and possibly an invocation to a positive future. He said that once he acknowledged that he was a tribal person, he gradually realized that he was part of a people who have survived against all the odds. His people had demonstrated an ability to endure and recover. He was a part of a people who have dignity and profound indigenous traditions and ways. He said that the rituals such as dances, prayers, and scratchings had facilitated his letting go of the anger he kept inside and the guilt he felt for having abandoned his traditional ways for so many years.

He recalled something he experienced during the stomp dance. He "danced the spirals" all night, and elders were astonished at his "dedication and stamina." He remembered the "call songs." It was a time when he "wasn't worrying about anything," and such a reprieve allowed him to come back to the world with renewed energy. The chanter, who was leading the dancers and intermittently turning toward the fire and singing directly to it, at one point stopped and allowed a turtle shell shaker (female) to take the lead. He said that he immediately thought of his mother and began to cry as he danced. He said he wanted to talk about her again.

I asked him if he was aware of any traditional Tsalagi stories about women. I began a story about Selu ("Grandmother Corn Maiden"), but he stopped me, telling me he knew the story well and that its theme of the importance of women was clear. He added that he knew that our tribe was historically matriarchal. He discussed his tribe's beliefs in balance, relationship, and the centrality of women. He said his mother had given him food, medicine, and shelter. For several sessions, we talked about whether he might have internalized male-dominant views, which could be contrary to his tribe's matriarchal views. He considered whether his scorn and contempt for his mother's quiet, peace-oriented ways had affected his attitudes and views, including his relationships with women. I gave him an assignment to consider what shifts in understanding he might have if he let himself appreciate or even identify with soft feelings, openly engaging in caring and intimate relationships?

Saloli reminded me that the spiritual healer had said we should talk about the ghost. He believed as the healer did, that it was "real" and that it was somehow both his mother and the tribe's corn maiden. He believed that she was trying to tell him to go back to school and come back to the tribe to feed his people just as the story of the corn maiden tells. Responding to questions about balance, he said that the vision was really about both his father's hard work and his mother's nurturance. He was tired of being angry at his parents. He wanted to internalize that part of his father that was self-assured and desirous of serving his community but reject his judgmental attitudes and his inability to accept the value of other cultures. He wanted to internalize his mother's humility, ability to sacrifice herself for others, and her love of the Tsalagi people and culture. Selu, the corn maiden, embodied both of the best qualities of his parents. In the story, she works hard for her family and eventually offers her body to be cut up and buried to later arise as corn for all the Tsalagi people to eat. She said that her words could always be heard in the wind for those who would wait and listen.

Follow-Up

I was able to work with this brilliant Tsalagi man for about a month after the last session presented earlier. He secured funding for college before we terminated our sessions. Contrary to his earlier point of view, he had learned that planting one foot firmly in traditional Tsalagi culture and the other in dominant culture had not fragmented his intentionality toward fulfillment and success but instead had provided him with rich resources and a new balance that both energized and consolidated his journey toward self-affirmation. He also expressed profound joy concerning his new connections with his traditional extended family members, with whom he could participate in traditional tribal ceremonies. I learned that there may be times when psychoanalytic theory could be united with traditional Native American ways to facilitate healing in Native American clients. I had also learned how important it was to relinquish my own needs for power as well as the inherent power imbedded in my theoretical framework to truly encounter another person and their culture.

Treatment Implications of the Case

Healing work with Saloli primarily entailed helping him to (1) become conscious of underlying emotional conflicts; (2) sense his powerful presence as a survivor of the unparalleled destructiveness of dominant society's attack on his people and himself; (3) value the nurturing peaceful part of himself and others, no matter their gender; (4) transcend the pressure to conform in response to the fear instilled in him by others; (5) reconstruct a tribal self and initiate a new life narrative; (6) view his tribal people and himself as being of worth; and (7) find opportunities to participate regularly in tribal rituals and ways.

Recommendations to Clinicians

There is potential for enriching our viewpoints, but this requires loosening the enclosed boundaries of our discipline. This allows for our expansion as human beings and professionals. Though Saloli and I did not totally abandon traditional psychoanalytic metaphors, interpretations, and defense mechanisms as guideposts, we did relax what might be considered the tendencies of logo-centrism in psychoanalytical treatment as we deconstructed language, values, and clichés while trying to make sense of Saloli's stories. The above case study is an example of how traditional psychoanalytical interpretations might be loosened to open space for a client experimenting with variations of meanings. Shifting theoretical perspectives can enrich therapy when done in a way that appreciates the value of all perspectives. With Saloli, it was not only perspectives provided by a theoretical model, therapist and client, but also the mythopoetic meanings offered in tribal stories and customs.

Considering Saloli's unique psychological struggles from only a psychoanalytic perspective allowed for complex but limited interpretations. While exploring the unconscious, the psychoanalytic conceptualizations with Saloli might have allowed for some rather fascinating points of elucidation. Many factors and perspectives were neglected, as was revealed when power dynamics and tribal perspectives were considered. There was a point while working with Saloli that I felt that, by subjecting him to psychoanalysis, we could arrive at only preconceived meanings. I wondered whether the repeated use of the psychoanalytic language resulted in interpretations that contradicted the variety of Saloli's experiences. Many psychoanalytic therapists, such as Nancy McWilliams (2011), are careful to acknowledge that the unconscious messages never fully yield themselves to psychoanalytic readings. However, many therapists, including myself, are susceptible to a lingering attachment to illusory psychoanalytic themes, which may offer powerful springboards for therapeutic discussions but are simply not identical to experience. As I worked with Saloli, it became increasingly clear to me that the restricted economy of psychoanalytic language was insufficient. Nonetheless, as a close reading of the earlier text reveals, efforts were made to broaden psychoanalytic conceptualization and treatment, making interpretations more tentative and treatment less authoritative.

To truly be present with Saloli, I empathized with the pressure he felt to assimilate the conventions, morals, and manners of mainstream American culture. When therapists, unaware of a tribal person's larger cultural identities, locate the problem only within the Native American client, they are guilty of imposing an incongruent conceptualization upon that client. Failing to recognize societal and client–therapist power asymmetry can negatively affect diagnosis, treatment, prognosis, and resource utilization. Furthermore, in clinging to their power and exclusive beliefs in Western healing practices, therapists, even in tribal behavioral health settings, are likely to ignore or avoid incorporation of Native Americans healing practices, activities, and ceremonies into their work with Native American clients.

On the other hand, I fear that if Saloli and I had exclusively focused on dominant external influences, he might have avoided dealing with unresolved internal psychic issues that were unavailable to him on a conscious level until they were brought forth with psychoanalytic therapy. Yet, as therapy with Saloli progressed, I became increasingly aware of theoretical and specialized problems with psychoanalytic theory. In the end, Saloli and I moved into working with his own tribal stories, symbols, and history to further his identity construction. Even when doing internal work with Saloli, I found that it was necessary to allude to external tribal wisdom. We brought in mythopoetic meanings regarding masculinity and femininity and connections between spiritual entities and human beings, place, and identity. I found that we often related his personal meanings to tribally given meanings.

Saloli came to therapy with only a vague understanding of why he was having a difficult time adjusting to the mainstream world, as well as a vague regret for his disconnect from his tribal ways. A therapist might have ignored these vague feelings and attempted to help him make adjustments so that he might become successful in the mainstream world. Without addressing tribal customs, beliefs, and spirituality, I might have been guilty of facilitating his assimilation into dominant culture. To limit the neocolonial influence, profound and systematic scrutiny of the assumptions of oppressive society and personal internalizations is necessary.

I could have superficially discussed his tribal customs with him, contributing to a kind of voyeuristic relationship with his tribal ways or, worse yet, nostalgia for lost ways. Therapists from every hue of psychological theory could probably advocate strongly for the effectiveness of their particular approach if they can demonstrate sensitivity, flexibility, and respect for many Native American clients' situational factors, beliefs, and values. However, they are strongly encouraged to seek consultation from people who are knowledgeable about the particular client's tribal ways.

REFERENCES

Beals, J., Manson, S. M., Mitchell, C. M., Spicer, P., & AI-SUPERPFP Team. (2003). Cultural specificity and comparison in psychiatric epidemiology: Walking the tightrope in American Indian research. *Culture, Medicine, and Psychiatry, 27*, 259–289.

Beals, J., Manson, S. M., Whitesell, N. R., Spicer, P., & Novins, D. K. (2005). Prevalence of DSM-IV disorders and attendant help-seeking in two American Indian reservation populations. *Archives of General Psychiatry, 62*, 99–108.

Bernstein, R. F. (2005). *The dependent patient: A practitioner's guide.* Washington, DC: American Psychological Association.

BigFoot, D. S., & Schmidt, S. R. (2010). Honoring children, mending the circle: Cultural adaptation of trauma-focused cognitive-behavioral therapy for American Indian and Alaska Native children. *Journal of Clinical Psychology, 66*, 847–856.

Brave Heart, M.I.H. (1999). Oyate Ptayela: Rebuilding the Lakota Nation through addressing historical trauma among Lakota parents. *Journal of Human Behavior and the Social Environment, 2*(1–2), 109–126.

Brave Heart, M.I.H., & De Buyn, L. (1998). The American Indian holocaust: Healing unresolved grief. *American Indian Native Mental Health Research, 8*(2), 56–78.

Cajete, G. (2000). Indigenous knowledge: The Pueblo metaphor of Indigenous education. In M. A. Battiste (Ed.), *Reclaiming Indigenous voice and vision* (pp. 181–191). Vancouver: University of British Columbia Press.

Debo, A. (1940). *And the still waters run.* Princeton, NJ: Princeton University Press.

Doering, A., & Veletsianos, G. (2008). What lies beyond effectiveness and efficiency? Adventure learning design. *The Internet and Higher Education, 11*(3–4), 137–144.

Evans-Campbell, T. (2008). Historical trauma in American Indian/Native Alaska communities: A multilevel framework for exploring impacts on individuals, families, and communities. *Journal of Interpersonal Violence, 23*(3), 316–338.

First Nation Histories. (2002). Retrieved from http://www.tolatsga.org/Compacts.html

Freud, S. (1955). *Totem and taboo* (Standard Edition 13). London: Hogarth. (Original work published 1913)

Freud, S. (2010). *Beyond the pleasure principle.* New York: Create Space. (Original work published 1922)

Freud, S. (1963). *Studies in para-psychology.* New York: Collier Books. (Original work published 1919)

Gone, J. P., & Trimble, J. E. (2012). American Indian and Alaska Native mental health: Diverse perspectives on enduring disparities. *Annual Review of Clinical Psychology, 8*, 131–160.

Grande, S. (2004). *Red pedagogy: Native American social and political thought.* Lanham, MD: Rowman & Littlefield.

Horney, K. (1950). *Neurosis and human growth.* New York: W. W. Norton.

McDougal, J. (1989). *Theaters of the body: A psychoanalytical approach to psychosomatic illness.* New York: W. W. Norton.

McWilliams, N. (2011). *Psychoanalytic diagnosis: Understanding personality structure in the clinical process* (2nd ed.). New York: Guilford Press.

Pace, T., Robbins, R., Hill, H., Blair, G., & Lacy, K. (2006). A cultural perspective on the validity of the MMPI-2 with American Indians. *Cultural Diversity and Ethnic Minority Psychology, 12,* 320–333.

Robbins, R., Hill, J., & McWhirter, P. T. (2008). Conflicting epistemologies. *Clinical Case Studies, 17,* 449–466.

Sue, S., Zane, N., Hall, G.C.N., Berger, L. K. (2009). The case for cultural competency in psychotherapeutic interventions. *Annual Review of Psychology, 60,* 525–548.

Trimble, J. E., & Gonzalez, J. (2008). Cultural considerations and perspectives for providing psychological counseling for Native American Indians. In P. B. Pedersen, J. G. Draguns, W. J. Lonner, & J. E. Trimble (Eds.), *Counseling across cultures* (6th ed., pp. 93–112). Thousand Oaks, CA: Sage Publications.

U.S. Bureau of Justice Statistics. (2006). *Race and crime in the United States.* Washington, DC: U.S. Government Printing Office.

U.S. Census Bureau. (2000). *The American Indian and Alaska Native Population: 2000* (Census 2000 brief). Retrieved from http://www.census.gov/prod/2002pubs/censr-28.pdf

U.S. Census Bureau. (2006). American Indian/Alaskan Native. Retrieved from http://factfinder.Census.gov/home/aian/index.html

Wendt, D. C., & Gone, J. P. (2012). Rethinking cultural competence: Insights from indigenous community treatment settings. *Transcultural Psychiatry, 49,* 206–222.

Whitbeck, L. B., Adams, G. W., Hoyt, D. R., & Chen, X. (2004). Conceptualizing and measuring historical trauma among American Indian people. *American Journal of Community Psychology, 33*(3–4), 119–130.

6

The Power to Recover: Psychosocial Competence Interventions with Black Women

Lani V. Jones

Power is often an avoided topic due to individuals' experiences related to power and/or powerlessness and what it has meant for them, which may involve discomfort and embarrassment (Pinderhughes, 1989). Early experiences of powerlessness, in which individuals felt dominated by parents, teachers, and other authority figures, can result in feelings of uncertainty about power. Failure to confront these feelings can lead to clinicians' inappropriate use of their endowed power in the clinical process (Pinderhughes, 1989). When therapists are unaware of their own sense of power and how it may operate in the clinical relationship, they are more likely to impose power and control on clients in the therapeutic relationship. Proctor (2008) discussed three forms of power within the therapist–client relationship. *Role power* is given to the therapist as a result of the authority inherent in their position and in the organization for which they work; *societal power* is reflective of the structural position of the therapist and client in terms of age, race, gender, and so on; and *historical power* is based on the therapist–client perception of past experiences of power and powerlessness and how it affected them. These forms of power illustrate how therapists are generally perceived to have more power than clients. The power dynamics may be inevitable; however, practitioners should seek to provide services with as little dominance as possible (Proctor, 2008).

Clinicians have traditionally been viewed as the expert helpers who diagnose, teach, and treat, whereas the client is seen as the one seeking assistance with his or her need. Cross-cultural clinical relationships may expose clients to double vulnerability by compounding the power differentials that exist between clinician and client as well as their respective cultural identities (Pinderhughes, 1989). Clinicians may use their power over clients to satisfy personal needs for power and recognition by viewing their clients as incompetent patients in need of help, thus bolstering their own sense of competence (Pinderhughes, 1989). Furthermore, practitioners, in attempting to attain or maintain their power, often label clients as different and in need of services that are separate from their own needs. Powerlessness among clinicians and clients can be decreased when the decision-making process is collaborative and shared. Grant and Cadell (2009) discussed the circular relationship of knowledge and power, noting that knowledge generates and sustains power and power creates and sustains knowledge. Practitioners must become aware of the effect that their knowledge and experiences may have on clients. In particular, for racial/ethnic minorities, power relations cannot be ignored, as clinicians may have to forfeit feelings of expertise to empower oppressed individuals. This vigilance is necessary in guarding against the clinicians' normal vulnerability to reinforce powerlessness in cross-cultural relationships. For instance, the helping relationship should be one of collaboration, trust, and shared power so that the same feelings of powerlessness are not replicated by the worker (Gutiérrez, 1990). The sharing of power creates a freedom from dominance whereby the sense of conflict, fear, stress, rigidity, and conformity are relinquished. Likewise, the freedom from the loss of power, the pressure to hold on to it, irrational thinking, and the intolerance of difference are unleashed (Pinderhughes, 1989).

Social work practitioners are in positions that place them in frequent contact with black women experiencing perceived powerlessness; hence, it is necessary to broaden our thinking about what it means to have power, to be powerless, and to empower. Further, while addressing issues of powerlessness, social work practitioners must simultaneously understand the consequences of these power dynamics for their clients and provide culturally congruent interventions that meet their complex psychosocial needs (Jackson & Greene, 2003; Shonfeld-Ringel, 2000).

This chapter proposes to briefly examine the core ideas of power and powerlessness that have traditionally guided mental health treatment in the United States. A contextualization of these concepts for black women, including how repeated psychosocial stressors may cause a cycle of powerlessness, is discussed (Jones & Warner, 2011). This chapter also discusses the framework of psychosocial competence as an empowerment-based approach to intervening with black women. A case vignette is offered to demonstrate the usefulness of culturally congruent, empowerment-based approaches aimed at enhancing cultural competence among black women. The psychosocial competence perspective calls attention to the positive resources (that is, skills, abilities, knowledge) that help people cope with stressful events, as well as those that contribute to goal achievement and psychological well-being. Lastly, future directions for research and practice are discussed.

LITERATURE REVIEW

Exploring Power and Powerlessness

Power, broadly defined, may entail the ability to bring about a desired effect on the micro (individual), mezzo (family, group), and/or macro levels (societal) (Hopps, Pinderhughes,

& Shankar, 1995; McCubbin, 2001). In the context of psychological recovery, power can also be defined as having the opportunity to access valued materials and psychosocial resources that satisfy basic human needs and also to experience a level of competence that may instill a sense of stability and predictability in life (Prilleltensky, Nelson, & Peirson, 2001). Further, power can be expressed as an internal capacity to generate change and is often perceived or manifested in one's sense of mastery or competence over self, environment, and others (Bruce & Thornton, 2004; Hopps et al., 1995). Prilleltensky et al. (2001) defined power as the presence of opportunities to achieve outcomes. Although individuals can have power, it is not an individual characteristic but instead is relational in nature. Hence, Prilleltensky et al. noted that power lacks meaning without relationship to others or the environment, which links power to social, economic, political, and cultural occurrences. Moreover, Tew (2006) discussed a framework for different types of power, including *protective power, co-operative power, oppressive power, and collusive power*, and how their effects can overlap with each other. Power that is used to guard an individual susceptible of harm is protective power. When similar or different values are supported for collective action, it is considered co-operative power and may have a positive effect. Negative forms of power, such as oppressive power or collusive power, entail exploitation and exclusion based on differences. At the same time, protective and oppressive power are demonstrated as having power over someone, whereas co-operative power and collusive power lead to shared and collaborative action. Caution is required in situations where too much power can lead to misuse and abuse and too little power can result in vulnerability and unmet needs (Prilleltensky et al., 2001).

North America's melting pot society privileges the lifestyles of people from specific class and racial groups (white, middle class) and ignores and devalues the lifestyles of racial and ethnic minorities and the poor (Pinderhughes, 1989). This is often considered cultural imperialism, whereby the dominant group's experiences and culture are seen as the norm of society. North American values have often embodied or idealized the notion of power as strength, perfection, gain, and possession of resources. Power is often illustrated in dominant–subordinate relationships, in which one's status and assigned role within their group (culture, class, and so on) or society often determine relationship interaction style (Pinderhughes, 1989).

Powerlessness Contextualized

Powerlessness is the inability to wield influence or gain needed resources such as income, education, and employment. This restricts a person's problem-solving abilities while simultaneously increasing feelings of despair, vulnerability, low self-worth, and physical and emotional distress (Hopps et al., 1995; Thomas & Gonzalez-Prendes, 2009). The perceptual experience of powerlessness can affect all humans at some point in their life span. Important here is that the vulnerability to powerlessness increases for many African American women as a result of their unrelenting exposure to intrusive, societally imposed oppression, as well as their frequent struggle with the juxtaposition of pride and shame.

Powerlessness as an experienced or perceived oppression is understood as a multidimensional and complex system of power, developed from social beliefs embedded in group superiority that justify privilege. Researchers have asserted that stressors associated with oppression or disempowerment act to suppress feelings of competence in black women; for instance, they may fear asserting themselves in social situations, set lower goals, experience more anxiety during competition, and express more dissatisfaction with their performance (Brown, 2000). These distinct oppressive challenges add a layer of complexity to black women's ability to function competently, and often result in serious psychosocial negative consequences (for example, depression, anxiety, strained resources, poverty, poor health outcomes, exposure to violence and drug addiction) that are associated with powerlessness. In fact, it has been found that black women experiencing powerlessness are at high risk for developing mental health and other psychosocial problems (Aiyer, Zimmerman, Morrel-Samuels, & Reischl, 2015; Lord & Hutchinson, 1993; Ryan & Deci, 2000; Zimmerman & Rappaport, 1988).

In attempting to understand the psychosocial context of powerlessness among black women in America, one may be abruptly confronted with grave misconceptions of identity, distortions of fact, and defensive attitudes. Historically and currently, African American women have been denied access to needed resources as a result of gender and racial oppression. This has made them susceptible to experiences of powerlessness, which, in turn, have placed them in unfavorable societal positions (Thomas & Gonzalez-Prendes, 2009). Many African American women in subordinate positions present with positions of powerlessness, sometimes expressed through behaviors that bring them a sense of authority. This exemplifies the cyclical nature of power and powerlessness in which individuals who feel powerlessness cope by developing power over others (Hopps et al. 1995; Pinderhughes, 1989). One common strategy often used by the powerless is to foster perceptions that they are better than others by achieving competence or mastery in an area of their life, like education or professional identity; others may display behaviors such as opposition, passive aggression, manipulation, accommodation, and identification to turn their powerlessness into power. For example, there may be two black women, living in public housing, both of whom work service jobs for the hospital. They both ride the same bus to and from work, their children are placed at the same schools, and they shop at the same neighborhood grocery store. However, one of the women has an associate's degree from a local community college. She is often overheard by other residents who work at the hospital talking about her neighbors. Although she boards the bus with her neighbors every morning, she chooses to make them invisible to her. Instead of acknowledging and reaching out to her neighbors to understand their similar life and work experiences, she prefers to disassociate herself from those aspects of her identity. On the contrary, some members of oppressed groups may not be aware of their powerless positions and present with overall feelings of dissatisfaction, whereas members of privileged groups may not be consciously aware of how they oppress others (Tew, 2006). Thus, there is a need to increase awareness of how power and powerlessness may affect one's life and to provide support in the development of empowering strategies.

Powerlessness has a blunt and often complex effect on black women. The internal experience of powerlessness is related to an individual's belief that she has no control over the causes of or solutions to adverse life circumstances. Often, blame is given to the transgressor (Thomas & Gonzalez-Prendes, 2009). Many inherent power dynamics in American society have become structural. Institutionalized power is seen when certain groups have privileged access to distributive resources, allowing them to exhibit power over another group (Tew, 2006). Institutionalized racism, sexism, and heterosexism are built into the norms, traditions, laws, and policies of society, compelling even those who have nonracist, nonsexist, and nonheterosexist beliefs to act otherwise. Institutionalized racism, sexism, and heteronormativity ensure that heterosexual white men and women benefit, regardless of the intentions of individuals in those institutions.

Many clients in treatment display powerlessness when they attempt to navigate economic, political, and social systems inherent in institutional oppression. Powerlessness implies that decision making is beyond the control of the individual and further holds the powerless person accountable for lack of power. For example, consider black women who reside in low-income communities and receive inferior educations in the public system. They are sent a message by American society that, as a result of their social status, they will never become the CEO of a large business or be admitted to a top college or university. In contrast, those who possess a positive sense of power implicitly feel empowered to make decisions that affect their life goals and outcomes.

Powerlessness that is ongoing, consistent, and intractable plays a significant role in the mental and emotional dysfunction of black people in America and often leads to negative coping responses (Hopps et al., 1995). Freeman (2008) discussed how some black Americans react to their powerless positions by creating personalities that are contrary to societal norms and the values of mainstream America. This form of negative coping has led to poor decision-making skills that have criminalized black Americans as a group. Pollack (2003) discussed how many imprisoned black women turn to nonviolent crimes and drugs and/or alcohol in an effort to cope with life stressors and oppressive circumstances. As Michelle Alexander (2010) so eloquently shared in *The New Jim Crow: Mass Incarceration in the Age of Colorblindness*,

> American society would rather portray Black women as criminals, unemployed, or single parents on welfare than place them in the context of their oppressive life experiences. A life experience that restricts affords few healthy options in attaining the "American Dream." (p. 54)

A comprehensive understanding of factors associated with powerlessness and psychosocial stressors among black women remains elusive; researchers have identified that oppressive social conditions such as institutional and ethnocentric practices are related to the development of mental health disorders for black women (Baldwin, Brown, & Rackley, 1990; Grote, Bledsoe, Larkin, Lemay, & Brown, 2007; Hopps et al., 1995). In particular, stress (Grote et al., 2007); negative thinking patterns (Delahanty et al., 2001); and institutional racism, sexism, and experiences of discrimination have been linked with depression among black women. In addition, research on the impact of stress on adverse health outcomes among black women is growing (Landrine & Klonoff, 1996). According to Geronimus, Bound, Keene, and Hicken (2007), the psychological and physiological responses to stress experienced by many American racial minorities over the life course led to chronic physical and psychological health problems. Studies reviewed by Thomas and Gonzalez-Prendes (2009) show a range of health problems created or exacerbated among African American women because of the association of anger and stress related to powerlessness. There are several other risk factors, including but not limited to, diastolic blood pressure (Artinian, Washington, Flack, Hockman, & Jen, 2006); low birth rates (Nuru-Jeter et al., 2009), pervasive mental health disorders (Williams, 2000), and lack of social support (Lincoln, Chatters, & Taylor, 2003; Thoits, 1984). Consequently, an important goal of practitioners is to reduce stress in an effort to promote positive health and mental health outcomes among African American women.

POWER AND THE CLINICAL RELATIONSHIP

Psychosocial Competence as a Construct for Empowerment

Over recent years, social work education and practice has been concerned with issues of power, particularly in relation to processes of oppression and empowerment (Gutiérrez, 1990; Karbon & Trotter, 2000). Although this strategy is a step toward acknowledgment and concern for disenfranchised groups in American society, little attention has been given to the unique psychosocial reality of black women in the United States. Consequently, the theoretical foundations of many established clinical practice models do not reflect the diversity of cultural values and worldviews found in the broader American society (Baldwin, Brown, & Rackley, 1990), especially those of black women. The exclusion of ethnic minorities in mental health outcome studies has been extensively documented (Brockting et al., 2006; Miranda & Cooper, 2004; Reay, Fisher, Robertson, Adams, & Owen, 2006). With the exception of a few studies that have focused on ethnic minority women (Miranda et al., 2003), research on prevention and treatment for women with mental health disorders has primarily focused on white women. This limitation of treatment outcome studies is problematic, as black women are increasingly entering public–private sector services, as opposed to more traditional methods (for example, the black church, familial support, neighborhood services), to address mental health difficulties associated with stress (Cooper-Patrick, Crum, Powe, Pratt, & Ford 1999; Snowden, 2001; Swartz et al., 1998). There is a need for culturally congruent, empowerment-based interventions that affirm the reality of black women with stressors that often lead to mental health disorders as a result of unrelenting exposure to oppressive conditions.

Empowerment perspectives assume that the role of power and powerlessness is integral to the experiences of black women (Gutiérrez, 1990). According to Browne and Mills (2001), empowerment is "the gaining of power by an individual, family group, or community" (p. 23). Empowerment assumes a position of powerlessness on the part of the client group. "Empowerment" is a broad term that has been used to help populations of disenfranchised people rise above situations as well as foster strength in individuals who experience feelings of powerlessness (Tew, 2006). Empowerment for people who occupy powerless roles in more than one area of their life can be perceived as double victimization and may require targeted and/or expanded strategies that are not required for those who are not in such roles (Pinderhughes, 1989). So-called double victims may have to work twice as hard to develop coping strategies, but it is possible that if one powerless role is linked with another powerlessness role, then modifications in one role may facilitate alterations in the other (Gutiérrez, 1990; Pinderhughes, 1989). For example, black women face double victimization as a result of racism and sexism in U.S. society. Hence, empowerment is a process of increasing personal, interpersonal, or political power so that people are motivated and encouraged to improve their overall well-being. In developing empowerment-based, culturally congruent interventions targeted for black women, methods must be structured so that they can experience themselves as competent within the context of a supportive environment (Jones, 2004). Empowerment techniques that enable people to experience themselves as competent, valuable, and worthwhile—both as an individual in society and a member of a cultural group—help create a sense of control in life. Effective empowerment strategies may require practitioners to become vulnerable by using strategies that eschew power derived from their position as expert and/or from a particular cultural group and by avoiding stereotypes (Pinderhughes, 1989).

Psychosocial Competence: Implications for African American Women Experiencing Powerlessness

One approach to mental health care that may have particular utility for black women experiencing stressors associated with powerlessness is embodied in the empowerment-based perspective of psychosocial competence. More recently, mental health researchers have identified the concepts of psychosocial competence (that is, locus of control, coping, and self-efficacy) and culture, race, and gender as constructs that are central to improved models for understanding and enhancing the psychological well-being of black women in mental health treatment (Jones, 2004; Tyler, Brome, & Williams, 1991; Tyler & Pargament, 1981). These key concepts are particularly relevant when working with black women experiencing a sense of powerlessness, given that their psychosocial responses are often related to feelings of loss of control and an inability to cope with their lives.

In social work, as in other fields, *psychosocial competence* is defined as an individual's ability to function effectively at the personal, interpersonal, social, and task levels. A psychosocially competent individual has an active coping style, a moderately internal locus-of-control orientation, and a moderate level of trust (Maluccio, 2000; Tyler et al., 1991). Psychosocial competence is a multifaceted configuration that includes a set of self-attitudes, world attributes, and behavioral attributes that are designed to promote effective functioning in human beings by focusing on their unique coping and adaptive patterns, actual or potential strengths, natural helping networks, life experiences, and environmental resources as major instruments of intervention (Maluccio, 2000). Within this configuration, individuals create for themselves a sense of self-empowerment, a sense of a relationship to the world, and a way of negotiating life events in light of these perspectives (Tyler et al., 1991).

Psychosocial competence has significant application to the planning and delivery of interventions for individuals confronted with psychosocial difficulties. Although there is a paucity of intervention research in the area of psychosocial competence and black women, the few studies that have been conducted have supported the presence of a shared constellation of personal attributes in individuals who successfully negotiate life with all its unexpected changes (see Evans & Tyler, 1976; Jarama, Belgrave, & Zea, 1996; Jones, 2004; Zea, Reisen, Beil, & Caplan, 1997). These findings suggest that interventions aimed at enhancing black women's sense of psychosocial competence during times of stress and adversity, or during less predictable environmental situations, may promote a more optimal pattern of functioning and promote greater well-being. Thus, black women are more likely to develop a personality and behavioral pattern that is characterized by strengths, capabilities, and resilience and is more adaptive to alternate circumstances. Psychosocial competence is a paradigm worth examining in black women dealing with multiple stressors or other mental health difficulties.

In an effort to expand opportunities for black women to engage in culturally congruent therapeutic interventions, I developed the Claiming Your Connections curriculum. The group curriculum draws on black women's cultural and spiritual traditions as vehicles for participants to gain self-awareness and a connection with others to alleviate symptoms of stress and depression and to develop problem-solving and coping skills. The group intervention consisted of 10 weekly, 90-minute sessions. The sessions are led by a licensed clinical social worker with experience working with black women. The protocol includes psychoeducational, support, and problem-solving approaches to competence enhancement. The sessions move from a predetermined structure focused on assigned readings to a progressively more open format. In later sessions, more intimate topics can be discussed while integrating supportive intervention techniques (see Jones [2008] and Jones & Warner [2011] for a detailed protocol).

The following vignette focuses on the early stages of the group process. It emphasizes the importance of the group leader's role as an interventionist using empowerment techniques and helping the members to affirm an anti-oppressive approach in problem identification, self-exploration, and problem solving in the alleviation of stress symptoms.

CASE VIGNETTE

Nia is a 48-year-old mother of four who is recovering from a history of childhood sexual abuse, domestic violence, and drug addiction. Her experience of multiple stressors has understandably led to the development of depressive symptoms. At the start of the group, Nia exhibited a low sense of self and flat affect, depressed mood, and passivity. She entered the group referring to herself as "second class" in her family life, work life, and social life. During the initial stages of the group, she barely spoke or offered feedback to the other participants. Nia appeared to be disengaged and disconnected from the group. When she did participate in group discussions, she displayed no emotion and was often critical and denigrating of others' experiences. Her emotional detachment was typical of someone who has experienced a sense of powerlessness in her life and is at high risk for developing mental health problems. Nia's detachment continued throughout the initial sessions of the program.

In the fourth session, which focused on the role of stress and coping in the lives of black women, the group worker provided a definition of psychological stress and asked the members to identify their emotional and physical reactions to stress. The group members listed several personal reactions, such as "confusion and disorganization," "overwhelmed," "used and abused," "I just shut down," and "irritable." As group members continued to explore the role of stress in their lives, Tanya said, "Emotionally I feel weighed down, like I can't go on." Nia abruptly stated, "Well, you're just going to have to learn how to move on; hard times come, hard times go, they come more often my way." Kendra responded, "I wish you would just stop pretending like you are all that. We all have problems, stress; that's why we're here." This statement made by another group member opened up the floor for Nia to engage in further disclosure. Nia stated, "You don't know me, who I am, what I have experienced. If you were in my shoes, you probably wouldn't be alive today. I am just so sick and tired of failing because I don't live up to what society wants, my family wants. No one cares about how I feel or how hard I work. I guess that's why I turned to drugs." Nia's feelings of despair settled in the room like a storm cloud.

As the group members listened to Nia's story filled with rejection, invasion, torment, and disappointment, they expressed their affirmation through silence and head nodding (a behavior traditionally learned in church or in discussion at the kitchen table). This indicated that it was a story they had heard many times before—a self-told story of feeling powerless, a story told by their mothers, aunts, sisters, and many other black women who had given and been taken from with great suffering. As she continued to tell her story, Nia shed not one tear; she stood firm and stoic. Although her body language lacked expression, the group worker could feel her spirit echo the pain she had endured.

Nia's story was rooted in the unfortunate internalized tradition that says that black women must be strong in the face of adversity and accept life's rejections as the products of their unalterable destiny. In breaking the group's silence and providing support for Nia's story, the group worker asserted, "Isn't it reasonable to consider that we can become 'tired and worn?'" Lisa, another group member, agreed, saying, "Nia, girl, I understand; we give everyone everything just to make other people happy, but we have nothing for ourselves; we are not happy. Yeah, alcohol was a way out. At least that's what I thought."

The group worker intervened by exploring the societal construction of black women as "mammies," "caretakers," and "superwomen," as well as women's acceptance of these roles. She discussed how the belief in the societal myths that black women are invincible and can endure any adversity without breaking down is psychologically damaging. She further explained, "The belief in these myths dates back to the days of slavery, when we had to ignore our emotional needs to survive. But today, black women continue to experience the emotional repercussions of slavery." With sincere conviction and emotion, Nia revealed, "I am that woman . . . but that's the only woman I know." Other group members agreed with Nia's identification with the forced role of the strong black woman. The group leader then said, "To reduce our psychological stressors, we must conquer denial and alter our defenses that lead us to pretend that we are always in control of our life circumstances and the behaviors of others, especially our family members. This will ultimately enable us to recover from psychological stress."

The support offered by the group gave Nia and the other members tangible tools for addressing such issues as stress and internalized oppression. The group leader stated, "Now that we have identified some of our causes and responses to stress in our lives, we can move our discussion forward and consider healing." The group further explored strategies for managing and healing from stressful life experiences. The group worker concluded by saying, "The more we as black women work on our self-recovery, increasing our self-esteem, ridding our lives of debilitating stress, and rejecting devaluation of ourselves, the less we will be drawn into self-destructive behaviors." By the end of the session, the group members began to understand, identify with, and support Nia. Realizing that her initial presentation of herself in the group was the mask of survival that she wore, Nia, in turn, became less defensive and more open to receiving feedback from the group for the remainder of the program.

During this session, the group members were able to receive acknowledgment and validation of both their current and historical realities of unrecognized, devalued, and oppressive relationships as black women and explore undue destructive criticism of normative difficulties. They learned to hear each other's deepest fears, insecurities, and mistakes in the context of informed, nonjudgmental support, and felt empowered to evaluate and change their life circumstances. The social worker's role as helper is to facilitate the empowerment process and nurture black women's resilience by sharing experiences and worldviews, encouraging self-definition and self-determination, and rejecting negative images and damaging stereotypes (Greene, 1997; hooks, 2005).

Knowledge of empowerment strategies to enhance psychosocial competence provides a foundation in which a student or professional might begin to think about interventions for this population. For example, empowerment-based perspectives draw on psychosocial competence rather than pathological or maladaptive behaviors (Jones & Warner, 2011). Thus, interventions in the mental health field should aim to help black women sort out the personal from the contextual by helping them recognize how the internalization of socially constructed identities has contributed to their depressive symptoms (Williams, 2005).

FUTURE DIRECTIONS: RESEARCH, PRACTICE, AND POLICY

Effective services that are aimed at increasing positive mental health outcomes for Black women experiencing societally imposed oppression should be an item of high importance to the social work profession. Given its potential applicability to black female recipients of services, the psychosocial competence paradigm offers a unique opportunity to work toward these goals. It also offers practitioners a useful method of providing services from an empowerment-based perspective. This differs from traditional medical models of stress and other related mental health disorders among black women. At the micro level, empowerment is the mobilization of the client's uniqueness and self-determination to take charge of her own life, to learn new ways of thinking about the problem situation, and to adopt new behaviors that result in positive outcomes. Social workers are often given the challenge of documenting the extent of a social problem and developing interventions to eradicate it. As I have highlighted here, it is clear that few data exist on the role of gender, race, ethnicity, and culture in the epidemiology, assessment, and treatment of mental health stressors. As social workers begin to apply empowerment-based concepts such as psychosocial competence to black women, they will be able to assess the concepts' utility (Jones, 2004). Furthermore, social workers must recognize that for interventions with black women and their families to be successful, clients need accurate information and professional service that demonstrate respect and care for the person, the family, and the values and traditions that they bring to the treatment process. Practitioners also ascertain whether members of a woman's microsystem, such as family members, friends, and small groups, can be linked to the roots of the problem.

On the macro level, there is a need to recognize potential links between problems and environmental factors. Macro-level empowerment recognizes the need for large-scale organizational and institutional change. Group empowerment involves the ability to work with others to change social institutions. For example, in work with black women, the absence of ethnicity-specific community organizations that offer culturally responsive treatment services can greatly affect the problem situations by contributing to the women's sense of isolation and alienation. Because it allows for a thorough analysis of multiple interactions between the micro and macro contexts, the psychosocial competence framework is also an important tool for policy and research that focus on addressing issues of importance to black women. Examining both micro and macro contexts allows for the development of policies and research that focus on both specific and general societal barriers to treatment of depression among black women.

REFERENCES

Aiyer, S. M., Zimmerman, M. A., Morrel-Samuels, S., & Reischl, T. M. (2015). From broken windows to busy streets: A community empowerment perspective. *Health Education & Behavior, 42*(2), 137–147. doi:10.1177/1090198114558590

Alexander, M. (2010). *The new Jim Crow: Mass incarceration in the age of colorblindness.* New York: New Press.

Artinian N. T., Washington, O. G., Flack, J. M., Hockman, E. M., & Jen, K. L. (2006). Depression, stress and blood pressure in urban African American women. *Progress in Cardiovascular Nursing, 21*(2), 68–75.

Baldwin, J. A., Brown, R., & Rackley, R. (1990). Some socio-behavioral correlates of African self consciousness in African-American college students. *Journal of African American Psychology, 17*(1), 1–17.

Brockting, C., Spinhoven, P., Koeter, M., Wouters, L., Visser, L., Schene, A., & the Delta Study Group. (2006). Differential predictors of response to preventive cognitive therapy in recurrent depression: A 2-year prospective study. *Psychotherapy and Psychosomatics, 75,* 229–236.

Brown, A. (2000). Rural black women and depression: A contextual analysis. *Journal of Marriage and the Family, 62*, 187–198.

Browne, C., & Mills, C. (2001). Theoretical frameworks: Ecological model, strengths perspective, and empowerment theory. In R. Fong & S. Furuto (Eds.), *Culturally competent practice: Skills, interventions, and evaluations* (pp. 10–32). Boston: Allyn & Bacon.

Bruce, M. A., & Thornton, M. C. (2004). IT'S MY WORLD? Exploring black and white perceptions of personal control. *Sociological Quarterly, 45*, 597–612.

Cooper-Patrick, L., Crum, R., Powe, N. R., Pratt, L., & Ford, D. E. (1999). Factors associated with help-seeking behavior for mental health services among whites and African Americans. *AHSR and FHSR Annual Meeting Abstract Book, 12*, 105.

Delahanty, J., Ranganathan, R., Postrado, L., Balis, T., Green-Paden, L., & Dixon, L. (2001). Differences in rates of depression in schizophrenia by race. *Schizophrenia Bulletin, 27*(1), 29–37.

Evans, D., & Tyler, F. B. (1976). Is work competence enhancing the poor? *American Journal of Community Psychology, 4*, 25–33.

Freeman, D. (2008). Kenneth B. Clark and the problem of power. *Patterns of Prejudice, 42*(4–5), 413–437.

Geronimus, A. T., Bound, J., Keene, D., & Hicken, M. (2007). Black–white differences in age trajectories of hypertension prevalence among adult women and men, 1999–2002. *Ethnicity & Disease, 17*, 40–48.

Grant, J. G., & Cadell, S. (2009). Power, pathological worldviews and the strengths perspective in social work. *Families in Society, 90*, 425–430.

Greene, B. (1997). Psychotherapy with African American women: Integrating feminist and psychodynamic models. *Smith College Studies in Social Work, 67*, 299–322.

Grote, N. K., Bledsoe, S. E., Larkin, J., Lemay, E. P., & Brown, C. (2007). Stress exposure and depression in disadvantaged women: The protective effects of optimism and perceived control. *Social Work Research, 31*, 19–33.

Gutiérrez, L. (1990). Working with women of color: An empowerment perspective. *Social Work, 35*, 149–153.

hooks, b. (2005). Sisters of the yam: Black women and self-recovery. Boston: South End Press.

Hopps, J. G., Pinderhughes, E. B., & Shankar, R. (1995). *The power to care*. New York: Free Press.

Jackson, L. C., & Greene, B. A. (2003). Review of psychotherapy with African American women: Innovations in psychodynamic perspectives and practice. *Psychoanalytic Quarterly, 72*, 524–526.

Jarama, S. L., Belgrave, F., & Zea, M. C. (1996). The role of social support in adaptation to college among Latino students, *Cultural Diversity and Mental Health, 2*, 193–203.

Jones, L. V. (2004). Enhancing psychosocial competence among black women in college. *Social Work, 49*, 75–84.

Jones, L. V. (2008). Preventing depression: Culturally relevant group work with black women. *Research on Social Work Practice, 18*, 626–634.

Jones, L. V., & Warner, L. (2011). Culturally responsive group work with black women. *Journal of Research on Social Work Practice, 21*, 737–746.

Karbon, K., & Trotter, J. (2000). *Boundaries and barriers: Promoting interprofessional education in social work.* Paper presented at joint conference at the International Federation of Social Workers and the International Association of Schools of Social Work, Montreal.

Landrine, H., & Klonoff, E. A. (1996). The Schedule of Racist Events: A measure of racial discrimination and a study of its negative physical and mental health consequences. *Journal of Black Psychology, 22*, 144–168.

Lincoln, K. D., Chatters. L. M., Taylor, R. J. (2003). Psychological distress among black and white Americans: Differential effects of social support, negative interaction and personal control. *Health and Social Behavior, 44*(3), 390–407.

Lord, J., & Hutchinson, P. (1993). The process of empowerment: Implications for theory and practice, *Canadian Journal of Community Mental Health, 12*(1), 5–22.

Maluccio, A. N. (2000). A competence-centered perspective on child welfare. In J. G. Hopps & R. Morris (Eds.), *Social work at the millennium: Critical reflection on the future of the profession* (pp. 160–174). New York: Free Press.

McCubbin, M. (2001). Pathways to health, illness and well-being: From the perspective of power and control. *Journal of Community and Applied Social Psychology, 11*, 75–81.

Miranda, J., Chung, J. Y., Green, B. L., Krupnick, J., Siddique, J., Revicki, D. A., & Belin, T. (2003). Treating depression in predominantly low-income young minority women: A randomized controlled trial. *Journal of the American Medical Association, 290*, 57–65.

Miranda, J., & Cooper, L. A. (2004). Disparities in care for depression among primary care patients. *Journal of General Internal Medicine, 19*(2), 120–126.

Nuru-Jeter, A., Dominguez, T. P., Hammond, W. P., Leu, J., Skaff, M., Egerter, S., et al. (2009). "It's the skin you're in": African-American women talk about their experiences of racism. An exploratory study to develop measures of racism for birth outcome studies. *Journal of Maternal & Child Health, 13*(1), 29–39.

Pinderhughes, E. (1989). *Understanding race, ethnicity & power: The keys to efficacy in clinical practice.* New York: Free Press.

Pollack, S. (2003). Focus-group methodology in research with incarcerated women: Race, power, and collective experience. *Affilia*, 461–472.

Prilleltensky, I., Nelson, G., & Peirson, L. (2001). The role of power and control in children lives: An ecological analysis of pathways towards wellness, resiliency and problems, *Journal of Community and Applied Social Psychology, 11*, 143–158.

Proctor, G. (2008). CBT: The obscuring of power in the name of science. *European Journal of Psychotherapy and Counselling, 10*(3), 231–145.

Reay, R., Fisher, Y., Robertson, E., Adams, E., & Owen, C. (2006). Group interpersonal psychotherapy for postnatal depression: A pilot study. *Archives of Women's Mental Health, 9*, 31–39.

Ryan, R. M., & Deci, E. L. (2000). Self-determination theory and the facilitation of intrinsic motivation, social development, and well-being. *American Psychologist, 55*, 68–78.

Shonfeld-Ringel, S. (2000). Dimensions of cross cultural treatment with late adolescent college students. *Child and Adolescent Social Work Journal, 17*, 443–454.

Snowden, L. R. (2001). Barriers to effective mental health services for African Americans. *Mental Health Services Research, 3*(4), 181–187.

Swartz, M. S., Wagner, H. R., Swanson, J. W., Burns, B. J., George, L. K., & Padgett, D. K. (1998). Comparing use of public and private mental health services: The enduring barriers of race and age. *Community Mental Health Journal, 34*, 133–144.

Tew, J. (2006). Understanding power and powerlessness: Towards a framework for emancipatory practice in social work. *Journal of Social Work, 6*(1), 33–51.

Thoits, P. A. (1984). Explaining distributions of psychological vulnerability: Lack of social support in the face of life stress. *Social Forces, 63*, 453–481.

Thomas, S., & Gonzalez-Prendes, A. (2009). Powerlessness, anger, and stress in African American women: Implication for physical and emotional health. *Health Care for Women International, 30*(1–2), 93–113.

Tyler, F. B., Brome, D. R., & Williams, J. E. (1991). *Ethnic validity, and psychotherapy: A psychosocial competence approach*. New York: Plenum Press.

Tyler, F. B., & Pargament, K. I. (1981). Racial and personal factors and the complexities of competence-oriented changes in a high school group counseling program. *American Journal of Community Psychology, 9*, 697–714.

Williams, D. R. (2000). Racism and mental health. The African American experience. *Race and Ethnicity, 5*(3–4), 243–268.

Williams, C. B. (2005). Counseling African American women: Multiple identities-multiple constraints. *Journal of Counseling & Development, 83*, 278– 283.

Zea, M. C., Reisen, C. A., Beil, C., & Caplan, R. D. (1997). Predicting intention to remain in college among ethnic minority and non-minority students. *Journal of Social Psychology, 137*, 149–160.

Zimmerman, M., & Rappaport, J. (1988). Citizen participation, perceived control and psychological empowerment. *American Journal of Community Psychology, 16*(5), 725–750.

7

Culture, Power, and Resistance: Testimonies of Hope and Dignity

Makungu Akinyela

What is power's relevance and meaning in relationships between mental health/ human service workers and working-class and poor black people in the 21st century? I contend that power and its meaning cannot be discussed outside of a conversation about culture, multi-culturalism, and the struggle for democracy. Antonia Darder (2012), in discussing the issue of power relations, argued that culturally democratic work must move beyond simple inclusion of diverse cultural information (multi-culturalism) and implement "the necessary shift in power relationships required in [communities] and society in order to involve [groups] in an active process of empowerment, assist them in finding their voice, and support the development of a spirit of social solidarity" (p. 57).

To have a voice—that is, to be able to give one's own testimony and feel that one is both comprehended and listened to as well as to be able to have the capacity to define oneself as an active agent in the world, rather than a passive victim—is a significant element of power appropriation. To have a voice and to be an agent of one's life is a minimal requirement for what Maulana Karenga (1980) in his cultural–political Kawaida theory, calls *kujichagulia* (self-determination). In a previous work, Delores Aldridge and I (2003) wrote:

> The history of resistance and movements for civil and human rights by African and other oppressed people in America make it clear that a central issue for oppressed communities is social, economic and political power and how it is distributed. Power is the ability of an individual or groups to make decisions

and to implement those decisions in relationship to another individual or group, even if the second individual or group resists the decisions being made. It is in these relations of power between dominant and subordinate groups that culture is constructed and cultural values defining behaviors and actions toward others are formed. Unevenly distributed power and privilege occurs within every social, cultural arena, including within the institutions and communities serviced by social workers. (p. 61)

In this chapter, I describe the actions and inactions that go into *infrapolitics* (Scott, 1990), or small acts of resistance used by the oppressed against powerful dominators. These infrapolitics are often judged by the powerful as simply laziness, mental ineptitude, or cultural deficiencies and are not recognized as legitimate acts of political resistance to oppressive power. Just as the infrastructure of a city provides the foundations and inner workings upon which a city is built, the infrapolitics of black family life provide the basis for the more overt political struggles and organized resistance within black communities and between black communities and dominant European American society. I argue here that the behaviors and responses to interventions by therapists and other human services workers that are labeled as oppositional are, in fact, efforts by people who experience themselves as powerless in the larger society to hold on to dignity. It is critical for human services workers to accurately identify these responses and to explore how their own experiences and biases affect their assessment of clients who are attempting to act with power in inherently disempowering situations.

Black parents, especially those who are poor and working class, are often considered by family service representatives and educators as unconcerned about their children's education or hostile toward teachers and social workers. Children are labeled as slow and as possessing inappropriate language skills, as reflected in the overrepresentation of low-income black children in special education programs (Blanchett, 2006; Gold & Richards, 2012). Child Protective Services workers are frustrated when they make appointments for home visits and repeatedly find no one home or find that when they arrive, family members are unprepared to receive them or fail to have key members present. Televisions are left on at full volume during home visits, and the neighbor's children or friends are brought along to office visits even though workers were explicit that this was a time for family members only. Beyond the common interpretations of these actions as inappropriate behaviors, these often frustrating, sometimes bewildering actions can be interpreted as representative of culturally grounded attempts to achieve justice in an unjust situation. These acts are directly descended (and learned) from the disruptive and destructive actions of enslaved Africans on southern plantations who "accidentally" broke farm tools, or overzealously beat plow mules to death, or worked much more slowly than production needs demanded. These behaviors were the basis of European American stereotypes of the shiftless and lazy Negro and of the black people who were too childlike and unintelligent to be allowed freedom. In the same way, human services, school, and other authority figures in poor and working-class black communities frequently develop stereotypes based on observed behaviors of black people with whom they interact.

The styles of resistance learned from generation to generation can be heard in the stories of everyday life as told by people from black communities. These stories are testimonies of "how we got over" and set the context for kinship interactions and intra- as well as intercommunal behaviors that may be observed from black people. Though these testimonies are critical to shaping the lives of the teller, they are rarely heard by human services workers. This is primarily because the everyday lives of the oppressed are considered to be insignificant.

Since 1996, my clinical practice has been ground in and committed to developing testimony therapy (Akinyela, 2008). *Testimony therapy* is a discursive therapy closely related to narrative and other storytelling therapies. The primary distinction is the focus on a cultural analysis of the meaning of the story in the context of the lives of black people.

In this chapter, the testimonies of four people are provided as examples of socially developed tools of counterhegemonic resistance to loss of dignity. These are the types of stories shared in the space provided by testimony therapy. These stories are examples of the hidden testimony that is rarely considered significant in working with black families. The hidden testimony is the story told by African American people in private spaces that feel safe from the judging gaze of racist oppression. Traditionally, the church, the barber or beauty shop, or the Friday fish fry might be examples of spaces for the hidden testimony.

The testimonies described in this chapter were evoked in discussions held with participants using the structured dialogue method of testimony therapy. In all cases, the names and identifying details of informants have been changed to ensure their privacy.

These testimonies reflect issues from the everyday lives of working-class and poor black people. These are the types of life issues that affect family relationships, shape the ability of individuals to carry out responsibilities and roles, and influence perceptions of success or failure in a person's life.

Though these testimonies might often be observed as evidence of pathology or enmeshment or other deficit-focused paradigms, they are not often listened to as testimonies to the cultural strengths of resistance to oppression that have been passed on from generation to generation within black family households. The stories and behaviors described here are not unfamiliar or unusual as accurate reflections of the lives of significant numbers of working-class and poor black people. Although there are likely many tactics or weapons of cultural resistance that may occur between poor clients and human services workers, the following eight are identified and briefly discussed in this chapter: (1) resigned fatalism, (2) noncompliance, (3) oppositional logic, (4) compliance to the letter, (5) rehearsed challenge, (6) emotional detachment, (7) stiff-necked independence, and (8) inferred potential violence.

These are all tactics of counterhegemonic resistance that are used by members of a subordinate community to resist perceived daily loss of dignity and injustice in a society where they otherwise have no significant power. These tactics are learned through the hidden testimony as it is constructed within households. They can be used to resist class, racial, ethnic, gender, or other forms of oppression.

The argument here is not that these weapons are in themselves always positive, good, or even beneficial in the long run for those who wield them. However, they represent a cultural legacy and style of institutional organization that has enabled Africans in America as a people to survive, develop, and maintain a cultural ethos, despite relentless social and political assaults against their cultural integrity. I believe that these behaviors and actions—which will seem familiar to many human services workers engaged in work in poor black communities—are efforts to maintain a sense of dignity in the face of what often can feel like permanent experiences of humiliation. For this reason, and because these weapons remain necessary and prevalent, they should be focused on for their value in helping us understand cultural resistance in African American communities.

WILLIAM

William is a 50-year-old retired black military veteran who has been on total disability since he was severely injured in combat on a tour of duty in Vietnam. He was diagnosed with posttraumatic stress disorder as a result of his war experiences. After his discharge from the military, he became heavily addicted to drugs and alcohol, until he became involved with Alcoholics Anonymous and Narcotics Anonymous.

Can you remember any particular time when you were made to feel "less than dirt" by somebody in authority?

I filed for disability, and they told me that I couldn't be having this much pain and I started becoming angry. Or they would make an appointment for me and I would have to sit waiting for the appointment all day.

How did you behave when you were feeling so disrespected?

So I would refuse to do certain things they told me to do, like dressing my wound certain ways or whatever. If they told me to take therapy, I wouldn't take the therapy. I just started being rebellious. You know, "If they don't believe anything is wrong with me, I'm not going to follow their orders." They would give me pills, I wouldn't take them, I'd just leave them there. I told them I didn't want them, I was already halfway addicted. Then they threatened me that if I didn't do this, I couldn't file for disability. Then I would do what they wanted.

If I had been waiting for an appointment all day, I used to stomp and cuss and demand to know, "Why I got to be here all day?" or go up to the desk and agitate the little person at the reception desk. I'd go up there and in a loud projected voice with my eyes bugged out, say something like, "I been here all day, I'm tired of waiting, so what's the problem?" And the little girl at the desk would get nervous and say that the doctor wasn't there. And I'd start yelling, "Well, somebody got to see me, I'm in pain!" And I wouldn't necessarily be in pain; it was just my way of making them pay attention to me so I could get out of there.

LISA

Lisa is a 39-year-old mother of two children, a 21-year-old daughter and a nine-year-old son. She and her 47-year-old husband, Melvin, have been married for six years.

Lisa grew up in the same neighborhood where the family continues to live today. She lived in a large household with five sisters and one brother. She said that her parents divorced when she was four years old, and her mother later remarried.

Can you remember any particular time when you were made to feel "less than dirt" by somebody in authority?

When my daughter was two years old, I got on welfare, and I was trying to find a job. The only job I could find was part time at a Burger King. While I was on welfare, I was getting a payment to help pay for my apartment. I saved my money to pay the deposit. They paid my rent, all except about 15 dollars. They paid me 72 dollars in food stamps. I'm working a part-time job, they were monitoring my hours, and I couldn't go over 20 hours. If I went one hour over, they would end up shortening my check the next month. So this went on until I said I was fed up with this.

How did you behave when you were feeling so disrespected?

I asked my manager if I could work some extra hours, 'cause I was so angry, I was determined I was going to get off welfare, even if they took money from me for working extra hours. I just kept on saying to myself that one day I was going to tell these welfare people where to go with their so-called help. One thing about my family, they can be busybodies, but when it's crunch time, they come together. My grandmother used to tell me, "You don't have to worry about groceries. Just make sure your rent is paid, and between me and your mother, we'll take care of your groceries."

When my manager gave me full-time, the social worker came to my apartment for her periodic inspection. I guess they was coming to see if a man is in your house, or something. Back in those days you couldn't have a telephone. That was considered a luxury.

The social worker told me they were going to cut my food stamps down to 24 dollars 'cause I was working too many hours at Burger King! I said, "Keep them! Y'all just go on and keep them! Keep the food stamp and keep the check!" And I wasn't nasty to her or nothing. When the social worker came through, I opened the door wide for her and told her to come right on in and showed her around.

I wanted them to know that they was not getting the best of me. I felt really pissed off that I was being put through so many tests and I was doing everything they asked me to do. It was folk who were really doing wrong who they weren't paying attention to, and here they were sending me through all these changes for 72 dollars in food stamps and a hundred and something dollars.

NADEERA

Nadeera is a 36-year-old single mother with a 16-year-old daughter, Nikita, in Oakland, California. She is a recovering alcoholic who, along with her daughter, has been homeless for the past three years. They currently live in a shelter for homeless families, where they are provided a studio-type apartment with a small kitchen and receive public assistance. Nadeera is also a film production student completing her final semester toward a bachelor's degree. She is deeply interested in going to law school to study entertainment law after graduation.

Can you remember any particular time when you were made to feel "less than dirt" by somebody in authority?

> When I was 22 or 23 years old, I was hired by [a California law enforcement agency], and my training officer [a white woman] who I allowed to humiliate me, embarrass me, and degrade me to the maximum, because I thought I wanted this job bad enough.
>
> Whenever any male officers were around, she would yell at me, criticize me, or say whatever she felt like. She just had a nasty attitude. She would treat prisoners bad, cursing them out and thrashing them around. She was cool as long as it was just the prisoner and her and me, but as soon as we got in front of the jail where other officers were . . . it was just brutality. One guy even said to me, "Thank you for treating me with respect," because I wouldn't go along with how she treated prisoners.
>
> She would yell at me in front of the other officers, "You can't even write a report?! This report is child's scratch!" Or if I took my uniform to a cleaners which she didn't use, she'd chastise me while we were at lunch with the other officers, "Why would you go to that place? You're going to look as dumb as you act if you wear that uniform like that." She'd try and find things to belittle me about. Even things I knew I was doing right and had improved on, she couldn't give me credit for it.

How did you behave when you were feeling so disrespected?

> I would just allow her to rant and rave like that and didn't say anything. I just accepted it because she was my training officer. I just eventually got to a point where I thought to myself, "Oh you fool!" and I thought, "I'll just let this fool run her course," but to her I would say, "Uh huh, yeah, OK." And I just did what she told me to do because she was my training officer.
>
> Then one day, something just snapped in me. We were in a break room, and there were two other officers sitting there. She came into the door and she just started yelling at me about my report. I just looked up at her, and I don't know what happened, but I think we both realized that I had a gun and she had a gun. I had a nightstick and she had one. And I just looked at her and I guess it was a death look. But she just shut up, and that was the last night that we worked together.

I finally left after I kept having my probation extended, and then they put me with a guy who could only talk about sex, no matter what the subject was. On the last day of my evaluation, he made a comment about a girl who had slept with her training officer so she could make it through, and he said, "Now you wouldn't do anything like that now, would you?" I just ignored him like I didn't hear him. Well, needless to say, I didn't get a good evaluation and so I ended up leaving and going back home to Oakland.

TINA

Tina is a single 34-year-old mother who had her first and only child six years ago. She and her son Rashad live alone in an apartment several miles away from the East Oakland community that she grew up in. Tina says that, as a child, she was not very happy because of ongoing arguments and fights between her mother and father. She says that though she did not notice it back then, she knows today that her mother is an alcoholic, which she attributes to her mother not being content in her marriage.

Can you remember any particular time when you were made to feel "less than dirt" by somebody in authority?

My son's daddy lives in San Francisco, but we don't socialize. I've never been his girlfriend or anything, but we were dating. Everything seemed OK, it's been a long time since I actually let anyone "claim" me, but everything was OK with him until he found out I was pregnant. And that's when things changed. He wanted to deny first of all that the baby was his, and that was just in the beginning. Even though he said it wasn't his, he tried to convince me to get an abortion! So I just told him like this, "You know you can deny it if you want, but it can be proven. I just wanted to let you know you had this baby since you claimed you didn't." I said, "I'll tell you what, you stay on that side of the Bay and I'll stay on this side. And I don't have to have anything else to say to you." And that's the way I left it. And I haven't had any problems with that person 'til this day. I've only talked to that person maybe three times, and he's only seen Rashad maybe twice, once when he was 21 days old and then when he was six months old. I don't have any kind of relationship with him at all, and it wasn't no arguing or fighting or anything.

How did you behave when you were feeling so disrespected?

When he tried to talk me into having an abortion and that kind of ticked me off and I just went on and decided to go through with [the pregnancy], 'cause I hadn't planned on any kids. If he wouldn't've tried to talk me into having an abortion, I would have gone on and had one, he just didn't know it, but he started denying that it was his and tried to get me to have an abortion, and I said, "If you feel that it's not yours, why would you want me to have an abortion with another man's child?" I said, "you obviously know that it's yours."

And then I told him, "I'm not going to do it." It was just the idea for him to just change on me the way that he did. You don't tell me what to do with my body, that's number one. I do what I feel is right, and it doesn't have to be right as far as abortion goes, but if that would have been my choice, then I would have did it. But it really irritated me for this man to be involved in the fact that I was pregnant 'cause it didn't happen by myself, that he would tell me to have an abortion. That had to be my choice, because I was the one carrying it. And that was an insult to me for him to even force that opinion toward me and then at the same time to deny that it was his.

DISCUSSION

Perhaps one of the most prevalent weapons of resistance, and one that has often been linked to the supposed "otherworldliness" of black religion, is the resigned fatalism that can be heard in the testimonies of William, Nadeera, and Tina.

When William was transferred from the Veterans Affairs (VA) in Carolina to one in Atlanta, he found himself in the midst of medical students who observed his every move, even when he was made to strip for doctors.

When the father of Tina's baby denies paternity, she reneges on her previous pact and decides to have the child.

In all of these testimonies, the tellers find themselves in stressful situations in which they feel absolutely powerless to make changes. Tina, confronted with the denial of paternity by the baby's father, felt compelled to hold on to some proof that would vindicate her dignity.

These stressful, often dehumanizing situations, of course, happen to all kinds of people, yet they are particularly likely to happen to those who lack the social, political, or economic power to fight back. And they are likely to happen more frequently to the powerless, which means that there must be a way in which the powerless can give meaning to these situations in their lives to overcome and move through them. This is the rationale for resigned fatalism. The oppressed hope for some explanation for their situation beyond the obvious, some higher and nobler reasoning for their suffering that gives them the strength and ability to hold on to sanity in the face of madness. They resign themselves to their fate in hopes that there is a greater reason that is currently unknown to them. Once this resignation has been achieved, the oppressed are able to let go of concern about the indignity of their situation and endure. They can wait for the greater good while holding on to a healthy sense of their own worth, even in the midst of chaos.

Noncompliance, likewise, is a weapon that can be used by the powerless in their struggle with the powerful in everyday life. This tactic can be seen in the testimony of Tina and again in William's story.

Tina makes a decision to keep her baby after the father begins to insist that she have an abortion. She asks him, "If you know that it's not yours, why would you want me to have an abortion with another man's child?" Then she adamantly tells him, "I'm not going to do it." William became angry after medical personnel attempted to convince him that he could not be in as much pain as he was describing to them. In response to their disbelief, he said, "I would refuse to do certain things they told me to do, like dressing my wound certain ways or whatever. If they told me to take therapy, I wouldn't take the therapy. I just started being rebellious."

Noncompliance is a weapon that the powerless use to negate the perceived injustice and indignities that come from the powerful. By refusing to "go along with the program," even in small ways, the oppressed attempt to hold on to a psychological advantage in the cultural warfare with their oppressors. Through this refusal, the oppressed, even as they remain in their subordinate condition, are able to construct a space in which they can feel a sense of freedom, independence, and dignity.

Noncompliance must be justified to have power. The ideological source of non-compliance is oppositional logic. This is "if/then" logic. Lisa reasons that if the welfare office insists on humiliating her by first forcing her to endure inspections of her house and then by cutting her allotment of food stamps because she adds hours to her work schedule, then she would simply reject any aid from the welfare authorities.

Tina, in recounting how she came to the decision to keep her child, says, "It was that he would deny it and then turn around in the same breath and tell me to get rid of it. That's when I decided that I would keep it and go on and deal with it." In other words, if the father would humiliate Tina by denying paternity and insist on a termina-tion of the pregnancy (in effect, acknowledging paternity), then she would refuse to give him what he wanted—that is, an end to potential responsibility through the abortion. William reasons that "if they don't believe anything is wrong with me, I'm not going to follow their orders."

Oppositional logic provides a reason to resist and a justification for noncompliance. It is a tactic through which the oppressed can gain a sense of moral authority over their oppressors. If the oppressor insists on heaping this unjust indignity on the oppressed, then the oppressed will frustrate the wishes of the oppressor through noncompliance. This oppositional logic may often not be in the long-term interest of the oppressed, yet it serves as a negation of perceived injustice and as an ideological basis for counterhe-gemonic cultural action.

On the other hand, the oppressed can take the opposite tactic and turn compliance into a weapon of cultural resistance. Compliance to the letter permits the oppressed a sense of inward power and freedom space even as they outwardly do exactly as they are told.

Lisa smiles conspiratorially as she recounts the home visits by her welfare worker. "I wasn't nasty to her or nothing. When the social worker came through, I opened the door wide for her and told her to come right on in and showed her around. I wanted them to know that they was not getting the best of me." Yet behind her congeniality and cooperation, she was seething with rage. "I felt really pissed off that I was being put through so many tests and I was doing everything they asked me to do," she said. "It was folk who were really doing wrong who they weren't paying attention to, and here they were sending me through all these changes for 72 dollars in food stamps and a hundred and something dollars."

Nadeera, recalling her reaction to her training officer's indignities, says, "I would just allow her to rant and rave like that and didn't say anything. I just accepted it because she was my training officer . . . I would say, 'Uh huh, yeah, OK,' and I just did what she told me to do because she was my training officer." Yet despite her apparent timidity in the public arena, Nadeera raged in the arena of the hidden testimony. "I just eventually got to a point where I thought to myself, 'Oh you fool!' and I thought 'I'll just let this fool run her course,'" she remembers.

By the outward cooperation with their oppressors, the oppressed create a space in which they can develop a rehearsed challenge to indignity. It is in the arena of the hidden testimony, whether in conversations with themselves or in actual or remembered conversations with family, that the oppressed are able to rehearse what they feel unable to say or do in the public arena.

Lisa recounts that, "I just kept on saying to myself that one day I was going to tell these welfare people where to go with their so-called help." Nadeera, though she does all she is asked to do and says nothing in response to the vile and dehumanizing attacks from her training officer, remembers how she allowed herself to mentally practice retorts against the indignities.

These rehearsals are not necessarily idle daydreaming. They are often precursors to counterhegemonic action. When Lisa finally does get fed up with the welfare system when they tell her that her food stamps will be cut because she works too many hours at Burger King, she tells the social worker, "Keep them! Y'all just go on and keep them! Keep the food stamps and keep the check!" Nadeera finally can take no more of her training officer's insults, and she remembers that, one day, "something just snapped in me . . . She came into the door and she just started yelling at me about my report. I just looked up at her and I don't know what happened, but I think we both realized that I had a gun and she had a gun. I had a nightstick and she had one. And I just looked at her and I guess it was a death look." In these rehearsed challenges to oppression, a doorway is left ajar between the hidden testimony that is passed down from generation to generation. This doorway always keeps open the potential for overt actions of resistance by the oppressed.

Often, the first steps through the doorway of the rehearsed challenge are behaviors that hold inferred potential violence. William, feeling frustrated by long waits and apparent lack of concern for his condition by the doctors of the VA hospital, stalks up to the reception counter and demands to know why he has to be there all day. He remembers, "I'd go up there and in a loud projected voice with my eyes bugged out, say something like, 'I been here all day, I'm tired of waiting, so what's the problem?' . . . And I'd start yelling 'Well, somebody got to see me, I'm in pain!' And I wouldn't necessarily be in pain, it was just my way of making them pay attention to me so I could get out of there." Nadeera believes that her torment by the training officer ended after the confrontation in the break room because of the way she looked at the other woman, which she calls a "death look."

In both these testimonies, the violence is never overt. It is only inferred and potential, yet it is a conscious effort to send a clear message to the oppressor that the oppressed will no longer tolerate a continued indignity. This sort of resistance does not occur without preparation both in the individual mind of the oppressed and in the arena of a remembered hidden testimony.

A seventh need of the oppressed in their effort to negate injustice in their lives is to have relief and independence from their oppressors. This is often accomplished in small ways through acts of stiff-necked independence performed by the oppressed in the face of their dependent situation. Lisa exhibits this independence when she refuses to be controlled by the welfare system and abruptly decides to detach herself from the program.

When Tina is insulted by the father of her child, rather than allow him to see her vulnerability, she exerts her own self-sufficiency and says to him, "I'll tell you what, you stay on that side of the Bay and I'll stay on this side. And I don't have to have anything else to say to you." She backs this statement up by refusing to have any contact with the man who so severely damaged her already fragile dignity. She continues to gain pride and a sense of self-worth in the knowledge that she does not need this man or any other to make it in her life. A folk term for this type of behavior might be "to cut off your nose to spite your face." However, it is an effective psychological defense against the dehumanizing indignities that are felt by poor and working-class black families.

Finally, and perhaps, most significantly, the oppressed develop the ability to maintain an air of emotional detachment both from their condition and from those whom they deem responsible for it. When Nadeera changed training officers and had to work with a man who forced her to deal with what would today be called sexual harassment, she recounts, "On the last day of my evaluation, he made a comment about a girl who had slept with her training officer so she could make it through, and he said, 'Now you wouldn't do anything like that now, would you?' I just ignored him like I didn't hear him." She had used similar tactics to deal with her previous training officer.

After explaining how she told her child's father to "stay on your side" of the San Francisco Bay, Tina (who seems to have relied on emotional detachment in most relationships in her life) says bluntly, "And that's the way I left it." Emotional detachment is in many ways the ultimate weapon of counterhegemonic resistance. It allows the oppressed the psychological space in which they can disassociate from any sense of connection or responsibility for the situation in which they are involved. To be disassociated emotionally from the oppressors and the acts of oppression means that the oppressed are not compelled to feel any part of the situation, nor do they have to believe that the behavior of the oppressor really has anything to do with them. "That's their trip and it ain't got nothing to do with me," they might be heard to say. Even if the immediate social effect is on the oppressed, emotional detachment enables them to disassociate from any cognitive or ethical relationship to the actions or behavior of the oppressor. Thus, they are enabled to feel no compunction to worry about what is being done.

CONCLUSION

All of these weapons of cultural warfare serve as tactics with which the oppressed attempt to negotiate power within an asymmetrical social order. Through these guerrilla tactics, they attempt to negate the injustices that are faced in everyday life and to create a sense of justice and self-determination for themselves (albeit at the risk of sometimes creating new conditions that prove as intolerable as the first). Yet, the oppressed are able to resiliently bounce back from adversity and maintain functional kinship networks and family structures over several generations.

The challenge and decision for human services workers and therapists engaged in work in working-class and poor and black communities is whether or not we are willing to side with the oppressed against their oppression. We must decide whether we are willing to refuse to contribute to the loss of dignity among those who are subject to institutional cultural violence and domination. Our challenge is to intentionally work in the interest of liberating clinical and service work to help the people we work with to gain power with dignity.

By learning to ask questions about experiences of damaged dignity and to listen to clients with a sense of not knowing (that is, to listen with fresh ears as if we are interested in being taught by the people we work with), we may be able to collaborate with them to find solutions in the search for dignity.

When we witness some of these tactics and recognize them as efforts to hold on to dignity, we are able to engage our clients with empathy in a collaborative manner. When clients seem to be submitting to resigned fatalism, we might empathize with their choice to accept their fate while inviting them to tell us about their hopes for an alternative outcome. If our clients seem to be practicing noncompliance or oppositional logic, we might acknowledge that what is being required can seem unreasonable; ask whether their present choices will get them what they really want; and, if not, invite them to work with you to figure out ways to get what they really want more effectively. When clients seem to be engaged in compliance to the letter, we might invite them to discuss with us what they are truly feeling about this situation and help them work through their challenges by providing a witness to their rehearsed challenges. We can do this with an eye to collaborating with our clients to find solutions that are more honoring of their dignity. When clients seem emotionally detached and uncaring about a situation, or begin acting with stiff-necked independence, we might express our understanding that it may seem scary to care too much about this situation. We might acknowledge and applaud their willingness to be self-reliant while at the same time expressing our sincere desire to work with them to find a solution to this particular problem that will allow them to keep the power and still benefit in a positive way. When clients are acting in ways inferring violent action, while ensuring our personal safety, we should also acknowledge the frustration and pain of our clients. Engage clients in dialogue about what they hope can come of the present problem and again sincerely invite them to collaborate with us to solve the problem together in a way that feels empowering and respectful of their humanity.

By creating relationships with the people we work with that reflect hidden testimony spaces and aligning ourselves with our clients for the purposes of their own empowerment and liberation, we honor their rights to be treated with dignity as human beings, and we refuse to align ourselves with institutional oppression and domination. In addition, by engaging the people we work with in these dialogical relationships, we nurture the experience of democracy centered on them as the subjects and agents of their own lives.

REFERENCES

Akinyela, M. M. (2008). Once they come: Testimony therapy and healing questions for African American couples. In M. McGoldrick & K. Hardy (Eds.), *Revisioning family therapy: Race, class and gender in clinical practice* (2nd ed., pp. 356–366). New York: Guilford Press.

Akinyela, M. M., & Aldridge, D. (2003). Beyond Eurocentrism, Afrocentrism and multiculturalism: Toward cultural democracy in social work education. *Journal of Race, Class and Gender, 10*(2), 58–70.

Blanchett, W. J. (2006). Disproportionate representation of African American students in special education: Acknowledging the role of white privilege and racism. *Educational Researcher, 35*(6), 24–28.

Darder, A. (2012). *Culture and power in the classroom: Educational foundations for the schooling of bicultural students* (20th anniversary ed.). Boulder/London: Paradigm Publishers.

Gold, M. E., & Richards, H. (2012). To label or not to label: The special education question for African Americans. *Educational Foundations, 26*(1–2), 143–156.

Karenga, M. (1980). *Kawaida theory: An introductory outline.* Inglewood, CA: Kawaida Publications.

Scott, J. C. (1990). *Domination and the arts of resistance: Hidden transcripts.* New Haven, CT: Yale University Press.

REFERENCES

8

Decolonizing Social Work Practice with Immigrants: The Power to (Re)define

Hye-Kyung Kang

Social work practice with immigrants in the United States is difficult to discuss without recognizing the global forces that produce international migration, including enduring legacies of colonialism (Massey et al., 1993). Although the era of colonialism in the formal sense may have ended, its influence is still present in global power relations, resulting in social, economic, and political inequities between the former empires in the West and the formerly colonized nations (Young, 2003). Postcolonial theorists call attention to these enduring effects, which they call neocolonial systems, as well as to how neocolonial systems are implicated in people's lives (Young, 2003). For example, in her influential book, *Decolonizing Methodologies*, Linda Tuhiwai Smith (1999) critiqued the colonizing effects of Western academic research on indigenous peoples and articulated a new indigenous research agenda. This postcolonial perspective is used in this chapter to examine power in social work practice with immigrants.

In this chapter, postcolonial and poststructural theoretical concepts provide a framework for elucidating the ways in which power operates in social work practice with immigrant clients. Although a full examination of poststructural and postcolonial theories is not the purpose of this chapter,[1] relevant concepts are first considered to scaffold the discussion of how social workers and other human service workers may use their power to facilitate or regulate change. Second, social work practice with immigrants is

---

[1] Neither poststructural theories nor postcolonial theories are a unified ideology, but rather a diverse critique of systems of knowledge; therefore, the use of the word "theory" here is not intended to suggest that they are coherent and discrete sets of grand theories.

situated within a historical context and postcolonial framework. Third, case examples are used to illustrate how power may be used in social work practice with immigrant clients. Finally, the chapter concludes with thoughts on decolonizing social work practice with immigrants.

THEORETICAL FRAMEWORK

Power and Discursive Construction of Subjects

Foucault conceptualized power as "a productive network which runs through the whole social body," which "induces pleasure, forms knowledge, produces discourse" (Foucault, 1984, p. 61). As such, power does not dominate subjects by force but rather absorbs them through shaping their sense of who they are, their social relations, and the way they generate knowledge about themselves (Rabinow, 1984). In this perspective, power does not reside in a single domain such as class domination but is interactional, fluid, and inscribed in all aspects of social relations.

An important component of Foucault's conception of power is *normalization*: "a system of finely gradated and measurable intervals in which individuals can be distributed around a norm—a norm that both organizes and is the result of this controlled distribution" (Rabinow, 1984, p. 20). Foucault was particularly concerned about the ways in which the system of normalization became the system of both regulation and judgment through the law and state practices. One example of how normalization operates in the United States is through immigration and naturalization policies. U.S.-born citizens constitute the norm, and immigrants are graded and distributed against this status (for example, naturalized citizens, permanent residents, temporary visa holders, asylum seekers, undocumented migrants, respectively). Not only does normalization assign different statuses to immigrants, but it also distributes differential rights and privileges such as voting rights, rights to travel, rights to employment, and financial aid qualifications for higher education, according to their grades. Furthermore, this normalization practice shapes how people talk and understand themselves and others ("an illegal immigrant," "a green card holder") and how they relate to one another, including who qualifies for ("deserves") social work services and who does not.

According to Foucault (1972, 1975, 1982), power operates through discourse to produce social realities and subject positions (such as "citizen" or "client"). Discourses scaffold how we see and interpret the world, how we structure our knowledge and social practices, and how we understand and make meaning of ourselves (Fairclough, 1992). In other words, who we are as social subjects is constituted through discourses. As agents of civil institutions, social workers hold much power over their immigrant clients because they moderate the client's understanding and social practices through the facilitating or regulating power of discourses (Ong, 2003).

Another important Foucauldian tenet of power and discourse is that discourses are constantly in flux (Fairclough, 1992). Thus, the social realities they produce are a version of what is considered true or real at particular moments and specific to certain social, political, and historical contexts (Carabine, 2001). Because discourses are shifting and dynamic, the subjects that they produce are also mutable. This mutability of discourses, theorists argue, leaves space for discursive and social change (Fairclough, 1992).

Resistance, Binary Discourses, and Discursive Change

Postcolonial theories arose out of recognition that Western ways of knowing and theorizing are not only limited but also radically consolidate and marginalize other ways of knowing (Ashcroft, Griffiths, & Tiffin, 2000). Thus, postcolonial writers are concerned about the ways in which dominant discourses produce and regulate social subjects in neocolonial systems. In extending discursive construction of subjects (Foucault, 1972, 1975, 1982), postcolonial theorists such as Hall (1996) and Bhabha (1994) have proposed that although people may not be able to completely escape the effects of the discourses that shape them as social subjects, they may still resist and possibly change those discourses (Ashcroft et al., 2000). One effective way in which postcolonial theories open up such opportunities is by calling into question the binary logic[2] of dominant social discourses (Ashcroft et al., 2000). Postcolonial and feminist critiques have argued that, in the binary system of language, two opposing terms are not equal; one term is always dominant (for example, "Western" over "non-Western," "civilized" over "primitive"), which establishes "a violent hierarchy" between those binary terms (Ashcroft et al., 2000, p. 24). Postcolonial theorists assert that such binary logic is how power operates in colonial discourses as they systematically privilege a specific version of social reality and suppress others. As these partial social realities are perpetuated through social and economic structures such as medical, educational, and social welfare systems, they establish a relation of dominance (Ashcroft et al., 2000).

One unavoidable problem of the binary system, however, is that social reality must fit into binary oppositions; thus, the system suppresses ambiguous spaces between categories, rendering any interstitial realities impossible (Ashcroft et al., 2000). When the lines of the binary oppositions start to blur, the system no longer makes sense; for example, mixed-status families in which parents are undocumented but children are U.S.-born citizens complicate the legal–illegal binary construction of immigration and deportation. This is why postcolonial critiques see interstitial realities as an effective way to destabilize the integrity of binary discourses and to create space for change (Bhabha, 1994).

SOCIAL WORK PRACTICE AND THE IMMIGRANT OTHER

In postcolonial framework, social work practice with immigrants in the United States cannot be considered without the nation's colonial history and its contemporary effects. The very construction of the United States as a "nation of immigrants" is entangled with

---

[2] Binary logic of discourses refers to Saussure's (1974, 1983) theory of language, which argues that each sign is distinguished not by its content but by its contrast to other signs in the system. (For example, "man" is not defined by any inherent meaning within m-a-n but by contrasting itself with "woman.") According to Saussure, the whole linguistic system works that way.

the devastation of an indigenous world and people (Hair & O'Donohue, 2009). It is important to remember that the nation's wealth was built upon its active participation in colonization, including slavery (Takaki, 1993). Furthermore, the U.S. military, political, and
economic hegemony, and involvement in marginalized (and often formerly colonized)
nations often trigger the migration from sending nations (Massey et al., 1993). Using a
postcolonial framework reminds social workers that these historical, social, and political contexts must be considered in their understanding of social work with immigrants.

Immigrants have been a major focus of social work practice since the earliest
days of social work history in this country. Two major institutions that constituted the
early U.S. social work profession, the Charity Organization Society and the Settlement
House, heavily engaged in practice with poor immigrants from Europe, who often lived
in slums, neglected by their city governments (Axinn & Stern, 2007; Gordon, 2002).
However, social workers' conceptualization of immigrants was fundamentally racialized
and pathologizing (Park & Kemp, 2006). Immigrants were constructed as the other:
culturally different, morally inferior, and in need of guidance from social workers who,
in turn, represented the unquestioned norm, morality, and knowledge (Gordon, 2002).
This echoes Rober and Seltzer's (2010) critique of the collusion of "benevolent helpers"
such as educators, missionaries, and social workers in imperial projects by taking on
the position of the knower and the helper vis-à-vis colonial subjects. In this sense, the
professional identity as a social worker is rooted in colonial discourses.

The conceptualization of immigrants as pathological and inferior led to interventions
that were "designed to educate, improve, and *adjust* immigrants to *American* ways of
life" [italics added] (Park & Kemp, 2006, p. 708). In this adjustment-oriented intervention
paradigm, the focus of the problem was the individual. With a few exceptions, such as
Jane Addams and her Settlement House colleagues' efforts to research and call attention
to failures of the local governments to provide adequate services and infrastructure to
poor immigrant neighborhoods (Axinn & Stern, 2007), social workers seldom questioned
the environment that assumed to uphold the "American ways of life," to which immigrant
individuals must adjust. Furthermore, what exactly constituted the American ways of life
went unquestioned. Rather, they were defined as normal and desirable in opposition to
immigrants' ways of life (which were a result of a complex interaction between structural
inequalities and divergent cultural traditions) that were consolidated and identified as
problematic and abnormal. Again, because social workers were part and parcel of the
American ways of life, this discourse was further normalized in their interactions with
clients.

The legacy of this individual adjustment–oriented intervention paradigm continues in contemporary social work discourses. Cultural adjustment, often referred to as
acculturation in the social work and psychology literature, has become a major area of
interest when it comes to practice with immigrants. For example, between the 1980s and
the 2000s, the number of scholarly articles on acculturation increased by nearly 700%
(Schwartz, Unger, Zamboanga, & Szapocznik, 2010). It is indeed important to study
the many challenges immigrants face when adjusting to a new environment and to help
them successfully navigate those challenges. However, the limitation of the adjustment-
oriented paradigm is that it privileges one way of understanding and intervening in

problems over other possible ways, which effectively consolidates and suppresses other ways of knowing. For example, in this paradigm, social, political, and historical contexts that are embedded in the environment are rarely critically considered. Given that the dialectical relationship between the person and the environment is the hallmark of the social work approach (Kondrat, 2002), this limitation poses significant challenges for social workers to imagine intervention strategies that might propose necessary changes in the environment.

However, the larger problem is located not in the intervention paradigm itself but in the positionalities of social workers in the paradigm, which reproduce the power relationship between the immigrant client and the social worker that are situated in the historically binary framework. The immigrant client is again constructed as the other whose knowledge and ways of life are subjugated and who therefore is in need of help and guidance. Social workers—even when they are immigrants themselves—are constructed as the norm, the experts whose knowledge is privileged. Social workers may easily occupy such a neocolonial position unless they actively and critically analyze the relations of power within which they and their clients are situated.

Similarly, whether or not contemporary social workers are conscious of how their power as professionals is used, they may easily participate in a neocolonial project of consolidating and marginalizing clients' realities by unquestioningly following and reproducing dominant discourses of policy and intervention (Kang, 2012). Historically, social workers' failure to critique and resist partial realities imposed by government policies involved them in such devastating injustices as the displacement of Native American children in the Indian Adoption Project of the 1950s (Hair & O'Donohue, 2009). However, there are counterexamples in which social workers and other human service workers collaborated with immigrant individuals and communities to resist and challenge marginalizing discourses (for example, the domestic workers' organizing in New York [Sen, 2010] and the Asian American Legislative Day activism work in Washington State [Kang, 2013]).

Because social workers occupy subject positions as professional helpers, they can also use their discursive power to create space for resistance and change. The following case examples illustrate how power operates in social work practice with immigrant clients. Both cases are composites, and all identities (except for the author's) are disguised to protect confidentiality.

CASE 1: MEANING OF MENTAL HEALTH

In the early 2000s, I was hired as a consultant/trainer by a community mental health agency, Agency A,[3] to conduct a series of community discussion meetings with marginalized immigrant and refugee groups to increase mental health treatment access for them. The meetings were conceptualized as a combination of community consensus building around mental health treatment and psychoeducation about integrated care (the model of

---

[3] Pseudonym.

care that places mental health clinicians in community health clinics for a seamless care). I designed a series of guiding questions to learn about community members' concepts about mental health and help-seeking behaviors as well as a description of integrated care. When I went over those outlines with the agency personnel, one of the directors (who was an immigrant herself) told me, "You *have to* tell them that mental illness comes from brain chemical imbalance, not from spiritual causes; it is a medical problem." When I asked why she felt it was so important to do so, she said that some immigrants and refugees believed that mental illness came from spiritual problems and therefore took their mentally ill family members to spiritual practitioners such as shamans and pastors. In many instances, the mentally ill family member did not get better through spiritual interventions and eventually deteriorated, often requiring hospitalization. She also said that some community members felt that having a mental illness, unlike physical ailments, produced stigma, which made it hard for people to seek treatments from a mental health agency. She wanted people to access mental health services without stigma.

In this example, the director privileged one (Western, medical) discourse over another (non-Western, spiritual) in her well-meaning concern for immigrant and refugee clients' access to what she believed was a less stigmatizing and superior model of mental health care. I understood her concerns and good intentions; however, by doing so, she inadvertently marginalized an important part of the immigrant and refugee communities' lifeworld (Summerfield, 2004). Furthermore, such construction of the cause of mental illness and what is proper care effectively placed her and other mental health professionals as knowledgeable helpers in opposition to the immigrant and refugee individuals who were constructed as ill informed and primitive, which reproduced the "benevolent helper" discourse (Rober & Seltzer, 2010).

I was not completely comfortable with her idea (after all, I could not find any scientific evidence that absolutely disproved spiritual etiology of mental illness) but agreed to add a psychoeducation component about the medical (brain chemical imbalance) model as another way of thinking about mental health. I believed I was presenting the model as one of many possible models without privileging it. However, as a social worker who convened and sponsored the meeting, I was already located in the position of an expert, and any idea I represented would become a privileged narrative. My lack of analysis of power dynamics obscured how I was reproducing and normalizing dominant discourses.

In one meeting, I asked the members of Community X[4] what they considered was the biggest barrier to mental health treatment, and one member said it was the lack of shamans. The number of shamans was rapidly decreasing in this refugee community because no young people were willing to carry on the shaman tradition. Even though shamans were highly respected in their home country, it was not seen as a viable career for young people who grew up in the United States. I thought this would be a good time to introduce the medical model of mental health treatment as an option to the shaman care model, because they couldn't easily find a working shaman in the area. As I presented the medical model, one elder interrupted me: "Listen, I know that Western medicine is strong and works well. But in order for it to work, you need a shaman to

---

[4] Pseudonym.

bless it to release its power. When we get medicine from [Agency A], we usually go to a shaman to bless it. Now we have to wait for a while before a shaman can do this. This is why we need more shamans!" By this conceptualization, this elder effectively deconstructed the binary (Western medical versus non-Western spiritual) discourse of mental health. He indeed created an interstitial narrative in which both models worked together. Furthermore, this narrative allowed the social worker (me) to imagine an innovative intervention strategy that combined both models. At the wrap-up of the meeting, I wrote down my recommendation for Agency A: "Support Community X's effort to recruit shamans in the area and collaborate with them." Community members were pleased to have taught this social worker how Agency A's services could be more accessible, which changed their subject position to experts and the social worker's position to a student.

CASE 2: ASIAN AMERICANS?

In the late 1990s, I was asked by the Health Education Office of Seattle Public Schools to develop and facilitate a young women's support group for Asian American students at a Seattle high school. Seattle is a white-dominant city; about 70 percent of its residents are white, according to the City of Seattle (seattle.gov, n.d.). Its largest racial minority group is Asian Americans (13.8 percent), followed by African Americans (7.9 percent). A fairly large share (17.3 percent) of its residents are foreign born (as compared to the national statistic, which is 12.9 percent), and more than 20 percent speak languages other than English at home (seattle.gov). As is true with many U.S. cities, Seattle was segregated by income and race in the 1990s (seattle.gov), with a heavier concentration of African Americans and Southeast Asian immigrants/refugees in the southern part of the city (the South End), whereas the northern part of the city (the North End) was predominantly white. In an effort to decrease educational segregation, Seattle Public Schools instituted busing from 1978 to 1999, and many students were bused to schools far from their neighborhoods (Tate, 2002). It was in this context that I was asked to develop this group. I was told by the school counselor at a North End high school that a group of Asian American female students had consistently complained about a dire lack of Asian representation in the school's teaching and other personnel and requested the school administration to hire an adult Asian female counselor to start a support group for them. I negotiated with the school to hire another Asian female social worker to co-facilitate the group to avoid a single representation.

At our first group meeting, my co-facilitator and I were surprised by the high number of students that showed up. There were 20 students waiting for us when we were expecting 10–12. As we did introductory exercises, two things became apparent: (1) students (rather than the school counselor) recruited their friends to join the group, which explained the unexpectedly high number; and (2) one half of the students could not stand the other half of the students, and vice versa. At the end of the first session, my co-facilitator and I suggested to the students that we run two groups because 20 was too many people for one group. We allowed students to self-select to form two groups (Group A and Group B). We predicted that students would divide themselves up by their own friendship networks, which was exactly what we saw when we showed up the next week. We also realized that their friendship groups echoed their neighborhood distribution (and, therefore, socioeconomic class), which was not surprising. Most of the Group A students lived in the North End and were from families with longer immigration histories and more resources: Chinese, Korean, and Filipina. All of the Group B students lived in the South End and were predominantly from Southeast Asian refugee families who were more recent immigrants with few economic resources: Vietnamese, Cambodian, Laotian, Hmong, Mien, and Cham.

Over the school year, both groups met every week and talked about a variety of topics related to their lives that they felt they could not share anywhere else. At one point, we (the co-facilitators) asked the students in Group A why they did not get along with the students in Group B. Group A students accused Group B students of "trying to be black" and not being "real Asian": "They act so black. Just look at the way they dress! The music they listen to! And the boys they date!" We asked Group B students the same question, and they accused Group A students of being "white-washed" and not being "real Asian" as well: "They think they are white! Look at the way they dress! The music they listen to! And the boys they date!" Each group reluctantly acknowledged that the other group probably saw them as being "white-washed" or "black-acting" but insisted that they were "acting real" and the others were being "fake."

It was not difficult to see that students in both groups were behaving in ways that were normalized in their respective neighborhoods and therefore believed their ways of being were genuine while the others' were not. These behaviors may well be seen as acculturation, specifically to their own immediate neighborhood environments. However, the acculturation framework does not explain why their experiences were underscored in racialized terms, why only certain sets of acculturative behaviors were available to each group of students, or why they were not able to articulate how their enculturation behaviors were different from those that they learned to acculturate.

Applying postcolonial insights may help us understand this phenomenon. The students' arguments exemplify what Ong (1996) describes as ideological "blackening" and "whitening" processes, in which different Asian immigrants are placed into different positions in the black–white binary racial scheme of citizenship on the basis of their social, cultural, and economic capital. Historically, the discourse of citizenship in the United States has been intertwined with the binary (white versus nonwhite) narrative of race, which was also interlocked with the deserving-versus-underserving narrative (Kang, 2010). Historically, immigrants who inhabited an ambivalent space in the black–white system of race (such as Asians) complicated this narrative. The history of racial prerequisite cases from 1878 to 1944 elucidates how U.S. courts enforced this binary discourse of citizenship by legally determining whether those immigrants were white (and, therefore, deserving an opportunity for citizenship) or not (Lopez, 1996).

Although the legal practice of "blackening" and "whitening" has stopped, the historical racialization and othering of subjects have been naturalized as the social order in the United States, and the racial binary discourse continues to construct the meaning and "criteria of belonging" (Ong, 1996, p. 738) within the nation. In this example, Group A students were constructed as white, whereas Group B students were constructed as black, which reflected their social, economic, and cultural contexts. Although there no longer was a singular entity such as the courts that determined their positions in the racial binary, these students learned to see themselves as occupying such subject positions and to perform intricate cultural inscriptions embedded within those positions through complex sets of social practices (Ong, 1996).

When we pressed the students to tell us what made them "real Asians," both groups had significant difficulty coming up with explanations. In other words, their conceptualization of Asian-ness was only in opposition to what they saw as "black" or "white." Overall, other than the fact that they were Asians because their families originated from Asia, they found it easier to agree on what they thought was not consistent with their idea of Asian-ness than what was. Through this discussion, students engaged in a critical deconstruction of hegemonic narratives of "Asian." For example, they were very clear that they did not see themselves as how Asians were portrayed by the mainstream media, which they scorned as hollow stereotypes (for example, "Come on; no one walks around with stupid chopsticks in their hair!" "Like I'm supposed to be a math nerd? I'm a cheerleader!!"). They also expressed that Asian-ness could not be defined by a set of essential behaviors or traits. As soon as someone came up with a behavior or a trait that she believed to be a mark of true Asian-ness, someone else stated why it was not necessarily so. For example, one student said that an important trait all Asians shared was their sense of obligation and loyalty to their family, including their extended family. Another student quickly countered this notion by pointing out that many of her African American and Latina friends felt the same way about their families. On the one hand, they agreed that narrowing down Asian-ness to a set of essential characteristics could actually spawn stereotypes; on the other hand, they wished there were some criteria or language to express what they felt identified them as Asian. Even as they resisted essentializing discourses of Asian, the absence of resonant discourses of subjectivity left them searching.

One source of this absence of discourse was the lack of representation with which students could readily identify as Asian American. Not only were there very few Asian American characters on TV or in movies, books, or magazines, but they were also excluded from the representations of Americans in the U.S. history class curriculum. Students spoke about how most of their U.S. history book was really about European Americans; African Americans received a few mentions either as victims of slavery or civil rights movement heroes. The few passages that did refer to Asians were not about Asian Americans but about the Japanese attack of Pearl Harbor or about the intercontinental railroad construction by Chinese railroad workers who were depicted as foreign labor. This lack of representation led some students to feel ambivalent about their claim as Americans; they felt that they, as immigrants or refugees, were less legitimately American than U.S.-born Americans. This reflects how students internalize historical discourses of citizenship that place white U.S.-born citizens and nonwhite immigrants at either ends of deserving-versus-undeserving binary oppositions (Kang, 2010). More importantly, this lack of historical representation erased the presence and history of Asian Americans whose immigration history goes back to as early as 1800s and produced a robust Asian American movement in the 1970s in the very city (Seattle) they lived in (Kang, 2010).

The discussion about their ambivalent subjectivity as Asian Americans led to an interesting discovery about the ways in which students constructed their own Asian American subjectivity by using an Asian American spectrum that incorporated age, generation from immigration, and language and other cultural performances. For example, both groups felt that they were not Asians in the same way their parents were; they saw their immigrant and refugee parents as "old-school" Asians or "Asian Asians" whose cultural beliefs and behaviors were different from their own. However, this differentiation was not simply about parent–child generational differences or whether one was born in the United States ("second-generation," "American-born Chinese," and so on) or was an immigrant ("first-generation" or "one"). They further differentiated Asian Americans using terms such as "boaters/FOBs" ("fresh off the boat," a pejorative and/or insider term that describes those who are recent immigrants and do not speak English well), "1.2" (those who immigrated in their teens and speak English proficiently but with an accent and are fluent in their first language), "1.5" (those who immigrated in childhood and are bilingual), "1.8" (those who immigrated in early childhood and are fluent in English but often do not speak their parents' language very well), and so on. These differentiations were not strictly about the age or language, but also about behaviors that were difficult to describe but apparently recognizable. For example, students talked about someone who immigrated as a toddler but behaved in a way that would be more typical of someone who immigrated much later in life in this way: "She's really a 1.8, but you'd think she was a 1.2 by the way she acts. That's because her grandmother raised her; she can totally speak [her parents' native language], even."

On the one hand, this differentiation may be interpreted as resistance against essentializing discourses of Asians as a singular group by generating a narrative about the internal diversity of performance of culture and identity. On the other hand, the same practice may be interpreted as students engaging in the Foucauldian concept of normalization (Rabinow, 1984) as they constructed those criteria of differences around a norm and distributed from the center to the periphery according to their proximity from the norm. This normalization practice reproduces the hegemonic discourse of "American" (U.S. born, English fluent) as the norm, set against the immigrant other as the periphery. Furthermore, this normalization intersects with the black–white binary discourse of Americans, which adds a dimension in terms of shaping students' conceptualizations about who they and their peers were and how they related to one another. In fact, students eventually came to the realization that these binary discourses and normalizing practices contributed to the animosity between two groups. This example demonstrates that although it is difficult it is to escape from and completely evade hegemonic discourses of subjectivity, one can still question and resist those discourses (Ashcroft et al., 2000).

As students recognized the larger societal discourses that shaped their understanding of and relationship with one another, both groups agreed to have an all-day conference together that addressed many of their common issues such as health, sexuality, relationship, and identity. We invited various Asian American women professionals as speakers, which students found very exciting. At the end of the conference, we held a reflection session during which students spoke about what they learned. One student from a refugee background spoke about what it was like to see so many different Asian

American adult women who represented such diversity; she always felt that she did not want to follow the path her mother and older sisters took (marrying young and becoming a mother) but did not have access to other role models as she saw that day. Many agreed; they were not sure what paths were available to them except for the usual doctor or lawyer track (which was often held up as the ideal but seemed remote for many of them given their family's socioeconomic status). When we asked who their Asian American women role models had been, most of them said "no one." However, when one student said "my girls," indicating her friends, many of them echoed this sentiment. These students were shaping their own subjectivity in reflection of one another, making meanings in vivo, and charting the course of an unknown map together. When we reflected this back to students, it was a powerful realization for them: that they were synthesizing what it meant to be Asian American young women, assimilating and deconstructing what was available in their environment. In the end, they recognized that they were constructing all different versions of Asian American young women: divergent, similar, constantly changing, and negotiated.

This case example illustrates how social workers may use their power by opening up spaces for questioning accepted narratives and helping clients generate counternarratives, which in this case led to clients' recognition of their own power of negotiating and redefining their subjectivity as immigrant Asian American women. This case demonstrates how social workers can use their power as agents of civil society to facilitate a discursive change rather than to regulate their clients' meanings and sense of who they are—and can be—according to normative discourses.

CONCLUSION

This chapter examined power in social work practice with immigrants from a postcolonial perspective. Postcolonial theories articulate how colonial discourses privilege one reality over another, radically consolidating and marginalizing other ways of knowing and being. The historical legacy of the relationship between social workers and their immigrant clients cautions us that contemporary social workers may reproduce such colonial models in their practice when they lack critical analysis of the relations of power between their clients and themselves. Social workers may impose dominant narratives of what is good, normal, and healthy on their immigrant clients through their intervention, which may result in subjugation of clients' lifeworlds (Summerfield, 2004).

However, postcolonial theories inform us that subversion and resistance are possible for those who are marginalized. Social workers can use their power to actively generate interventions that embrace resistance and produce counterdiscourses. They may critique accepted realities produced by dominant discourses and show how they limit immigrant clients' subjectivity. They may help clients negotiate their positions in a creative way by opening up spaces where contradictions can occur and destabilize hegemonic realities. Because both social workers' and clients' subjectivity are implicated and intertwined in the process of discursive construction, the discursive changes that social workers and clients produce affect not only the client, but also the social worker.

REFERENCES

Ashcroft, B., Griffiths, G., & Tiffin, H. (2000). *Post-colonial studies: The key concepts.* London/New York: Routledge.

Axinn, J., & Stern, H. (2007). *Social welfare: A history of the American response to need* (7th ed.). White Plains, NY: Longman.

Bhabha, H. K. (1994). *The location of culture.* London: Routledge.

Carabine, J. (2001). Unmarried motherhood 1830–1990: A genealogical analysis. In M. Wetherall, S. Taylor, & S. J. Yates (Eds.), *Discourse as data: A guide for analysis* (pp. 267–307). London: Sage Publications.

Fairclough, N. (1992). *Discourse and social change.* Cambridge, UK: Polity Press.

Foucault, M. (1972). *The archaeology of knowledge and the discourse on language.* New York: Pantheon Books.

Foucault, M. (1975). *Discipline and punish: The birth of the prison.* New York: Vintage Books.

Foucault, M. (1982). The subject and power. In H. Dreyfus & P. Rabinow (Eds.), *Michel Foucault: Beyond structuralism and hermeneutics* (pp. 208–228). Chicago: University of Chicago Press.

Foucault, M. (1984). Truth and power. In P. Rabinow (Ed.), *The Foucault reader* (pp. 51–75). New York: Pantheon Books.

Gordon, L. (2002). If the Progressives were advising us today, should we listen? *Journal of the Gilded Age and Progressive Era, 1*(2), 109–121.

Hair, H., & O'Donohue, K. (2009). Culturally relevant, socially just supervision: Becoming visible through a social constructionist lens. *Journal of Ethnicity and Cultural Diversity in Social Work, 18*(1–2), 70–88.

Hall, S. (1996). Introduction: Who needs "identity"? In S. Hall & P. du Gay (Eds.), *Questions of cultural identity* (pp. 1–17). London: Sage Publications.

Kang, H.-K. (2010). *Cultural citizenship and immigrant community identity: Constructing a multi-ethnic Asian American community.* El Paso, TX: LFB Scholarly Publishing.

Kang, H.-K. (2012). Re-imagining citizenship, re-imagining social work: U.S. immigration policies and social work practice in the age of AZ SB 1070. *Advances in Social Work, 13,* 510–526.

Kang, H.-K. (2013). Claiming immigrant cultural citizenship: Applying postcolonial theories to social work practice with immigrants. *Critical and Radical Social Work, 1*(2), 233–245.

Kondrat, M. E. (2002). Actor-centered social work: Re-visioning "person-in-environment" through a critical theory lens. *Social Work, 47,* 435–448.

Lopez, I.F.H. (1996). *White by law: The legal construction of race.* London/New York: New York University Press.

Massey, D., Arango, J., Hugo, G., Kouaouci, A., Pellegrino, A., & Taylor, J. E. (1993). Theories of international migration: An integration and appraisal. *Population and Development Review, 19,* 431–466.

Ong, A. (1996). Cultural citizenship as subject-making: Immigrants negotiate racial and cultural boundaries in the United States. *Current Anthropology, 37,* 737–762.

Ong, A. (2003). *Buddha is hiding: Refugees, citizenship, the new America* (Vol. 5). Berkeley: University of California Press.

Park, Y., & Kemp, S. P. (2006). "Little alien colonies": Representations of immigrants and their neighborhoods in social work discourse, 1875–1924. *Social Service Review, 80*, 705–734.

Rabinow, P. (Ed.). (1984). Introduction. In *The Foucault reader* (pp. 3–29). New York: Pantheon Books.

Rober, P., & Seltzer, M. (2010). Avoiding colonizer positions in the therapy room: Some ideas about the challenges of dealing with the dialectic of misery and resources in families. *Family Process, 49*(1), 123–137.

Schwartz, S. J., Unger, J. B., Zamboanga, B. L., & Szapocznik, J. (2010). Rethinking the concept of acculturation: Implications for theory and research. *American Psychologist, 65*, 237–251.

Saussure, F. d. (1974). *Course in general linguistics* (W. Baskin, Trans.). London: Fontana/Collins. (Original work published 1916)

Saussure, F. d. (1983). *Course in general linguistics* (R. Harris, Trans.). London: Duckworth. (Original work published 1916)

Seattle.gov. (n.d.). *About Seattle: Race and ethnicity quick statistics.* Retrieved from http://www.seattle.gov/dpd/cityplanning/populationdemographics/aboutseattle/raceethnicity/default.htm

Sen, R. (2010, September 2). *Domestic workers lead the way to 21st century labor rights.* Retrieved from http://colorlines.com/archives/2010/09/domestic_workers_lead_the_way_toward_21st_century_labor_rights.html

Smith, L. T. (1999). *Decolonizing methodologies: Research and Indigenous peoples.* London: Zed Books.

Summerfield, D. (2004). Cross-cultural perspectives on the medicalization of human suffering. In G. M. Rosen (Ed.), *Posttraumatic stress disorder: Issues and controversies* (pp. 233–245). Chichester, UK: Wiley & Sons.

Takaki, R. (1993). *A different mirror: A history of multicultural America.* New York: Back Bay Books.

Tate, C. (2002, September 7). *Busing in Seattle: A well-intentioned failure.* Retrieved from http://www.historylink.org/index.cfm?DisplayPage=output.cfm&file_id=3939

Young, R.J.C. (2003). *Postcolonialism: A very short introduction.* Oxford, UK: Oxford University Press.

9

The Power to Create Equity and Justice

Patricia Romney

Each year, the town of Greenfield, Massachusetts, holds an annual health fair. Hosted by the Fire Department and the Public Health Department, the fair brings together a wide array of community agencies. The community health center, the sheriff's office, the public library, the local hospital, the medical reserve corps, the community emergency response team, the disaster animal response team, the public health coalition, the regional emergency planning committee, and the local branch of homeland security are all partners in the effort to improve the health of their community. Town citizens who attend the fair receive free flu shots, health information, and medical and dental screenings, including a blood pressure clinic. They are able to witness sprinkler house demonstrations, safe-house demonstrations, house numbering, and are informed by emergency notification ideas, themed book displays, and more.

One year, the annual fall event was scheduled on Yom Kippur, the highest holy day in the Jewish calendar, a day when Jews typically engage in prayer and fasting and do not participate in secular events. The conflict caused by the scheduling was not intentional, nor was it even noticed by the planning committee. The Jewish population of the town that year was approximately 15 percent—neither infinitesimal nor mammoth, but arguably large enough to have led the officials to take the date into consideration. Many of the medical staff at the hospital were Jewish but, likely because none of the planners were Jewish, the conflict did not emerge.

That year a new president, Steven Bradley, was in his first year at the local hospital. At a meeting of the hospital's leadership team, Steven was told about the annual fair and its scheduled date. When it was announced in the meeting, the Jewish doctors on his medical leadership team lamented that the fair had been scheduled on Yom Kippur. They

129

said this meant they would not be able to participate and that most Jewish members of the community would be unable to attend.

The hospital president surprised everyone at the table when he quickly and decisively responded by saying, "We won't participate. We can't participate in a fair that de facto excludes members of our staff and members of our community!" Some members of his team protested that, as the hospital representatives, their absence at the health fair would be noticed. "Exactly," the president responded. "We have to send a message. We will tell them we are not participating and we will tell them why. Yes, our absence will be noted. Next year, they won't choose a date that is in conflict with the spiritual and cultural needs of our staff and our patient population." And so, that year the hospital did not participate, and yes, its absence was noted.

In my work as an organizational consultant focused on social justice, I have had the opportunity to work with leaders like Steven Bradley and the other leaders and staff mentioned in this chapter. Their use of position power has deepened my understanding of power and its just use. This chapter presents some of what I have learned. Its purpose is to deepen understanding of power's place in organizational life and to present examples of power constructively used.

What does Bradley's action teach us about power? The power and authority of his position made his decision possible. Position power is connected to one's role. The higher one's role is in the organization, the more one's position power increases. What is less common, perhaps, is the use of position power to advance an equity agenda, an agenda that takes into account the needs and priorities of those who are marginalized (in this case, those of the Jewish faith and culture in a predominantly Christian town and nation). In his new role, the hospital president, who was not himself Jewish, used his position power to signal community leaders that the self-identified community hospital was there to serve the needs of all members of the community, and to do so they needed to pay close attention to inclusion.

Position power, as Bolman and Deal (2013) pointed out, is synonymous with authority. It is perhaps the most obvious type of power that leaders hold. It is visible and observable. Because it is observable, it has its risks. Bradley, as he has done throughout his career, took a risk in the interest of advancing equity.

Just Associates of England (http://www.justassociates.org/) use the well-known idea of "power to" which they define as "the unique potential of every person to shape his or her life and world." This senior hospital executive used his "power to" to shape his organization. He used his "power to" to enact change. He knew his action would be noticed. He knew his decision would be listened to in years to come. Without verbalizing it, he told everyone to check their calendars when they planned this event in the future to be sure no constituent group would be excluded.

A HEAD OF SCHOOL BUILDS THE PIPELINE

Dennis Bisgaard began his work as the new head of school at Kingswood-Oxford School in Connecticut in 2006. He established himself in his position, and three years later initiated a program "to help ensure that rising stars do reach the top." One of a very few heads of color nationally, he distinguished himself and his school by establishing a new leadership institute for educators of color. The goal of the institute is

> to provide education, resources, and networking opportunities for people of color on the path toward becoming Senior Administrators or Heads of independent schools. The Leadership Institute was created in response to a stark reality in the independent school profession: Out of 1,400 schools that belong to the National Association of Independent Schools, only 4 percent—50 schools—are led by a person of color. The percentage of female Heads, while not quite as low, is still surprisingly small, especially at the high school level. The mission of the Leadership Institute is to help educators of color explore, prepare for, and position themselves for passageway into leadership roles within independent schools. (Kingswood-Oxford, n.d.)

When Dennis later won a fellowship to the prestigious Klingenstein Center, he engaged in research to "explore schools and 'variables' that have allowed schools . . . to embrace diversity and actively and deliberately diversify the leadership top" (D. Bisgaard, personal communication, February 1, 2015).

David Thomas and John Gabarro of Harvard Business School wrote in their 1999 book, *Breaking Through: The Making of Minority Executives in Corporate America*, that "reaching the executive level cannot happen if opportunity is not provided in . . . the upper-middle management phase, for individuals to prepare, audition, and prove themselves qualified to succeed to the executive level" (Thomas & Gabarro, 1999, p. 221). This head of school used his position power to provide just that opportunity, and his wisdom led him to expand beyond a one-by-one mentoring approach.

In 2015, the Kingswood-Oxford Leadership Institute educated its third cohort of educators of color. Dennis Bisgaard uses his power to encourage annual cohorts of aspiring leaders, and the institute serves young professionals of color from schools across the region who come together to learn and, in the process, build relationships and a frame of reference that helps them to work together to create change and advance equity in their institution. In the process, they generate power together.

"Power together," sometimes called "power with," is another aspect of power often examined by scholars. From social worker and management theorist Mary Follett, who differentiated "power over" from what she also called "coactive power," through the work of the scholars at the Jean Baker Miller Training Institute at Wellesley College, who define "power with" as the idea that "more can be accomplished through collaborative efforts than through hierarchical arrangements, building on the notion that creativity and action develop in good connections" (Jean Baker Miller Training Institute, n.d.), power continues to be studied. Tew (2006), in his discussion of emancipatory power, wrote that a productive mode of power is "power together," in which collective action is taken stemming from mutual support and challenge, which occurs through valuing commonality and difference. The model of power illustrated by Dennis Bisgaard might look like what VeneKlasen and Miller (2007) called "power within" ("the capacity to imagine and have hope"; Miller, VeneKlasen, & Reilly, 2006, p. 6). His internal power led him to action: the creation of a program in which participants could gain "power with" and "power together," which strengthened their "power to" and enabled them to become heads and assistant heads of schools.

But how can we access power when others have so much power over us, especially if they have position power and we don't? What do we do when someone in the position of authority operates in unjust and oppressive ways? When we are treated unfairly by a person (or a group) with position power, and thus authority over us, does this mean we are powerless? I argue that it does not. My work as an organizational consultant has made me aware that power does not exist in dualities. It is not an all-or-nothing entity. The characterization of targeted and disenfranchised groups as powerless is disturbing and erroneous. Power is the ability to do or act, the capability of doing or accomplishing something. Suggesting that an individual or a group is powerless is an act of disempowerment. The following example illustrates this point.

STAFF UNITE TO OUST AN OPPRESSIVE LEADER

Twenty-five staff members of a drug treatment facility used their "power to" to collaborate and oust a tyrannical leader. The problems at the organization had a long history. Several years before, 90 percent of the staff had resigned and announced their resignation to the local newspaper. They cited difficulties and differences with management as the cause. Although some changes were made, and many staff (but not all) returned to work, morale issues persisted, worsening as the years passed.

It took some time, but little by little, the staff came together again, albeit secretly and cautiously. They took the risk of approaching the agency's board of directors with a letter of no confidence in the director. The board president called on me to help the board assess the situation. Because of the staff's fear of reprisals, the board president introduced me as an organizational development consultant who was going to do an organizational assessment. No mention was made of staff complaints, and there was no suggestion that the executive director (ED) was being evaluated in any way.

My first step was to interview the staff who spoke candidly, though fearfully, about their experiences. One by one, they spoke about what they experienced: the ED's emotional unevenness, sometimes crying, sometime yelling at staff, and then later being charming. They spoke of poor treatment, ranging from unfairness to bullying, as well as demeaning and degrading treatment. They reported her negative reputation in the community, specifically referencing her not showing up for meetings with vendors and not paying bills on time. They cited her withdrawal from many community collaborative efforts. They spoke of their excessive workload, with additional responsibilities being added on a regular basis.

Staff also reported that it was difficult to get reimbursed for expenses. One employee reported being quoted one salary on being hired and then being paid a different, lower figure after starting the job. Staff complained about a level of secrecy and a lack of transparency. They described file cabinets that were kept locked so that staff members could not access needed information. Staff did not know how the ED spent her time during the day, where she went when she left the building, or even when she was going on vacation.

There was significant fear of retaliation on the part of many staff members. They informed me that when they tried to speak with the chief executive officer about their concerns, she would reportedly turn things around to make it appear that the person raising an issue was at fault. In my interviews, I heard things like: "I'm afraid to ask her things; she makes me very uneasy"; "I was afraid that she'd punish me, if I asked too many questions"; "She could talk her way in and out of anything, and often things I had said would come back to bite me." The entire staff shared horror stories about the ED's leadership, and they were unanimous in their critique. I interviewed the ED, as part of the assessment, asking her about organizational functioning and her vision for the agency. Although I, of course, could not verify what staff had said, I did get a sense of an executive who was neither stable nor forthcoming.

In my report to the board, I described these behaviors and concluded that staff's outreach to the board was well grounded, and the problems they described could be attributed to poor leadership and management on the part of the ED, as well as insufficient oversight on behalf of the board (whose duty it is to regularly evaluate the director). The board received most of their information about the agency from the ED's monthly and annual reports and, therefore, was unaware of these issues until the staff identified them. It is optimal for boards to review directors on an annual basis, and at least biannually, this review should include feedback from staff and clients, either through the use of surveys or through interviews. My report included several future recommendations. The board then took action, dismissing the ED and prohibiting her from returning to the workplace for any reason.

Power, or more specifically, abuse of power, was a key theme in this case. The ED was in the position to exercise power over her employees, and she derived benefit from keeping information from them. Her use of "power over" exemplified what Tew (2006) described as a "limiting type," power that is oppressive because she used that power to enhance her own position and resources at the expense of her staff.

Just Associates, a feminist group of activists and scholars from 13 countries who focus on the study of power, provide a careful consideration of power over, which they describe as having invisible, visible, and hidden dimensions. They define *visible power* as observable decision making done in the open, using strategies such as research, analysis, lobbying, and use of media. It is open, uncorrupt, and serves the interests of all. *Hidden power* is the setting of the political agenda. Hidden power controls the agenda and determines whose voices are heard. It excludes and marginalizes in a way that is not easily visible and is used by the powerful to control the conversation. Just Associates call *invisible power* the "most insidious of the three dimensions of power" (Miller et al., 2006, p. 10). In this dimension, information is held secret. Both problems and ideas are intentionally held back, and thus those who are privy to knowledge can shape the discussion and its meaning. They also get to define what is normal.

The ED had not only failed, her leadership was arbitrary, abusive, and interfered with the staff's power to do their best work. She closed off opportunities for them. Both hidden power and invisible power operate in closed space, a space "where decisions are made by an elite group . . . behind closed doors without any pretense of public participation" (Miller et al., 2006, p. 5). This director's insidious use of power was invisible to the board of directors and to the clients. Her actions suggest that she saw her employees as powerless, and clearly that is how they felt as individuals, individuals who loved their work and were dependent on the salaries for their livelihood.

But power has many expressions and forms and "can range from domination and resistance to collaboration and transformation" (Miller et al. 2006, p. 4). In response to their boss's treatment, through talking with one another and sharing their stories, these individual employees built what relational cultural theory calls "power through connection" and what Tew (2006) called "co-operative power," power strong enough to defend themselves and the agency itself. They used "power with" ("finding common ground among different interests in order to build collective strength"; Miller et al., 2006, p. 4) and "power to." What began as oppressive power was turned around by the staff's ability to develop power-generating relationships among themselves. In the face of abusive control and restriction of information, the staff took collective action, reclaiming their own power as workers and human beings entitled to respect and fair treatment.

As I work with social justice concerns in organizations, the examination of power is essential. As I consider power and seek its appropriate usage in organizations, theoreticians and practitioners like those discussed earlier have informed my thinking and my practice. Bolman and Deal (2008) are two other authors who have been major contributors to my thinking. They too identify types of power that appear in organizational life: position power (or authority), control of rewards, coercive power (the ability to constrain, block, interfere, or punish), information and expertise, reputation, personal power, alliances and networks, access and control of agenda, and framing control of meaning and symbols. Most significant for my work, however, has been their identification of four frames (structural, political, human resource, and symbolic) with which to think about and assess organizations. Their illustrations of how these frames inform leadership and relate to power have been indispensable to me.

The *structural frame* (the organization as factory) is a way of understanding organizations from the perspective of rules, structures, and hierarchy. Framing organizations from a human resources point of view (the organization as extended family) focuses on people, their needs, and their energy. In the *human resource frame*, there is an inclination to enable a good fit between systems and individuals to ensure personal and organizational success. The *political frame* (the organization as jungle) highlights the competition that exists in organizations: competition for resources, saliency, and competing interests between individuals and interest groups. From the perspective of the *symbolic frame* (the organization as theater), signs, symbols, and images are important. This perspective focuses on meaning and on the importance of meaning in helping an organization find its direction and generate hope and confidence. This is also the frame that highlights vision and values and builds motivation.

Bolman and Deal (2013) advised those who seek a deep understanding of organizations to integrate these frames. Though leaders, consultants, and others may have preferred ways of knowing, all of the frames or perspectives provide a different view of the organization.

The operation of power is highly central to the political frame, which is conceptualized as a jungle where people compete for resources. When an individual constructs or conceives of an organization from a political frame, power dynamics are inevitably a part of that. Bolman and Deal wrote that political power is "how competing groups articulate preferences and mobilize to get what they want" (2013, p. 201). Power in organizations is, for example, often about the distribution of resources.

As Bolman and Deal (2013) wrote, "At every level in organizations, alliances form because members have interests in common and believe they can do more together than apart. To accomplish their aims they need power" (p. 201). This need of power to accomplish goals is, of course, true of all individuals, groups, and organizations; however, each frame provides its own way of thinking about and using power. According to Bolman and Deal, "Human resource theorists place less emphasis on power and more on empowerment" (p. 201). In the symbolic frame, power resides in the development of meaning, vision, values, symbols, and in the creation and usage of heroes and heroines that will move an organization and its people. In the structural frame, power resides in the design of structures and in those who make the rules. Excellent leaders know how to use the power of each of the four frames. In my consultancy, I worked with a college president whose leadership and attention to her school's mission and vision embodied all of these frames.

A COLLEGE PRESIDENT SHIFTS THE LENS

Something had to happen when three members of the National Collegiate Athletic Association conference, to which Spelman College belonged, left the conference and joined another. Their move threatened the survival of the original conference, which required the membership of seven schools. Spelman College tried to join another conference, but they were limited in choices due to the necessity for conference members to be in relatively close geographic proximity so they could compete without onerous and expensive travel arrangements—arrangements that would necessitate some overnight stays and require students to miss classes. Membership in a new conference would also be much more expensive. Projections of the cost ran close to a million dollars.

Beverly Daniel Tatum, the college's president at that time, began her research. She examined participation in intercollegiate sports and discovered that only about 80 students competed in intercollegiate sports. This was a very low number in a black women's college whose enrollment topped 2,000 students. Wellness classes at the college, she discovered, had higher enrollments (278 students) and seemed to be of more interest to the students, but scheduling them was a problem because the old gym built in the 1950s was small and usually in use for team practices.

Weighing the challenges of greater expense and a benefit to less than 100 students, President Tatum began to think about having the college withdraw from intercollegiate sports. However, she wondered whether doing this would negatively affect enrollment.

She conducted research on black women and sports, the relationship between health and competitive sports, and the data on black women's health. She thought about the college's old gym and the lack of their own athletic field. She realized either Spelman would have to spend a lot more money to continue in intercollegiate sports, or they would have to get out of the business altogether. In my conversation with her that this decision, she told me that her research revealed that black women tend to be sedentary and in addition tend to make poor food choices.

This information sparked an idea in this famously creative and innovative leader. She decided to flip it? Why not take the resources and engage in a campuswide wellness program to benefit everyone. Why not introduce students to activities they could engage in throughout their lives (running, walking, yoga, and so on) rather than prolonging a program of high school and college sports activities that could not follow them into their adult years?

To make this idea work, she had to persuade people. She first went to the faculty resource committee and presented the choices and the pros and cons. She went to the trustees with the same presentation. She went to the trustees one by one and spoke to each of them to explain what she wanted to do. She recalled one trustee whose alumnae daughters did not exercise and how he was persuaded because of his concern for their health. With data in hand and her vision in mind, she worked to persuade every trustee.

She knew the athletes would not be happy. She knew she could not just lead the college to walk away from the athletic conference and offer nothing to replace it. To get everyone's attention, generate enthusiasm, and provide a picture of where she was heading, she dubbed her plan the "wellness revolution." She drew on the image of the college's founders, two women who spoke about their goal to educate black women so that they could educate others. They spoke about helping their students to develop literacy in the black community, starting with their own graduates. Spelman's wellness revolution, as she envisioned it, would be in the same vein; it would develop fitness literacy. "If we could help our students to be literate in fitness, they would spread that knowledge to the community" (B. Tatum, personal communication, September 8, 2013).

The idea was met with both excitement and resistance. Perhaps the biggest issue was that they still had an old gym that could not support the kind of fitness revolution the president had in mind, so she went to work to raise $18 million to build a new gym where the old gym stood. Two years into the plan, she reported that the fitness revolution was finding its legs. Participation in wellness programs at the college increased from 278 students to 1,300 students, and the president exemplified that success by walking with students in an annual 5K Wellness Race that was part of the "Wellness Revolution."

Beverly Tatum's success in this effort is a powerful example of both the use of position power and the power of expertise. Posed with a challenge, she was in the position to influence a change in direction. She did the research and gathered relevant, persuasive information. She shared that information with others, packaged in a compelling way, and also offered a promising solution.

Her work exemplifies each of Bolman and Deal's (2013) four frames. Always expert at the use of the symbolic frame, this president framed the change as a wellness revolution, a powerful and energizing image. She used the founders' idealism and charge to educate black women to educate others as a way of undergirding the image of the fitness revolution. She supported her imagery and vision with financial strategies, and she brought together different points of view to connect to a shared interest in creating wellness among black women who suffer high rates of obesity, high blood pressure, and diabetes. This was the power of the political frame, engaging in what Bolman and Deal call "the realistic process of making decisions and allocating resources in a context of scarcity and divergent interests" (p. 190). Using the structural frame, she thought of where classes would be held as the revolution began and before the new gym could be built, and she raised the money to make it happen. The outcome of the wellness revolution would be the empowerment of all students through improvement in the quality of their health and well-being.

All of this was accomplished through the very visible use of power: the power of the president's role and her ability to frame, innovate, educate, envision, and persuade. No back-room negotiations. No private deals. Rather, the elegant development of a vision that would open possibilities and serve the good of all students and the skill to make it happen. Facing declining participation in intercollegiate sports and the high costs of maintaining the athletic programs at a small liberal arts college, the college president shifted the lens of the community and used the power of all four organizational lenses to enact a change in the interest of all.

CONCLUSION

Bolman and Deal (2013) called organizational power "the capacity to make things happen" (p. 190). These two definitions are at the heart of an understanding of positive position power. With power, we can accomplish our goals. Without it, we cannot.

Although we often think of power as something that belongs solely to individuals, organizations and other groups of people with a particular purpose also have power. Created to accomplish a vision and a mission, organizations' right use of power takes the form of commitment to an ethical mission and vision.

Achieving success in organizations is not easy. Organizations are complex; people's needs vary; hierarchy matters (in pay, decision making, authority, benefits, hours); and the needs of managers, workers, and those they serve often differ and may even compete. Competing needs and unequal benefits may, and often do, interfere with the completion of the mission. Abusive bosses undermine the health and well-being of employees.

In the face of challenges, power reveals its complexity; its seemingly clear and straightforward definitions are now complicated and controversial. We live in a world of inequity with an increasing incidence of power distance (a measure of inequality between bosses and subordinates) in organizations. However, some organizations make positive use of power.

The aforementioned leaders and staff members who use power to serve and empower offer compelling, positive examples. These examples of people who achieve power within themselves and with others and who make right use of power in ways that serve social justice and the common good are worthy models for us all. Lifting up these exemplary leaders and continuing the quest for a "unifying theory of power" (Clark, 1974) will help us to achieve power sharing and right use of power.

We cannot understand organizational life without attention to power, and we cannot consult to organizations without attention to power dynamics. The consultant's role is a unique example of position power. Consultants do not have direct power. That is, we are not the decision makers, but we can cultivate the power to influence an organization by educating our clients and by building relationships. We always retain the power to take on an engagement or to withdraw from one. And by designing principles of practice to guide our work and sharing these with our organizational clients, we can strengthen our ability to engage in ethical practice grounded in the principles of social justice.

An awareness of power in its multiple forms and a clarity that power can strengthen and accomplish, as well as constrain and oppress, will help us to serve our clients well. To ignore power dynamics in the construction and facilitation of organizational consultation ultimately sabotages the goal of organizational development. Power is a necessary energy, an important concept, and an ever-present dynamic. Yes, there are inequities of power and abuses of power. These must be noted and rectified, but we must not eschew the concept of power in an effort to avoid exploitation.

REFERENCES

Bolman, L. G., & Deal, T. E. (2013). *Reframing organizations: Artistry, choice, and leadership.* (5th ed.). San Francisco: Jossey-Bass.

Clark, K. (1974). *Pathos of power.* New York: Harper & Row.

Jean Baker Miller Training Institute. (n.d.). *Glossary of relational-cultural theory key terms.* Retrieved from http://www.jbmti.org/Our-Work/glossary-relational-cultural-therapy#power%20with

Kingswood-Oxford. (n.d.). *KO leadership institute for educators of color.* Retrieved from http://www.kingswoodoxford.org/page.cfm?p=2946

Miller, V., VeneKlasen, L., & Reilly, M. (2006). *Making change happen: Power. Concepts for revisioning power for justice, equity and peace, #3.* Retrieved from http://www.powercube.net/wpcontent/uploads/2009/11/making_change_happen_3.pdf

Tew, J. (2006). Understanding power and powerlessness: Towards a framework for emancipatory practice in social work. *Journal of Social Work, 6,* 33–51.

Thomas, D. A., & Gabarro, J. (1999). *Breaking through: The making of minority executives in corporate America.* Boston: Harvard University Press.

VeneKlasen, L., & Miller, V. (2007). *A new weave of power, people, and politics: The action guide for advocacy and citizen participation.* Warwickshire, UK: Practical Action.

10

The Joy of Sharing Power and Fostering Well-Being in Community Networks

Ramon Rojano

As reported by the U.S. Census Bureau, by 2012, there were 46.5 million people living in poverty in the United States, and the official poverty rate was 15.0 percent of the population, 2.5 percentage points higher than in 2007 (DeNavas-Walt, Proctor, & Smith, 2013). Facing such challenges requires not only major changes in social policy but also the collaboration of different sectors of the community. Health and human services providers have the opportunity to make a contribution by helping low-income clients transform their lives, conquer poverty, and achieve holistic well-being. This chapter offers some paradigms and strategies to work toward the achievement of such laudable goals.

The proposed framework starts with the assumption that a practitioner is the facilitator of a process of individual and family self-development. This definition provides enough flexibility to work hand in hand with clients, solving problems and building supportive infrastructures, while simultaneously developing their psychological strengths. This agenda targets ambitious goals such as creating a supportive and enriching social network, adopting healthy lifestyles, enhancing resilience and leadership skills, and attaining holistic well-being. The approach presented is the result of the integration of lessons from different masters of the field; from community workers; and, most especially, from clients themselves. Let me share the experience.

LESSONS LEARNED

I was born in Colombia, South America, in a small rural town without electricity or potable water. However, I was blessed with a supportive and inspiring family. My father, a telegrapher, worked hard and was an avid reader. My mother, always very affectionate and hardworking, was also very involved in the Catholic Church and had a positive mind set. She used to say, "Faith comes first, everything else will come after," a saying that stuck in my head forever. When I was about seven, my father got sick with diabetes and could not work anymore. Without medical care available, he used only home remedies that were not effective. The family finances deteriorated. My mother made the decision to move to the city to work as a seamstress. She made money by sewing clothes for children and put me in charge of going downtown to deliver the products. After my father died when I was 16, we became poorer. Sometimes I had to go to a food pantry for resources. I remember how embarrassing it was to be in those lines, but my mother made sure that I had the right attitude. According to her plans, this was just temporary. We prayed the rosary every evening and ended each day energized by her messages of hope. We felt encouraged to talk about our great plans in life. I spoke about my desire to become a medical doctor. My mother smiled with the certainty that it would happen. There were days when we did not have anything to eat, but my mother still woke up singing, as if she were possessed by a strong spirit. She always found a solution. She would sit at the sewing machine and work until she finished one or two items of clothing. I delivered them, coming back with money and groceries.

Eventually, my mother's predictions came true, and I graduated as the first doctor from my town. Subsequently, I graduated as a psychiatrist well versed in classical forms of psychotherapy. I trained in family therapy, for which I had developed a special passion. Being the only family therapist in a big city, I had a very successful private practice. Several years later, while visiting relatives in Connecticut, I received the offer to move to the United States to work for the University of Connecticut at a community mental health center. This was a major cultural shock. I went from being a therapist of the upper-middle-class in the third world to becoming a helper of the poor in the richest country in the world.

HARTFORD'S ENVIRONMENT

Back in 1986, Hartford, Connecticut, was a city of about 125,000 people and only 17 square miles. The place that was then described as the insurance capital of America was becoming poorer and more diverse. During the housing boom of the 1980s, the Irish, Jewish, and Italian families that had populated the city for decades purchased bigger and newer homes in the surrounding suburbs, and Hartford's white population decreased to less than 30 percent. At the center of the wealthy Hartford County, in one of the richest states in the country, this historic town became one of the poorer state capitals. Its unemployment rate was double the national average, and it had a median family income of $24,000, just a third of the average income of families in the state. The child poverty rate was 47 percent, and single-parent households were prevalent. Food stamps and child welfare caseloads soared, neighborhoods became dilapidated, and gang violence was rampant.

FOLLOW-UP WITH SUCCESSFUL FORMER CLIENTS

For a therapist who used to treat primarily an upper-middle-class clientele, this environment was challenging. However, being open to listen and learn from clients yielded enormous returns. One of the initial lessons I learned was from Rose, a 36-year-old Caribbean woman who had been referred for counseling because of allegations of physical and verbal abuse toward her three children. She was unemployed, receiving welfare support, and living in a dangerous housing project. After combining counseling with parenting education, she became compliant and started to use nonabusive ways to discipline her children. However, the rest of her circumstances remained the same, full of stagnation and hopelessness. I felt powerless. I kept thinking about her situation until I challenged myself with the question: What would I do if she were my sister whom I had not seen in 15 years? The answer hit me like a lightning bolt. I realized that I was not seeing her as an equal but as a "different" type of human being. Because of this, I was depriving her of many opportunities. At the next session, I started praising her three beautiful children and invited her to make plans to give them a better life. She felt energized and talked about her dreams. She found motivation to attend English classes and to use other community resources. Two years later I found her in a train station. She had improved her English, had a small business, had a meaningful relationship with her new husband, and had moved to a better house. This case was transformative for me. I learned about the power of believing in people and treating them as equals.

As a strong believer of the importance of social medicine and social psychiatry, I made great strides adjusting to the new environment and became active in the community. In a small city, I always had easy access to my former clients. Seeing some of them prosper in life made me wonder if the former therapeutic interventions had anything to do with their progress. I decided to do a very informal inquiry and had conversations with 10 of them. I asked, "What helped you move forward?" To my astonishment, none mentioned therapy but, instead the following factors: supportive families, a circle of friends, community resources, strong faith and engagement in church, mentors, experiencing love, a good job, getting education and training, increased income, a geographical move, removal of stressors, engaging in cultural activities, and helping other people. This experience taught me the value of going beyond the traditional role of a "therapist" to recognize the influence of other factors. I thought that if I wanted to succeed with my cases, I needed to combine therapy with other variables.

Miriam's Story

Miriam's story helped shape my form of practice. She was born in a remote Puerto Rican town, the sixth child in a family of 10. Since age 8, she had assumed responsibility for household chores, spending her Saturdays washing clothes in a nearby river and ironing them on Sundays. Her father traveled to the United States to do farm work for six months every year, while her mother ran the family with an iron fist. Miriam resented this life and dreamed of a way out. At age 14, her mother pulled her out from school to only do housework. In protest, she ran away, moving to Chicago with a friend. At age 16, she had her first son, and at age 20, she had twin boys. Two years later, she left her boyfriend, registered in a GED program, and went to work in a factory. She completed her GED and was accepted at Northeastern University for undergraduate studies. She remembers surviving financially using a combination of government assistance and income generated from a work–study program. At school, she learned about Puerto Rican history and started to develop a positive identity as a Latina-Caribbean woman. She discovered a passion for early childhood education, but juggling employment and college as a single mother was not easy. She lived in a rundown, gang-infested inner-city neighborhood. Despite her intentions of protecting her children from this negative environment, at age 14, her oldest son was shot dead as an innocent bystander during a gang feud. This experience broke her down, causing major grief. According to her report to a *Family Therapy Networker* writer in 1987, she felt guilty for not having enough income to live in a better neighborhood (Markowitz, 1997). She spent hours just walking and crying. Following the recommendation of a friend, she moved to Hartford looking for a new life. Unfortunately, she rented an apartment in a neighborhood that was also poor and riddled with gang activity. But she was ready to fight for her children. She lived on government assistance and volunteered in the development of a new culturally competent child care center. This is where I met her. Back then, I was a clinician at a child guidance clinic, assigned to work 12 hours per week at the high school where her twins attended as special education students. The boys had been referred for behavioral problems and low educational performance. I found her still grieving the death of her son. Her children had developmental disabilities that had not been adequately treated. I supported her fight against a failing educational system. As described by the reporter, "in therapy, she found enough respite from the pressure to be the strong mother to let down her guard and mourn for her son. She says therapy renewed her energy, and then she became determined to improve life for her twins" (Markowitz, 1997, p. 5). Miriam had strong leadership skills. She started to organize parents of other children in special education, to learn about their rights, and also to advocate for appropriate programs. I watched her successfully sue the school system, forcing them to place her boys in vocational programs in mechanics and auto body repair. Miriam founded an advocacy organization called Parents Opening Doors that eventually grew to be a statewide agency that has helped educate thousands of parents and advocated for substantial changes in several school systems in Connecticut. This volunteer work was a platform for Miriam to develop her own supportive network. She became a prestigious and credible community leader with child development expertise. She became the director of a child development center, earned a master's degree in education, bought a home in a stable neighborhood, and eventually got married.

While writing this chapter, I decided to call Miriam to ask her permission to write her story and to get updated information. She is now a very successful 59-year-old woman, enjoying a middle-class status. Her two adult sons have steady jobs and good families, and she is a proud grandmother. Her résumé shows a victorious trajectory of progress. She is an assistant professor of child development at a community college and also the owner–founder of a school readiness agency that serves 72 children. I asked her for her recipe to success. According to her, the ingredients are: having clear goals, working hard toward such goals, developing a solid cultural and gender identity, accessing community resources, and maintaining a strong set of moral values. She emphasized the value of altruism, highlighting the importance of using personal achievements to benefit other people. When asked about how therapy helped her in her journey, she said that it was a critical part of her life. It enabled her to grieve the death of her son, and also receive validation as a woman of color and emotional support for her ambitious dreams. She insisted on talking about the importance of being treated with respect and having an empathetic therapist.

From her I learned that clinical work, although very important, is only a piece of the puzzle. I also learned that for people in poverty, the consequence beyond not having enough resources is losing control over their own circumstances. I also learned that becoming a community leader provides a sense of external power that also generates a personal experience of self-efficacy.

CONCEPTUAL FRAMEWORK

The proposed practice builds on the concept that, under the right conditions, everyone has the potential to develop into a healthy, productive, and happy citizen. Within this framework, deficient levels of personal and social development are believed to foster dysfunction. The combination of a lack of resources and experiences of abuse or neglect causes disempowerment that triggers unhealthy habits, behavioral problems, and life dissatisfaction. The equation is simple:

$$\text{Low level of development} + \text{Deficient resources} +$$
$$\text{Exposure to abuse and trauma} = \text{Individual and family dysfunction}$$

In simple terms, *power* is defined as the ability or right to control people or things (Merriam-Webster, n.d.). Unfortunately, when working with low-income minority individuals, we frequently find very low levels of power and see people struggling to achieve within the context of disempowering and threatening societal infrastructures. Clearly, certain levels of power are indispensable to effective functioning.

There are two categories of power. *Extrinsic power* refers to external assets such as material possessions and resources, titles, positions, family, and social circles or connections. *Intrinsic power* refers to internal assets such as knowledge, experience, values, thoughts, and feelings. Normally, individuals have a combination of internal and external assets and develop habits that could be power generating or disempowering. Examples of empowering habits include working hard, accessing available resources, being persistent, establishing good relationships, practicing healthy behaviors, and thinking positive thoughts. Examples of disempowering habits are sedentary lives, unhealthy eating, alcohol/drug use, verbal or physical conflicts, avoidance of responsibility, social isolation, and poor levels of effort.

Unfortunately, beginning in childhood, many people are bombarded with disempowering messages that cause preoccupations with negative self-perceptions. Living in toxic and unsafe environments, their mental status tends to be a combination of sadness for what happened before, anxiety for what is going on, and fear for the future. They attempt to navigate a never-ending ocean of hopelessness. Clearly, they need to be helped to deconstruct the past and create internal and external conditions that are conducive to the development of healthy, productive, and satisfactory lives. The good news is that the passion and beliefs of a helper could serve as a means of summoning the best of a person.

HOLISTIC WELL-BEING

The concept of well-being offers a good paradigm that encompasses all aspects of life, including good socioeconomic conditions, quality relationships, positive emotions, physical health, resilience, realization of potential, happiness, and overall life satisfaction (Centers for Disease Control and Prevention, n.d.). Achieving well-being requires a basic infrastructure that includes adequate income, good education, marketable skills, good health, a nurturing family and social network, productivity, and a safe environment.

A comprehensive action plan could cover the following four bases: physical conditions, socioeconomic status (SES), family and social networks, and psychological strengths (see Table 10.1). The equation looks like this:

$$\text{Physical conditions} + \text{Socioeconomic status} + \text{Social networks} + \\ \text{Psychological strengths} = \text{Well-being}$$

TABLE 10.1:   Types of Factors Included in the Four Bases

Building Blocks			
Socioeconomic Conditions	Social Networks	Physical Conditions	Psychological Strengths
Income and assets	Close family	Healthy eating	Clear goals
Job and/or own business	Extended family	Physical activities	Self-efficacy
Education and training	Circle of friends	Preventive health care	Optimism
Financial literacy	Support/education groups	Stress reduction	Coping skills
Health care	Cultural groups	Sobriety	Emotional intelligence
Housing	Faith congregations	Health information	Persistence
Other social resources	Civic engagement	Disease management	Spirituality

The correlation between well-being and the previously mentioned four bases has been validated by many research projects.

Socioeconomic Factors

Many studies have demonstrated the association between subjective well-being and SES. Cooper, McCausland, and Theodossiou (2013) found that individuals with the lowest percentile of income also had lower levels of well-being. Adamkiewicz et al. (2014) found evidence that poverty and deteriorated housing conditions are associated with poor health. These and other studies not only show the detrimental impact of poverty on well-being but also suggest that improving well-being helps increase SES. Luo and Waite (2005) found that low SES since childhood was linked with poor health conditions in later life but also found that this negative impact could be ameliorated if SES was improved in adulthood. Contemporary research findings support the development of the social determinants of health concept that have become a centerpiece of public health practice (World Health Organization, n.d.).

Social Networks

A positive association between social interaction and health conditions has been described. Mukerjee (2013) found that enjoying an active network of friends increased the possibility of being in very good or excellent health. Pinderhughes, Nix, and Foster (2001) found that, disregarding race and ethnicity, living in distressed neighborhoods and experiencing social isolation affected the quality of parenting.

Healthy Lifestyles

The positive correlation between physical and psychological conditions has been documented. Ariza-García et al. (2013) found a negative association between physical activity and fitness and depression, anger, fatigue, and blood pressure. The 2002 World Health Survey showed that, globally, individuals with diabetes had increased odds of an episode of depressive symptoms compared with those without diabetes (Mommersteeg, Herr, Pouwer, Holt, & Loerbroks, 2013).

Psychological Strengths

This term is used interchangeably with the concept of resilience (Brownlee et al., 2013). *Resilience* is defined as the process used by people facing adversity to recover successfully or adapt and meet whatever demands are required to cope (Werner & Brendtro, 2012). Contemporary studies have shown its impact on the transition to adulthood (Nikitin & Freund, 2008), college achievement (Masten, Cutuli, Herbers, & Reed, 2009), and social mobility (Weidenfeller, 2012).

In conclusion, the studies point to the importance of targeting healthy lifestyles, network development, and social mobility as expected outcomes of holistic interventions.

Intervention Strategies

The following are some strategies that could help achieve the aforementioned goals.

Coaching. Building on principles of family life education, life coaching is a popular approach that assists individuals in designing and implementing a life plan, maximizing potential, and growing and achieving success and well-being (Allen, 2013). It is geared toward the clarification and definition of goals and helping clients stay focused, removing obstacles, and monitoring the plan implementation.

Therapy. Mental health interventions are crucial, as they lend clients a sympathetic ear and provide emotional support. The therapeutic goals could include debriefing and deconstructing previous negative and traumatic events, managing current personal and family problems, cognitive reframing of self-perceptions, reexamining and clarification of previous dreams, validating identity, and promoting positive outlooks on life. An effective therapeutic intervention could help develop key psychological strengths such as goal setting, persistence, self-efficacy, coping, emotional intelligence, and optimism.

 Goal setting involves the capacity and motivation to commit to specifically defined outcomes (Carroll, Gordon, Haynes, & Houghton, 2013). *Persistence* relates to self-control and endurance, the ability to bring a task from start to completion, and postponing immediate gratification for the sake of future reward (Halkjelsvik & Rise, 2015). *Self-efficacy* is the confidence that one will successfully master difficult tasks or situations (Weiss, Freund, & Wiese, 2012). *Coping* refers to a psychological process by which individuals effectively navigate and manage challenging or threatening demands (Leipold & Greve, 2009). *Emotional intelligence* is manifested by an array of skills that allow individuals to successfully deal with interpersonal situations, including the capacity to perceive and understand others' emotions and to reflectively regulate their own (Buvoltz, Powell, Solan, & Longbotham, 2008). *Optimism* is the tendency to expect positive outcomes even when such expectations are not rationally justified (Hmieleski & Baron, 2009). All these factors could be developed in therapeutic, counseling, or educational settings.

Case Management. Growing out of social work models, case management is an intervention that evolved in the 1970s and 1980s to assist children living in families with multiple problems. It aims at helping clients access a variety of services. It starts with an assessment of needs, and, among others, its strategies include linking and facilitating access to resources and advocating on behalf of individuals (National Association of Social Workers, 2012).

Healthy Lifestyles. Promoting healthy lifestyles is also a critical component. The research shows that good eating habits, physical activity, and healthy weight are related to better mental health, including mood, vigor, and decreasing fatigue (Olabi et al., 2015), and lack of physical activity and unhealthy diet have been found to be associated with low motivation and depression (Lee, Lan, & Lee, 2012). The large amount of available scientific evidence calls for the incorporation of health promotion as a critical part of comprehensive interventions.

Networking. Helping families that face multiple challenges requires the development of a large intervention team, which eventually should be comanaged by clients themselves. An initial comprehensive assessment of the four bases could help identify the necessary components of such a network. These networks need to be tailored and assembled like a personalized quilt. It is recommended that practitioners spend some time developing their own treasure chest of community resources. These partnerships could be established first by accessing local, state, or national directories of community resources, identifying the most important services needed, spending time reading about programs, visiting agencies, or attending community fairs. Time spent upfront building a personal network will yield returns in the future. Sharing power through collaboration could be one of the most effective ways of developing an effective network.

Leadership Development. Practitioners could help clients gain leadership skills through the following three strategies: (1) attending local or national leadership training programs, (2) signing up as volunteers in local organizations, or (3) engaging in campaigns that advocate for neighborhood improvements or other related causes.

Integrative Approaches

Socioeconomic progress could be influenced by five different factors: (1) the macro socioeconomic structure (Abelev, 2009); (2) family and social supports (Folger & Wright, 2013); (3) the opportunity to access educational, employment, and other resources (Johnson, Brett, & Deary, 2010; Rogers, Creed, & Searle, 2009); (4) dispositional biological factors (Viinikainen, Kokko, Pulkkinen, & Pehkonen, 2010); and (5) the internal psychological strengths or resilience (Khan, 2013). The discussed interventions could help make substantial improvements on factors 2, 3, and 5. In addition, promoting healthy lifestyles could enhance biological and dispositional factors. Through advocacy, some changes in local social and economic infrastructures could be achieved.

Using a simpler approach, and from a power perspective, the intervention goal will aim at facilitating success and holistic well-being using this formula:

$$\text{Intrinsic power} + \text{Extrinsic power} + \text{Healthy habits} = \text{Success and well-being}$$

From a coaching/therapeutic perspective, the formula will look like this:

$$\text{Clarity} + \text{Preparation} + \text{Effort} = \text{Realization of dreams}$$

The proposed action plan aims at embracing healthy lifestyles, changing internal concepts and personal attitudes, building a supportive personal and social network, and fostering socioeconomic progress. A potential therapeutic sequence could begin with weekly appointments, spacing out the remaining sessions over the course of one or two years. A few phone or electronic contacts could be useful.

Clinicians might benefit from training focused on the following four objectives: (1) learning about available community resources and understanding the requirements of social policies, (2) developing minimal life coaching skills to help clients develop a good life plan, (3) learning methods of developing resilience factors in a clinical settings, and (4) improving cultural competency levels and self-checking to identify biases and stereotypes. In addition, a positive client–therapist relationship is paramount for positive outcomes (Lambert & Barley, 2001). It is important to value clients as equals and believe in their potential to conquer adversities.

Professional Commitment

For these interventions to be effective, there is a set of beliefs and attitudes needed:

- Believing that social change is possible
- Having the conviction that people have the potential to progress in life
- Self-reflecting and being willing to get rid of racism or other biases
- Not working alone but always enlisting other people to be part of a larger team
- Making clients true partners and sharing the professional power with them
- Being happy with large or small victories in only a portion of the clientele
- Being patient and committed for the long run

There is the need to restructure internalized negative schemas about the community and to process biases and negative assumptions about people different from ourselves. Unfortunately, research has shown that many well-intentioned therapists have internalized feelings leading to ethnic microaggressions toward their diverse clientele (Owen, Tao, Imel, Wampold, & Rodolfa, 2014). Constant self-checking and conceptual restructuring will necessarily foster the development of inclusive, equitable, and culturally sound approaches to community practice. To ensure this, it is recommended to always ask clients how they are experiencing the relationship.

Community Family Therapy

The community family therapy (CFT) model offers a potentially useful platform for action (Rojano, 2004). This strategy combines mental health techniques with case management and fosters the development of clients' leadership and advocacy skills. CFT was developed out of a conviction that therapists' attachment to traditional treatment methods is a fundamental obstacle for working effectively with low-income and disenfranchised families. This theory postulates that conventional ideas about job descriptions, clinical protocols, and therapeutic boundaries function as the walls of a constricting box that limits the effective treatment of low-income families. CFT was developed in response to the need to address five primary factors historically not considered a part of therapists' responsibilities: (1) moving family income above the poverty line, (2) increasing availability and access to community resources, (3) formulating a plan for personal and professional growth, (4) fostering personal responsibility and self-sufficiency, and (5) developing leadership skills and capacity for civic engagement (Rojano, 2004).

In summary, the intervention sequence comprehends the following seven steps: (1) conducting a comprehensive assessment; (2) partnering with clients, enlisting them as coproducers of the intervention process; (3) codeveloping a comprehensive action plan; (4) developing and consolidating a supportive and nurturing network; (5) consulting and assisting clients in the implementation of plans; (6) managing emerging problems and crises; and (7) celebrating victories. The CFT approach has been successfully replicated in Cali, Colombia (Terranova-Zapata, Acevedo-Velasco, & Rojano, 2014).

Middle-Class Express

After many years of practicing CFT, I wanted to make use of the institutional power I had as director of Hartford's Department of Health and Human Services. I wanted to develop a large-scale social mobility program that could be implemented and replicated by other human services professionals. With technical and financial support from the Annie E. Casey Foundation, the Middle Class Express (MCE) started in 2001 (Ubinas, 2001). From its inception, the concept was successful. In partnership with the Hartford Housing Authority, this program helped former housing projects residents become homeowners. In the process of redoing public housing and promoting home ownership, the Housing Authority needed to help former tenants develop the mind-set, skills, and habits necessary to keep up with their new responsibilities. Dozens of individuals were assisted, and they were able to purchase and maintain their homes. Subsequently, I moved to Raleigh, North Carolina, to become the director of Human Services for Wake County, a jurisdiction of 900,000 people. I was able to negotiate political support for the initiative. In 2008, the Board of Commissioners adopted a policy called the Human Capital Initiative, with MCE as its centerpiece (Lagrone, 2008). This policy provided the support needed to get MCE to a higher level. Thanks to the passion and commitment of dozens of human services workers who embraced the idea and made it their own, this program quickly became successful. I served primarily as a program consultant and trainer, and human services workers were in charge of leading and implementing this program, which ended being recognized as a model by the National Association of Counties. In addition, it has been embraced by several local community agencies that adapted the concept and developed their own models.

Using the metaphor of a train station, MCE was conceived as a process to help people go from poverty to middle-class status. Coaches and clients cocreate a life plan conducive to achieving a desired and personalized lifestyle. At least 40 hours per week of sweat equity are required, in the form of work, education, training, or other efforts. The program focuses on eight specific developmental tracks:

1. Employment
2. Financial literacy and entrepreneurship
3. Formal education
4. Training/skill sets
5. Attitude/mind-set
6. Access to and use of resources
7. Healthy lifestyle
8. Family and community engagement

Clients are provided with individual or group coaching sessions, educational sessions and also are helped access a network of existing community resources. Two case vignettes are used to illustrate how MCE works.

Carmen's story. In early 2000s, while working on my master's in family therapy, I worked as an intern at a mental health agency, where I had the opportunity to test the MCE approach with Carmen, a 35-year-old Puerto Rican. Carmen had three children, was unemployed, but sometimes worked as a foster mother. She felt trapped in her home, feeling depressed and hopeless about her ability to improve her skills, get a job, and change her life. I worked in collaboration with a doctor who prescribed antidepressant medication and with other community agencies. Cognitive techniques helped her develop a healthier mind set, and by integrating coaching strategies in the process, we developed a multiyear life plan. She started by attending English classes and getting training in child care. Subsequently, she enrolled in community college, graduated as a child development specialist, and ended with a full-time job at a preschool center. Her depressive symptoms remitted, and she did not need medication. Eventually, she was able to buy her own home. This intervention lasted about three years and included a total of 29 sessions. From Carmen, I learned that achieving a life change requires a multiyear commitment to a life plan.

Clementine's story. Clementine is a 44-year-old African American woman who was brought by a friend to the MCE program in Raleigh. She lived with her 38-year-old boyfriend, an alcoholic and drug user who abused her verbally and emotionally. She had lost several jobs because of problems with anger management, attendance, and punctuality. She was unemployed, living on food stamps, and had no health insurance. Previously, she had been diagnosed with obesity, hypertension, and type II diabetes, but was without medical treatment. She attended group coaching for several years. Following a life plan, she enrolled in a community college and, three years later, completed an associate degree, secured a job in a medical clinic, and moved independently. After participating in a health promotion group, she lost weight and became more physically active. She no longer needed medication for hypertension but continued to be treated for diabetes and was in good compliance with medical recommendations.

MCE has produced good results for clients who persevere in the process. In 2011, a follow-up survey revised data from 40 of the most engaged participants and showed the following results: 87.5 percent reported progress in employment, 82 percent maintained stable housing, 84 percent were working on their life plans, and 82 percent reported compliance with sweat equity requirements. To this date, MCE has a caseload of about 300 clients and continues to produce tangible outcomes, including the fact that several clients have purchased their own homes.

LIMITATIONS

Although these approaches have been proven to work, there are conditions and limitations that need to be considered. The social and economic macrostructure of the country, and the absence of national and local agendas destined to foster human development at a larger scale, are sociopolitical realities that tend to perpetuate poverty and disempowerment among low-income communities. For people of color, the constant exposure to open or tacit experiences of racism tends to result in low motivation, resentment, and isolation. The existing fragmentation of health and human services systems makes it difficult to implement well-coordinated integrative service plans. Current funding and reimbursement schemes are based on medical models. This fact makes it hard to access appropriate funding for the comprehensive programming needed. However, this model would work well for clients willing to work hard on changing their lives, with the help of passionate and relentless practitioners willing to make some personal sacrifices to help them.

CONCLUSIONS

Notwithstanding our potential professional brilliance, sustainable therapeutic breakthroughs are just not possible in the absence of the fundamental pillars of individual and family life. Promoting empowerment and fostering well-being in underserved populations is possible only by using integrative approaches that encompass economic, physical, social, and psychological factors. Internal and external assets need to be codeveloped with clients through stronger partnerships with several agencies, institutions, and community groups. Both clients and practitioners need to learn new paradigms; overcome the remnants of internalized oppression; and, through shared leadership, advocate for community transformation. This chapter offers some potential blueprints and prototypes for action. Practitioners have the option of directly following the models presented here, organizing programs such as MCE, or using some of the ideas provided to enhance their practices. Attaining the expected outcomes requires hard work, enthusiasm, and persistence. Nevertheless, the rewards are plenty. Helping clients beat the odds and seeing them successfully go from point A to point Z is a refreshing and inspiring experience. When the passion of practitioners and the dreams of clients are fully aligned with a supportive and enriching network of resources, miracles happen, hopes are restored, lives are enhanced, and professional purposes are rekindled.

REFERENCES

Abelev, M. S. (2009). Advancing out of poverty: Social class worldview and its relation to resilience. *Journal of Adolescent Research, 24*(1), 114–141. doi:10.1177/0743558408328441

Adamkiewicz, G., Spengler, J. D., Harley, A. E., Stoddard, A., Yang, M., Alvarez-Reeves, M., & Sorensen, G. (2014). Environmental conditions in low-income urban housing: Clustering and associations with self-reported health. *American Journal of Public Health, 104*, 1650–1656.

Allen, K. (2013). A framework for family life coaching. *International Coaching Psychology Review, 8*(1), 72–79.

Ariza-García, A., Galiano-Castillo, N., Cantarero-Villanueva, I., Fernández-Lao, C., Díaz-Rodríguez, L., & Arroyo-Morales, M. (2013). Influence of physical inactivity in psychophysiological state of breast cancer survivors. *European Journal of Cancer Care, 22*, 738–745. doi:10.1111/ecc.12101

Brownlee, K., Rawana, J., Franks, J., Harper, J., Bajwa, J., O'Brien, E., & Clarkson, A. (2013). A systematic review of strengths and resilience outcome literature relevant to children and adolescents. *Child and Adolescent Social Work Journal, 30*, 435–459. doi:10.1007/s10560-013-0301-9

Buvoltz, K. A., Powell, F. J., Solan, A. M., & Longbotham, G. J. (2008). Exploring emotional intelligence, learner autonomy, and retention in an accelerated undergraduate degree completion program. *New Horizons in Adult Education & Human Resource Development, 22*(3–4), 26–43.

Carroll, A., Gordon, K., Haynes, M., & Houghton, S. (2013). Goal-setting and self-efficacy among delinquent, at-risk and not at-risk adolescents. *Journal of Youth and Adolescence, 42*, 431–443.

Centers for Disease Control and Prevention. (n.d.). *Well-being concepts. Health-related quality of life (HRQOL).* Retrieved from http://www.cdc.gov/hrqol/wellbeing.htm#three

Cooper, D., McCausland, W. D., & Theodossiou, I. (2013). Income inequality and well-being: The plight of the poor and the curse of permanent inequality. *Journal of Economic Issues, 47*, 939–958. doi:10.2753/JEI0021-3624470407

DeNavas-Walt, C., Proctor, B., & Smith, J. (2013). *Income, poverty, and health insurance coverage in the United States: 2012.* (U.S. Census Bureau, Current Population Reports, P60-245). Washington, DC: U.S. Government Printing Office.

Folger, S., & Wright, M. (2013). Altering risk following child maltreatment: Family and friend support as protective factors. *Journal of Family Violence, 28*, 325–337.

Halkjelsvik, T., & Rise, J. (2015). Persistence motives in irrational decisions to complete a boring task. *Personality and Social Psychology Bulletin, 41*(1), 90–102. doi:10.1177/0146167214557008

Hmieleski, K. M., & Baron, R. A. (2009). Entrepreneurs' optimism and new venture performance: A social cognitive perspective. *Academy of Management Journal, 52*, 473–488. doi:10.5465/AMJ.2009.41330755

Johnson, W., Brett, C. E., & Deary, I. J. (2010). The pivotal role of education in the association between ability and social class attainment: A look across three generations. *Intelligence, 38*(1), 55–65. doi:10.1016/j.intell.2009.11.008

Khan, A. (2013). Predictors of positive psychological strengths and subjective well-being among North Indian adolescents: Role of mentoring and educational encouragement. *Social Indicators Research, 114*, 1285–1293. doi:10.1007/s11205012-0202-x

Lagrone, S. (2008, March 10). Wake program aims to fast-track participants to middle class. *News & Observer*. Retrieved from http://www.ncpolicywatch.com/2008/03/10/wake-program-aims-to-fast-track-participants-to-middle-class/

Lee, P., Lan, W., & Lee, C. C. (2012). Physical activity related to depression and predicted mortality risk: Results from the Americans' Changing Lives Study. *Educational Gerontology, 38*, 678–690. doi:10.1080/03601277.2011.598410

Leipold, B., & Greve, W. (2009). Resilience: A conceptual bridge between coping and development. *European Psychologist, 14*(1), 40–50. doi:10.1027/1016-9040.14.1.40

Luo, Y., & Waite, L. J. (2005). The impact of childhood and adult SES on physical, mental, and cognitive well-being in later life. *Journals of Gerontology, Series B: Psychological Sciences and Social Sciences, 60B*(2), S93–S101. doi:10.1093/geronb/60.2.S93

Markowitz, L. (1997, November). Therapy and the poor: Ramon Rojano won't take no for an answer. *Family Therapy Networker, 21*(6), 24–35.

Masten, A. S., Cutuli, J. J., Herbers, J. E., & Reed, M. J. (2009). Resilience in development. In S. J. Lopez & C. R. Snyder (Eds.), *Oxford handbook of positive psychology* (2nd ed., pp. 117–131). New York: Oxford University Press.

Merriam-Webster. (n.d.). *Simple definition of power*. Retrieved from http://www.merriam-webster.com/dictionary/power

Mommersteeg, P. C., Herr, R., Pouwer, F., Holt, R. G., & Loerbroks, A. (2013). The association between diabetes and an episode of depressive symptoms in the 2002 World Health Survey: An analysis of 231,797 individuals from 47 countries. *Diabetic Medicine: A Journal of the British Diabetic Association, 30*(6), e208–e214. doi:10.1111/dme.12193

Mukerjee, S. (2013). An empirical analysis of the association between social interaction and self-rated health. *American Journal of Health Promotion, 27*(4), 231–239.

National Association of Social Workers. (2012). *NASW standards for social work case management*. Washington, DC: Author.

Nikitin, J., & Freund, A. M. (2008). The role of social approach and avoidance motives for subjective well-being and the successful transition to adulthood. *Applied Psychology: An International Review, 57*, 90–111. doi:10.1111/j.1464-0597.2008.00356.x

Olabi, A., Levitsky, D. A., Hunter, J. B., Spies, R., Rovers, A. P., & Abdouni, L. (2015). Food and mood: A nutritional and mood assessment of a 30-day vegan space diet. *Food Quality and Preference, 40*(Pt A), 110–115. doi:10.1016/j.foodqual.2014.09.003

Owen, J., Tao, K. W., Imel, Z. E., Wampold, B. E., & Rodolfa, E. (2014). Addressing racial and ethnic microaggressions in therapy. *Professional Psychology: Research and Practice, 45*(4), 283–290. doi:10.1037/a0037420

Pinderhughes, E. E., Nix, R., & Foster, E. M. (2001). Parenting in context: Impact of neighborhood poverty, residential stability, public services, social networks, and danger on parental behaviors. *Journal of Marriage and Family, 63*, 941–953.

Rogers, M. E., Creed, P. A., & Searle, J. (2009). Social class and work-related decisions: Measurement, theory, and social mobility. *Journal of Career Assessment, 17*(3), 266–270.

Rojano, R. (2004). The practice of community family therapy. *Family Process, 43*(1), 59–77.

Terranova-Zapata, L. M., Acevedo-Velasco, V. E., & Rojano, R. (2014). Intervención en terapia familiar comunitaria con diez familias caleñas de la ladera oeste [Community family therapy intervention with ten families from Cali]. *Revista Latinoamericana de Ciencias Sociales, Niñez y Juventud, 12*(1), 23–38.

Ubinas, H. (2001, August 27). *Ramon Rojano's Middle Class Express picks up steam.* Retrieved from http://articles.courant.com/2001-08-27/news/0108270370_1_welfare-regular-jobs-poor-residents

Viinikainen, J., Kokko, K., Pulkkinen, L., & Pehkonen, J. (2010). Personality and labour market income: Evidence from longitudinal data. *LABOUR: Review of Labour Economics & Industrial Relations, 24*(2), 201–220. doi:10.1111/j.14679914.2010.00477.x

Weidenfeller, N. K. (2012). Breaking through the glass wall: The experience of being a woman enterprise leader. *Human Resource Development International, 15*, 365–374. doi:10.1080/13678868.2012.688361

Weiss, D., Freund, A. M., & Wiese, B. S. (2012). Mastering developmental transitions in young and middle adulthood: The interplay of openness to experience and traditional gender ideology on women's self-efficacy and subjective well-being. *Developmental Psychology, 48*, 1774–1784. doi:10.1037/a0028893

Werner, E., & Brendtro, L. (2012). Risk, resilience, and recovery. *Reclaiming Children & Youth, 21*(1), 18–22.

World Health Organization. (n.d). *Social determinants of health.* Retrieved from http://www.who.int/social_determinants/en/

11

Cash & Counseling: Empowering Elders and People with Disabilities to Make Personal Care Decisions

Kevin J. Mahoney and Erin E. McGaffigan

People who experience disability face daily obstacles, but those around them are often uninformed regarding the societal barriers that impede autonomy. Individuals' obstacles are compounded by assumptions made by those who surround them, including friends, family members, and strangers. As a society, our assumptions are also embedded in our institutional practices and policies. People who do not have disabilities are typically in control of the design of policies and practices and, as a result, often remove choice and dictate decisions for many people with functional limitations. Many people with disabilities have made it their lifelong mission to advocate for a meaningful role in addressing the barriers they face. Concrete examples breathe life into these theoretical concepts. Cash & Counseling provides a real-life example of how empowerment at the individual, interactional, and institutional levels can occur. Our lessons learned can support empowerment across a wide range of social services models.

THE POWER TAKEN FOR GRANTED

Today, people who need assistance to perform important activities of daily living, such as bathing, dressing, toileting, transferring, and/or eating, often access Medicaid-funded services to help meet their needs. Sometimes referred to as "traditional personal care services," these services are often managed by an agency serving individuals across the age span who have varying physical, social, and emotional needs and live in diverse geographic locations. Individuals in licensed positions, often nurses, conduct functional need assessments, and on the basis of that assessment, determine the duration and type of care provided to individuals. Worker availability, geographic location, and safety protocols typically dictate who comes to the house to provide care and the type of care they perform.

Now, let's step back a moment and reflect on power. The majority of the individuals reading this book decided, over the past few days, how many showers to take, when to take them, and who was present during these intimate moments. You may be an early riser who chooses showers before breakfast, or, maybe you prefer a bath as part of your evening ritual. Maybe you eat your meals every night at 6:00, or maybe you eat at 9:00 as you watch your favorite television drama. Now imagine, after decades of routine, you acquired an acute illness. Your recuperation, now that your body has broken down, is taking far longer than you ever expected. Or, consider your life after a serious (and obviously unplanned) car accident. You are now attempting to maneuver through your home in a wheelchair for the foreseeable future (and possibly permanently). Your medical bills now far exceed any income or savings you had. You are now forced to rely on the long-term care system (long-term services and supports, or LTSS).

From now on, your bath, your meal, and your transportation will need to fit within an agency's calendar. Most likely, your needs are now being met between the hours of 9:00 A.M. to 5:00 P.M., before or after the needs of others, and through the lens of an individual with professional training and their own favorite routines. Weekend care is even harder to find; and for some, completely unavailable. Also, the person who helped you in and out of the tub yesterday (someone has deemed it unsafe for you to take showers) may not be the person who comes today. Modesty is a thing of the past.

For years, people with disabilities have been saying, "If I had more control over my services, my quality of life would improve. Not only could I get my needs met, I could meet them for the same amount of money or less." Since the 1970s, states like California and Massachusetts have administered models, often referred to as "consumer or participant-directed care," that allow individuals to do just this by accessing public funds to hire workers to meet their personal care needs. Some advocates and policymakers, over time, have questioned the quality and outcomes associated with this type of care. In the early 1990s, consumer groups led by the World Institute on Disability advocated that a "consumer-directed alternative" be included in the long-term care section of the Clinton administration's health care reform proposal. That bill never passed. Officials at the U.S. Department of Health and Human Services (HHS) Office of the Assistant Secretary for Planning and Evaluation and leaders at the Robert Wood Johnson Foundation thought the idea had merit but needed to be tested on a large scale in a controlled experiment. The Cash & Counseling Demonstration and Evaluation (CCDE), as a result, evaluated one of the most unfettered forms of consumer direction: offering consumers a budget of comparable value in lieu of agency-delivered services. This model puts the money—and, as a result, the power—in the hands of the individual in need (and/or their direct representative) to make personal care decisions and purchases. The person often chooses to hire a friend or family member to assist with baths, prepare meals, help with shopping, and provide transportation to doctor appointments and stores. The person also can purchase home modifications and equipment to support independence and minimize the need for workers, most of which, typically, are not included on a standard medical supply list.

MODELS OF PARTICIPANT-DIRECTED CARE

"I like this program because I'm the boss." These are the telling words of Lillian Brannon, known to all her friends as "Ms. Lillie." At age 88, with multiple chronic medical conditions and severe functional disabilities, Ms. Lillie was among the first enrollees in Arkansas' Independent Choices program, one of the three pioneer state programs that made up the original CCDE. She lived alone in subsidized housing for older adults on only the income provided by a monthly Supplemental Security Income check. She was confined to her home, and more specifically, her bed and a reclining chair.

Despite her physical limitations, Ms. Lillie was strong-willed. She thought she could—and ought to—have the right to make decisions about how to live her life, including how to meet her own disability-related personal assistance needs. She delighted in telling visitors how she had previously "escaped" nursing homes four times. She also made it clear that she had little use for the well-meaning but, in her view, condescending professionals who routinely sought to convince her that she belonged in a nursing home.

Ms. Lillie's experience is just one example of participant-directed services. This model of service delivery offers public program participants opportunities to exercise choice and control over the LTSS that they need to live as independently as possible at home, rather than in facilities. There are two basic types of participant direction, differentiated by the scope of choice and control they offer program participants: *employer authority* and *budget authority*. The former affords program participants the authority to hire, fire, and manage individual paid workers of their choosing rather than being required to obtain services through personal care agencies. The latter expands program participants' range of choice and control by providing a monetary allowance (a "budget") that can be used to pay workers and to purchase other goods and services, such as assistive technologies and home modifications, incontinence and other personal care supplies, transportation, and meal services. The first phase of Cash & Counseling was the efficacy test. Between 1998 and 2003, Cash & Counseling was tested in three states: Arkansas, New Jersey, and Florida. Each of these states tested the model with elders and other adults with disabilities. Florida's model also included 1,000 children with developmental disabilities. Overall, approximately 6,700 people volunteered to participate in this controlled experiment, with half being randomly assigned to traditional agency-managed care and half managing their own supports and services. The evaluation, conducted by Mathematica (Dale & Brown, 2007), examined the model's effects on participants' access to care, satisfaction with discrete aspects of care, unmet needs, health outcomes, and overall life satisfaction. The evaluation also examined the model's effects on primary unpaid caregivers (such as physical, financial, and emotional strain and overall satisfaction with care), paid workers (with a direct comparison to agency-hired workers), and costs. A separate ethnographic study, following 25 participants and their caregivers, was conducted by researchers at the University of Maryland, Baltimore

County, to gain a deeper understanding of the findings. In Phase II, the efficiency study, 12 additional states (Washington, New Mexico, Alabama, Minnesota, Iowa, Illinois, Michigan, Kentucky, West Virginia, Pennsylvania, Rhode Island, and Vermont) replicated the model in their Medicaid programs, resulting in additional examination of the fidelity to the model, participation rates, and participant satisfaction.

CASH & COUNSELING RESEARCH RESULTS

So, what did the CCDE teach us? By allowing beneficiaries to hire family members and friends during a time when agency workers were in short supply or undesired, Cash & Counseling increased individuals' ability to obtain the paid care for which they were eligible. The program offered control and flexibility, which, in turn, greatly increased individuals' satisfaction with care and with their overall quality of life. The link between satisfaction and power is obvious: People were able to choose who entered their homes, what time they came, and how their nonmedical care was provided, and this, in turn, increased access to care, addressed unmet needs, and made people more satisfied. The question commonly asked next is, "Was quality of care sacrificed?" Not according to this research. Individuals directing their own care had the same or even lower incidences of care-related health problems. Participant direction increased access to care because those who directed their care often had local friends, family members, or neighbors who could be hired to provide the care needed. Participants' outcomes also were measured on the basis of 11 health indicators, including number of bed sores, contractures, and falls. Never, for any of the measures, did those receiving care from agencies fare better in a statistically significant way than those receiving participant-directed care. In 30 percent of the cases, those with participant-directed budgets actually fared 20 percent to 50 percent better (Benjamin & Fennel, 2007).

The results for unpaid primary caregivers and paid workers also were fascinating. Primary caregivers experienced less physical, emotional, and financial stress than their counterparts. Participant-hired workers (often family members) were far more likely to feel positively toward their jobs compared with their agency-hired counterparts. In two of the three original demonstration states (New Jersey and Florida), the participants even chose to pay the workers better, on average, than agencies. Even so, costs per member per month were generally lower. One state, Arkansas, realized an 18 percent reduction in nursing home use when comparing the experiences, over three years, of the treatment and control groups (Dale & Brown, 2007).

HOW DID CASH & COUNSELING EMPOWER?

As discussed in earlier chapters, a practitioner's effectiveness depends on his or her understanding of people's constraints on their own use of power. Individuals who rely on others to get their basic and most intimate living needs met often lack power when they are limited by the availability of caregivers and necessary supports, license restrictions, and agency policies. Cash & Counseling, in an attempt to address this power differential, allocates power typically held by agencies to the individuals being served. The theory, supported by the demonstration and evaluation, is that this reallocation of power improves access, quality, and satisfaction and allows the individual to tailor a plan consistent with his or her own preferences and cultural background. The research findings shed light on the benefits of enhanced individual choice and control within LTSS and possibly even within the broader health and human services system. Even with the impressive outcomes that surfaced, Cash & Counseling's process evaluation uncovered power barriers at the individual, interpersonal, and institutional levels that can obstruct the effective adoption of Cash & Counseling and other participant-directed approaches.

Power Barriers at the Individual Level

Participant direction is built on the (tested) assumption that an individual who has power is able to make sound decisions about his or her care. There are a few key factors that make this possible. For one, individuals need information to make informed decisions, such as information about their condition, about the resources available to meet their needs, and about how to hire and manage their workers. Some individuals will come with some or all of this knowledge, whereas others will not. Practitioners, in a successful participant-directed model, work with individuals to assess their information needs, provide access to desired training, and develop backup plans to meet contingencies. This role, often termed a "counselor" or "support broker," is a critical element to making Cash & Counseling (and the allocation of power) work.

Cash & Counseling also highlights the importance of decision-making tools and supports to assist individuals to effectively use power because, without these tools, many would face personal barriers to successful participation. For instance, support brokers often share helpful handbooks on how to recruit, manage, and even dismiss workers as well as tools to guide individuals to create effective job descriptions. Individuals also access financial management services to support adherence to employment laws and tax responsibilities, which then allows the individual to focus on making important decisions pertaining to care. Finally, the representative option allows individuals to appoint a person to make the hiring and managing decisions on their behalf, which makes Cash & Counseling available to individuals who face extensive barriers to accessing personal power and decision making, such as individuals with cognitive limitations. The importance of each of these supports surfaced during focus groups and surveys of representative samples of home care recipients before the start of Cash & Counseling.

Power Barriers at the Interpersonal Level

Although participant-directed services may not be for everyone, such services can be assumed prematurely without a deeper analysis of the power barriers that exist at the interpersonal level. Take enrollment as one example: Despite the participant-directed nature of Cash & Counseling, someone is responsible for introducing a client to the model, assessing the client's eligibility, and informing him or her of the boundaries of the program. Intake coordinators who lack training on the benefits of personal autonomy and the availability of decision-making supports may make assumptions that have a direct impact on who is offered the chance to self-direct. In fact, there are concrete examples of some intake workers referring the "easiest" clients, whereas other practitioners were referring the "difficult" clients who were refused services by agencies. There also is evidence of some service professionals using scare tactics, such as threatening the loss of trusted workers, to discourage individuals from enrolling in Cash & Counseling because of their own fear of what the program's success would mean for their job. Similar interpersonal barriers can exist within the family unit. Loved ones, such as adult children of aging parents or parents of individuals with cognitive disabilities, may have an established role in making decisions, which may contradict the desires of their loved one (making participant direction difficult at best).

Power Barriers at the Institutional Level

The 1999 *Olmstead v. L.C.* Supreme Court decision, stemming from a Georgia case advocating for community options for two women with mental health conditions, changed the course of LTSS. This decision placed more responsibility on the state and federal government to provide people with disabilities opportunities to access less restrictive community-based options for publicly financed LTSS. Subsequently, more flexible, community-based service delivery models such as Cash & Counseling have slowly emerged to address the increasing demand for community options.

The National Inventory of Participant-Directed Supports and Services shows that over 815,000 people in publicly funded programs across the United States are involved in one or more forms of participant direction (National Resource Center for Participant-Directed Services [NRCPDS], 2014). Every state has at least one program in which participants can hire their own workers, and 45 states have programs in which the participant has control of a budget. Overall, there are more than 266 such programs nationwide. Much of the recent growth is attributable to the advent of Veterans-Directed Home and Community-Based Services at 47 Veterans Affairs medical centers around the country. Still, participant direction is unavailable to many who require LTSS because many of the existing programs are small (with only 1,000 to 5,000 people enrolled). Even so, some states have made participant direction a major component of their LTSS continuum. For instance, 85 percent of participants in California's In-Home Supportive Services program choose participant direction (NRCPDS, 2014).

Institutional barriers also are apparent in the design and oversight of programs in which the individual voice is often weak or nonexistent. Program administrators designing Cash & Counseling programs have faced their own challenges with meaningfully engaging recipients of services in the design and oversight of these programs. The original three Cash & Counseling programs and the 12 expansion programs were all expected, as a funding requirement, to engage users of service in their program design; most, if not all, faced significant challenges obtaining and maintaining this involvement. We saw firsthand the repercussions of such disengagement: Grassroots advocacy for Cash & Counseling was weak, and new state and federal laws presented hurdles to this purest form of LTSS choice and control.

What do we do as practitioners to address institutional-level barriers to power? The National Program Office (NPO) for Cash & Counseling, which has now morphed into NRCDPS, allocated time and resources to identifying and working directly with Cash & Counseling recipients across the nation to assume a lead role in the model's refinement, expansion, and advocacy. Interested participants were offered the opportunity to join the NPO as liaisons and, in this role, support the development of a national network of Cash & Counseling participants (later termed the National Participant Network [NPN]). The goal was twofold: (1) Ensure that the NPO's work was appropriately informed by those we sought to empower at the individual service level, and (2) form a national network of Cash & Counseling participants who could lead the development of meaningful local participant networks across the country. Since its creation in 2007, NPN has grown to over 2,000 members in 30 states and has incorporated as an independent nonprofit to ensure the voice of participants in the expansion and improvement of participant direction options across the country.

Cash & Counseling research (McGaffigan, 2011) points to participant engagement at the program and policy level as a complex topic requiring a great deal of attention to power dynamics. For one, administrators responsible for engaging program participants need to buy in to the process and the sharing of power because they already control (and are held responsible for) program design and management. These same individuals, who are often without disabilities, need to be comfortable reaching out to and engaging people who may live and think differently than they do. Also, Cash & Counseling program participants face their own personal barriers to attending meetings that they have to overcome to participate in the process. They also need to have the esteem to face powerful people, the ability to access helpful information, and effective communication and conflict resolution skills that make engagement work. According to this research, it is not just the people that matter, but the process and environment as well. Engagement methods, such as committees, advisory groups, and public forums, need to be accessible to people with disabilities. Constructive and neutral facilitation strategies also are critical given the power differentials that exist between those who lead programs and those who depend on the services being provided. Finally, a government led by a leader who values transparency and is contemplating politically charged financial decisions may run toward (rather than away from) stakeholder engagement strategies, whereas more closed government climates, more averse to risk, may focus less on grassroots priorities (Bens, 1994).

Many practitioners miss the direct link between individual choice and control and the policies and procedures that make a program. Program administrators leading Cash & Counseling programs have benefited as much, if not more, from expanding individuals' power to the program and policy arena. This is how they learned that the majority of their program participants did not have Internet access to retrieve forms or fax machines to submit invoices and time sheets. Advisory groups also provided program administrators with ideas on how to simplify language and even hands-on assistance drafting their guidebooks. Some program administrators would not have had a Cash & Counseling program (or employment) if not for the grassroots advocacy to rescind budget cuts. It was engagement at the program and policy level that actually made choice and control at the individual level viable.

IMPLICATIONS FOR SOCIAL WORK TRAINING

In a recent article examining the education and training of support brokers in three Cash & Counseling states, Jeon, Mahoney, Loughlin, and Simon-Rusinowitz (2014) found that nursing and social work professionals and other so-called caring professions were more apt to face challenges with the empowerment paradigm required for Cash & Counseling, whereas individuals from professions like occupational therapy or education found the transition easier. Whereas the social work tradition is built on our roots in Hull House and the empowerment approach of Jane Addams, the Cash & Counseling model requires new empowerment competencies that emphasize social workers' roles as facilitators and coaches rather than experts. This requires advanced skills in areas such as brainstorming, weighing the pros and cons of options, and developing mutual agreements that clearly identify participants' risks and plans to minimize risk. Social workers also need to be informed of effective ways to engage participants at the program and policy level as well (for example, through the effective use of advisory groups). One particular situation that occurred early in the replication of Cash & Counseling in Minnesota provides a cogent example. A case manager, who had historically assumed the role as expert and service plan decision maker, was working with an elderly man who had stopped eating. His family, in complete desperation, had heard of the new Cash & Counseling approach and asked that it be given a try. When the man was able to hire a family member who cooked the way he liked, he started to eat. When the worker took him in her car to go grocery shopping at one of the stores closest to him, they were able to take a short detour so he could visit his wife in the nursing facility; then he truly started to thrive. The case manager, who soon assumed a role as coach and facilitator rather than decision maker, became a convert and helped record a video to convince others like herself to give the new model a try. McInnis-Dittrich, Simone, and Mahoney (2006) were pioneers in the development of training modules that help social workers to make the shift from expert to facilitator, adopting an adult learning approach grounded in self-awareness exercises and case examples. More recently, the New York Community Trust funded the Council on Social Work Education and NRCPDS to work with nine social work programs (and their agency partners) to develop curriculum models for infusing person-centered planning and participant direction training into bachelors and master's-level social work courses. This training is intended to inform social workers who assume many different roles and to inform the training of other professionals who work in interdisciplinary teams. Moving forward, some key steps that states and federal agencies can take to further the growth of participant direction include sharing best practices; developing and offering training to assist case managers and their supervisors to move from a "professional knows best" approach to an empowerment approach; setting quality standards reflective of participant direction; and requiring the collection of data to assess participant direction-specific quality benchmarks. Pinderhughes's (1989) "powerful/powerless processing" can be beneficial to supporting this paradigm shift. Workers often feel powerless in many aspects of their work, which may cause them to maximize the power and control that they wield (consciously or unconsciously) over service users.

CONCLUSION

This chapter has examined participant direction—more specifically, the Cash & Counseling approach—as a model that supports empowerment at the individual, interactional, and institutional levels. A review of LTSS's purest form of personal choice and control sheds light on the significant barriers to power that exist even when a program is intended to provide full choice and control to individuals who are typically disempowered. The types of power that were enhanced included decision-making power and financial power at the individual level; the power to engage in a more meaningful way, giving as well as getting, at the interactive level; and the power to play a meaningful leadership role in the design of programs and policies at the system level. Harkening back to the opening chapter, power is a fundamental concept critical to people's health and mental health. Powerful people act more, use more variable behavior, and more readily prioritize and engage in effective goal pursuit. In the arena of home and community-based services, the power relationship is becoming more unstable. Many participants are understanding and exerting their rights. Social workers have the opportunity to engage what Tew (2006) called co-operative power sharing. Paradoxically, this power sharing can lead to enhanced respect, new roles, and power for social workers as society attempts to find new ways to integrate acute, behavioral, and long-term services and supports. By helping service users to set their own agendas, social workers can encourage a sense of "power to" for the people we work with.

A number of factors bode well for the future growth of participant direction, including the growing diversity of the U.S. population and the aging of a baby-boom generation that will demand more choice and control than their parents did. In addition, aspects of health care reform emphasize person-centered planning and participant direction. For instance, Section 2402a of the Patient Protection and Affordable Care Act (2010) prompted HHS to issue guidelines regarding person-centered planning and participant direction that cut across all programs and populations served by that department. More recent efforts to integrate acute care and LTSS under the managed care umbrella encourage a tendency to remedicalize participants into "patients" for whom someone else is responsible. Even so, there is a continued movement toward large-scale participant direction offerings as states are recognizing participation direction as an important component of rebalancing long-term care budgets and addressing institutional bias (Wenzlow, Borck, Miller, Doty, & Drabek, 2013).

As one individual reported:

> I sleep much better. I feel much better. You know, my biggest fear is to be stuck in the damn bed and waste my life away. . . . I want to get out and get back into society and do lots of things.

In the words of a second participant, "It's my own money, I'm more careful with it. I'm building skills and have to do research to see how much things cost. I try to do as much as I can myself."

REFERENCES

Benjamin, A. E., & Fennell, M. L. (2007). Putting the consumer first: An introduction and overview. *Health Services Research, 42*(1 Part 2), 353–361.

Bens, C. (1994, Winter-Spring). Effective citizen involvement: How to make it happen. *National Civic Review,* 32–39.

Dale, S. B., & Brown, R. S. (2007). How does Cash & Counseling affect costs? *Health Services Research, 42*(1, Part 2), 488–509.

Jeon, H., Mahoney, K. J., Loughlin, D. M., & Simon-Rusinowitz, L. (2014). Multi-state survey of support brokers in Cash and Counseling programs: Perceived roles and training needs. *Journal of Disability Policy Studies 26,* 24–32. doi:10.1177/1044207313516494

McGaffigan, E. E. (2011). *It's not so simple: Understanding participant involvement in the design, implementation, and improvement of Cash & Counseling programs* (Doctoral dissertation, University of Massachusetts, Boston). Retrieved from http://scholarworks.umb.edu/doctoral_dissertations/55

McInnis-Dittrich, K., Simone, K., & Mahoney, K. (2006, April). *Consultant training program.* Retrieved from https://nrcpds.bc.edu/details.php?entryid=275&page=1&topics=&types=&keyword=Consultant%20training&population=

National Resource Center for Participant-Directed Services. (2014, September). *Facts and figures: 2013 National Inventory Survey of Participant Direction.* Retrieved from https://nrcpds.bc.edu/details.php?entryid=445

Patient Protection and Affordable Care Act, 42 U.S.C. § 18001 (2010).

Pinderhughes. E. (1989). *Understanding race, ethnicity and power: The key to efficacy in clinical practice.* New York: Free Press.

Tew, J. (2006). Understanding power and powerlessness: Towards a framework for emancipatory practice in social work. *Journal of Social Work, 6,* 33–51.

Wenzlow, A., Borck, R., Miller, D., Doty, P., & Drabek, J. (2013, July 1). *An investigation of interstate variation in Medicaid long-term care use and expenditures across 40 states in 2006.* Retrieved from http://aspe.hhs.gov/daltcp/reports/2013/40State.pdf

12

Teaching Power beyond Black and White: Recognizing and Working with Student Resistance in Diverse Classrooms

John Tawa and Jesse J. Tauriac

Increasingly, educators, clinicians, and researchers, are recognizing the need to include a power analysis in their understanding of human differences (for example, differences between racialized groups, differences in sexual orientation) (Goodman, 2001; Pinder-hughes, 1989; Suyemoto et al., 2009). To be a racialized minority in the United States means not only having comparatively different cultural values than those of the majority group but also existing within a context that devalues the cultural values of the racial minority group and normalizes the cultural values of the dominant group. Therefore, mere analyses of cultural difference are insufficient to explain, for example, mental health disparities between black and white people. A more complete analysis considers the influence of racial minority status on racial minorities' mental health, including experiences of racism and the impact of being stereotyped, devalued, and slandered.

As teachers of multicultural curricula in psychology (for example, Asian American Psychology, Psychology of the Black American Experience), we recognize the need to impart on our students a multilevel analysis of power and its multiple effects. We teach how power differentials affect the intrapsychic, interactional, and social experiences of Asian and African Americans. In our experience, teaching power is much more difficult than teaching culture (for example, cultural values). Students will relatively easily accept, for instance, that Asian Americans tend to be more family oriented when compared with European Americans. They will be less inclined to see, however, that Asian Americans' family orientations put them at a structural disadvantage within a social system that privileges individualism. The latter seems to touch a nerve in students, and they frequently balk in resistance; it seems the notion that some groups are favored challenges a deeply internalized view of the world as safe and just.

Furthermore, as racial minority educators (the first author is a multiracial Asian American, the second author is a multiracial African American) with experience teaching in a diverse, urban context, with student bodies composed of multiple minority group members (for example, black, Latino, Asian, and multiracial students[1]), we recognize that an "absolute power" analysis is insufficient and frequently brings about resistance from members of minority groups. Framing white people as the absolute oppressor, with all of the power, and minority groups as the absolute oppressed, with none of the power, does not allow for more complex analyses of power relations between minority groups. I (J. Tawa), for example, can recall teaching a workshop on racism toward Asian Americans with a primarily Asian student body. After the workshop, a black student wrote on the evaluation, "It was hard to hear everyone complaining about Asian racism because it does not compare to black racism." On the other hand, discussions of racism that are often black–white dominated frequently bring up for Asian students a feeling of being left out of the race dialogue and a sense that their experiences of racism are invalidated (Sue et al., 2007). Thus, while teaching within a racially diverse, urban educational context, we felt the need to frame power as a complex, problematized construct rather than an absolute, either/or construct.

In this chapter, we share our pedagogical approaches to teaching power in diverse urban contexts. We begin by defining power as it has been articulated by leading theorists. In addition, we share a framework for a complex conceptualization of power that we have found to minimize resistance from students who may struggle to see how power as a concept can simultaneously validate the diverse experiences of oppression of multiple minority group members. We then examine more closely students' psychological resistance to learning about power, including some theory behind such resistance, and how it manifests in student behavior. Finally, we share some strategies and exercises for teaching power that we have found adaptive within a diverse, urban context.

WHAT IS POWER?

Power, perhaps most simply put, is a capacity to control or influence others for one's own benefit (hooks, 1984; Pinderhughes, 1989). It is a multileveled construct such that imbalances of power play out within the individual psychology of both the oppressed and the oppressor, and in interactions between oppressed and oppressive members and

---

[1] We use the language schema of "Asian," "black," and "Latino" to reflect groupings of people and ethnic groups based on shared experiences of racialization and racism within the United States. Despite the vast ethnic and generational diversity within these broad categories, people and ethnic groups who are perceived to fall within one of these umbrella labels are frequently assumed to possess specific—and often inferior—cognitive, behavioral, and even moral dispositions. "Multiracial" includes people with membership in two or more racialized groups.

groups (for example, families, social groups) (Pinderhughes, 1989). Within a person's psychology, power can be felt as a sense of agency and a sense of control of others and of situations (hooks, 1984; Pinderhughes, 1989). Conversely, powerlessness can be experienced as "an absence of choices" (hooks, 1984) or lack of free will, sense of shame, and an internalization of negative perceptions of one's self (van Vorhis, 1998).

At group and institutional levels, power establishes a code of normalcy and an assumption of a disproportionate right to resources (that is, an assumption that the lion's share of resources is deserved) (hooks, 1984; Pharr, 1988; Pinderhughes, 1989; van Vorhis, 1998). Institutional power may be best depicted as a circle, in which the group in a position of power is placed at the center, and relatively powerless groups are placed at the margins (hooks, 1984). Although people from groups on the margins can move toward the center, to do so, they often must conform to the expectations of those in the center, including accepting negative stereotypes of themselves or internalizing beliefs that features of their cultural backgrounds are deviant, defiant, or dysfunctional (Ayvazian & Tatum, 1994; hooks, 1984).

The relationship between the oppressed and the oppressor (people and groups) is symbiotic; the powerful rely on the powerless as "system balancers" (Pinderhughes, 1989), as a yardstick to infer one's superiority in relation to (Turner, Brown, & Tajfel, 1979), and as a source of, scapegoating for social problems (Pharr, 1988). Benefits reaped by groups in positions of power come at the expense of the powerless and inherently rely on their exploitation (van Vorhis, 1998). The powerless, too, begin to take form and shape in relation to the dominant group; for example, many cultural values of oppressed groups (for example, black cultural value on cleanliness and hygiene) may originate as a response to oppressive demands (for example, European Americans' depiction of black people as unclean) and later may crystallize into a cultural value (Pinderhughes, 1989).

Teaching about race-based power is challenging given that it is often personally salient for students in both privileged and oppressed positions. Moreover, teaching about power within a diverse, urban context with multiple racial minority groups (for example, Asian, Latino, black) presents an additional challenge, given that it is often unclear which group is the oppressed and which group is the oppressor. In our experience, teaching about power within this context requires moving beyond a binary (oppressor/oppressed) conceptualization of power.

A FRAMEWORK FOR MOVING BEYOND A BINARY MODEL OF POWER

Despite the fundamental contributions of previous literature toward articulating the concepts of the powerful and powerless, we find it necessary to further problematize power. In this chapter, we depict power as multidimensional and differentiate between actual and ascribed power and between universal and context-specific power. These three concepts related to power provide us with a framework that has been helpful for us in being able to teach and validate experiences of power and powerlessness of multiple minority group members.

Multiple Dimensions of Power

From a binary model of power, it is relatively easy to conceptualize a relational dynamic between a single majority group (for example, European American) in relation to a single minority group (for example, African American). However, when additional minority groups (for example, Asians, Latinos) are considered, it becomes more difficult to conceptualize who has power in relation to whom. Multicultural educators are likely to be familiar with the impossible debate among minority students about which group is more oppressed, and in our experience, such conversations are futile and even problematic in that they often engender resistance from one group and block empathic stances toward another groups' plight of oppression. One effective solution is to discuss multiple dimensions on which racial minority groups may be afforded more or less power in relation to one another.

For example, black (and white) people are often racialized as privileged in relation to Asian people on an "insider/outsider" (dimension that is, perceived to be insiders and not stereotyped as foreigners in the U.S. context). Asian people (and white people) are racialized as privileged in relation to black people on a "merit" dimension (that is, perceived to be models for success in the U.S. meritocracy and not stereotyped as unintelligent) (Kim, 1999; Tawa, Suyemoto, & Tauriac, 2013). By explicitly teaching about these different areas of ascribed privilege, we have found that black students, for example, are more easily able to empathize with racism toward Asians based on "perpetual foreigner" experiences (Uba, 1994), without feeling as though such discussions obscure their own experiences of oppression. And likewise, Asian students can more easily empathize with black students' experiences of being treated as unintelligent and lacking merit.

Actual versus Ascribed Power

Teaching power within a context of multiple minority groups can be facilitated by differentiating power that has an actual basis versus power that is ascribed to people simply because of their membership in a racialized group. For example, an Asian American student from a wealthy family may have actual power and privilege in the sense of having greater access to resources. By contrast, an Asian American student from a poor family may not have actual power and privilege in relation to access to resources, yet, because Asian Americans are often racialized as having economic parity with white Americans, may be granted some privileges, such as being assumed by guidance counselors to be a potential candidate for expensive colleges or graduate programs. Similarly, a West Indian immigrant is likely to be less familiar with the values, customs, and mores of a U.S. context compared with a fourth-generation Japanese American. However, because of how members of these groups are racialized, the West Indian immigrant, who is racialized as "black" with an extended history in the United States, is ascribed relative power on the insider dimension. The fourth-generation Japanese American, who is racialized as Asian and thus a "perpetual foreigner" in a U.S. context, is not given the same power.

Often it is not easy for students from racial minority groups to see how they are actually afforded relative power when they lack power in a more absolute sense. Being explicit about the difference between actual and ascribed privilege may make it easier for a Southeast Asian student, from a refugee family living in poverty, to see how they may have some educational privilege (ascribed, not actual) relative to the black racialized group members.

Universal versus Context-Specific Power

Power relationships are affected by the contexts in which the power dynamics play out. Most people can recall a situation that they have been in where they felt different or unable to just be themselves. A white person in a black church or a heterosexual person at a gay pride event may feel momentarily that they are in a powerless position; for example, they may feel that they are being judged and that the ways they present themselves need to be consistent with the expectations of others in this particular context. Of course, for people in positions of power on a more national scale (for example, a white person or a heterosexual person), their feelings of powerlessness are frequently limited to specific contexts as those in the previous examples. Many minority students at diverse urban schools have co-resided with other minority group members in inner-city communities and may have had previous experiences of feeling powerless within a specific racial minority context. These previous experiences of powerlessness, which are context specific, often contribute to students' resistance to understanding another groups' oppression.

As an example of resistance, an Asian American student in a workshop on black and Asian relations co-led by the authors was resistant to seeing black experiences of racism in the United States. She had grown up in a primarily African American housing project, and, indeed, in this context she felt relatively powerless; to be friends with some of the other black residents, she could not be fully "Asian" and instead needed to adopt, in her words, a "crossover" identity and fluency in black culture. For her, understanding that her relative powerlessness in relation to black people was context specific enabled her to move past her personal experience and develop an analysis of anti-black racism on a more national scale.

In the next section of this chapter, we consider more closely the process of working through students' resistance. For educators, the first steps to working through resistance are identifying it in the classroom and having some understanding of the causes of students' resistance.

IDENTIFYING AND UNDERSTANDING RESISTANCE

We believe that resistance is a normative process of learning about power and privilege. In this section, we discuss theoretical understandings of what resistance is, how it manifests and can be identified by teachers, and why students resist learning about power and oppression. We consider resistance at a more universal level (as it is experienced by all students learning about power and oppression), and also resistance specific to diverse, urban contexts with representations from multiple minority groups.

Resistance in the classroom is a student's (largely subconscious) opposition to learning new material and/or changing or revising old views about the self and the world (Chan & Treacy, 1996; Davis, 1992; Deal & Hyde, 2004; Higginbotham, 1996). From a psychodynamic perspective, resistance is seen as a defense mechanism against new information that is deemed threatening to one's worldview. Thus, it is not surprising that learning about power and oppression—concepts that frequently challenge students' views of the world as safe and just—can often engender resistance in the classroom. Despite the negative connotations of the word, we do not believe resistance is a bad thing; in fact, we would go as far as to say that it is a normal function of learning about power and oppression and can be indicative of the first stages of a true transformative process. For resistance to be a healthy learning process, educators need to work toward developing a classroom environment that is perceived by students as safe enough to take chances and explore their complex feelings about power and oppression.

In the absence of fostering safe environments and developing tools for challenging oppression, healthy resistance (which is likely momentary and can be worked through) may be replaced by "paralysis" (Davis, 1992); discussions may become unfocused, and students may express hopelessness in relation to responding to social challenges. Failure to foster safe environments and to provide students with tools for addressing oppression can also lead to "enraged" classes in which minority students misdirect their anger and frustration about white racism at a nearby representative of the oppressor group, such as an outspoken white student (Davis, 1992). Similarly, minority students may misdirect their anger by scapegoating other minority students as the primary source of social problems. For example, in a reflection paper, one of my (J. J. Tauriac) Asian students described being denied entry at a prestigious undergraduate institution (presumably due to full quotas) and expressed frustration toward black people for pushing affirmative action policies. Last, students in classroom environments that are not considered safe spaces to work through resistance may become disengaged. In such occurrences, students may no longer willingly share personal views and may hide during personal discussions by avoiding eye contact and allowing themselves to be distracted. At a conceptual level, it is important for teachers to differentiate resistant classroom climates from paralyzed, enraged, and disengaged classroom climates; unlike the latter three, the former is likely to be a normal process of learning about power and oppression that can be worked through.

How Do Students Resist?

Student resistance can manifest in multiple forms; it may be reflected in students' behavior, or the content of their speech or writings, or even by their lack of certain behaviors. We offer some of our observations about manifestations of resistance to learning about power in general and resistance specific to diverse, urban contexts. Much of the content in this section of this chapter comes from both formal and informal discussions with our colleagues and supervisors (see *Authors' note*).

Student resistance to learning about power can be both content based and process based. Content-based resistance manifests in the perspectives that students share in their writings and during in-class discussions. Students, for example, may take a position on the current state of society by pointing to how "conditions are improving" (Higginbotham, 1996) or "racism isn't like it used to be." Students may also declare a moral stance about their views of human difference, for example, stating, "I don't see color" and "I treat everyone the same." Although these views are outwardly positive and even humanistic, students' persistent focus on these views may function to minimize the harsh realities of accepting that, for most people in society, color does matter and that even though conditions may be improving for some, power differentials and oppression still exist. Resistant students also frequently talk about or focus on "exceptions" or individual cases that challenge the notion that oppression exists on a societal level (Higginbotham, 1996). For example, students may highlight the achievements of a wealthy CEO who is a person of color. Individual cases can also be used to minimize or deny one's personal oppressiveness; for example, a student might suggest: "How can I be racist if one of my best friends is black?" In diverse, urban classrooms, we have seen minority students try to "one up" other minority students when sharing experiences of racism. For example, in one class discussion, a black student shared how her mother was treated disrespectfully at a doctor's office. An Asian student followed her comment with a discussion about how his grandmother was not even able to see a doctor because of her citizenship and health insurance status. In exchanges such as these, students may become overly focused on comparing their experiences and may lose sight of the larger context of institutional oppression operating to disempower minority groups.

Process-based resistance is reflected in the students' behaviors inside and outside of the classroom. Students may resist both actively, such as criticizing or directly challenging the teacher or other students, and passively, such as disengaging with the material or missing classes (Chan & Treacy, 1996; Higginbotham, 1996). Actively resistant students may accuse the teacher of working from a personal agenda or bias and may claim that they are being victimized by reverse racism (for example, stating that because of the expectation of political correctness, their right to free speech is challenged) (Davis, 1992). Passive process-based resistance may be hardest to identify. Students may tend to stay at an abstract, intellectual level and avoid personal narratives or memories that may be affectively charged (Davis, 1992). Students with laptops may hide behind the screen or pretend to be engaged in note taking. In addition, students may simply excuse themselves from class or fail to attend classes they anticipate to be emotionally charged. Although such behaviors are likely accurately interpreted as resistance, instructors need to be cautious when choosing to push students to work through their resistance. Such defenses are likely in place for a reason, and learning to see power and oppression can be disrupting to students' worldviews.

Social justice educators can facilitate students' processes of working through resistance by normalizing the pain and emotional rawness of engaging this material, emphasizing the importance of self-care during periods when students are learning about privilege and oppression, offering case studies and online videos of people describing their own process of coming to terms with their privilege and oppression, describing the actions of social justice allies who work to affect change, and planning self-care exercises (for example, asking students to describe one thing they will do to practice self-care; leading relaxation exercises) during transition points as classes are ending.

Why Do Students Resist Learning about Power and Oppression?

Learning about power and oppression can often cause major disruptions in students' fundamental meaning making about the self and society. For example, many students who have been socialized in Western individualist contexts maintain a view of the self as bounded, independent, and unaffected by societal contexts such as racism and oppression (Markus & Kitayama, 1991; Tawa & Suyemoto, 2010). Thus, for students socialized in a primarily Western individualist context (for example, European American students), learning about power and oppression—and their effects on people's psychology—can threaten their very basic view of self (Chan & Treacy, 1996). It is not surprising then, that students may, at least initially, resist accepting that power imbalances and oppression exist in our society.

Learning about power and oppression can also challenge students' fundamental views about society. For many students socialized in Western contexts, learning that power imbalances and oppression exist within our society is discordant with a view of the world as safe and just (Chan & Treacy, 1996; Deal & Hyde, 2004). During the 1980s, the Reagan administration triumphed with self-help, personal success, and "rags to riches" narratives, perpetuating a view of the U.S. economic structure as meritocratic. Students raised during this time may be particularly wed to a view of the United States as an "even playing field" and may reject the idea that racial disadvantages are inherent in the system (Davis, 1992). We have also recognized that for students socialized in more collectivist contexts such as many societies in Asia, learning about power and oppression requires the development of a perspective that is often critical of authority (for example, the government, legal institutions), which may be discordant with cultural values that emphasize deference and acceptance of authority.

Minority students may also resist learning about and accepting other minority groups' experiences of oppression. About eight years ago, we conducted a series of focus groups with black and Asian students on campus. One black student commented that Asians had gained social status since the civil rights movement (and largely due to the efforts of black civil rights activists), but now that they (Asians) were in a position of power, they had "turned their backs" on black people. Attention to the plight of other minority groups' continued struggles may trigger an associated belief that resources allocated to minority groups are "zero sum" and that attention to another racial minority group inherently disadvantages one's own group. This sentiment may be a particularly deeply ingrained assumption among minority students raised in the 1980s, a period that gave rise to a view of "special interest groups" (for example, women, Asians, black people, gay people) as selfish and competing for limited resources (Davis, 1992). Asians who have internalized the model minority stereotype that perpetuates the notion that Asians have succeeded within the U.S.-based meritocracy through hard work and intelligence may be particularly resistant to seeing anti-black racism. In the final section of this chapter, we discuss strategies and exercises that we have found helpful for moving past students' resistance in teaching power and privilege.

LESSONS ON POWER: PRACTICE AND THEORY

Combining experiential exercises with readings on power can be a particularly effective method of teaching about power and privilege. Rather than merely reading or listening to lectures about particular ideas, taking part in activities enables participants to draw on their lived experiences and observations to grasp concepts or appreciate the emotions stemming from social dynamics (Dorn, 1989). However, social justice educators facilitating these interactive exercises should foster learning environments that feel safe enough to take risks and engage this material at cognitive and affective levels. Furthermore, they should thoughtfully consider the complexities of power dynamics, lest they run the risk of alienating and overwhelming participants. Educators can work toward a safe classroom by, for example, setting discussion guidelines, discouraging more vocal students from dominating class conversations, validating complex and intense emotions (for example, anger), encouraging students' self-awareness of nonverbal communication during interaction with other students, and thoughtful debriefing after the close of each exercise.

Depending on the exercise, one or more mechanisms of change are designed to enhance student understanding. These mechanisms can be broadly categorized as cognitive or affective (Dorn, 1989). Experiential exercises influence participants cognitively by linking abstract concepts (such as social stratification or oppression) to their personal experiences and observations within the activity. Activities also have great potential to foster affective learning through processes such as building empathy toward oppressed group members or developing participants' awareness of emotions related to resistance, thereby allowing them to confront and challenge previously held values or assumptions (Harlow, 2009). Follow-up reflection on these activities (whether through debriefing, process questions following the activity, or writing reflections papers) further enhances this conceptual and affective learning (Coghlan & Huggins, 2004).

In the following section, we describe three activities we have used in our classes that we believe demonstrate the complex model of power we seek to teach, ways in which these activities can help with working through students' resistance to understanding power, and some of the mechanisms of change previously described.

Exercise 1: Dynamic Stereotyping

Because we teach about power in an ethnically diverse, urban context when engaging students in learning about power, we select not only activities that illustrate dynamics of absolute power, but also those that attend to multidimensional and ascribed power. For example, I (J. Tawa) engage students in my Asian American Psychology class in a "dynamic stereotype" activity in which students brainstorm stereotypes associated with the terms "black" and "Asian" and consider the socially constructed nature of these stereotypes and how they are interrelated. First, I ask students to list stereotypes that are associated with Asian people, and I write down this list on one side of a whiteboard or chalkboard. I then ask students to list stereotypes that are associated with black people and write this list in a column near the Asian stereotypes list. To address students' discomfort when soliciting stereotypes, I use very precise language to emphasize that I am not asking them to indicate which stereotypes they believe but instead am asking what societal stereotypes exist about particular group members, regardless of whether participants believe them to be true or not. I even go as far as to say that to challenge stereotypes, we must first know what they are. In my experience, these statements reduce students' discomfort about mentioning stereotypes and potentially being perceived as holding racist views.

Once these lists are written down, I ask students to make observations about these lists, and inevitably, one or more students observes that the stereotypes associated with each of these groups are often oppositional (for example, Asian people as hardworking, black people as lazy; Asian people as asexual, black people as hypersexual; Asian people as smart, black people as unintelligent; Asian people as unathletic, black people as athletic). I then ask students where they believe society would place white people along each of these dimensions, and, invariably, students respond that white people would fall in between these two groups, constituting normality for particular characteristics. To debrief, I end this exercise by leading a discussion about the development of these stereotypes; the ways in which one aspect of power is the ability of the dominant group to define normalcy with itself as the referent; and the sociohistorical origins of these stereotypes, for example, the colonizer's divide-and-conquer tactic of positioning minority groups against one another.

This exercise works through both cognitive and affective mechanisms and yields a number of desired effects. Because students were involved in generating the lists of stereotypes and recognizing the contrasts between the lists and their relative association with whiteness, they gain a better understanding of the socially constructed nature, meaning, and function of stereotypes. There is a greater appreciation for these insights because they were evoked from students themselves, rather than imposed by teachers. Thus, at cognitive levels, students' grasp of these abstract concepts is appreciably stronger and better retained, because students participated in the discovery of the dynamic construction of these stereotypes. With regard to affective change, racial minority students who previously internalized racist beliefs may experience a sense of liberation as they discover the origins of stereotypes about their groups and greater feelings of empathy toward other racial minority groups who are also stereotyped.

Exercise 2: Simulation Gaming

A number of innovative simulation games have been used to enhance student understanding about institutional oppression and unearned privilege. Simulation games used in teaching about power have been designed so that elements of the game represent or model social structures, which role players can experience or observe firsthand (Dorn, 1989). These exercises include modified versions of games (such as Jenga [see

Lichtenwalter & Baker, 2010] and Monopoly [see Coghlan & Huggins, 2004]), simulated disproportionate distribution of academic resources (for example, time to take quizzes) (Eells, 1987), contests in which certain group members have distinct advantages over other members (for example, Harlow, 2009), and the Level Playing Field exercise (also commonly referred to as the Privilege Walk, Step Forward/Step Back Exercise, Horatio Alger exercise, Class-Race Exercise, or Bootstrap Exercise[2]).

Recently, I (J. Tawa) have been conducting a class exercise that uses virtual world technology to enable students to participate in social interactions as a member of a racial background different from their own. The Virtual Immersion Project (VIP) uses the virtual world, Second Life, an online program that allows users to develop relatively realistic avatars—of diverse gender and racial backgrounds—and interact with other live participants around the world. The program is free and relatively easy for students to download on their personal computers (students also have the option of using computers owned by the university). In this class project, students select from a group of six avatars (provided by me) one that is likely to have a different racialized experience from their own. Students are required to spend a total of two hours interacting with other avatars and are required to visit three locations within Second Life that were previously selected by me because they have relatively high user traffic (thus ensuring social interactions) and relatively different levels of diversity. During their two hours in the virtual world, students are asked to keep a written log of their experiences and emotions. The following week, students are required to turn in reflection papers describing how their experiences in Second Life may have shaped their understandings of their real-life racial experience.

An examination of students' reflection papers suggests that for some students, the VIP facilitated subjective access to other people's racial experiences. For example, white students operating avatars of color described feelings of alienation and frustration related to experiences of microaggressions. One white student described how the VIP enabled him to subjectively understand minorities' experiences of "dual consciousness": the constant need to be aware of the possibility of racism and the constant ambiguity around whether or not their racial appearance influenced other people's actions and behaviors. For minority students, experiencing life as another minority group member can be influential in understanding the impact of discrimination among people of color; for example, one Japanese international student, operating a black avatar, visited a Japanese-speaking location in Second Life but was surprised to find that, despite speaking (that is, text-based chatting) fluent Japanese, his authenticity was constantly challenged because of his racial appearance.

Exercise 3: A Community Visit

Another activity that we frequently use is the Community Visit exercise (Suyemoto, Liem, Kuhn, Mongillo, & Tauriac, 2007). This exercise was introduced to us by Dr. Karen

---

[2] This activity was originally developed by Martin Cano, Valerie Tulier, and Ruth Katz of "World of Difference" and was subsequently adapted several times by Ellen Bettman, Paul Kivel, and a number of others.

Suyemoto as part of our graduate training, so we both have had experience in this exercise as both participant and facilitator. Students are instructed to attend an event or community activity made up predominantly of members from a racialized group other than their own. This event or activity should be a culturally meaningful event that is geared toward members of a specific racial/ethnic community (rather than, for example, a retail event or showcase focused on attracting outgroup members). Students are instructed to interact with community members in culturally sensitive ways, attend to their own internal experience, observe their responses toward others and others, responses toward them, and write a reflection paper about the experience (Suyemoto et al., 2007). For many, this exercise arouses a great deal of discomfort, particularly for majority-group members who rarely are part of the numerical minority and who have rarely experienced context-specific powerlessness. This discomfort frequently fosters greater self-awareness and reflexivity, and students emerge with a greater understanding of the impact of their own socialization.

This activity was particularly meaningful for me (J. J. Tauriac) during my graduate training. As a multiracial African American, my worldview had been shaped by my racial identity development and experiences of racism, contributing to a more developed awareness of racial oppression. However, I lacked awareness of my areas of privilege (for example, being male, middle-class, heterosexual, and a U.S. citizen) and the ways they affected others' perceptions of me. Thus, as a graduate course requirement, I had an eye-opening community visit to an urban park where more than 80 first- and second-generation Cambodian immigrants were taking part in a volleyball tournament. I assumed that those I encountered would perceive me as a fellow person of color and perhaps feel some sense of alliance with me. However, after several failed efforts at starting conversations and encounters with others who seemed dismissive, I was able to engage in a conversation with a young, acculturated, Cambodian American woman. After I commented on the attitudes others seemed to be taking toward me, she shared that many in the park mistrusted my motives for being there and feared that I was connected to a local government agency that would contest their right to use the park because of their immigration status. While in the park, before this conversation, I was completely oblivious to this area of difference and the privileges ascribed to me as one who was perceived as an insider, with a multigenerational U.S. history. My community visit provided me with a lived experience that I could connect to several power-related concepts (for example, the lack of awareness of one's own privilege, the different dimensions of privilege and oppression experienced by different racialized groups, and the ways areas of oppression are often more salient and central to one's identity, relative to areas of privilege).

CONCLUSION

A comprehensive understanding of multiple aspects of power is critical for those working in the health, education, and human service fields. Learning about power, however, is frequently met with resistance, perhaps because understanding injustice often requires challenging people's foundational views of themselves and the world. Working through resistance is a vital part of the process of understanding power. For many racialized minority students, however, a more nuanced framing of power as a multifaceted construct allows them to better work through this resistance and emerge ready not only to grasp these concepts but also to take action in advancing social justice. Conceptualizing power as multidimensional, ascribed, and context specific has made teaching about power appreciably more effective in diverse, urban contexts. Furthermore, we have found that engaging these topics through experiential exercises has better prepared students to accept and work through their own privilege and oppression.

Authors' note: The concepts, observations, theories, and stories presented in this book chapter have emerged from extensive dialogues and previous scholarship with a team of our mentors and colleagues with whom we share an interest in teaching diversity. Thus, we would like to share ownership of the ideas offered in this chapter with the following people: Dr. Karen L. Suyemoto, Dr. Grace S. Kim, and Dr. Vali Kahn. We would like to give a special acknowledgment to our colleague and friend, Dr. Karen Suyemoto. J. Tawa first met his mentor, Dr. Suyemoto, 14 years ago as an undergraduate student in her Asian American Psychology class. J. J. Tauriac met Dr. Suyemoto more than 13 years ago, when he took her course on culture and mental health during his first semester as a graduate student.

REFERENCES

Ayvazian, A., & Tatum, B. D. (1994). Women, race and racism: A dialogue in black and white. *Work in Progress, 68,* 1–10.

Chan, C. S., & Treacy, M. J. (1996). Resistance in multicultural courses: Student, faculty, and classroom dynamics. *American Behavioral Scientist, 40*(2), 212–221.

Coghlan, C. L., & Huggins, D. W. (2004). "That's not fair!": A simulation exercise in social stratification and structural inequality. *Teaching Sociology, 32,* 177–187.

Davis, N. J. (1992). Teaching about inequality: Student resistance, paralysis, and rage. *Teaching Sociology, 20,* 232–238.

Deal, K. H., & Hyde, C. A. (2004). Understanding MSW student anxiety and resistance to multicultural learning: A developmental perspective. *Journal of Teaching in Social Work, 24*(1–2), 73–86.

Dorn, D. (1989). Simulation games: One more tool on the pedagogical shelf. *Teaching Sociology, 17*(1), 1–18.

Eells, L. W. (1987). So inequality is fair? Demonstrating structured inequality in the classroom. *Teaching Sociology, 15,* 73–75.

Goodman, D. J. (2001). *Promoting diversity and social justice: Educating people from privileged groups.* Thousand Oaks, CA: Sage Publications.

Harlow, R. (2009). Innovations in teaching race and class inequality: Bittersweet candy and the vanishing dollar. *Teaching Sociology, 37*(2), 194–204.

Higginbotham, E. (1996). Getting all students to listen: Analyzing and coping with student resistance. *American Behavioral Scientist, 40*(2), 203–212.

hooks, b. (1984). *Feminist theory: From margin to center*. Boston: South End.

Kim, C. J. (1999). The racial triangulation of Asian Americans. *Politics and Society, 27*(1), 105–138.

Lichtenwalter, S., & Baker, P. (2010). Teaching about oppression through Jenga: A game-based learning example for social work educators. *Journal of Social Work Education, 46*, 305–313.

Markus, H., & Kitayama, S. (1991). Culture and the self: Implications for cognition, emotion, and motivation. *Psychological Review, 98*, 224–253.

Pharr, S. (1988). *Homophobia: A weapon of sexism*. Inverness, CA: Chardon.

Pinderhughes, E. (1989). *Understanding race, ethnicity, and power: The key to efficacy in clinical practice*. New York: Free Press.

Sue, D. W., Capodilupo, C. M., Torino, G. C., Bucceri, J. M., Holder, A.M.B., Nadal, K. L., & Esquilin, M. (2007). Racial microaggressions in everyday life. *American Psychologist, 62*, 271–286.

Suyemoto, K. L., Liem, J. H., Kuhn, J. C., Mongillo, E. A., & Tauriac, J. J. (2007). Training therapists to be culturally sensitive with Asian American women clients. *Women & Therapy, 30*, 209–227.

Suyemoto, K. L., Tawa, J., Kim, G. S., Day, S., Lambe, S. A., Nguyen, P. T., & AhnAllen, J. M. (2009). Integrating disciplines for transformative education in health services: Strategies and effects. In L. Zhan (Ed.), *Asian American voices: Engaging, empowering, and enabling* (pp. 209–228). New York: NLN Press.

Tawa, J., & Suyemoto, K. L. (2010). The influence of race and power on self-construal in bicultural Asian Americans. *Asian American Journal of Psychology, 1*(4), 275–289.

Tawa, J., Suyemoto, K. L., & Tauriac, J. J. (2013). Triangulated threat: A model of black and Asian race-relations in a context of white dominance. In S. Pinder (Ed.), *American multicultural studies* (pp. 229–247). Thousand Oaks, CA: Sage Publications.

Turner, J. C., Brown, R. J., & Tajfel, H. (1979). Social comparison and group interest in ingroup favouritism. *European Journal of Social Psychology, 9*, 187–204.

Uba, L. (1994). *Asian Americans: Personality patterns, identity, and mental health*. New York: Guilford Press.

van Vorhis, R. M. (1998). Culturally relevant practice: A framework for teaching the psychosocial dynamics of oppression. *Journal of Social Work Education, 34*, 121–134.

13

Discovering and Building RESPECT: A Relational Model Addressing Power and Difference in Medical Training

Carol Mostow*

Pinderhughes's work on difference and power reminds us that who we are shapes what we notice and what we think we know (Pinderhughes, 1989). This socially embedded perspective helps illuminate the personal origins and development of the RESPECT model, an innovative relational training model that addresses race, difference, power, and empathy in health care communication (Bigby, 2003; Mostow et al., 2010). We start with the critical incident that led to the formation of the Diversity Curriculum Task Force at the former Boston City Hospital (now Boston Medical Center), an urban safety-net academic medical center. The underlying power dynamics illustrate why we need educational interventions specifically targeting the relatively low-power position of medical trainees within the medical hierarchy, as well as the disempowered position of the many poor and racially/ethnically diverse patients they serve. Pinderhughes's work also clarifies how personal experiences with power and difference of the nonphysician founder and the racially/ethnically diverse Diversity Curriculum Task Force contributed insight regarding power, race, and other relational factors that are missing from most prior cross-cultural communication models. Clinical and educational applications of the model to interactions with patients, medical trainees, colleagues, and teams are described. Lessons learned include the need to manage power dynamics on personal, clinical, collegial, and institutional levels to optimize contributions by and outcomes for patients, learners, educators, teams, and a diverse health care workforce.

---

*Special thanks to Jane Shanny, MA, MSW, for reviewing the manuscript.

PROLOGUE

A trainee enters the room where the communication skills seminar mandated for all medicine interns takes place and immediately starts to complain about the "politically correct" in-service examination he just took. A graduate of a top medical school and now almost five months into his internship, he is dealing with the grueling and often sleep-deprived training years, seemingly endless hours of menial busywork for patients whose symptoms, diseases, and suffering he is now responsible to diagnose and treat. He continues to speak frankly to me, his instructor, and to a fellow intern in the room. Because of the open learning climate established the previous week, as well as my nonthreatening position as a communications specialist and social worker without evaluative role or faculty rank, he seems to share freely, unconcerned about being judged. "These guys, if they weren't up to no good in the first place, wouldn't have gotten shot." Without elaboration, I know to whom he refers. Our setting was a large public safety-net hospital serving the poorest neighborhoods of the city. The "guys" he refers to are the mostly black and Latino young men, the city's most frequent gunshot victims. "When I was their age, I never would have chosen to hang out with those folks," he continues.

Flabbergasted by this young white man's statements, I ask where he grew up and learn that he comes from an out-of-state, middle-class, and predominantly white suburb. Speechless and filled with righteous anger, I think about the kids I counseled for many years at a community clinic and urban middle school in the same city as our hospital. The 12-, 13-, and 14-year-olds at the school had told me about the street violence risks surrounding them. Some had even resorted to bringing guns to school in the hopes that a reputation for toughness might protect them. One 13-year-old student had spent two months hospitalized with massive internal injuries after being struck in a drive-by shooting while he was simply socializing with friends. Another patient, a 14-year-old Jehovah's Witness who had aspired to become a law enforcement officer, arrived late one day to therapy after being stopped and searched by police and falsely accused of criminal activity for the fifth time in his young life. We both came to realize that, unlike his white therapist, he could not safely assert his constitutional rights. My work also had attuned me to the media's differential treatment of attacks on children of different races or from different neighborhoods. Coverage of missing or injured white children appropriately conveyed shock, compassion, or outrage. In contrast, media coverage of injuries or deaths of black or Latino youth was often limited to brief, impersonal, back-page descriptions that frequently conveyed implicit and numbing normalization and blame.

How could I convey to this young intern the reality of these boys' lives? How could I help him understand the vastly different risks, opportunities, and privilege of their world and his own?

The intern continues: "I know not to say this in front of the attendings but you want us to be honest, right?"

Again, I pause. This is what I want, right? Honesty? Trust of me as a teacher? Isn't this what is called a "teachable moment?" How do I use my own power as a teacher, not to silence or overpower this new doctor but to increase his awareness of and openness to the lives of the patients he will be treating throughout his career? What would it take for him to feel empathy for them?

He continues, "I'm sick and tired of these patients changing my scripts" (to get extra narcotics).

"Well you don't have to put up with that, that's illegal."

"Yeah, well, I get off late at night and have to walk to my car. . . ."

I hear his sense of powerlessness, his ignorance of how to treat substance abuse, his confusion about poverty, race, addiction, and violence. I also hear his own long hours and personal deprivation translated into displacement and blame, targeting his even more disenfranchised patients.

Why does he choose to disclose to me views he knows are antithetical to the stated aims of both his profession and my own? I realize that it may be largely as a result of my own powerlessness in the medical hierarchy—I have so little standing or control over his rewards and sanctions—that he is less afraid to tell me the truth. I also realize that he is actually confiding in the right person. It is my responsibility to him, and to the patients he will encounter throughout his career, to help him learn what he does not currently know how to do.

What I realized that day was that I did not have a readily available approach to provide. I was an inadequate teacher for the great problem he had presented, potentially as unable to help him as he was to help his patients. I brought this dilemma to national medical education conferences to consult with seasoned medical faculty. Their initial well-meaning response immediately diagnosed the problem; If only I had more power, in their view, I could make this overtly unprofessional intern comply with the desired views.

But, I pointed out, if what I was seeking was not obsequious parroting of my own or others' views but rather a radical openness by the trainee to his patients' experiences, an awareness and respect for them, and a skill set to connect more effectively to obtain better outcomes, then coercion was not the answer. Without thorough educational preparation, how can we expect medically trained but often socially inexperienced and ethnically sheltered young people to bridge the often great differences between their own and their patients' social background, privilege, and racial and cultural experiences? How can we make sure trainees have the knowledge, skills, and attitudes necessary to untangle the relevant factors, especially in the setting of poverty, limited resources, and often overwhelming psychosocial problems that so easily strain the capacities of both patient and providers? What should we teach them to do to build trust effectively with patients to promote optimal outcomes? It was my responsibility not to silence the learner but to identify how best to engage him and then what to teach him.

As I began to search for answers, I found myself grateful that social work training teaches us to connect with those we serve rather than distance ourselves from them. "Start where the client is" was the mantra I recalled from graduate school. This deceptively simple but profound instruction recognizes the authority of clients over whether and in what ways they may want and choose to change. How could I manage the power dynamics in my teaching to truly engage learners and, in turn, to facilitate their engagement with and management of the power dynamic with their patients?

LOOKING FOR WHAT AND HOW TO TEACH: THE FOUNDING OF THE DIVERSITY CURRICULUM TASK FORCE

With these kernels of questions but no answers, I turned to physician faculty colleagues at my own hospital. Boston Medical Center (BMC) had grown from a merger of a private hospital with the former Boston City Hospital, which for centuries had been the city's public hospital and haven of care for Boston's poor, including neighboring African Americans and Latinos, other multicultural immigrants, and low-income whites. Affiliated with Boston University School of Medicine, BMC combines academic rigor with an overt mission to serve patients with the greatest unmet medical and social needs. BMC attracts a particularly diverse group of top doctors and trainees from around the country and the world who are drawn by this combination of purpose, challenge, and intellectual resources. Most feel this mission to be a worthy and satisfying use of their skills and talents. This rich legacy includes a cadre of seasoned physicians and other clinicians committed to developing innovative and effective ways of serving patients with complex medical and social needs. These veteran clinicians often cite their patients as the most sustaining part of what has remained challenging, often underresourced work. What were these doctors doing that allowed both them and their patients to invest and trust in the therapeutic alliance and its effectiveness? What was that skill set, and what would be the best way to teach it to trainees?

Founded in 2000 within the Section of General Internal Medicine, the Diversity Curriculum Task Force initially consisted of approximately 30 mostly physician colleagues from several departments who assembled to help identify the knowledge, attitudes, and skills needed to effectively engage and treat patients how to teach these to medical trainees. We were fortunate to have physicians with vast direct patient experience as well as expertise developing services and programs to better serve their complex needs. Early members included Dr. John Rich, a pioneer in engaging young black men to seek health care at the Young Men's Clinic as well as in researching young black men as victims rather than perpetrators of violence (Rich, 2011). The group also included the medical directors of Interpreter Services, Latino Clinic, Refugee Health, and Haitian health services. We had clinicians with expertise in substance abuse and women's health and those who practiced at community health centers in the city's diverse cultural, ethnic, and class enclaves. The Task Force members included immigrants as well as U.S.-born physicians from a variety of racial, ethnic, and cultural backgrounds and life experiences.

This combination of colleagues with intellect, expertise, and commitment along with differing experiences regarding power, race, and culture inspired stimulating exchanges. Our diverse prior experiences shaped our awareness and contributions. Physicians of color who had experienced racism in their personal and professional lives shared their experiences. The physician serving a poverty-stricken, heroin-plagued white neighborhood prompted further discussions of the role of class. A physician who treated torture victims in the refugee clinic added the issue of international abuse of power to our rich exploration of the contributions of race, class, poverty, and inequity to health disparities.

We started to examine existing educational materials to identify what knowledge, attitudes, and skills to focus on in our curriculum. What would help the naïve and sheltered learner recognize that disparities in health and health care exist; that these issues have real medical consequences; that patients and doctors do not approach each other on an equal playing field; that poverty, race, and culture elicit disparate treatment in this country; and that trust across difference and power inequity cannot be assumed but must be earned?

KNOWLEDGE, ATTITUDE, AND SKILLS

To engage data-driven, pragmatic new physicians, we focused first on knowledge and evidence regarding the scale of health care disparities. Learners needed to recognize the significance of the problem whose solution demands new approaches to change the status quo. In deference to the evidence-based culture in which medical training takes place, we assembled materials regarding disparities in health and health care as well as in social determinants of health.

A cultural awareness sharing exercise adapted by Swaby-Ellis, Salazar, and Pololi from Pinderhughes's work (1989) was introduced to foster learners' insights regarding the impact of difference and power in their own lives and in those of their colleagues. Early on, we introduced this exercise for use with medical students. For use with residents and practicing clinicians, we eventually added the fifth question to encourage reflection on the way one's own background affects work with patients and to help make more explicit the connection with clinical work.

Reflection Questions: Difference and Power

The following questions are designed to help participants reflect on their own experiences of difference and power. The answers are not handed in or, if used in a facilitated sharing exercise, shared without the consent of the participants.

1. With what cultural/class/other background(s) do you identify?
2. What do you like and dislike about your background/identity?
3. Reflect on an experience when you felt different.
4. Reflect on your experiences with privilege and power, either having it or lacking it.
5. In what ways can your background help and pose challenges in connecting with patients?

These questions also served as the basis for a carefully facilitated sharing exercise with role modeling by leaders from different cultural backgrounds, ground rules regarding confidentiality, and other guidelines for attentive listening and respectful intercultural dialogue.

Facilitator guidelines and learning objectives are available in Mostow, Gorosh, Crosson, and White (2016).

This exercise is stimulating even in groups without overt differences and provides a wonderful way to help health care providers and trainees reflect on the role of privilege and power in their lives and recognize the power dynamic in the doctor–patient encounter. The sharing exercise is also universally enjoyed by students, trainees, and staff as well as faculty serving as role models and facilitators. Experiencing and sharing cultural differences as a positive and enriching way to learn relatively quickly about somebody that you might already think you know is itself a powerful message in a medical culture that prioritizes quick, data-oriented interactions. Similarly, valuing difference counterbalances powerful messages that personal identity doesn't matter and that ethnically diverse trainees should seek to assimilate rather than bring the richness of their background into their work. It also creates a positive and trusting learning climate in which to address more challenging issues. Awareness of power and privilege is often most challenging for those who have it; a supportive and carefully facilitated group with a diversity of racial, ethnic, and class backgrounds can help provide greater insight to those who might be less experienced, more naïve, or oblivious to these issues. The tendency to stereotype is also countered by the discovery that many differences among people are not visible and that what is most salient to any individual is usually not what others may assume. Because self-awareness per se is not inherently a value in most medical settings, we also distribute to participants a written educational rationale and learning objectives, with the goal of reducing potential resistance.

Knowing that there is a problem and gaining awareness of the role of difference and power in one's own and others' lives provides a valuable beginning. But to improve communication, the relationship with the patient and, hopefully, health care outcomes, practitioners' personal knowledge, and awareness alone are insufficient; they must improve their interactions by demonstrating behaviors that will produce better results. It was in the area of skills that our group ended up making our biggest contribution, resulting eventually in the creation of the RESPECT model.

Searching for Skill Set

A review of the literature on cross-cultural skills revealed a range of approaches, from potentially simplistic approaches focused on learning a few basic characteristics of different cultural groups to approaches identifying how to prompt the patient to disclose his or her own cultural beliefs, practices, and expectations. This latter inquiry approach, pioneered by Arthur Kleinman (Kleinman, Eisenberg, & Good, 1978), avoids stereotyped assumptions about the patient's beliefs and practices and instead focuses on eliciting the patient's explanatory model of the illness and approach to the treatment. The subsequent LEARN model (Berlin & Fowkes, 1983) built on these elements and included the need to negotiate with the patient regarding potential conflicts between the patient's and doctor's perspectives. ESFT (**e**xplanatory model, **s**ocial context, **f**ears and concerns, **t**herapeutic alliance) (Betancourt, Carrillo, & Green, 1999) added important content to these questions, including social context, fears, and concerns, and included therapeutic alliance, which is akin to the LEARN (**l**isten to patient's perspective, **e**xplain own perspective,

acknowledge the differences and similarities, **r**ecommend treatment, **n**egotiate mutual agreement on plan) negotiation process. The focus of these and other contributions, however, remained primarily on a cognitive-oriented data-gathering activity, with a series of questions directed at the relatively passive patient.

Adding Power, Empathy, and Trust to Build RESPECT

However, as our task force continued to work with these existing models in teaching sessions and in our own meetings where we role-played patient encounters, we began to feel that our successful interactions with patients involved more than the elements identified in previous models. In one particularly pivotal session, an African American faculty member role-playing a young black male patient identified the moment when the person playing the doctor "came down to my level" as the moment that built trust. We continued to explore the significance of this moment, and what was communicated nonverbally and verbally, and we began to recognize the role of respect in mitigating differences in power and building trust, especially with a population who often experiences stigma, oppression, and disrespect. We realized that so-called cross-cultural approaches too often skip the power dynamics, emotions, and relationships involved with race, ethnicity, power, and inequity. Successfully treating our patient population involves more than a merely cognitive process of eliciting data points of difference regarding health beliefs and practices in a power-neutral setting. Instead, in a setting of patient distrust and power inequity, we must take proactive, relational steps to build trust. The imperative to do everything possible to build effective relationships with all patients becomes even more urgent given disparate outcomes in health and health care for these underserved groups.

Pinderhughes's work identified the relational and affective elements so salient to our understanding. Adding the elements she highlights—power and empathy—we formulated RESPECT, a relational model to build trust that focuses on both patient and doctor. Beyond just what data and questions we ask, what do we do to build trust? In the face of inequity and disparities, we need to take action. We need to show respect, show empathy, share power, and build trust, not assume it. This emphasis on respecting and empowering patients also exemplifies our interest in patient strengths, a concept that too often is missing from a traditional medical prioritization of pathology. So in the social context component of the RESPECT model, we encourage the elicitation of strengths and spirituality, along with stressors, to help understand how patients' illness affects their lives; how their lives affect their illness; and what personal, family, and communal resources and potential resilience the patient can draw on.

How to RESPECT the Patient

- **R**espect: Show respect by maintaining appropriate eye contact, following cues about personal space and greetings. Welcome the patient and introduce yourself. Ask how he or she prefers to be addressed. Recognize and affirm the patient's strengths and efforts.

- Explanatory model: Ask the patient what he or she thinks is causing the illness and what will alleviate symptoms. Listen without judgment.
- Social context: Elicit the impact of the patient's life on his or her illness and the impact of the illness on his or her life, including strengths, stressors, and spirituality.
- Power: Reduce inherent power discrepancy by reducing physical barriers, sitting during conversations, listening attentively, and limiting interruptions. Elicit patient's preferences and active participation in discussion, decision making, and treatment planning.
- Empathy: Show empathy by listening attentively and responding accordingly. Name and validate the patient's emotions by conveying specific understanding of what the experience means to the patient.
- Concerns: Ask the patient about worries regarding symptoms, diagnosis, treatment, or other issues. Use open-ended questions supported by receptive nonverbal cues.
- Trust: Notice and respond to any signs of distrust. Ask about expectations. Reassure, clarify next steps, and follow through on promised actions.
- Team: Flatten hierarchy to elicit diverse perspectives and solutions. Collaborate with other members of health care team.
- Therapeutic alliance: Search for specific common goals, identify differences, and, when needed, collaboratively negotiate mutually agreeable alternatives (adapted from Mostow et al., 2010, p. S148).

Subsequent to development of the model, surveys revealed evidence supporting the RESPECT elements and their relevance to health care disparities. Factors that had been intuited by task force members turned out to have empirical evidence supporting their validity in studies of patient responses and physician behaviors, demonstrating differential experiences of patients in terms of respect, empowerment, and trust. Differential behaviors of white physicians with patients of color included greater dominance, less warmth, and less information sharing. More than 30 percent of white patients thought their doctors would experiment on them without consent. However, that level of distrust was twice as high for patients from racial and ethnic minorities (see Mostow et al., 2010, p. S148, Table 1).

Using RESPECT for Clinical Training

We quickly discovered the wide utility and clinical applicability of RESPECT as a training model. It serves as a core framework in the four-year cultural competence curriculum for the University of New Mexico School of Medicine and has survived 14 years of curriculum revisions at Boston University School of Medicine. The observational exercise for preclinical medical students to use when observing doctor–patient interactions (see Table 13.1) focuses on how successful relationships are built rather than on just the data documented in the medical history and physical exam.

TABLE 13.1: Clinical Observation Exercise

Looking for **RESPECT:** *A clinical observation exercise or assessment tool*
The RESPECT model conveys a value essential to clinical practice and required for all effective communication. It also offers a handy list of essential components to optimize health care encounters for both patient and physician, especially important when facing additional differences of culture, race, class, etc. between the parties. NOTE: Make sure to observe nonverbal as well as verbal clues regarding the following.

R	Did the physician convey *Respect*? If so, in which ways? What seemed to be the patient's reaction?
E	What did the doctor learn about the patient's *Explanatory* model of the illness and ideas of what might help? (e.g., What's wrong with me and what do I think will make me better?)
S	What did the doctor learn about the *Social* context of the patient, including *Stressors, Supports, Strengths,* and *Spiritual* beliefs and practices which might affect health, treatment, expectations, or relationships with the doctor and healthcare system? How does the patient's life affect his illness and how does his illness affect his life?
P	What expectations and preferences did the patient and doctor each seem to have for the *Power* relationship? Notice both non-verbal and verbal cues. Pay attention to displays of deference, control, hierarchy. Who does the talking? Who determines the agenda? What did the doctor or patient do or say during the encounter which seemed to em*Power* or disem*Power* either party? Does the doctor seek the patient's input and preferences or simply announce to the patient what will happen?
E	What opportunities were there for the doctor to convey *Empathy*? What did the doctor do or say to which conveyed an understanding of the patient's experience and its significance to the patient? What were the patient's responses?
C	Are there any *Concerns* and fears which underlie or coexist with the patient's presenting problems? What prompted the patient to share these? What did the physician do to elicit or facilitate this fuller, possibly more emotional disclosure?
T	What seemed to be the patient's initial level of *Trust*? (What verbal and nonverbal indicators did you notice?) What did the doctor say or do during the interview which seemed to modify the patient's level of *Trust*? Was a *Therapeutic* plan created? i.e., Did the doctor and patient reach common ground regarding the problem and the approach to diagnosis and treatment? Are there any indications that there might be obstacles to and/or disagreements about the next steps? What evidence do you have that the patient understands, can and will adhere to the treatment regimen? If there remained divergent preferences at the end of the interview, was the doctor able to negotiate a partnership based on other shared goals?

Adapted with permission from Springer Science+Business Media: Mostow, C., Crosson, J., Gordon, S., Chapman, S., Gonzalez, P., Hardt, E., et al. (2010). Treating and precepting with RESPECT: A relational model addressing race, ethnicity, and culture in medical training (Box 1). *Journal of General Internal Medicine, 25*(Suppl. 2), S145–S154. © 2010 by the Society of General Internal Medicine.

The RESPECT model has also been readily applied to a wide range of medical problems, settings, and training audiences, including breast cancer community outreach workers, online alcohol training modules, and faculty responsible for training eye-care professionals.

Precepting with RESPECT

From an early stage, our group of clinician educators wanted to bring the training process out of seminars and to the examination room and bedside. We made an additional exciting discovery about the RESPECT model when we recognized that medical faculty could use it to improve their supervisory communications and relationships with trainees by using RESPECT to address power dynamics and parallel process with them during clinical supervision (known as "precepting"). We began to recognize that respecting the resident was the most effective way to help the resident respect the patient. Although this parallel process in supervision is a well-known component of social work training, a relational focus on teaching is a newer approach in medical training. Given the model's explicit focus on power dynamics, it should not be surprising that RESPECT can help build trust within the hierarchical training relationships of medical culture.

The stakes are high for patients and for trainees, especially given the accumulating evidence that both empathy for patients and personal well-being decline starting in the clinical years of medical school and continuing through residency (Bellini & Shea, 2005; Hojat et al., 2009). The personal deprivation in terms of sleep, control over one's time, and access to usual supports and sources of meaning no doubt increase vulnerability to stress; this is heightened by a curriculum that frequently fails to exemplify empathy for residents or patients (Hafferty, 1998). For disenfranchised patients particularly vulnerable to powerlessness, it becomes even more important that the residents who treat them are in turn supported and empowered to be effective by empathic and respectful supervising physicians.

See Table 13.2 for the ways supervisors can learn to precept with RESPECT, followed by an example of an actual educational encounter and clinical outcome.

CASE EXAMPLE: HOW RESPECTING THE TRAINEE HELPED HIS PATIENT

"I don't know how to help these people," admitted an intern to a preceptor at a large urban safety-net hospital. He went on to describe an encounter with a Haitian patient that had left him feeling inadequate and frustrated. After a history of the symptoms and the appropriate physical exam, the intern had found nothing of medical significance. "I told the patient that there was nothing wrong with her, but I know she left dissatisfied." The preceptor expressed empathy for the intern's frustration, compounded by his social context of fatigue and concern regarding his own helplessness in the face of so many patients' overwhelming problems. She showed respect for his recognition of the

TABLE 13.2:   Ways Supervisors Can Learn to Precept with RESPECT

Precepting with RESPECT	
RESPECT	Approach the learner with respect.
	Builds resident confidence, preceptor resident relationship. Reduces defensiveness.
	"I know how hard you've been working to try and get his diabetes under control".
EXPLANATORY MODEL	Elicit the resident's thoughts about the patient and interest in the patient's perspective.
	Helps preceptor learn what resident knows and has asked as starting point for further discussion. Conveys interest in resident's perspective while supporting resident's interest in patient's perspective.
	"What do you think is going on with the patient?" "What does patient think is causing his symptoms?"
SOCIAL CONTEXT	Check re residents' well-being and context. Explore possible professional and personal stressors.
	Builds preceptor-trainee relationship. Models how to act with patients.
	"How are things going for you these days?" "What clinical rotation are you on?"
POWER	Find ways to share power and support resident self-efficacy. Resist the temptation to take over in the face of learner's uncertainty.
	Helps assess clinical judgment, build problem-solving ability and increase investment in solution.
	"How might you find out why this patient has a hard time taking his medicines daily?"
EMPATHY	Let resident know their frustrations and emotions are heard
	Documented decline in residents' mood and empathy for patients as well as differences from their patients' background make this step essential. Faculty support may enable residents to engage more effectively with patient.
	"After all your effort, I can imagine how frustrating it is that she didn't fill her prescription."
	"Particularly when I'm tired, it can be hard to put aside my own frustration to find out what's going on from the patient's perspective."
CONCERNS	Elicit and address residents' concerns about situations they don't feel confident handling or fear will make visit too long.
	Help residents strategize about possible solutions and educate about relevant data
	Replaces anxiety with information to improve quality and efficiency
	"I know you were worried about eliciting more of the patient's concerns but eliciting them doesn't mean you or the patient can tackle them all in one visit."
	"Let's discuss how to identify your and the patient's top priorities, come up with a plan for today and bring him back for follow-up and to address the other issues."
TRUST	Building on all the skills above fosters trust in the preceptor-resident relationship. Learners may become more willing to identify areas of challenge.
	"I admire your openness and ability to share with me that your patient was so frustrated that she wanted to change doctors." "How can I help you?"

Adapted with permission from Springer Science+Business Media: Mostow, C., Crosson, J., Gordon, S., Chapman, S., Gonzalez, P., Hardt, E., et al. (2010). Treating and precepting with RESPECT: A relational model addressing race, ethnicity, and culture in medical training (Box 2). Journal of General Internal Medicine, 25(Suppl. 2), S145–S154. © 2010 by the Society of General Internal Medicine.

difficulty in connecting with patients from unfamiliar cultures and his wish to overcome barriers of difference and distrust. Then the preceptor began to partner with the intern, empowering him regarding what skills he could use to learn more about his patient and attempt to engage her more effectively. "Did you ask her what she thought was wrong and what concerned her the most? What she thought would help?" queried the preceptor, proceeding to introduce elements of the RESPECT model.

An indication of the clinical and training value of the model was affirmed by the greeting received by the preceptor when encountering the intern the following week. "I tried the approach we discussed and it worked," he declared, describing how he had treated a patient differently than he might have otherwise. This time, in an outpatient encounter with an elderly, homeless African American man complaining of chronic diarrhea, the intern made efforts to elicit the patient's concerns and social context and express genuine empathy. He learned of the patient's job loss several months earlier and the sorrow and shame the patient felt about his current situation. "The patient hates living in the shelter and thinks that he got diarrhea because it's so dirty there." It was clear from the admiring way that the intern referred to the patient's strengths and hardships that the intern had treated the patient with dignity and respect.

The patient, who had previously avoided doctors and the medical system, not only remained for the collection of multiple stool samples for the lab but also felt enough empowerment and trust to follow through with a colonoscopy recommended by the intern. A finding of a tumor at an early treatable stage led to a successful surgical outcome. What could have been a disconnect between a white intern, at once powerful and disempowered, and a disenfranchised patient of color became a mutually satisfying partnership, forging a life-saving bridge between differences of power, race, culture, and class.

Funding for a pilot project applying the RESPECT model to selected precepting clinics allowed us over the course of a year to use the observational exercise as an assessment tool, bring the cultural awareness exercise into the resident teams to build their connections with nurses and attendings across hierarchies, design and role-play teaching interventions using the RESPECT model, and apply them with residents in the clinic. As described more fully by Mostow et al. (2010), there were statistical limitations in the analysis, but resident-administered pre- and postintervention surveys demonstrated increased awareness and self-assessed skills connecting with patients from backgrounds different than their own.

COMING TO TERMS WITH OUR POWER

Surveys and exit interviews with participating preceptors in the faculty development project showed a positive impact on confidence and efficacy as faculty in addressing race and culture with trainees. A more surprising finding, perhaps, was that our experienced and diverse faculty participants all spontaneously remarked on improved communication with their own patients. Clearly "cultural humility" (Tervalon & Murray-García, 1998) rather than "cultural competence" more accurately describes the process in which we continually journey to collaborative understanding with patients and other people rather than achieving mastery of a fixed data set and understanding that remains static over time.

Pinderhughes (1989) reminded us that all helping professions need to contend with the power dynamic inherent in our roles. To the extent that we focus more on our agenda than our patients', that we hear what we want to hear rather than what the other person is saying, and that we hold the authority to have our perspective defined as the truth, we all need reminders to actively seek to share power with our patients.

A growing literature about shared decision making in medicine advises against totally abdicating the powerful role we have in terms of responsibility and expertise with our patients. Situations with particularly complex decisions and conflicting evidence pose tremendous challenges to comprehension and clarification of personal preferences, especially when the patient may be critically ill and need swift and compassionate care that respects their priorities as much as possible. Perhaps the ultimate solution to this dilemma is to embrace the power of both the patient and the doctor in this situation, building trust and sharing the respective expertise each has regarding medical knowledge and personal, family, and cultural values and preferences (Tuckett, Boulton, Olson, & Williams, 1985).

Increasingly, medical culture is recognizing the importance of addressing the power dynamic in the multiple settings of patient care, teaching, and teamwork. The development of motivational interviewing and its supporting base of evidence indicates that we cannot make others change but rather can offer support and facilitate their examination of their choices. Nonconfrontational exploration of patients' decision making and support of their self-efficacy are critical elements to effecting changes in health behavior. Educational leaders recognize that learners' "critical consciousness" requires honest dialogue and exchanges about controversies rather than the repression of dissent (Kumagai & Lypson, 2009). As with the intern from the opening anecdote, silencing a learner is not the same as helping him or her change and, indeed, can block learning.

Hierarchy also poses a risk to patient safety. Studies from the aviation industry, critical care, and other team settings have demonstrated that without proactive measures, hierarchy can inhibit communication up the chain of command and prevent optimal decision making by the team. Managing power dynamics on teams by flattening the hierarchy is now widely recommended (Kohn, Corrigan, & Donaldson, 1999). Recent work applying the RESPECT model to teams has helped create a safe place to appreciate and respect strengths, better understand differences, express empathy and support, empower team members, and find ways to address concerns together (Mostow et al., 2016).

Taking a larger view of institutional power and powerlessness, it is revealing that our task force formed and discovered our truths through mutual support and collaboration rather than more hierarchically based forms of power. Without external funding for a number of years, it was mostly primary care providers with less power within the institution and with racial and ethnic experiences most similar to those of their patients who were willing to commit time and creative energies to collaborate and share insights. In other words, it was not coincidence that the views of the less powerful yielded insights that were new to those with power; it was not coincidence that it was a social worker and a racially and ethnically diverse group of physicians at an inner-city hospital who integrated Pinderhughes's attention to race, power, and empathy into existing discussions of culture. Sharing these discoveries within the safety of a protected peer structure that supported our teaching provided a source of renewal, validation, and recommitment to our work with patients and learners. Sharing these discoveries in public, in turn, empowered the participants, who have continued to have increased influence within the spheres of their own careers. Academic medical centers often award the greatest prestige to bench researchers who bring in the largest number of grant dollars, but our experience reinforces the value of including and supporting diverse perspectives, including the voices of those who care directly for patients, especially when the mission involves improving care for diverse populations. We are continually reminded that who we are shapes what we know—or may be blind to—and that it is essential to consider all perspectives to create the best outcomes.

As I think back to the burned-out intern who began my journey, I see another opportunity to reflect on assumptions, power, respect, empathy, and trust. His sharing of his very real struggle opened my eyes and eventually made me confront the helplessness we shared; neither of us knew how to help those for whom we had responsibility. My self-righteous anger reflected the misplaced arrogance of my power position, as well as other cultural baggage, and my assumption that despite the difference in our life experiences, he should see things the way I did. Finally, because I do believe that physicians have an obligation to learn the skills needed to help their patients, this floundering intern inspired me to do my job and get help from those who have discovered ways to make a difference with their patients. My colleagues and I empowered one another to make useful discoveries and build the trust necessary for our patients and learners to share their challenges, teach us about their worlds, and discover together how we can help.

REFERENCES

Bellini, L. M., & Shea, J. A. (2005). Mood change and empathy decline persist during 3 years of internal medicine training. *Academic Medicine, 80,* 164–167.

Berlin, E. T., & Fowkes, W. D. (1983). A teaching framework for cross-cultural health care. *Western Journal of Medicine, 139,* 934–938.

Betancourt, J. R., Carrillo, J. E., & Green, A. R. (1999). Hypertension in multicultural and minority populations: Linking communication to compliance. *Current Hypertension Report, 1,* 482–488.

Bigby, J. A. (Ed.). (2003). *Cross-cultural medicine.* Philadelphia: American College of Physicians.

Hafferty, F. W. (1998). Beyond curriculum reform: Confronting medicine's hidden curriculum. *Academic Medicine, 74,* 403–407.

Hojat, M., Vergare, M. J., Maxwell, K., Brainard, G., Herrine, S. K., Isenberg, G. A., & Gonnella J. S. (2009). The devil is in the third year: A longitudinal study of erosion of empathy in medical school. *Academic Medicine, 84,* 1182–1191.

Kleinman, A., Eisenberg, L., & Good, B. (1978). Culture, illness and care: Clinical lessons from anthropologic and cross-cultural research. *Annals of Internal Medicine, 88*, 251–258.

Kohn, L. T., Corrigan, J. M., & Donaldson, M. S. (Eds.). (1999). *To err is human: Building a safer health system.* Washington, DC: Institute of Medicine.

Kumagai, A. K., & Lypson, M. L. (2009). Beyond cultural competence: Critical consciousness, social justice, and multicultural education. *Academic Medicine, 84*, 782–787.

Mostow, C., Crosson, J., Gordon, S., Chapman, S., Gonzalez, P., Hardt, E., et al. (2010). Treating and precepting with RESPECT: A relational model addressing race, ethnicity, and culture in medical training. *Journal of General Internal Medicine, 25*(Suppl. 2), S146–S154.

Mostow, C., Gorosh, M. R., Crosson, J., & White, M. (2016). High performance teams: Diversity and RESPECT. In D. Novack, W. Clark, C. Daetwyler, & R. Saizow (Eds.), *DocCom—An online communication skills curriculum* (*M38*). Lexington, KY: American Academy on Communication in Healthcare.

Pinderhughes, E. (1989). *Understanding race, ethnicity and power.* New York: Free Press.

Rich, J. (2011). *Wrong place, wrong time: Trauma and violence in the lives of young black men.* Baltimore: Johns Hopkins Press.

Tervalon, M., & Murray-García, J. (1998). Cultural humility versus cultural competence: A critical distinction in defining physician training outcomes in multicultural education. *Journal of Health Care for the Poor and Undeserved, 9*(2), 117–125.

Tuckett, D., Boulton, M., Olson, C., & Williams, A. (1985). *Meetings between experts: An approach to sharing ideas in medical consultations.* London: Tavistock Publications.

14

Deconstructing Power to Build Connection: The Importance of Dialogue

Boston Institute for Culturally Affirming Practices (BICAP)[1]

We are the Boston Institute for Culturally Affirming Practices (BICAP), a multicultural, multiracial group of eight family and systems clinicians, supervisors, consultants, teachers, and activists, along with our mentor and consultant, Elaine Pinderhughes. We are committed to a culturally affirming stance, learned together from the nuanced cultural experiences and contexts we embody as a heterogeneous group and from the power dynamics that emerge among us as a result of our respective multiple, intersecting social locations. We began as a teaching team. Though we no longer co-teach regularly, we still meet, learn, write, train, and consult together. We rely on mutual support and respect to help us expand our practices of social justice, based on the aspirational concepts of human rights, dignity, and equality at all levels of society.

As BICAP, we strive toward greater awareness of our respective, complexly intersecting power locations (related to gender, racialized identity, ethnicity, and so on) and toward responsiveness to their effects on our work and relationships. Because microaggressions and other problematic power-related processes in BICAP reflect and reproduce larger social processes, discourses, and structures, we address them at personal, group, and societal levels. This task is not easy. Because all relationships involve the

---

[1] Rather than replicating academia's usual power-infused practice of having a first author, with all other authors lost in "et al.," we write as BICAP. We are, in alphabetical order (reflecting neither the size nor importance of our respective contributions nor power differentials among us): Gonzalo Bacigalupe, Mary-Anna Ham, Hugo Kamya, Jay King, Jodie Kliman, Roxana Llerena-Quinn, Patricia Romney, and David Trimble. We all contributed meaningfully to this chapter.

workings of power in multiple domains, they are fraught with tension related to complicated dimensions of power.

The fact that, despite our collective social justice commitment, our group has had need for repair reflects the importance of life-long cultural humility (Tervalon & Murray-García, 1998),[2] One of us, Jay, says we do better to discuss how to recover from our mistakes than how to avoid them. Our accountability to and mutual affirmation of each other, in the context of friendships and collegial relationships, constitute a messy, cherished, work in progress.

This chapter is our response to Elaine Pinderhughes's challenge to apply a power analysis to BICAP's own history and processes. We have worked on this task for years, learning about each other, our group, and ourselves in the process. We have tried to explore which operations of power close down meaning and which help reopen dialogue. The struggle to make sense of how power operates among us has been difficult, but its rewards keep us engaged. In the process, we are learning how we use power to accomplish things we can only do in BICAP, as well as how power operations among us sometimes make it difficult to go forward.

UNDERSTANDING POWER

Power is many things and resides in many places. It consists of incalculable types and forms of expression and operation. Rather than repeating others' efforts to define a phenomenon as complex as power, we direct the reader to Pinderhughes's chapter in this volume. That said, how we identify and experience power within and between ourselves can be the difference between our withering and blossoming. How we use power with or over others is crucial, as is how we express it in our lives. Do we use power to oppress or liberate, to bind or release, to harm or heal?

Power has many types: political, economic, social, cultural, and more. It exists at every level, from the intercellular to the cosmic, from micro to macro. We argue that power, which is in itself neither good nor bad, must be used to create equity. This is important in part because one can feel (and can actually be) powerful and powerless at the same time, because power exists in relationship—in degrees, in different contexts—and not in a zero-sum game.

Baker-Miller (1987) and others have effectively analyzed the differences among oppressive power ("power over") and positive, collaborative power ("power with"). She argued that "power-over" transactions interfere with people's abilities to see and engage with each other. Through Elaine Pinderhughes's mentorship, we came to understand that BICAP's goal of engaging in liberatory practice (Tew, 2006) with clients, students, and organizations was not achievable without examining how power operates within our own group.

---

[2] Cultural humility, according to Tervalon and Murray-García, embodies four principles to which we aspire: (1) lifelong learning, (2) critical self-reflection, (3) recognition and challenge of power imbalances, and (4) institutional accountability.

This chapter describes some of what we are learning in our collective examination of power and efforts to make our own practices more just. We hope our story can inform others' efforts to engage in the difficult work of collaborating across complex and layered differences of privilege and identity and the power relations they reflect. We will provide a brief history of our group and situate ourselves as individuals so as to contextualize how power has influenced some instances when we have worked well together and some when we have been (or remain) stuck in our efforts to be effective.

A BRIEF HISTORY OF BICAP

BICAP began as a team teaching a family therapy course at a multicultural psychology training program. The team had regular meetings and occasional retreats, developed a course, and led classes together and in subgroups. After challenges from interns and each other, we began examining our process and our multiple privileged and marginalized social locations in seminars and faculty meetings. Power issues and microaggressions emerged across multiple differences in our individual social locations.

BICAP offered us a culturally and racially diverse collegial setting in the segregated professional world of Boston. We came together through our commitment to a shared mission; collaboration, transparency, and accountability helped us forge strong personal bonds. We learned, often painfully, how to be held, and to hold each other, accountable for microaggressions that emerged in our work, while also affirming and validating each other. We have watched each other's children grow. We have witnessed and supported each other through life cycle events, including illness and the loss of loved ones. It has affirmed and reassured us to share our experiences of marginalization, silencing, or targeting in work situations characterized by a dominant discourse that can leave any of us feeling invisible, threatened, or questioning our own realities. We value our relationships and our hard-learned accountability practices at least as much as our official work together.

In its 11th year, the teaching team included Andrea[3], David, Gonzalo, Hugo, Jay, Jodie, and Roxana. After difficulties with the training program, five members left the program; Andrea and David continued the family therapy seminar. Nevertheless, we then continued as a group, teaching, consulting, and writing (Bacigalupe, 2002; Kamya & Trimble, 2002; Kliman & Llerena-Quinn, 2002; Llerena-Quinn, 2001; Llerena-Quinn & Bacigalupe, 2009) to advance understanding of power, equity, and social justice. In writing this chapter, we have learned more about our different reasons for staying with the group. We share some of those reasons, in our individual voices, over the course of this chapter.

We have worked to develop a culturally affirming stance embracing both openness to diverse cultural experience and commitment to social justice. We share similar perspectives as system thinkers committed to social justice and multiculturalism. Our intragroup diversity, embodying multiple and intersecting social locations of relative privilege and marginalization (Kliman, 2010), allows us to learn from polyphonic

---

[3] Andrea Canaan, who identifies as an African American lesbian, left for the West Coast a few years later.

explorations. The differences among us are continuously co-constructed in multiple relational contexts, in ways that can promote our health and well-being or destroy us. They are also vital for our survival and growth as biological, social, cultural, and spiritual beings (Llerena-Quinn, 2001). We have brought into our conversations struggles in serving vulnerable families in hospitals and private practices; difficulties with promotion, tenure, marginalization, and silencing in academic institutions; the dilemmas of caring for family members who live abroad; and wrenching family losses.

When Jay invited the group in 2007 to join a consultation with the Boston Red Sox about organizational difficulties around immigration and race, we named ourselves the Boston Institute for Culturally Accountable Practices. In 2009, we renamed ourselves the Boston Institute for Culturally Affirming Practices to better embody a discourse of appreciation rather than of judgment. In the next two years, two new members, Mary-Anna and Pat, joined BICAP, and we gained our consultant, Elaine.

SOME OF OUR REASONS FOR BEING IN BICAP

We are four women and four men, all straight and cis-gender, with a range of class backgrounds. Five of us are U.S.-born, with African American, Caribbean Islander, Latin American, Scots-Irish-American, Jewish American, and Chinese-Transylvanian-American ancestry, respectively. Three of us are immigrants or refugees, from Uganda, Chile, and Peru. Our elder-consultant, who attends meetings regularly, is African American. Writing this chapter has challenged us to learn more about the differences and similarities in our reasons for being in BICAP, helping us to better understand our group process and history. Some of our multiplex social locations will be described in the context of particular stories of group and subgroup process in BICAP; others are found just below. We situate ourselves in the service of exploring how our respective areas of relative power and privilege, and of marginalization, have shaped our group processes.

Patricia Romney

My identity has shifted over the decades, sometimes seeming to shift from day to day. It is more a question of naming than of experience. One constant has been my struggle to maintain a multicultural worldview while rooting out the internalized racism that is my familial and national legacy. I was born a West Indian child (as defined by my family) in the Bronx. At age eight, the parents of a new playmate in the previously all-white neighborhood my family had moved to identified me as colored. Neither my new playmate nor I knew what "colored" meant, but in any case, her family soon moved out in response to my family's presence. I was the Frantz Fanon of the family: introduced to concepts of race only when I entered the wider world.

My ethnic heritage is Trinidadian, Mexican, and Scottish, with more of Mother Africa shining through in my phenotype and in me than in any other member of my immediate family. How perplexing to have a father and brother who passed for white and Latino, respectively, and a mother who later in life married an Italian and was often seen as Italian by others in her community. Their reality was not mine. Colored, Negro, black, African American (even Negress in Finland) were the terms attributed to me. Almost invariably, I have been denied the power to name myself.

I care much more about culture than I do about race, but I live in a society that constantly racializes. I am deeply connected to my Caribbean heritage, appreciating the many islands my family members came from, the languages they spoke, the foods they cooked, and their indomitable instincts to survive and thrive. I am delighted by the multicultural, multireligious, multiracial, multilingual family of which I am currently a member.

I asked to join BICAP because I wanted to be a part of a group with the demonstrated ability to explore and understand culture through a social justice lens. My experience is not perfect. I am sometimes misheard and misidentified. I am sometimes distanced by those I deeply care about; yet I also have the experience of being deeply held while sharing parts of myself I am unable to voice or explore in other places. In BICAP, I work with my colleagues to deepen my understanding, improve my therapeutic skill, and strengthen my commitment to justice and love. *A luta continua.* (The struggle continues.)

Gonzalo Bacigalupe

I became a member of what became BICAP soon after beginning my faculty role at UMass Boston in 1996. Without my comrades, I am not sure I could articulate questions of intersectionality and equity with any complexity. Having come to the United States to complete a doctoral degree and to breathe after living most of my adolescence and young adulthood under an oppressive military dictatorship, being a South American immigrant was never in my consciousness in my first years as a student. Becoming an immigrant, with focus on the verb "becoming," was truly a process. The solidarity and continuous challenge and support of BICAP enabled me to speak and write about this process. What in our actions and reflections in action had such a profound impact on how I construe my identity today?

As a Chilean who had worked tirelessly to resist a military dictatorship, the questions of "power over" and "power with" have been on my mind since I was a child. Politics is in my veins and informs my understanding of power as resistance and emancipation, but also as oppressive and tyrannical. My mind has always received the assumption that we are equals, or that a turn in discourse makes us all collaborative, with a large dose of skepticism. The worst for me is the unacknowledged silence about such thinking in psychology and psychotherapy. Many of BICAP's challenges in presenting to, consulting with, or writing for others have always been centered around constitutive power relations.

BICAP is never a perfect, enlightened place, but for me it is always the necessary place for reflecting, whether serendipitously or very intentionally, about how we each operate in weaving and living power. Personally, the most difficult form of oppressive power, and the one that still surprises me, is that I can be instantly categorized by my skin color and accent. I am still being socialized into something I was never prepared for. BICAP has been a place for experimenting, sometimes painfully but often graciously, with those experiences. It is a place where I can stop and think, listen and reflect, where some of my unfinished thoughts become articulated into knowledge. Why is that essential? Because for those not in the "appropriate place," knowledge creation is often denied. Tenure and promotion, for instance, one of the most power-infected processes, have been a source of angst, and not only because they are hard in themselves. For some of us, becoming legitimate members of the knowledge class is seen with suspicion and is packed with the double burden of proving we are "better than." Being able to unpack those power dynamics and dialoguing and writing about them are essential. There are, indeed, few spaces for honest, although at times injuring, dialogues.

MaryAnna Domokos-Cheng Ham

I call myself MaryAnna, although the name on my birth certificate states: "Baby girl born to Mary Domokos." On the U.S. census, I check "other." My mother is Transylvanian Hungarian and my father is Chinese. I call myself a "mixed-blood" person who is racially mixed, and I reject identifying with racial labels that historically have been assigned by political consensus of the dominant culture. Several themes have meandered throughout my personal and professional life, only to converge and leave bare my most vulnerable psychic parts. At these times, I have often been left defenseless to wrestle with my feelings of inadequacy to cope with the shadow of invisibility, the precariousness of marginalization, and the disorientation created by multiple perceptions of reality. I have been willing to grapple with these issues yet find myself pursuing a lifelong quest of self-definition and identity. I am no different from other mixed-blood people uncertain about their relational position as either an insider or outsider (Ham, 2008). I have learned to be vigilant and to exercise caution in defining my social position with others.

Before joining BICAP, I had known several members through shared membership in another professional organization. I saw BICAP as residing within a closed unit, like a friendship circle whose boundaries had been previously determined. Then a member asked me if I would like to join BICAP. Previously an outsider, I was being asked to become an insider. Although I might be a member of BICAP, I would historically be an outsider. I wondered then, as now, whether I would ever be a real insider. I admit that I still feel marginal to the group. I struggle to find a bridge from their insider's reality to mine as a former outsider. Often, I continue to feel like an outsider and wonder whether I should leave the group, yet, I continue to stay. I may not be an original BICAP insider, but through the group's genuine caring and compassion for each other, I experience BICAP's capacity to maintain a "good-enough" container for all of the members' idiosyncratic perspectives.

David Trimble

As a heterosexual white man of 70, my external attributes afford me privilege. My experiences of marginalization are invisible: I was targeted as the neuroatypical child of socialist parents in a Republican suburb in the McCarthy era; along with Jodie, I am a bereaved parent. The coping strategies I developed in childhood shaped my current vulnerability to perpetrating unconscious microaggressions. Active in the early peace and civil rights movements, I started graduate school as the husband of an African American/Native American working-class woman and the father of my first multiracial child. My experiences of race and class were invisible in graduate school; my voice was silenced. I could not be whole in a monocultural white world; I was dying spiritually. I trained at the nascent multicultural psychology training program, the Center for Multicultural Training in Psychology at Boston University Medical Center (where BICAP was later born), which was and remains a lifeline and professional home base for me.

As an invisibly multiply acculturated white man with multiracial children and as a Jewish convert long married to a Jewish BICAP member (Jodie), my need to live in a multicultural world involves painful complexities. I sometimes say and do things that hurt people I care about. Most valuable to me about BICAP is the opportunity and commitment to stay at the table and explore together the complexity of our group process. In our wrestling together to make sense of power in relationships, I have come to believe that to do so, we also must consider love.

Jay King

I was a college freshman when Martin Luther King was shot. My father had me at 18 and went from a technical high school into the army while my mother, a high school senior, Catholic, and pregnant before marriage, became a full-time guilt-ridden mother. My father could pass for white, as he was a very light-skinned West Indian/Canadian/Cherokee who never referred to himself as colored or Negro or black or African American until after I was 40. He considered himself to be "better than those people." He was never subtle about his desire not to live in a neighborhood with "those people." My parents were racist. Academics prefer to identify them as people with "internalized racism." I find this differentiation counterproductive. Unaware of the implications for their children, they wanted us to understand that we should avoid dark-skinned people and associate with white people whenever possible. I was a foreigner in my birthplace.

For me, BICAP represented an opportunity: power and liberation from the shame introduced by parents and their extended family that was embedded in a liberal white supremacy and vigorously reinforced by the all-white schools that my parents, with good intentions, desperately wanted their children to attend. Ironically, it was a very dark-skinned black 18-year-old from Nashville and a native-born Ugandan who turned my shame and my mother's shame into pride about the African part of our ethnicity.

As David wrote about how love keeps us at the table, fear is also a factor that keeps me at the table. I live every day acutely aware of a world that hates to talk about bigotry. The legal system protects men who murder men and boys who look like me.

As a person who works in hostile environments where inclusive philosophies are discouraged, the affirmation that I experience with BICAP is indispensable to me. I believe, as I suggest to my students, that normal human behavior is not culturally competent, culturally affirming, or culturally humble. The inevitable microaggressions that occur in our process are not intentional, but they are not to be ignored. Affirmation and accountability continue to be vital to the survival of our group. They both must be symbiotically attached to every injury.

POWER WITH

Through the years, we observed our group grappling with power in ways like those of any group with diverse perspectives, worldviews, positions of privilege, and life experiences. We may be more intentional and explicit about attending to the workings of power in multicultural relationships, except when we are not. We use this understanding to help us limit—if not altogether prevent—conflicts, injuries, and microaggressions among ourselves and to avoid personalizing those injuries that do occur in BICAP's projects and in our relationships with one another. We have come to appreciate how power, "operates in all the levels of human functioning and is critical to all relationships, [including] those between individuals in our group, as well as interactions among us all" (E. Pinderhughes, personal communication, September 9, 2014).

Our group is not a static, completed phenomenon, which makes description difficult. Our process embodies dynamic tensions emerging from our multiple social locations and particular individual qualities. There is also dynamic tension between the need to pay deep attention to our group process and to produce the work that we want and need to complete (including this chapter!). These sometimes competing, sometimes complementary tendencies of attending to process as well as to tasks both suppress and sustain us. In the face of the complex power implications of our diverse multiple social locations, no one wants to be in charge. Overloaded in our professional and personal lives, we struggle to function as a leaderless group.

Despite these obstacles, we have enjoyed many experiences of productive "*power with*": productive, cooperative power with real effects in the world, embodying values of cultural sensitivity and social justice. In the training program where we began, we were mostly effective multicultural family therapy co-teachers. We prepared and debriefed together and so could respond appropriately when, for instance, our students told us we were spending too much time in seminars engaging with each other, at the expense of supporting their voices. We believed that power should be shared equitably among all the seminar participants. Our transparency enabled the students to exercise their power to challenge our teaching practice, and our response helped them cultivate experiences of power within (see Pinderhughes's chapter in this volume).

In what follows, we invite the reader into several experiences that embody BICAP, as we struggle, successfully or not, to make sense of who we are as a multicultural group in a challenging world. We do not suggest that we are a perfect group. We still struggle to make sense both of how we have injured each other in our practices of power, exemplified in some of the ruptures described as follows, as well as how we can best repair them. Such self-examination is fundamental to our group identity.

ROXANA'S PRESENTATION OF "PABLO"

As we developed the chapter, we presented our cultural self-understanding to each other and offered an example of work shaped by our cultural experience. Roxana's presentation was particularly influential on our understanding of power. Here is Roxana's example, preceded by her own self-location.

Roxana Llerena-Quinn

Born in Peru, I have lived in the Boston area since age 17. My identity has been shaped by a multiplicity of languages, passports, worldviews, and meanings derived from simultaneous membership and participation in a variety of contexts[4] and social locations. I was born to difference through my parents' interethnic (Peruvian and Italian), interracial marriage (white, African, Indigenous) in the early 1950s, in a country where legacies of colonization and slavery had left profound social inequalities. Blessed with multiple identities and a quiet, observing stance that allowed me to travel safely across contexts, the valences attached to difference revealed themselves in the politics of language,[5] nationality, geographic region, skin color, and gender, which tacitly served as markers of class and power in those I encountered. A permeable membrane developed between what I noticed outside and inside my family, but most important, inside myself. The complicated algebra of mixed-blood children showed up in the skin, but if confronted within, one could hope for a quiet revolution.

My mother's European heritage granted me a benefit that others in my family did not have. This social benefit disappeared with my passport as I entered the United States for school. New social identities greeted me at the door, as others disappeared. The first to go was national identity: I became Hispanic, Latina, erasing as current and historical within- and between-group fissures of the previous context were erased. Boxed into a racialized pan-ethnic group (Hispanic, though we are many races), a first-generation immigrant, I acquired minority status, which expanded my positive connection to many groups here.

As the only Latina in my college classes, I learned to speak the language of the dominant discourse, noticing how other voices fell silent. In the meantime, Latino families continue to come to see clinicians before they can find the words to describe their experience in a borrowed language, relying on our "good listening" to hear the stories embedded in multiple contexts erased by a "box." The price of not hearing the voices of the heart that have become fragmented or remain unknown can range from silence to many forms of quiet death. BICAP remains a place I keep coming back to, despite our misrecognitions, with glimmers of hope that we can see and hear each other better the next time.

---

[4] These include historical, economic, social, political, and geographic contexts, which give meaning to language: rural, urban, and suburban settings; race, ethnicity, and socioeconomic status; age, gender, religion, and nationality; and employment, education and occupation, and political ideology.
[5] Italian, Spanish, Quechua, other disappeared languages, and the "desired" English.

The case of Pablo. I met Pablo, a talented, 19-year-old Puerto Rican college student on scholarship, halfway through his sophomore year at a prestigious college. Pablo was taking time off from school to "pull myself together."[6] His difficulties were not academic at first but progressively developed as he had trouble sleeping, was late for early classes, and then stopped attending altogether. Worries about home kept him up at night. He called home nightly to ensure doors were locked and the stove turned off. Crying spells worried him. When thoughts of suicide became unbearable, he sought help.

Pablo had excelled in school without his mother's academic assistance. His mother, equipped with only a second-grade education, became responsible for housework at age seven, while her parents worked in the fields of rural Puerto Rico. She taught herself and several siblings to read and write. Individual and family work focused on safety, reducing depression, and personal and family concerns around leaving home. Later, I came to understand how closely Pablo's fear was connected to worries about "losing home" through his growing and educationally privileged distance from family.

Pablo re-entered school feeling ready, only to return home his junior year, questioning whether he would return to school at all. This time, he handed me an essay he had written, "We Are Fragmented People." He said to me, "These are the things I really want to talk about." Here is an excerpt:

> I am *mestizo*, one part Taino (native of the Caribbean region), one part Spanish and yet another part African. Made up of thirds. A fragmented person . . . I have learned to express myself in the way the white man upstairs tells me to. I see things his way. I see my other two thirds in the way he wants me to. . . . I have learned to utilize only one of my fragments. I will never be able to rationalize my world in the way the starving two thirds would have. . . . I wonder if I will ever be able to get the white man to stop growing and give my other two-thirds a chance to develop. I wonder if I can just knock him out of me.

With this insight of Pablo's, the silence of dormant voices was broken. It seemed that a larger kind of "family therapy" was needed among the inhabitants of our world, with their loud and silenced voices, all fragmented inside Pablo. His early thoughts of suicide now remind me of the fragments that had been dying in him, crying out for restored wholeness.

Pablo's essay leaves us with many questions: How does the dominant voice in Pablo's writing inform how the other two thirds of his identity evaluate themselves or tell their stories? If they all had voice, what would they say? How does it come about that one body of knowledge becomes privileged over another? What is the history of that knowledge? What are the economies of these arrangements? How do these arrangements affect us all? And finally, what are the complex meanings of education to him, and what was the nature of the knowledge he was acquiring at school?

---

[6] Another Latino student, mourning a Latino classmate's suicide, told me Latino students cannot afford time off to figure things out because this would not be seen as depression but as an inability to do the work.

The questions Pablo brought to my office involved multiple social identities affecting his view of himself, his family, and his place in the world. Because all groups are not valued equally, questions like, "Who are my people?" and, "Where do I belong?" take on special significance. When their answers come through the eyes of others, without critical analysis of others' assigned meanings, such imposed identities can be destructive to the individual. Thus, we had to re-examine the politics of language, class, culture, affirmative action, the experience of the "sun children,"[7] "scholarship boys," and the death of confidence. Pablo examined visible and invisible discourses that attempted to define him and affected his own sense of power. Late in our work together, he shared many other essays. Here is one excerpt:

> The product of a mostly American and entirely Western education, I am frequently visited by intense feelings of sadness and despair when I think of my childhood, living in what I *now* understand was poverty. I am then too quick to arrive at the conclusion that as a child in our home I suffered from what others have called "intellectual starvation," amongst other unwanted things.
>
> . . . In poverty, no, in spite of poverty, my childhood was filled with moments of intense learning and joy. This is not to negate the horrid effects of poverty, or to justify its insidious causes, but to celebrate my childhood as one worthy of having been lived. Too often I have bought the lies, believing that which negates my life by claiming that some other person has lived her or his childhood "the right way." . . . Yet in this home devoid of what I am told (of what I believed!) are proper things, gifts were given me plenty.

Pablo's writings triggered many questions of my own personal and professional acculturation that had remained invisible. Pablo became my powerful teacher without realizing his own power. Pablo reclaimed his silenced histories and his right to define himself, restoring wholeness to a fragmented self.

Hugo's reflections on Pablo's work with Roxana. Pablo's writing and Roxana's reflections on her conversations with Pablo resonate deeply with us in BICAP. All of us are either in multicultural/multiracial families, or ourselves of mixed descent, or both. Roxana, who has always gently challenged us to attend to what voices are absent from our conversations, challenged us with her account of Pablo to pay attention to the power struggles and silencing processes among our own inner voices.

I ask: How do we re-invent ourselves when the world does not mirror our image or value someone we recognize as ourselves? Maya Angelou (1989) described the power to define oneself, writing, "I decided many years ago to invent myself. I had obviously been invented by someone else, by a whole society, and I didn't like their invention" (p. 108).

In his writings and his work with Roxana, Pablo grew into his sense of agency, of "power to" and "power within," thereby questioning dominant culture's invention of him. His own fragmentation of identity (Ruiz, 1990) was central to his self-perception, but

---

[7] The "sun children" refers to the children of the "Sun God" in many ancestral civilizations of Latin America.

in finding ways to reintegrate the fragments of his life, he began to find himself and his sense of power. As he reconnected to his mother while also finding comfort in learning, he found his own sense of connection and a way of giving back to her. Affirming the value of that connection helped him to feel the "power to" and the "power with" he had experienced with his mother.

Throughout this work, Pablo constructed power for himself and his mother. His writing, revealing some visible power, was perhaps one of his strongest instruments in life. The power of language can be transformative, not only for speaker and decoder, but also for the interpersonal space(s) between them. That interpersonal space reveals the sacred within us. I argue that real power is that which honors the sacred within each of us. It is the shared reality into which we are all invited to play with each other, to love and own our own vulnerabilities.

The notion of agency is central to narrative therapy, which holds that without agency, we are helpless in the face of dominant, oppressive discourses—the single-story, deficit model of identity (White, 2007). Agency—and solidarity with those who struggle alongside us—allows us to thicken our stories, adding the knowledge that comes from our preferred values and practices, many of which are derived from subjugated cultures.

White (2007) wrote of how "re-authoring conversations" help people to "include some of the more neglected but potentially significant events and experiences that are 'out of phase' with their dominant storylines" (p. 61). Pablo engaged in such re-authoring in these essays, inventing his own understandings of his identity. Though his identity had been injured, it had also been strengthened by the solidarity and creativity in which his family engaged in the face of stark poverty.

THE RED SOX CONSULTATION

Reflecting Boston's history of ethnic and racial polarization, the Boston Red Sox was among the last professional baseball teams to recruit black players. The organization shows little critical awareness of the power-over processes controlled by its predominantly white management, or of the invisible power of the white normative discourse dominating their conversation, action, and experience. Their stands at Fenway Park remain unfriendly to people of color, particularly African Americans.

The Red Sox had recently relied heavily on talent from the Dominican Republic, where baseball is prized as a sport and as an opportunity for economic success in the United States. Cultivating and enlisting Dominican talent for the Red Sox resonates with traditions established during colonialism and the slave trade. The Red Sox had work to do to assimilate and accommodate Dominican players from impoverished lives to the cultural, linguistic, economic, and racial differences they encountered on immigrating and joining the team.

In this context, the Red Sox recruited some high-profile players from Japan, with enormous publicity. The contrast between the public attention to facilitating the Japanese players' cultural transition and the neglected challenges of Dominican players' transition created organizational strain. A new, more progressive general aanager, recognizing the need for a consultation about foreign players' cultural marginalization, sought an organizational consultation. Jay, approached for consultation, clarified their objectives and approached BICAP to participate in the project.[8]

The process of preparing for the consultation embodied BICAP practicing "power with" at its best. Excited by the opportunity, we addressed the complexities of identity and availability of resources. The Red Sox were willing to pay for three BICAP consultants. Given the organization's dominant male, white culture, we saw it as important to have both female and immigrant BICAP members on the consultation team; Roxana, our only female immigrant member, did not have time. We agreed that Hugo, from Uganda, and Gonzalo, from Chile, would join Jay's team. All the current BICAP members brainstormed on planning the consultation, entrusting Gonzalo, Hugo, and Jay with discretion and autonomy in representing us.

Their consultation began with an attempt to give the dominant members of the organization an experience similar to that of an immigrant recruit, such as hearing people talk in a language that they could not understand. Therefore, Jay welcomed everyone in English; Gonzalo extended a welcome in Spanish; Hugo did so in Swahili.

Some of us were surprised when the consultation fees were distributed among all six of us (power with), including those who had not traveled to the Red Sox Florida training camp for the consultation. Gonzalo, Jay, and Hugo explained that, since we were all involved in the planning process, we were entitled to share the proceeds.

Our meeting to debrief the Red Sox consultation went well, until we learned that the Red Sox had offered some tickets for choice seats. David enthusiastically bid for some tickets, driving the conversation to an apparent agreement about ticket distribution. This contradicted Hugo's, Gonzalo's, and Jay's understanding that the tickets were intended to compensate them and their families for weather delays in their flight home after the consultation. Nothing was said at the meeting, but that evening, Jay sent us all an e-mail clarifying that intention. I (Jay) wonder if my silence in the actual meeting emerged from my racial socialization. Did I assume that I did not have a voice when a white man claimed what was mine?

I (David) immediately withdrew my bid for the tickets, taking responsibility for narrowly focusing on my own interests. In the e-mail, I asked that we "make sense of the process and outcome involved in the misunderstanding." Reading the e-mail nearly eight years later, I can see how I had bid to set the agenda for the group, a (failed) performance of power over. That is not a new issue for me, either in general or in our group. It involves an unfortunate convergence of my white privilege and my neurobiological challenges, which make it difficult for me to sit with incomplete tasks.

We moved on for some time without examining our process over the tickets. As I (David) tried to make sense of the event on my own, I wondered if I had been unconsciously applying an earlier template to BICAP. Had I assumed that the group would automatically check my performances of white privilege? In the mid-1960s civil rights movement in Mississippi, African American activists routinely called out white allies

---

[8] The Red Sox generously gave BICAP permission to write about the consultation.

for acting entitled, and white allies were expected to change their behavior accordingly. I had similar experiences with my African American/Native American former in-laws.

Moreover, I wondered if I had responded with Mississippi-based assumptions of a binary black/white racial dynamic, despite BICAP's multiracial composition and different historical moment. I now know that I must acknowledge my responsibility for a microaggression as soon as I recognize it, whether I am challenged or not, and then all I can do is ask the person I have injured to agree to processing the event. That person has exclusive power to allow that processing, which involves being transparent, and therefore vulnerable, about having been injured. This practice ensures that the injured person, by exercising the power to choose whether to grant permission, has power within to manage the internal experience of injury, regardless of consequent discomfort to the microaggressor.

What stopped Gonzalo, Hugo, and Jay from objecting in the moment to David's claim on the tickets? Was our collective reluctance to process the event resistance to David's claim of "power-over" privilege? Was it an example of limiting, collusive "power with," enabling us to avoid an uncomfortable conversation? Did it involve the intersectionality of our individual social locations? Did our avoidance set the stage for difficulties that emerged later when we began our planning for a presentation on *Caramelo* (addressed later in this chapter)? Processing difficult conversations involves concerns over trust and vulnerability, natural concerns in the evolution of a group when it incorporates new members. Was processing of the event delayed by developmental transition, as Pat and MaryAnna joined BICAP very shortly after this event?

Did what ensued about this event reflect what we found so entrenched in the Red Sox nation? What responsibility did we have to engage these issues in consultations when we struggled with the same issues? Finally, how might our "behind-the-scenes" experiences reveal what was happening internally for the Red Sox?

INJURY AND REPAIR BETWEEN HUGO AND JODIE, IN TWO VOICES

Here, we discuss an injury between two BICAP members, Hugo and Jodie, and the long healing process that followed it. For an *AFTA Monograph*[9] on social justice in training, I (Jodie) proposed a piece on my visual model of intersecting domains of privilege, marginalization, and collective identity (Kliman, 2010). Knowing me to be white and Jewish, the editors suggested adding another author's perspective, from a different social location. I asked Hugo, who is black and Ugandan, to reflect on my article. He knew the model, and I had always appreciated and learned from his reflections. Hugo accepted, asking me to send him my draft for his reflections before sending it to the editors. I agreed, welcoming both his presubmission feedback and his written reflections.

---

[9] The American Family Therapy Academy (AFTA) is an academy of teachers, researchers, and practitioners in family and systems work; all BICAP members are also members.

Still struggling with organization and writing two years after a second concussion, I underestimated the time needed to finish the draft. Two weeks past deadline and stressed by the pressure to submit my draft, I developed a sort of tunnel vision; my promise to send Hugo the manuscript before sending it to the editors became invisible. My memory shifted, distorted by mild traumatic brain injury (TBI) and racial privilege. Misremembering our agreement, I submitted the paper. The next morning, I sent him the manuscript, unaware of breaking our agreement or of overlooking Hardy's (2002) concept of harmful impact trumping good intentions in relationships across power differentials.

I (Hugo) was stunned and hurt. I doubted whether Jodie actually wanted my reflections. After several weeks on hold, I also doubted that I could write reflections on such short notice. I let Jodie know of my surprise, distress, and pressing deadlines.

With horror, I (Jodie) saw the seriousness of my error and the relational injury I had caused my beloved colleague and friend. I reached out to repair the injury, but Hugo had other deadlines and did not feel ready for that conversation. I remorsefully accepted Hugo's decision, saying I was ready to revisit these events whenever he might feel ready. I realized that pressing for rapid resolution and healing when Hugo was unready would exacerbate the injury. Doing so would relieve me of guilt more than it would serve Hugo's need for my accountability; that would replicate the power dynamic's relational injury. Hugo's choosing not to engage for the time and my accepting that choice rebalanced power somewhat.

In a recent healing conversation, spurred by writing the current chapter, we co-constructed the aforementioned events. In the following text, we describe our respective and shared meaning making around those events and the lessons we take from them and hope to share with BICAP and the reader.

Hugo's Initial Perspective

Jodie's neglecting to send me the paper in advance ruptured for me our personal and professional relationship. I felt disorganization and a mix of hurt, anger, frustration, disappointment, and confusion. I was confused about how to continue with that collaboration and with Jodie herself, yet I knew that Jodie's actions, however hurtful to me, did not embody who I knew her to be; that was all the more confusing. Did she disinvite me from giving her early feedback on her paper because she did not trust my writing in English, which is not my first language? Did she not trust or value my ability to conceptualize or reflect? Was she oblivious to the hurt her actions would cause me? Was her original request self-serving rather than truly collaborative?

Since the article and the model were hers, didn't she have the right to disinvite me? But why would she, without discussing it with me in advance? What was the role of power, including power related to race, nationality, and language in Jodie's blind disregard for our agreement? How much power had she shared with me? How much had she taken away? Had I misunderstood something when we first agreed to my contributing to her work? Who am I to Jodie? Also, because I had my own deadlines to deal with and

Jodie had kept me waiting only to go ahead without my feedback, why should I feel any urgency to reflect on a fait accompli?

Deadlines were the least of my reasons for pulling back, however. Mostly, it involved my pain and new distrust of my understanding of our relationship. I was filled with self-doubt about what I had, and what Jodie thought I had, to contribute to her work, whose mission we shared. One reason I pulled back from writing my reflections or talking with her was self-protective. I wanted to protect myself from the doubts I thought Jodie must have about me. I also wanted to protect her; I cared about and enjoyed working with her, and would need to continue doing so in BICAP and elsewhere. I appreciated that Jodie did not push me to process the injury, given my self-doubt and mixed emotions. I decided I could still collaborate well with Jodie in other areas, which preserved BICAP. Still, this major relational injury left me feeling undervalued. I did not know how to talk about these events in the face of such complexity.

My own background combines several intersecting narratives, each with inter-nested connections. I am a refugee from Uganda, one of 11 children, a black African man born during a colonial era, for whom English is my fourth language. From a very early age, church, religion, and spirituality were very important to my parents, and they worked hard to develop faith values in us. My life was profoundly shaped by the narrative of Uganda as a colony of Britain. Growing up in a postcolonial country, where whiteness symbolized privilege and power, I struggled to understand the so-called benevolence of Uganda's colonial masters and their sanitized oppression. Colonialism found other names that justified itself. Uganda was Britain's "protectorate" rather than its "colony." As a member of the country's largest tribe, I felt a sense of power, checked by the helplessness I felt throughout postcolonial Uganda, where an oppressive government targeted my tribe.

Important formative life events steered me toward who I am today, strongly influencing my worldview. An attack on our family when I was a boy forever altered our family life. After shots were fired into our home, only a crack in the window and a streak of blood on the floor remained in the room where our father had run from the soldiers. There was no sign of our father. My father's disappearance, capture, and detention for several years left an indelible mark on me. His disappearance left our family with few options beyond hoping for his return. With my mother as the sole breadwinner, our family turned to faith to find a place of comfort and solace. Our faith became the backbone of our life and the lens through which we engaged various forms of power as we struggled with a sense of voicelessness.

This enabled me to understand the powerlessness embedded in retaliatory discourses. Perhaps more pressing was the intense anger I felt in struggling to construct "the other" in those who oppressed my family. Although this anger gave me a means of dealing with my pain, I could not, and chose not to, live consumed by anger defining my relationship to power and hope, especially in the face of struggle and pain. The crack in the window then, and now, became a metaphor through which I felt a sense of hope and deliverance.

I have suffered many untimely losses in my family of origin, most of whom are an ocean away from me. In another important life story, on realizing that my eldest brother, Joseph, was hearing impaired, unable to speak, and struggled with many challenges, I came to appreciate the blessings in my life and family. Joseph's difficulties with communication alienated him from all of us as a family, perhaps including from himself. His inability to speak was a silence that affected us all, coming with a costly pain as we all struggled to make sense of it. Growing up with Joseph, I saw what it meant to live with such challenges. This experience allowed me to imagine some of what Jodie articulates below, in relation to her head injury. I, in contrast, have been blessed with generally good health.

Of note, I am about a decade younger than Jodie; once, as a young academic, I took her class at a local institute. I am now a full professor of social work, with advanced degrees in theology, social work, and psychology, yet my voice, that of a black African man at predominantly white colleges, often goes unheard in academic settings, my ideas taken up only when white colleagues speak them (Kamya, 2005, p. 105). Often, when I question white students, they respond to my white colleagues, not to me. I am left to wonder: Whose voice carries weight, and why? I therefore wondered during this breach with Jodie: Did my voice carry weight with her?

Jodie's Initial Perspective

Two head injuries in middle age, one not long before the events between Hugo and me, had left lasting effects on my organizational and visual ability, reading speed, and cognitive set. These deficits are subtle but painful to an academic; they provide one way to understand my grievous injury to Hugo. Once I realized how I had hurt Hugo, I wanted to talk with him, so we could both understand and repair the relational injury and clear a path toward his continued and valued involvement in the writing. My experiences of shame and marginalization around my recent cognitive challenges helped me appreciate what I imagined to be Hugo's relationship to marginalization and vulnerability to shame. Moreover, my childhood protecting and interpreting for my late brother, whose voice had been largely ignored due to difficulties with speech, cognition, and illness, forced me to confront how my actions had silenced Hugo's (written) voice and diminished his agency.

I had to respect, however, the fact that Hugo was neither ready to talk nor ready to reflect on my article. I knew I had harmed him but not how he experienced our interactions. BICAP and other social justice work had taught me the importance of people with greater power and privilege engaging accountably about injuries committed, regardless of good intentions (Hardy, 2002). I am white and U.S.-born; English is my first of three languages. These aspects of identity gave me greater privilege than Hugo, as did the fact that I had asked him to reflect on my article and model.

I am ethnically and religiously Jewish. Jews were marginalized as I grew up in the 1950s and 1960s, but we are fairly privileged today, at least in the United States. My mixed-class family had gained class privilege by my childhood. I grew up among and was deeply influenced by Jewish refugee great-grandparents and family friends; I strongly identify with today's refugees and immigrants but have far more power, privilege, and safety. As a child, I protected and interpreted for my brother, whose dwarfism, cognitive challenges, illnesses, and impaired speech most people did not bother to understand. He was my first inadvertent teacher of the social justice importance of being an ally. My first intentional teacher of allyship was my father, a 1940s-era civil rights activist who had been partly raised by his grandmother, whose entire family and Jewish village had been massacred in an anti-Semitic pogrom in pre-Soviet Ukraine.

I am in my sixties, heterosexual, married, and stepmother to two multiracial (African American, Native American, and white) children. I am the bereaved mother of a son whose voice died with him at age 19. As an adult, I have had great privilege, which I have often performed, including toward my BICAP comrades, despite my best intentions. My privilege has been somewhat diminished in recent years as my bereaved parent status can frighten some people away. Chronic health problems and a significantly slower postconcussion work pace have interfered with academic productivity, leaving me more vulnerable at my doctoral program, which is only now developing faculty rank and has no tenure. My health and my post-TBI struggles are areas of marginalization relative to Hugo's robust physical and cognitive functioning.

I thought that Hugo must have felt terribly hurt and marginalized by my serious oversight and that he likely saw the injury through lenses of race and national origin (I never imagined his doubting his linguistic or conceptual abilities, which I see as brilliant). At the time, my heartfelt apology was not enough to engage him with me around this injury, though I said I hoped for reparative conversations in the future. Later, as BICAP discussed our group process around various other injuries, I privately asked Hugo if he wanted to talk about these events. He said no.

I had to take responsibility for letting external pressure to produce my manuscript distract me from my agreement with Hugo. I felt remorse and shame over my racial and cultural microaggression against Hugo and the lasting consequences to both him and BICAP. But I also viewed my injurious tunnel vision as reflecting post-TBI cognitive deficits, something I have never written about, as it (still) feels professionally risky. I felt shamed by invisible cognitive deficits making me so vulnerable to a mistake with such disempowering effects on a dear friend.

I wondered: Could someone so agile of mind as Hugo understand the role of cognitive challenges in my actions? Did that even matter, given the racial power differential or the harm I had done? Was I using disability as an excuse for performing racial privilege or the power of "owning" a conceptual model I could invite (or accidentally disinvite) him to engage with? I felt both humiliated and guilty, since the focus of the article and the monograph itself was social justice. I wept at injuring Hugo and railed at what I harshly judged as my cognitive inadequacy. In response to Hugo's stance, I retreated. The article was published, without Hugo's enriching feedback or reflections, and was well received. The pain re-emerged; did I deserve that positive reception, when submitting the article as I did, had injured my friend?

Our Conversation of Healing, Accountability, and Affirmation

External pressures and deadlines (for classes, articles, talks, and consultations) have facilitated BICAP's productivity (power with and power to) but also impeded the important work of attending to our group process (another form of power with). They did both in this situation. When this book's editors invited BICAP to delve into how we manage power issues, Hugo invited Jodie into a healing conversation of repair, validation, and accountability. This time, we used the external time pressure well to process and start repairing power-involved injury. What follows is our shared and consensual meaning making and the lessons we have taken from these painful events.

I (Hugo) shared my complex feelings at the time of the painful events of five years earlier for the first time and heard Jodie reiterate her sorrow and remorse. She asked me how much my silence and withdrawal had been to protect her from my anger, out of caring, and how much it had been to protect myself by protecting her, the person with greater power, from discomfort (Hardy, 2002). I replied that my protecting her was grounded in my caring and that I knew she did not need protection from my anger. I also shared that I remembered that Jodie had showed true respect for my contributions in BICAP and elsewhere.

I (Hugo) realized I also had been protecting myself with my silence, as our shared commitment to BICAP required us to stay committed to, and work with, each other as members of BICAP and AFTA and as Multicultural Family Institute Culture Conference faculty. I wondered, on reflection, if my silence had been an attempt to protect BICAP itself; suppressing my distress had allowed me to continue collaborating with Jodie on a team we both cared so much about.

I (Jodie) validated how deeply I had injured Hugo and shared how I understood and appreciated his experience of the breach my actions had created. I told Hugo how much I had wanted and valued his reflection and presubmission editorial feedback, my tunnel vision notwithstanding. Together, we had a caring and helpful "both/and" conversation about how Hugo's social location as an immigrant of color for whom English was a fourth language intersected with my longstanding linguistic and U.S.-born privilege and painful new marginalization because of brain injury.

We asked how to make room for power together (power with)—effective work in the service of social justice and mutual caring and respect, collaboration, and co-constructed meaning, given the power differentials our complex social locations engendered. We asked how to repair the damage when one of us injures the other in the context of such complexly layered power arrangements. How do we heal the self-doubt we each felt about our respective abilities (Hugo's because of cultural and linguistic, and Jodie's because of cognitive, marginalization)? And when is a good time to engage in processing an injury shaped by and deriving meaning from power imbalances?

I never intended to have power over Hugo, effectively disinviting his participation in a shared writing venture, but power I had. I (Hugo) never intended to injure Jodie with the power of my long silence about these events, but I too had power over Jodie in relation to the healing process. Our conversation in the service of this chapter helped bring us back to a place of power with (collaborating mindfully) and power within (resisting the internalization of marginalization), rather than power over each other.

Growing together. The initial injury came when I (Jodie) allowed the pressure to produce an article distract me from a deeply valued collaboration with Hugo. The healing came when the pressure to produce this chapter opened up a true dialogue in the service of examining how power over can distort power with and power within. Such opportunities to learn, grow, and heal together through true dialogue with colleagues and friends I can trust to act with integrity and compassion, even in responding to power-infused injuries, keep me committed and grateful to BICAP.

In BICAP, I (Hugo) have a group or circle/community of care among well-intentioned individuals who choose to work collaboratively to find a sense of purpose and connection. My life has been one of feeling voiceless or silenced, including, at times like the one described earlier, in relation to some members of BICAP, yet we have made efforts to work through these challenges. BICAP has allowed me to live the stubborn, optimistic dream that has brought me so far. BICAP offers conversational opportunities that help shift "power-over" relationships to "power with." Such opportunities have helped me continue to find that crack in the window, sometimes occasioned by a BICAP member, sometimes self-claimed.

THE *CARAMELO* PRESENTATION

The Multicultural Family Institute's[10] Culture Conference offered an important opportunity to expand our transparency with a trusted but not intimately involved audience. The Culture Conference affords support and validation for marginalized, culturally sensitive practitioners nationwide, including us. At the Culture Conference, we had previously shown some films to stimulate discussions of racism, authoritarianism, and oppression on the basis of race, social class, and gender. During one such discussion, we accepted Hugo and Jay's last-minute invitation to hold an open BICAP meeting at the conference, demonstrating our practices of transparency and accountability.

Although spontaneous unplanned transparency was successful in that presentation, our next, planned attempt was an unequivocal failure. Years later, our struggle to understand what happened is still a work in progress. Writing this chapter has helped us, and we hope will help the reader, understand the imperative of persistence, ultimate reconciliation, and rejuvenation in the face of the obstacles that power issues create for a multiracial, multicultural group.

The conference organizers requested that, rather than presenting a film, we share a clinical case. BICAP is not a group practice or a training institute. When we were unable to choose a suitable case from our individual practices, we decided, at Roxana's suggestion, to explore the intergenerational stories and identity issues in the Mexican family depicted in Sandra Cisneros's novel *Caramelo* (2003). To put it succinctly, we "bombed." To make it worse, we did not fully understand why. Neither our message nor our focus was clear. The conference conveners were disappointed, and we were embarrassed.

The *Caramelo* episode embodied a tension intrinsic to much of what we do as a multicultural group. The tension between needing to explore our group process and performing the necessary task of the moment can be generative or a source of disconnection and the demise of dialogue. Tension from the pressure to produce a presentation

---

[10] For information on this program, see www.multiculturalfamily.org/.

led to polarization between those group members who pressed urgently for concrete agreements about the task and Roxana, who urgently sought deeper conversation about the implications of the *Caramelo* story for the particularities of identity, history, context, and social justice in Latino/a family life. Before the conference, our interactions had devolved to the point that David asked for a decision by vote, an abrupt departure from our usual collaborative method.

The uncertainty about what to do played itself out at the conference, right up to the moment we appeared on the stage. Today, through the lens of power, we see how a toxic runaway feedback of "power over" had captured us.

Since the conference, we have periodically tried to understand more about what happened around the *Caramelo* presentation. At a retreat five years later, we collectively reflected on our performances of power and privilege when we heard Roxana say, "At some point, I lost my team and I lost my voice." We further understood how privilege and microaggressions (by non-Latino/as) had shaped our group's performance when she reminded us, "This can happen when you are dis-membered." We realized that we needed to continue processing conflicts and injuries to go on as a group.

In writing this chapter, a trove of essays, minutes, and audio recordings of meetings, and e-mails have helped us reconstruct events from various perspectives. One recording stimulated a recent reparative conversation around Jodie's having once equated her identification with her great-grandparents' and other-mothers' refugee experiences with Roxana's personal immigration experience, thus inadvertently disqualifying Roxana's lived experience. This repair raised an important concern beyond the need for relational accountability. It speaks to the need for affirmation of the complex particularity of cultural identity. Such understandings come from deep, honest, and courageous exploration of our experiences, witnessed across all of the individual differences our diverse group embodies.

THE PROCESS OF WRITING THE CHAPTER

It took five years to write this chapter, during which time we produced enough pages for a book. We began by sharing detailed presentations of our individual experiences of cultural and class history and identity. Our narratives included early life histories, including power relationships with family members and community; early encounters with social, educational, and religious structures; migration and immigration stories; workplace interactions with colleagues, students, and clients; and how they all influenced our respective constructions of personal identity.

These presentations stimulated rich conversations from which we learned and grew as speakers and witnesses. We have learned more about each other's cultural and class histories and tried to resist seeing one another as a member of a category. We have seen how our cultures' values and practices and teachings converge and conflict.

Our group discussion of individual stories helped us comprehend each presenter's experiences of power and powerlessness, including within BICAP. We bore witness to expressions of deeply vulnerable and personal thoughts and feelings. In the process, responding to each other's meaning making, we held and honored each other's vulnerabilities at deeper levels.

Intrinsic to our writing, as in all our shared history, was the dynamic tension between task performance and deep exploration and processing. Our struggle with the tension between production and processing in the writing of the chapter has been generative, expanding our discourse beyond the "power over" of microaggression and the "power with" of repair to include "power within." Exploring the many inner voices emerging from our respective multiple social locations has invited us into deeper understanding of power within. How can we enhance our individual "power to" through honest exploration of how the "power over" wielded by some of our inner voices can silence others' inner voices, which must be heard for us to be whole individually and as a group? How can we bring all the inner voices forth, to be wholehearted in our actions for cultural sensitivity and social justice? At the same time, Elaine Pinderhughes has cautioned us not to expect power to change just because you tell a story. We have persevered through relational ruptures and focused on the importance of dialogue (Romney, 2005) and the development of allyship.

Power's manifestations intensify in the context of resource scarcity; as the time left to submit our chapter shrank, time was a scarce resource for each of us. Under pressure to produce, we fell out of the practice of checking in about our personal lives, a process that has sometimes absorbed entire BICAP meetings. Late in the project, needing to complete the task, we stopped meeting in person, instead meeting electronically and exchanging e-mails. This meant fewer opportunities to attend to our relationships, our process, and each other. This loss has been poignant, as nothing has slowed the pace of life and its inevitable experiences of personal and family health problems, crises, and major losses.

Inspired by Roxana's attention to voice when she has asked, "What voices are not in the room, what voices are we attending to, and what voices are we ignoring?" Jay offers this closing reflection:

> Is there a time when voice is noise
> Is there a time when silence is power
> When voice is choice AND when silence is choice
> And when is silence very loud
> And when is voice inaudible
>
> When is voice a matter of courage
> And when is it a matter of defense, fear and flight
> And when is silence a matter of courage
> And when is silence a matter of defense, fear and flight
>
> When is the imperative of "voice" the coercive path to imperialism
> In defense of the dominant monologue
> And when is it the resistance to oppression
> And when is it both . . . and . . .
> And when are both impotent and redundant
> AND when are both dynamic, empowering and transformative

When are we listening to
And (who do we be[11]) listening *with*
Are we hearing ourselves
While we are hearing the other

How did we learn to think
Either, Or
How do we feel protected and empowered by "right" and "wrong"
How does *write* (voice) and wrong (silence) move us from
Lost to found and from found to lost
And from visible to invisible
And from invisible to visible

Listening, are we?
Or is voice and being heard the only discourse to power
Some say silence is death
When i am listening am i an activist, am i learning
Am i silent or
Am i dead?

REFERENCES

Angelou, M. (1989). *And still I rise.* New York: Little, Brown.

Bacigalupe, G. (Ed.). (2002). Relational conversations in the face of trauma and political terrorism: Professional training, and personal reflections in the aftermath of September 11. *Journal of Systemic Therapies, 21*(3), 1–7.

Baker-Miller, J. (1987) *Toward a new psychology of women.* Boston: Beacon Press.

Chang, J. (2014). *Who we be: The colorization of America.* New York: St. Martin's Press.

Cisneros, S. (2003). *Caramelo.* New York: Vintage.

Ham, M. D. (2008). Biracial legitimacy: Embracing marginality. In M. McGoldrick & K. V. Hardy (Eds.), *Re-visioning family therapy: Race, culture, and gender in clinical practice* (pp. 213–225). New York: Guilford Press.

Hardy, K. (2002). *From borders to bridges: Strategies for addressing cross-cultural conflict* [Keynote address]. Presented at the Annual Culture Conference, Multicultural Family Institute, New Brunswick, NJ.

Kamya, H. (2005). African immigrant families. In M. McGoldrick, J. Giordano, & N. Garcia-Preto (Eds.), *Ethnicity and family therapy* (3rd ed., pp. 110–116). New York: Guilford Press.

Kamya, H., & Trimble, D. (2002). Response to injury: Toward ethical construction of the other. *Journal of Systemic Therapies, 21*(3), 19–29.

---

[11] With acknowledgment, both the common phrase, "who we be," and the book by Jeff Chang, *Who We Be: The Colorization of America* (2014).

Kliman, J. (2010, Winter). Intersections of social privilege and marginalization: A visual teaching tool [Special issue]. *AFTA Monograph Series, 39*–48. Washington, DC: American Family Therapy Academy.

Kliman, J., & Llerena-Quinn, R. (2002). Dehumanizing and rehumanizing responses to September 11. *Journal of Systemic Therapies, 21*(3), 8–18.

Llerena-Quinn, R. (2001). How do assumptions of difference and power affect what and how we teach? *Newsletter of the American Family Therapy Academy, 82,* 22–26.

Llerena-Quinn, R., & Bacigalupe, G. (2009). Constructions of difference among Latino and Latina immigrants and non-Hispanic white couples. In K. D. Killian (Ed.), *Intercultural couples: Exploring diversity in intimate relationships* (pp. 165–186). New York: Routledge.

Pinderhughes, E. (1989). *Understanding race, ethnicity, and power: The key to efficacy in clinical practice.* New York: Free Press.

Romney, P. (2005). The art of dialogue. In P. Korza, B. Schaffer Bacon, & A. Assaf (Eds.), *Civic dialogue, arts & culture: Findings from animating democracy.* (pp. 57–79). Washington, DC: Americans for the Arts Press.

Ruiz, A. S. (1990). Ethnic identity: Crisis and resolution. *Journal of Multicultural Counseling and Development, 18*(1), 29–40.

Tervalon, M., & Murray-García, J. (1998). Cultural humility versus cultural competence: A critical distinction in defining physician training outcomes in multicultural education. *Journal of Health Care for the Poor and Underserved, 9*(2), 117–125.

Tew, J. (2006). Understanding power and powerlessness: Towards an emancipatory practice in social work. *Journal of Social Work, 6,* 33–51.

White, M. (2007). *Maps of narrative practice.* New York: W. W. Norton.

15

Power and Research

Sarita Kaya Davis

The concept of power in research is similar to the notion of democracy in America. Participants in each system are indoctrinated with promises of truth, objectivity, and fairness. However, when lived out in the experiences of marginalized and vulnerable populations, clear patterns of oppression, victimization, and even genocide become painfully apparent. Power in research and democracy in America share a lengthy and ignoble history when viewed through the eyes of marginalized peoples. In 2002, Louis Menand penned an article on the origins of scientific racism in the United States. Menand documented that long before anthropologist Franz Boas empirically established that intellect is largely attributed to exposure and environment, two Harvard professors, Louis Agassiz and Samuel George Morton, taught students and promoted among scholars the notion that people of African descent were subhuman and inherently inferior. Their findings were largely based on the measurements of interior skull capacity of more than 600 skulls collected from across the world in the 1830s. The results were published in a collection in 1849 that ranked the human races by cranial capacity. At the top of the ranking were Caucasians, and at the bottom were Negroes, Hottentots, and Aboriginal Australians. Coupled with anthropological travel literature, Morton concluded that the Ethiopian (Negro) was at the far extreme with the lowest grade of humanity. The scholarship of Agassiz and Morton influenced medical and social scientific research for many years to come.

In her 2007 book *Medical Apartheid: The Dark History of Medical Experimentation on Black Americans from Colonial Times to the Present*, medical anthropologist Harriet Washington charted the history of America's horrendous treatment of people of African descent as unwilling and unknowing experimental subjects at the hands of the medical establishment and experimental researchers. *Medical Apartheid* is the most comprehensive history of medical experimentation on African Americans. Beginning with the earliest encounters between the descendants of Africans and Western medical researchers and documenting the racist pseudoscience that resulted, it details the ways people of African descent were used in hospitals for experiments conducted without their knowledge—a tradition that continues today within some communities (DuBois, Kraus, & Vasher, 2012; Fanelli, 2009). It reveals how black people have been prey to grave robbing; unauthorized autopsies; the pseudoscience of eugenics; social Darwinism; experimental exploitation; and inferior medical treatment that treated them as inhuman, oversexed, and unfit for adult responsibilities. These medical atrocities were conducted by the government, the armed services, prisons, and private institutions. *Medical Apartheid* reveals the hidden underbelly of scientific research and makes transparent the unjust and unethical treatment of people of African descent. Washington's book provides the fullest possible context for comprehending the behavioral fallout that has caused black Americans to experience power in research as systemic and sanctioned abuse.

Power in social scientific research is no less problematic. The social scientific method of constructing knowledge evolved out of medical experimentation. Consequently, medicine and the social science methodology share the same underlying assumptions. Early social scientific research in Western society was rooted in the observations and stories of travelers, who were typically white men, whose interactions with indigenous people were constructed around their own cultural views of gender, race, and sexuality (Smith, 2002). Memmi (1965) noted that early scientists typically used zoological terms to describe primitive people. The dispassionate and dehumanizing ways of viewing the other have become so embedded in the fabric of doing research that they are nearly transparent to the uncritical eye.

In this chapter on power in research, I discuss where, why, and how power shows up in social science research and how power issues in research can be mediated. I explore this topic in the following three sections: (1) the philosophy of social science research, (2) the practice of research, and (3) democratizing research. I also include examples from my own research in HIV prevention education to help contextualize the narrative. The first section discusses the philosophy underlying social science research. The goal of this section is to offer the reader a careful examination of the roots and branches of social science research, after which the reader should understand how power is embedded in the research process, including its foundations, methodological assumptions, rules, and explanations.

THE PHILOSOPHY OF SOCIAL SCIENCE RESEARCH

Before addressing the philosophy of social science research, it is important to understand how researchers come up with ideas for research projects. There is no singular method, but three primary sources are constant—practical problems, the literature, and culture. Some researchers devise research problems independently, but because they do not live in a vacuum, their ideas are influenced by their personal circumstances (background, culture, education, class, and so on) and the world in which they live (Creswell, 2007; Guba & Lincoln, 2005). Social science research questions generally evolve out of a context, be it professional or personal experience, practice, or a specific discipline. Despite the historical claims that research is objective, we see that the process of research problem formulation is often informed by a situation, incident, or event (Creswell, 2007). Because these frameworks are all guided by the interpretation of the receiver, it is safe to assume that research questions come from a place that is informed by value positions. This finding inspires questions about whose values are (or are not) being considered and how those values influence power in research.

Logical Reasoning

Contemporary research is rooted in philosophy and logical reasoning (Kuhn, 1962). In the past, philosophers and scientists were primarily concerned with trying to understand the world around them, thereby generating knowledge and truth. *Epistemology* is the philosophy of knowledge or of how we come to know. Early philosophers and scientists who laid the foundation of research assumed that there was a single objective reality. Understanding the epistemological debate at the core of research gives us insight as to how the notion of power is introduced into the research context. Although the epistemological schools of thought undergirding social science research have multiplied over the years, they all can be placed under one of the following two broad categories: positivism and postpositivism.

Evolutions in Philosophy

Positivism asserts that the purpose of science is simply to observe, measure, and report what is seen. A positivist would argue that knowledge (truth) beyond what can be observed is impossible. Because we cannot directly observe feelings, thoughts, perception, and so on, positivists believe that behavior is the only legitimate source of knowledge. Disciplines that embrace positivism include medicine, public health, biology, anthropology, and some branches of education and psychology.

In contrast, the postpositivist believes that there is an independent reality that can be studied. The postpositivist asserts that all measurement is fallible, so high importance is placed on multiple measures and observations as a way to reduce error and get a better understanding of what's happening in reality. The most important belief of the postpositivist is that all observations are theory laden and that scientists are inherently biased by their cultural experiences, worldviews, and other personal factors. Some of the other theories that fit under the umbrella of postpositivism include relativism, hermeneutics, constructivism, and feminism. The emergent theories generally agree that there are multiple realities based on consciousness, gender, and experience. Some, however, differ as to whether our realities can be mutually understood or even reconciled. Disciplines that lean in the direction of postpositivism include sociology, nursing, history, and social work. However, these categories are not ironclad. Some disciplines, like education and psychology, have a place in both schools of thought.

The primary differences between the positivist and postpositivist are found in the notion of a singular reality (truth) and the objectivity of the researcher. On the basis of our understanding of epistemology and its role in research, we see that power is embedded in the very fabric of a discipline or field of study.

Most researchers are socialized in the values and practices of their discipline during their academic education and professional development. Gatekeepers such as faculty, staff, licensing bodies, and professional societies indoctrinate researchers in the history, goals, practices, and expectations of their chosen field. As previously mentioned, most disciplines clearly fall under one of the two primary epistemological schools of thought. As a result, some disciplines inherently regard the values, beliefs, customs, and practices of a community as barriers to research, whereas others embrace them as opportunities to engage in self-determination, decolonization, and social justice (Smith, 2002).

Scholars and researchers have noted that the lack of critical reflection about one's field can create a schism or bifurcation within the researcher, especially if the researcher is a member of a marginalized group. Patricia Hill Collins refers to this disconnect as "the outsider within" positioning of research (Collins, 1991). I can best explain this concept by using myself as an example. As a black female social worker and evaluator who was raised in South Central Los Angeles, I have some understanding of and proximity to oppression based on race, class, and gender inequities and its effect on the sexual decision making of black women. However, my education and training suggest that neither my personal experience nor the social and historical context of black women's relationship with their bodies is relevant to the landscape of my own HIV prevention research. My own struggle is not uncommon for a great many black researchers. They struggle with the disconnections between the demands of their own research and the realities encountered in working with other marginalized communities with whom they share lifelong relationships.

To reconcile the outsider-within struggle in my own research, I learned how to move the lived experiences of black women and HIV from the margins to the center of the conversation. This simply means I privilege the social context of black women's experiences in framing HIV prevention research. Among women in the United States affected by HIV, black women bear the greatest burden (Kaiser Family Foundation, 2014). Although black Americans represent only 12 percent of the U.S. population (Kaiser Family Foundation, 2014), they accounted for 44 percent of new HIV infections and an estimated 44 percent of people living with HIV in 2010. Black Americans also accounted for almost half of new AIDS diagnoses (49 percent) in 2011 (AIDS being the most advanced form of HIV). The rate of new HIV infections per 100,000 among black adults/adolescents (68.9) was nearly eight times that of white adults/adolescents (8.7) and more than twice that of Latino adults/adolescents (27.5) in 2010. The rate for black men (103.6) was the highest of any group, more than twice that of Latino men (45.5), the second highest group. Black women (38.1) had the third highest rate overall and the highest among women (Centers for Disease Control and Prevention [CDC], 2012). HIV was the fifth leading cause of death for black men and the seventh for black women ages 25–44 in 2010, ranking higher than for their respective counterparts in any other racial/ethnic group (CDC, 2014).

In light of the disproportionate burden of HIV among black women, it is more important than ever to understand why black women now account for over half of women living with HIV. As a social worker, I observed that HIV as an issue has been largely defined by the medical and public health professionals. This means that problems and solutions to HIV are generally seen as behavioral (for example, condom usage, number of partners, shared needles). As such, the social determinants of HIV have been given little attention. *Social determinants* refers to the conditions under which people live, work, play, and so on. These social conditions have immediate and long-term effects on the quality of people's health.

Several researchers have suggested that social determinants of health may be more salient to black women and may increase their sexual risk of HIV. Evidence indicates that the social and economic contexts of life differ dramatically for black women compared with white women in regard to income, education, housing, neighborhood quality, political power, morbidity, mortality, and sexual oppression (Adimora & Schoenbach, 2005) Social context is clearly an important influence on sexual behavior (Friedman, Cooper, & Osborne, 2009; Rothenberg, 2007). Sexual oppression and experiences of racial discrimination have been associated with black women's risk of other health conditions (McNair & Prather, 2004) and HIV risk (Wingood & DiClemente, 2000). Several authors have postulated that black women's risk of HIV may be a function of larger social and structural factors, such as sexual exploitation (Collins, 1991), segregation (Massey, 2005), economic marginalization (Zierler & Krieger, 1997), and mass incarceration (Braithwaite & Arriola, 2003; Mauer, 2003; Rothenberg, 2007). The ways in which black women in the United States experience, resist, and internalize these factors are unique but rarely explored. Placing the lived experiences of black women at the center of my research agenda has helped me to develop a more comprehensive approach to understanding black women's risk for HIV, one that takes into account the influence of sexual oppression, as well as larger social and structural influences.

In summary, for the researcher, the primary allure of scientific inquiry is its potential to provide information that fills a gap in knowledge. Whether the researcher is a positivist and believes in an objective truth or a postpositivist who seeks to provide the best possible answer available at the moment, the research is vulnerable to assumed knowledge and preconceptions. In addition, research questions are value-laden propositions that are reinforced through disciplinary training, education, and professional development—which may be experienced differently by researchers who identify with marginalized populations. As a result, we see that researchers encounter issues related to power regardless of their epistemological stance or social location. The following section explores how power shows up in the practice of research.

THE RESEARCH PROCESS

This section details where and how power issues manifest in the process of conducting research. In so doing, I define the five broad stages of the research cycle and discuss how power manifests itself in each stage. At the end of this discussion, the reader should understand how social scientists invite power dynamics into the research process through westernized thinking and the use of colonized methods.

How Do Issues Related to Power Show Up in the Research Cycle?

The social science research cycle occurs in the five sequential following stages: (1) problem/opportunity identification, (2) purpose, (3) conceptualization, (4) implementation, and (5) interpretation.

Problem/Opportunity

In this stage, the individual or entity that frames the research is exercising power. The notion of the "problem" is typically how research begins. A friend of mine added the "opportunity" part of the phrase several years ago because she felt defining everything as a problem was pathological. I agreed and continue to use it. This thinking supports Pinderhughes's one-up one-down scenario in the power theory (1989). This occurs in research when those who are the focus of the research become the saved objects of the benevolent researcher. As a result, the research subjects become a vulnerable population, chronically impaired by the very attention designed to help. No matter how good the principle behind such research, it is essentially impossible to implement without the built-in complications of the projection process. Pinderhughes went on to say that this dynamic can keep the victim, or research group, in relatively powerless positions where they serve as a balancing mechanism for the systems in which they exist.

Purpose

Purpose is where the goals, aims, and benefits of the research are explained.

Where power shows up. Much of research is formulated, designed, and executed without the input of the researched. This practice creates another power dynamic by placing the researched in a purely reactive situation. The researched are unable to exercise initiative, set goals, make choices, plan, or assume leadership (Pinderhughes, 1989). Consequently, the research subject fails to create a sense of mastery over life. In the final section, I explore more innovative approaches to research that attempt to remedy this imbalance.

Another power dynamic at this stage has implications for the researcher. Pinderhughes said that the result of having a position of power includes being controlling and/or dominating; expressing arrogance; and displaying paranoia that result from delusions of superiority, grandiosity, and an unrealistic sense of entitlement. The outcome may be vulnerability to having distorted perceptions and being unable to realistically assess one's own reality and that of the powerless. So in applying Pinderhughes's power theory to the research context, the pure gratification of having this type of power may encourage researchers to isolate and distance themselves from the researched, which, in turn, can result in a comfort with sameness and an intolerance of differences. Moreover, having power can create or satisfy a psychological need to have a victim, someone to scapegoat and control to maintain one's equilibrium. For example, in the case of black women and HIV prevention, behaviorally based perspectives rooted in the fields of medical and public health research tend to explain racial differences in HIV in terms of promiscuity among black women, which invokes notions of sexual tropes such as the Jezebel.

An example of how stereotypes influence scientific inquiry is Sarah Bartmann, also known as the Hottentot Venus. Bartmann, an enslaved African woman, was objectified and placed on public display for exhibition to the masses because scientific experts considered her genitalia and buttocks sensational and extraordinary. Commentators considered the genitalia of Bartmann and other African women as primitive and a sign of their sexual appetites. These beliefs became the foundation of Western thinking about and treatment of the black female body. According to Hammonds's (1995) scholarship, at the end of the 19th century, European experts in fields ranging from anthropology to psychology concluded that black female body embodied the notion of uncontrolled sexuality.

It was also during this time that the myths of the "Jezebel" and "Mammy" were born. African American women were seen as loose or whores and carried this label along with others such as "mammy" or "caretaker" in the eyes of their oppressors. Regardless of their free or enslaved status, these myths become closely associated with black women. They were seen as either nonsexual (Mammy) or hypersexual (Jezebel), but they were never seen as normal or human (Wallace, 1996).

As rates of sexually transmitted infections (STIs), especially syphilis, grew in the United States in the mid-19th century, black women were identified as the site of corruption and disease (Hammonds, 1995). The labels of "savage" and "primitive" justified the ideology that black women could not control their own bodies and, therefore, reinforced the need for male ownership and domination. The images of black women as savage and hypersexual remain with us in popular culture today. According to Kahn (2008), black women are generally portrayed as "Vixen," in sexist terms that conjure meanings similar to that of "Jezebel."

Rose (1994) puts black women's displays of their bodies in broader perspective when she argues that the black buttock has an especially charged place in history as a sign of sexual perversity as well as inferiority. The image invokes a nuanced history of white fascination with black female behinds, exemplified in the exhibition of Sara Bartmann as The Hottentot Venus in the early 1800s and the eroticized fascination with Josephine Baker's buttock-centered dances in the early 1900s. The image of the black female behind is revered and disdained at the same time by European standards.

The black female body has been and remains the site of a deeply rooted struggle for both black women and larger society. Although some research has reported that black women are protected from the adverse effects of these historical notions and contemporary media images (Fitts, 2008; Hudson; 1995; Miller-Young, 2008), others have highlighted that the sense of inferiority that many black women internalize when compared with the majority can put them at mental and physical risk (Hall, 1995; Krieger, 1990; McLune, 2008; Stephens & Phillips, 2003, 2005). The significance of this example is that it highlights how purpose sans historical context can perpetuate pathology-driven approaches that continue to oppress rather than liberate.

Conceptualization and Implementation

Conceptualization is the point in the research process where the project is detailed, including the sample, design, measurement, and data analysis. The research is executed in the implementation phase. Because conceptualization and implementation function together as idea and plan, I discuss them here jointly.

Where power shows up. I think the second most critical appearance of power in research occurs at the juncture of conceptualization and implementation. It is an interactive level characterized by dominance, obedience, or equality. Ultimately, this is the location at which the researcher decides the roles to be played by himself/herself and the researched, and the value of each. These choices have implications for all stakeholders on multiple levels.

A controversial example of the long-term consequences of the dominant–subordinate stance can be found in the Moynihan Report. In March 1965, a young political appointee in the Labor Department named Daniel Patrick Moynihan wrote a report warning of high levels of out-of-wedlock births in the black community. *The Negro Family: The Case for National Action* (Moynihan, 1967) noted that nearly a quarter of all black children were born out of wedlock, a ratio that had been rising since the end of World War II. Such a trend, Moynihan (1967) warned, could deepen black poverty rates and lead to a "tangle of pathologies." Although the Moynihan Report acknowledged structural factors such as slavery and growing urbanization for the state of the black community, it is remembered more for its criticism of black mothers and absentee fathers.

Interpretation

Interpretation is the point in the research process when the researcher translates the results in the context of the purpose of the research.

Where power shows up. Without the input of the researched, the interpretations of the researchers are vulnerable to internal biases or projections. Epistemology, as discussed in the first section, is the concept of an objective reality belonging to a school of thought that believes researchers are unbiased. Consequently, one can argue that the singular interpretations of a researcher can act as projections that are then used to provide justification for maintaining power and control over research participants. People in power then can blame the powerless for assuming these roles. If the powerless fail to do so, those in the more powerful roles can perceive them as having done so anyway or can become angry with them.

In summary, I share an African proverb: "Never let the lion tell the giraffe's story." This proverb means that the giraffe can never be the hero in a story told by its hunter. The problem begins with the research problem statement and is exacerbated throughout the remaining four stages of the research process. The voices of the researched are absent in the framing of the research questions, the methods used to find the information, and the interpretation of the results. This deficit-based approach to research is exemplified in the Moynihan Report.

DEMOCRATIZING RESEARCH

Finally, this section illustrates how power in research can be democratized by using practices and concepts that center the research question in the historical and social context of a person or group. This discussion is designed to show that using the liberating lens to focus on self-empowerment and opportunity shifts the problematic research paradigm to one that is empowering and inherently affirming.

The past 60 years have witnessed a surge in research approaches that are designed to be inclusive, affirming, and empowering for both the researcher and the researched. For that reason, I limit my discussion to three types of research methods that reflect my own social location as an African American woman trained as a social worker and program evaluator: Africentric research, feminist research, and community-based research.

Africentric Research

Several scholars have made important contributions in defining the concept of African-centered epistemology. An African-centered perspective is an orientation to data that places African people as key participants and agents in their shaping of their life opportunities and experiences (Asante, 1987; Karenga, 1989). Nobles (1985) said

> Afrocentric, Africentric, or African centered are interchangeable terms representing the concept which categorizes a quality of thought and practice which is rooted in the cultural image and interest of African people and which represents and reflects the life experiences, history, and traditions of African people as the center of analyses. It is their own scientific criterion for authenticating human reality. (p. 47)

Africentric scholars generally agree that there is a centering of the research in the lived experience of African people. To be centered simply means being well grounded in the history, culture, and understandings of African people and having their best interests at heart. Ruth Reviere (2001) developed the most concrete definitions of Africentric research to date. She outlined several canons based on the principles of Ma'at (quest for justice and harmony) and Nommo (productive word). The canons are Ukweli, Utulivu, Uhaki, Ujamaa, and Kujitoa.

- Ukweli: Grounds research in the experiences of the community being researched.
- Utulivu: Requires the researcher to actively avoid creating, exaggerating, or sustaining divisions between or within communities and strive for harmony within and between groups.

- Uhaki: Requires that the researcher ensure that the research process is fair to all participants, especially those being researched.
- Ujamaa: Requires the researcher recognize and maintain community and reject the separation between the researcher and participant.
- Kujitoa: Requires the researcher to make a commitment to the objectives and outcomes of the research.

All elements of the research process, from the framing of the research question to the data collection and analysis, are closely integrated with the five canons. Researchers are required to pay close attention to the role of power throughout the research process, from the source of the research question to the social and historical contexts of its existence. Critiques of Africentric research could argue that this approach does not specifically advocate for a gender-based perspective, which still makes it biased. However, one could use the overarching principle of Ma'at (justice) as a counterpoint.

Feminist Research

Feminist research acknowledges that patriarchal values and beliefs in our social world shape both the construction and definition of how research is done and how knowledge is determined. According to some postmodern researchers, male bias in the world determines how and why research is done and shapes the interpretation of data (Bowleg, Belgrave, & Reisen, 2000; hooks, 1984). The bias is usually that of white, middle-class, heterosexual men (Hawkesworth, 1989). Traditional social science research, with its claims to objectivity (in both qualitative and quantitative methods), is fundamentally flawed, because it does not recognize how its own biases affect the research process, from the choice of a topic to the final presentation of data.

Methodologically, feminist research differs from traditional research in three ways: (1) It actively seeks to remove the power imbalance between research and subject; (2) it is politically motivated and has a major role in changing social inequality; and (3) it begins with the standpoints and experiences of women. Sandra Harding (1987) argued that studying women from their perspective, recognizing the researcher as part of the research subject, and acknowledging that the beliefs of the researcher shape the research are the defining features of feminist research. I explore this concept further by examining the relationship between the researcher and subject.

First, the unequal power relationship between the researcher and the subject is restructured to validate the perspective of the participant. The premise is to remove the hierarchical relationship between researcher and participant. Second, feminist research is also defined by its use of feminist concerns and beliefs to ground the research process. Feminism takes women as its starting point, seeking to explore and uncover patriarchal social dynamics and relationships from the perspective of women. Third, feminist research is also committed to social change, arising from the actions of women to refuse the patriarchal social structure as it stands in favor of a more egalitarian society. Fourth, feminist research addresses the power imbalances between women and men and between women as active agents in the world. Finally, feminist research uses feminist principles throughout all stages of research, from choice of topic to presentation of data. These feminist principles also inform and act as the framework guiding the decisions being made by the researcher.

Community-Based Research Principles

Community-based research takes place in community settings and involves community members in the design and implementation of research projects (Minkler & Wallerstein, 2008). Such activities should demonstrate respect for the contributions of success that are made by community partners, as well as respect for the principle of doing no harm to the communities involved (Wallerstein & Duran, 2006). To achieve these goals, the following principles are used to guide the development of research projects involving collaboration between researchers and community partners, whether they are community-based organizations or informal groups of individual community members.

- Community partners should be involved at the earliest stages of the project, helping to define research objectives and providing input into how the project will be organized.
- Community partners should have real influence on project direction—that is, enough leverage to ensure adherence to the original goals, mission, and methods of the project.
- Research processes and outcomes should benefit the community. Community members should be hired and trained whenever possible and appropriate, and the research should help build and enhance community assets.
- Community members should be part of the analysis and interpretation of data and should have input into how the results are distributed. This does not imply censorship of data or of publication, but rather the opportunity to make clear the community's views about the interpretation before final publication.
- Productive partnerships between researchers and community members should be encouraged to last beyond the life of the project. This will make it more likely that research findings will be incorporated into ongoing community programs and therefore provide the greatest possible benefit to the community from research.
- Community members should be empowered to initiate their own research projects that address needs they identify themselves.

Each of the three research approaches discussed addresses issues of power in research from their inception. They acknowledge that history, context, and the active engagement of participants are central in mediating power differentials and producing relevant and useful research.

An Example

An example of how I incorporate context in my HIV prevention research is by using Linda Smith's indigenous research model (Smith, 2002). Smith's model is specifically designed to work with marginalized communities and deliberately seeks social justice, action, and self-determination. It includes a process of orientation and social justice identification. The orientation process includes four phases that move from survival, recovery, development, to self-determination. These phases serve to orient the research question toward an outcome that is in the best interest of the community. The social justice identification uses healing, decolonization, transformation, and mobilization to understand the phenomenon from the lived experiences of the community. When applying Smith's model to HIV prevention education, the research lens moves beyond the limited focus on behavior to include the historical sexual oppression of black women and its influence on individual and community perceptions. The example below combines elements of Africentrist, feminist, and community-based research.

The first orientation phase, survival, is represented by one-dimensional intervention approaches, such as protection-only HIV/AIDS strategies (for example, the distribution of condoms and dental dams). Barrier methods are important tools in preventing the spread of HIV. Unfortunately, tools without education have little sustained impact.

The second orientation phase, recovery, represents a return from a setback—that is, obtaining a state of normalcy. In the context of this conversation, normalcy is present in the form of instruction or education. To be instructive means that enough experience and information have been gained so that proactive rather than reactive measures can be taken. HIV education strategies are typically guided by theory or values (for example, cognitive–behavioral, health belief, faith based). However, behavior-driven frameworks minimize the importance of context. For example, ABC is a popular faith-based framework that emphasizes abstinence for youths. Although this HIV educational approach informs participants about the history and consequences of the disease, it advocates a narrow response that has little appeal beyond specific populations (such as fundamental Christians and public school officials).

The third orientation phase is development. In the context of HIV education, the combination of information, skill building, and use of protective methods allows individuals to gain knowledge and create skills that increase safe sex practices. Although these approaches facilitate efficacy around sexual relevance, they are generic in their knowledge base and thus lack cultural grounding. Consequently, they do not allow individuals to see their sexual choices in the context of culture and historical events.

Finally, the fourth orientation phase is self-determination. When self-determination is placed at the center of the HIV/AIDS education in the black community, the issue transcends socially imposed constructs of HIV to address issues of nonjudgmental, affirming definitions of sexual rights, behavior, and the practice of acts of self-love. Issues of healing, decolonization, transformation, and mobilization crystallize in the face of the historic struggle of ownership of the black body and its offspring.

This example illustrates the historical and social context that influenced the sexual experiences of black women for more than 400 years, as well as our understanding of how the myths of oppression may continue to influence our sexual thoughts and behaviors today. This approach to inquiry allows for the development of socially constructed knowledge rather than socially imposed knowledge. In centering the phenomenon of HIV prevention in the lived experiences of black women in America, other culturally relevant research questions emerge that otherwise would not have been raised. Those questions include, but are not limited to, the following: How have the effects of enslavement disconnected black men and women from their bodies? What is the extent to which oppressive myths have shaped our contemporary body images? How do these historical factors influence our gender identities and sexual practices? How can we reclaim and transform negative body images? How can we mobilize to reclaim notions of self?

CONCLUSION

This chapter was not intended to be an exhaustive overview of the multiple ways in which power and research manifest in the social science research process. Rather, its intention was to contribute to the discussion on power and research and illuminate ways in which oppressive ideologies and methodologies are embedded in the social science process and obscure other truths from view.

To cross over into the land of powerfree research, one has to commit transgressions against epistemological beliefs, leap over disciplinary hurdles, and slay internalized notions of objectivity. Although I learned these lessons long ago, it is good to be reminded of them as I continue on my research path. Sometimes it is important to be reminded that the struggle is not imagined.

REFERENCES

Adimora, A., & Schoenbach, V. (2005). Social context, sexual networks, and racial disparities in rates of sexually transmitted infections. *Journal of Infectious Disease, 191*, 115–122.

Asante, M. K. (1987). *The Afrocentric idea.* Philadelphia: Temple University Press.

Bowleg, L., Belgrave, F. Z., & Reisen, C. A. (2000). Gender roles, power strategies, and precautionary sexual self-efficacy: Implications for black and Latina women's HIV/AIDS protective behaviors. *Sex Roles, 42*, 613–635.

Braithwaite, R., & Arriola, K. (2003). Male prisoners and HIV prevention: A call for action ignored. *American Journal of Public Health, 93*, 759–763.

Centers for Disease Control and Prevention. (2012). *HIV surveillance supplemental report* (Vol. 17, No. 4). Atlanta: Author.

Centers for Disease Control and Prevention. (2014). *Fact sheet: HIV among African Americans.* Atlanta: Author.

Collins, P. (1991). *Black feminist thought: Knowledge, consciousness, and the politics of empowerment.* New York: Routledge.

Creswell, J. W. (2007). *Qualitative inquiry & research design: Choosing among five approaches* (2nd ed.). Thousand Oaks, CA: Sage Publications.

DuBois, J. M., Kraus, E., & Vasher, M. (2012). The development of a taxonomy of wrongdoing in medical practice and research. *American Journal of Preventive Medicine, 42*(1), 89–98.

Fanelli, D. (2009). How many scientists fabricate and falsify research? A systematic review and meta-analysis of survey data. *PloS One, 4*(5), e5738.

Fitts, M. (2008). "Drop it like it's hot": Culture industry laborers and their perspectives on rap music video production. *Meridians: Feminism, Race Transnationalism, 8*(1), 211–235.

Friedman, S., Cooper, H., & Osborne, A. (2009). Structural and social contexts of HIV risk among African Americans. *American Journal of Public Health, 99*, 1002–1008.

Guba, E. G., & Lincoln, Y. S. (2005). Paradigmatic controversies, contradictions and emerging confluences. In N. Denzin & Y. Lincoln (Eds.), *Handbook of qualitative research* (3rd ed., pp. 191–216). Thousand Oaks, CA: Sage.

Hall, C. C. (1995). Beauty is in the soul of the beholder: Psychological implications of beauty and African-American women. *Cultural Diversity and Mental Health, 1*(2), 125–137.

Hammonds, E. (1995). Black (w)holes and the geometry of black female sexuality. *Differences, 6*, 126–145.

Harding, S. (1987). Introduction: Is there a feminist method? In S. Harding (Ed.), *Feminism & methodology* (pp. 1–14). Bloomington: Indiana University Press.

Hawkesworth, M. (1989). Knowers, knowing, known: Feminist theories and claims of truth. *Signs, 14*, 533–557.

hooks, b. (1984). *Feminist theory: From margin to center.* Boston: South End.

Hudson, B. (1995). Images used by African Americans to combat negative stereotypes. In H. Harris, H. Blue, & E. Griffith (Eds.), *Racial and ethnic identity* (pp. 135–172). New York: Routledge.

Kahn, K. (2008). Critical debates on the politics of representing black American women in musical video productions. *Muziki, 4*(2), 263–270.

Kaiser Family Foundation. (2014). *Women and HIV/AIDS in the United States.* Retrieved from http://kff.org/hivaids/fact-sheet/women-and-hivaids-in-the-united-states/

Karenga, M. (1989). *The African American holiday of Kwanzaa: A celebration of family, community & culture.* Los Angeles: University of Sankore Press.

Krieger, N. (1990). Racial and gender discrimination: Risk factors for high blood pressure. *Social Science Medicine, 30*, 1273–1281.

Kuhn, T. (1962). *The structure of scientific revolutions.* Chicago: University of Chicago Press.

Massey, D. (2005). Race, class, and markets: Social policy in the 21st century. In D. Grusky & R. Kanbur (Eds.), *Poverty and inequality* (pp. 117–132). Palo Alto, CA: Stanford University Press.

Mauer, M. (2003). *Comparative international rates of incarceration: An examination of causes and trends.* Retrieved from http://www.sentencingproject.org/publications/comparative-international-rates-of-incarceration-an-examination-of-causes-and-trends/

McLune, J. (2008). *Celie's revenge: Hip-hop's betrayal of black women.* Retrieved from http://www.saidit.org/archives/jan06/article4.html

McNair, L. D., & Prather, C. M. (2004). African American women and AIDS: Factors influencing risk and reaction to HIV disease. *Journal of Black Psychology, 30*, 106–123.

Memmi, A. (1965). *The colonizer and the colonized.* Boston: Beacon Press.

Menand, L. (2002). Morton, Agassiz, and the origins of scientific racism in the United States. *Journal of Blacks in Higher Education, 34,* 110–113.

Miller-Young, M. (2008). Hip-hop honeys and da hustlaz: Black sexualities in the new hip-hop pornography. *Meridians: Feminism, Race Transnationalism, 8*(1), 261–292.

Minkler, M., & Wallerstein, N. (Eds.). (2008). *Community-based participatory research for health: From process to outcomes* (2nd ed.). San Francisco: Jossey-Bass.

Moynihan, D. P. (1967). *The Negro family: The case for national action.* Washington, DC: U.S. Department of Labor, Office of Planning and Research.

Nobles, W. (1985). *Africanity and the black family: The development of a theoretical model.* Berkeley, CA: Institute for the Advanced Study of Black Family Life and Culture.

Pinderhughes, E. (1989). *Understanding race, ethnicity, and power: The key to efficacy in clinical practice.* New York: Free Press.

Reviere, R. (2001). Toward an Afrocentric research methodology. *Journal of Black Studies, 31,* 709–728.

Rose, T. (1994). *Black noise: Rap music and black culture in contemporary America.* Middletown, CT: Wesleyan University Press.

Rothenberg, R. (2007). Maintenance of endemicity in urban environments: A hypothesis linking risk, network structure and geography. *Sexually Transmitted Infection, 83*(1), 10–15.

Smith, L. (2002). *Decolonizing methodologies: Research and indigenous peoples.* London: Zed, Ltd.

Stephens, D. P., & Phillips, L. D. (2003). Freaks, gold diggers, divas, and dykes: The sociohistorical development of African American female adolescent scripts. *Sexuality and Culture, 7,* 3–47.

Stephens, D. P., & Phillips, L. D. (2005). Integrating black feminist thought into conceptual frameworks of African American adolescent women's sexual scripting processes. *Sexualities, Evolution, and Gender, 7,* 37–55.

Wallace, M. (1996). *Black macho and the myth of the superwoman.* New York: Verso.

Wallerstein, N., & Duran, B. (2006). Using community-based participatory research to address health disparities. *Health Promotion Practice, 7*(3), 312–323.

Washington, H. (2007). *Medical apartheid: The dark history of medical experimentation on black Americans from colonial times to the present.* New York: Doubleday.

Wingood, G. M., & DiClemente, R. J. (2000). Application of the theory of gender and power to examine HIV-related exposures, risk factors, and effective interventions for women. *Health Education and Behavior, 27,* 539–565.

Zierler, S., & Krieger, N. (1997). Reframing women's risk: Social inequalities and HIV infection. *Annual Review Public Health, 18,* 401–436.

16

Re-methodologizing Research: Queer Considerations for Just Inquiry

Julie Tilsen

I go through the world with the wind at my back for the most part: white, American, educated, able-bodied, cisgender, middle-class, professional. As a queer-identified, Jewish (nonreligious) woman, I also occupy locations that are marginalized to varying degrees in varying contexts. When approaching any research project, it is important to me to remain cognizant of ways in which my age, class, and position as a professional represent privilege and authority to those participating in research with me. It is important to construct a research process that disrupts the opaqueness around issues of power and authority that typically are required by conventional research methods.

In this chapter, I describe a queer theory–informed,[1] constructionist research project that I facilitated with a group of queer youths. In Part 1, I discuss the philosophy, principles, and practices that guided this research and that inform a queer analysis of power. In Part 2, I tell the story of this research as an endeavor that brought to life the "doing" of power as a discursive achievement—that is, an exercise of power—I shared with the youths.

DESCRIPTION OF THE RESEARCH

The research focused on the question, "How do queer youths construct a queer identity within a homonormative context?" My intention was to center queer youths' experiences

---

[1] Queer theory is a set of critical practices intended to complicate hegemonic assumptions about the continuities between anatomical sex, gender identity, sexual identity, sexual object choice, and sexual practice. It rejects biological theories of sexual identity. For a useful introduction, please see Jagose (1996).

of identity by creating a queer space for conversations. I approached their insider knowledges as one of two discursive frames that I would draw on to articulate a queer therapeutic practice. The other discursive frame was that of academic literacies from queer and poststructural theories. The research attempts to bridge the gap between the practice of therapy and the bodies of scholarship generated within interdisciplinary fields of study, such as queer theory and cultural studies (Tilsen, 2010). The research was done for my PhD program through the Taos Institute in collaboration with Tilburg University.[2] The program is explicitly focused on constructionist methods of inquiry and practice.

PART 1: FROM METHODOLOGY TO RE-METHODOLOGIZING

Power Is What We Do, Not What We Have

How is power conceptualized when engaging in queer theory–informed constructionist forms of inquiry? Constructionists are interested in language practices[3] and what people make together through their engagements (whether or not this making leads to something desired or planned). We view language as productive, not as merely descriptive. In other words, language does things (Austin, 1962). Power, then, is the capacity to proliferate discursive possibilities. As a nonessentialist, discursively focused frame, social construction understands power not as an attribute or commodity contained within a person or held by an institution; rather, power is about discourse, where discourse is understood as what gets to be said, by whom, with what authority, and with what effects.

Foucault (1970) defined *discourse* as a "social practice" that circulates through culture. Discourse acts as a governor on what may or may not be said and done. We cannot speak, think, feel, or act outside of the influence of discourse. Even resistance to the regulating effects of discourse gains its meaning through its relationship to discourse.

As a queer theory–informed poststructuralist, Foucault (1978a, 1978b, 1985, 1986; Gordon, 1980; Morris & Patton, 1988) is a major influence on my analysis of power. Foucault's conceptualization of power is notable for its opposition to the structuralist notion of power as being held by dominant groups in society. Rather, Foucault maintained that power is multidirectional and contextual. Power is deployed by people in particular situations and may produce new outcomes in the form of resistance to dominating discourses. Power is an action, something that is exercised and not possessed. One of the tenets of Foucault's (1978b) analysis is that "where there is power there is resistance" (p. 95). This notion, in particular, affords subjugated people's participatory status in the production of meaningful discourse that gives visibility to their lived experiences while exposing oppressive social apparatus.

Although power is multidirectional and discursively produced, that does not mean that all exercises of power are equal in their scope and ability to exert social–political influence. Indeed, this is precisely why the Foucauldian analysis of discourse as power

---

[2] http://www.taosinstitute.net/phd-program; http://www.tilburguniversity.edu/
[3] Language practices are all embodied social interaction.

is compelling: It breathes meaning and possibility into both hegemonic and counterhegemonic exercises of power. By situating acts of resistance within the broader narrative of subjugating exercises of power, these often small acts may be read as significant and ripe with rhizomatic possibilities.[4]

Undoing Assumptions in Research

What are the implications for research when one is equipped with a Foucauldian analysis of power situated within a constructionist worldview? To begin with, I approach research with an eye toward disrupting conventional assumptions about research, knowledge, and truth. I view the Western scientific notion of research as one possible discursive frame—albeit an authoritative one—which may be questioned to create paths for new ways of understanding and making meaning in the world. This perspective unhinges ontological and epistemological assumptions of Western science and thus makes room for other forms of inquiry. Research is revealed as culturally contingent, reflecting the local understandings and values of those involved (McNamee & Hosking, 2012; Smith, 1999; Wilson, 2008). Thus, I am interested in doing research that resonates culturally and ethically with the communities in which I engage.

Another assumption (within positivist and postpositivist research) is that the goal of research is to discover the objective truth about something. Constructionist inquiry is instead interested in giving voice to the multiple realities of people's lived experiences, whereby value is not placed on a singular truth but on consideration of the possibilities generated. Furthermore, constructionists acknowledge that inquiry is productive of new possibilities and that the very goal of research is to be generative, not definitive.

Finally, assumptions about methodology are exposed, leading to what I call "re-methodologizing": a reimagined fluid process that is informed by, and responsive to, the local values and experiences of research participants. Linguistically, moving from the static noun, "methodology" to the dynamic verb, "methodologizing" emphasizes the ongoing, emergent process of this inquiry.

What does this mean for the actual practice of research? It means positioning oneself as refusing to maintain fidelity to any particular methodology or protocol. My commitment is to my participants and to the facilitation of a conversational space that would allow them to bring as much of themselves as they want to bring to the process. Insisting on adherence to a methodology (that is created outside of the inquiry itself) would undermine the values that I seek to bring to this endeavor. These values include:

- Accountability to relations of power: This means treating participants as experts in their lives and ensuring space for the performance of these knowledges. My commitment to upholding this value is informed, in part, by Foucault's (1978a,

---

[4] Deleuze and Guattari (1987) use the metaphor of the rhizome (a root system of plants characterized by their underground, decentralized, horizontal shoots with multiple entryways) as a way to resist hierarchical, linear, and finite conceptualizations of identity, relationship, and making meaning. It is a common conceptual resource among poststructural practitioners and researchers.

1978b) critique of knowledge production based on systems of discipline and punishment. By attending to the power relations inherent in research, I am focused on finding ways to produce knowledge that resist disciplinary or confessional practices.

- Transparency: This means involving participants in my inner dialogue as well as situating my ideas and questions. Being transparent by making available to the research participants my ideas, plans, thoughts, and purposes is a practice of accountability.

- Self-reflexivity: This refers to what Parker (2005) described as "enthusiastic self-questioning rather than fanatical certainty" (p. 21). This is a contextualization and examination of what's going on within me so that I may make accountable decisions in the research process and in my relationships with the participants.

- Responsiveness: This means that I am providing respectful, relevant, non-tokenizing responses to participants' comments and concerns.

- Social poetics/conversational imagination: By allowing the process to unfold without the imposition of external methodological constraints (that is, constraints embodied within a methodology that is produced before and outside of the research conversation itself), the possibilities for a proliferation of identity performances, new knowledges, and emergent meanings gain freedom. McNamee (2000) stated, "to talk of the poetic is to give wing to the imaginative" (p. 146). Poetics is a crafting of new meanings, and social poetics points to how people create meaning together.

These principles serve as the ethical guidelines for my research encounters. At the center of these ethics is a decentering of expert knowledge to bring forward knowledge of the participants. McNamee (1994) pointed out that so-called research subjects are chosen because of their expertise in the area of inquiry. By intentionally making space that centers on this expertise, I hope to acknowledge "that there are multiple forms of description" (p. 73) as I seek to construct an inquiry process in which the inevitability of my own descriptions are mitigated by the voices of the participants. Thus, constructing a discursive space that allows participants to bring the multiplicity of their voices to the conversation is essential to the ethical constitution of the inquiry process.

From Therapist to Researcher: Blurring the Lines of Practice

Another assumption that permeates conventional notions of research is that research is distinct from practice. As a therapist-cum-researcher, I sought ways to break this binary to open up possibilities within both disciplines.

By specifically discussing research practices that blur the line between therapy and research, McNamee (1988, 1989, 2000) provided a useful link between the two domains. Contending that therapy, at its best, is a discovery process, and that research, at its best, provides a therapeutic experience, McNamee (2000) argued for a research that is free "from the constraints of traditional forms of practice" (p. 146). McNamee (2000) envisioned research that is relationally engaged, unencumbered by "specific techniques or strategies that will produce valid research" (p. 148). Research becomes not a search for truth but a conversation through which participants perform multiple truths. Indeed, in terms of validity, McNamee (2000) asserted, "validity is an issue of the politics of the research (of the rhetoric within which it is constructed)." This articulation of research as intervention—and, more pointedly, that "useful or generative research and useful or generative therapy are more similar to each other . . . than they are different" (McNamee & Tomm, 1986, p. 18)—has provided me the conceptual support and methodological validation to engage in research in a manner consistent with my preferred ethics.

A relationally engaged process cannot be contained or constrained by predetermined methods. Smith (1999), Parker (2005), and Diversi and Moreira (2009) argued for the use of methodologies that originate from and are generated by the communities being researched. In McNamee's constructionist terms, this involves choosing a discursive frame for our research that is valid to the communities we are working with as they constitute validity. Constructionist research seeks to create ways of generating knowledge, as well as giving recognition to the kinds of knowledges that go unrecognized. The way in which knowledge is generated and *what* is generated cannot be separated, as they exist in a recursive, discursive relationship. Imposing adherence to recognized methodologies is a colonial act that functions as a dividing practice (Foucault, 1965, 1973).[5] By unhinging research from the hegemonic hold of the received view of science (Woolgar, 1996),[6] an opportunity for other people, their ways of generating knowledge, and their ways of knowing may be created. By definition, any adherence to a methodology will always render fidelity to that methodology rather than to the individuals involved.

At the heart of such a process is an intentional undoing of conventional notions of power and positionality that define traditional research practices. By entering into a relational, dialogical process with others within a community that will have its own notions about and preferences for how we are positioned with power and authority, we are surrendering "the much-denied yet prevailing academic ideology of 'scholar knows best'" (Diversi & Moreire, 2009, p. 31). This undoing is facilitated by asking questions such as:

- Who has the authority to ask research questions?
- Who has the authority to intrude into people's lives to do research?
- Who owns the concept of research?
- Who is granted the authority to name and claim some practices as legitimate research and others as illegitimate?
- Where does this authority to name and the power to define certain practices as research come from?

---

[5] Dividing practices are methods of objectification through social and spatial regulation that gain authority through the institutional power of science (or pseudoscience) and impose specifying identities on individuals. I am expanding on Foucault's original meaning here and arguing that those with the power to impose specifications on individuals also do so when some practices are deemed worthy of being called research while others are not. The consequence is that some knowledges are made invisible because of their lack of compliance with accepted methods.

[6] The received view of science refers to the Western post-Enlightenment tradition of empiricism and logical positivism.

By asking critical questions, thus exposing the dominant paradigm of research and its effects on people, constructionist research holds the promise of being radical and liberatory, subversive and transformative (Parker, 2005).

Resources for Liberatory Research

Constructionist philosophy and a Foucauldian analysis have opened the door to other theoretical resources that inform my approach to power relations. Looking outside of the traditional tropes of social science research provides both philosophical and methodological resources for a liberatory research pedagogy that centers discursive production as a means of exercising power. These are the very same resources that I had been engaged with as a therapist and educator for many years before I carried them into the research realm.

For example, youth–adult partnership approaches (Norman, 2001; Zeldin, McDaniel, Topitzes, & Lorens, 2001; Zeldin & Petrokubi, 2006) have informed my position on creating experiences with youths that embody mutuality in learning, leadership, and participation. Similarly, ideas from liberatory education (Freire, 1999; hooks, 1994) have further fueled my commitment to practices that are transparent, responsive, and reciprocal.

Finally, my training as a narrative therapist contributes immensely to my resolve to stay reflexively engaged with issues of representation, inclusion, and power. As a narrative therapist, I owe much to pioneers in cultural anthropology. For example, Bruner (1986a, 1986b) challenged the distinction between researcher and researched, paving the way for a therapeutic practice premised on "co-research" (Epston, 1999) that is at the heart of narrative therapy. Geertz (1973, 1985) suggested that the anthropologist's task is to bring forward insider knowledges and to invite "thick descriptions,"[7] a practice essential to narrative therapy that I also place at the center of research.

Interestingly, many therapists espouse an unyielding postmodern ethic—up to the point of research. This kind of theoretical incoherence is somehow rationalized by the hegemonic status of the scientific method. For me, this begs a litany of questions, such as:

- How can one espouse a constructionist philosophy and embrace the practices informed by it up to the point of research and then abandon those ideas as summarily inappropriate, less than, useless, and meaningless when it comes to research?
- What does one's willingness to renounce postmodern principles and relational ethics when it comes to research suggest about one's relationship with their postmodern principles and ethics?
- Isn't a cornerstone of the postmodern project to unhinge the unquestioned authority embedded within language and move from fixed to fluid, rigid to pliable, to make room for a proliferation of possibilities, including (especially?) those from nondominant locations or with nonorthodox ways?

---

[7] Geertz, in introducing this term to ethnographic research, credits Ryle (1949) with the original usage. *Thick description* refers to a situated description that extends beyond observation of behavior to one that brings forward the meaning and significance of what is described.

- Who benefits and who suffers from the accepted construction of legitimate versus illegitimate research?
- How did "research" become synonymous with "empiricism" and exclusive of all other forms of knowledge?

Questions such as these can help to further deconstruct the assumed superiority and universality of modernist epistemologies and methodologies and thus create space for other forms of inquiry.

Queer Theory, Radical Research

Because this research was an inquiry with queer youths about how they construct a queer identity, finding a methodology that was culturally consonant required a queer process.[8] I wanted to engage in an inquiry process that would be both philosophically congruent with the basic tenets of queer as well as resonant with queer youths' lives. This was not merely for purposes of theoretical consistency; it also was about creating a process that would be accountable to and inclusive of the queer lives of the youths with whom I would be working. This act alone would stand in opposition to standard research practices and, as such, would embrace a queer politic of resisting norms. Similarly, *to queer* something is an emergent process of disrupting expected norms in such a way that, while new possibilities unfold, standard practices—reified through discourse and methodically unquestioned—become open for interrogation. Thus, a queered research is not for queers only. It is for those who seek to resist the normalizing project of modernity and exercise power through the discursive production of emergent narratives.

Halberstam (1998) provided a critical treatment of what a queer methodology might entail in her description of her interdisciplinary research. Queer methodology, according to Halberstam, "attempts to remain supple enough to respond to the various locations of information . . . and betrays a certain disloyalty to conventional disciplinary methods" (p. 10). Halberstam maintained that central to the queerness of such a methodology is its refusal to participate in conventional methodologies. Furthermore, Halberstam suggested that a "queer methodology . . . is a scavenger methodology that uses different methods to collect and produce information on subjects who have been deliberately or accidentally excluded from traditional studies. . . . Queer methodology . . . refuses the academic compulsion toward disciplinary coherence" (p. 13). Halbertam's articulation reflects both a *queer methodology*—one that embodies fluidity and refusal to be clearly defined in accepted (acceptable?) terms—and a *queering of methodology*: an emergent process of troubling standard practices.

Whereas Halberstam is guided by disciplinary "disloyalty" as a matter of political resistance, Parker (2005) argued against fidelity to a particular methodology on the

---

[8] *Queer* is a critique of identity categories, an act of resistance against naming and dividing practices that demand stable, essentialist binary notions of identity. Also, *queer* stands in opposition to "normal" (Warner, 1999) as a political statement and embodiment of resistance. Thus, queer research will not be compliantly constrained within the methodological parameters of a particular research methodology.

basis of a rather resistant and queered version of best practice. Asserting that "the best research does not allow itself to be defined by its methodology alone" (p. 11), Parker campaigned for a dialogical (Bakhtin, 1981) process characterized by collective participation. A dialogical methodology invites us to ignore/blur boundaries between different approaches to create a process that emerges relationally among coresearchers. Such a process is constituted in the interview process, taking pieces of certain methods that invite conversations that are meaningful to participants and refusing to be limited by maintaining fidelity to one method.

Parker (2005) staked his position, in part, on the same theoretical ground that undergirds queer theory: feminism and the work of Foucault (1978b, 1985). Noting that feminist theory (for example, Harding, 1987; Hartsock, 1987; Rowbotham, Segal, & Wainwright, 2013) has provided the most significant innovation in qualitative research, Parker highlights the illumination of power available through feminist analysis. Parker stated that the feminist assertion that "knowledge is different for the powerful than it is for the oppressed" is the "key methodological point" (p. 2). Whose knowledge will be privileged in any given inquiry becomes a political and ethical question. In my inquiry, I attempted to create a process that would center the knowledges of queer youths, a constituency whose knowledges typically are not privileged.

Parker also points to Foucault's ideas about the production of knowledge, or how we know what we know. Foucault (1978a, 1978b; Gordon, 1980; Morris & Patton, 1988) argued that history is always represented through a contemporary lens. This serves to legitimate what we do and how we think about things. Professional disciplines and traditional research methodologies function as what Foucault (1978a) called "regimes of truth" that circulate knowledge produced by the practices through which they are known. Thus, the production of knowledge becomes even more important than the knowledge itself. The research implication of a Foucauldian analysis of knowledge production asserts that it is more critical to focus on the *process of research rather than the objects we attempt to know*" (Parker, 2005, p. 3). Parker's favoring of a feminist critique and a Foucauldian analysis points to a radical shift from conventional power operations of research methodologies.

PART 2: THE STORY OF THIS RE-METHODOLOGY

Part 1 outlined the philosophical and theoretical foundations that inform re-methodologizing research and how power relations are understood. Part 2 tells the story of the research project with a group of queer youths in which these ideas were put into action.

Language

Rejecting the use of the term "subject" (a misnomer even in traditional research, as subjects really serve as objects of study) for "participant" or "coresearcher" better reflects the collaborative and relational nature of both the ethic and the practice of this research.

I referred to the group of youths who worked with me as "the research team," as it felt more inclusive and representative of my hopes that collectively we would all experience the endeavor as something that needed each of us, if in differing capacities. I was clear in my head and my gut that they were not objects of study, and I fully believed that we all had things to teach and learn from each other. As the process unfolded, there were ways in which the language became more and more cumbersome for the simple yet significant reason that the relationships I was developing were becoming ones for which I felt great fondness. These were the individual relationships I was in with Daniel, Roberto, Marco, Carly, and Sophie.[9] And, it was the relationship I had with the collective: who we were as a gathering of six people, embodying the axiom, "the whole is greater than the sum of its parts."

As a result of the connection I had with the group and the five youths who composed it, I named the team The Q-Squad.[10] Our mission: to engage in a queering[11] process that destabilizes traditional understandings of research to privilege the knowledges and lived experiences of queer-identified youths in a way that is coherent in its methodology with those experiences. The Q-Squad functioned as (a) a signifier describing the wholeness that was produced by our coming together; (b) an expression of my affection for the individuals, the group, and the process; and (c) an expression of a sense of irony and humor for an endeavor that is typically wrought with inflexibility and self-importance.

The Creation of The Q-Squad

An inquiry based on insider knowledges required some insiders to recruit a research team. I borrowed on my relationship with Carly and Sophie, two queer youths I had met previously at a queer youth camp. Carly had graduated with her degree in women's and gender studies, and Sophie was in her last year of the same program. As such, they brought with them a combination of insider knowledges and academic literacies, the two discursive frames that would inform the dissertation.

We met to talk about moving forward. Of particular interest to them was the focus on homonormativity.[12] Sophie and Carly both thought that this focus would bring a critical edge to the conversation, and they saw value in bringing forward queer youth resistance to homonormativity because they both were living that struggle.

Sophie and Carly were also interested in influencing the process of the inquiry. Together, we identified broad topic areas of discussion, including ideas about queer

---

[9] These are pseudonyms.

[10] For a full description of each Q-Squad member, as written by each of the youths, see Tilsen (2010) and Tilsen (2013).

[11] I think of "queering" as an action that is always occurring, never complete, defined nor definitive, rather than as the adjective "queer" that describes a fixed process.

[12] Homonormativity (Duggan, 2002) describes "a politics that does not contest dominant heteronormative assumptions and institutions but upholds and sustains them while promising the possibility of a demobilized gay constituency and a privatized, depoliticized gay culture anchored in domesticity and consumption" (p. 179).

identity and homonormativity, sex, experiences with therapists, and pop culture. These would end up guiding the inquiry meetings and serving as the chapters of the dissertation. We also discussed providing ways for the reflections and feedback of the research team members to be written in response to my writing. For me, including their writing served as an act of accountability: Asking them to author responses to what I had written served as a further privileging of their voices. It also extended the conversation in both content and process, furthering the possibility for the generation of ideas. In addition, the inclusion of research participants' comments in the final document continued the project of destabilizing traditional notions of research that privilege so-called expert knowledge. And, as such, it's a queer practice.[13]

During our planning meeting, we discussed issues of representation and safety in consideration of whom to invite to join us. For example, we talked about wanting to include queer youths from a variety of social locations while also being mindful about the experience of "being the only one" in a group. One idea they offered to mediate this was to organize a group of participants who knew each other and who would agree collectively to form the team. This way, we speculated, individual participants might find some support and safety already embedded within their relationships with each other. Also, we agreed that, although representation is important in a queer conversation about homonormativity (given that homonormativity embodies a middle-class, white, consumer-culture experience), we didn't want the group to become unwieldy in numbers. We fully realized that there was no such thing as full representation of every possible social location. The focus of the inquiry and its limitation could be named, and we still could assemble a group that offered diverse perspectives.

They contacted three friends who they thought would be interested in participating and who would represent various queer ways of being. This included a pair of siblings, Marco and Roberto, and another mutual friend, Daniel, who also happened to be Marco's roommate. When we met, I was interested in finding out why they were interested in participating in the research. Here are some of their comments from that meeting:

- Everyone I know has different experiences; no one is the same.
- I don't see myself represented in a lot of the TV shows and movies about gay people.
- It's about time people had a better grasp of who queer youth are.
- The stereotype is that we're defined by the bar. I could never define myself there. (Tilsen, 2010, p. 69)

We discussed anonymity. All five participants wanted to have their names associated with their comments. They were clear that they felt that "having a voice" also included claiming their voice. I assured them that we would revisit this before the ink was dry and the document sent to press. Parker (2005) challenged the research practice of maintaining anonymity as a matter of convenience, not ethics.

---

[13] Sophie and Carly wrote reflections/responses that were published in my dissertation and book.

> To conceal the identity of research participants might be the most convenient and easiest option, but not actually the most ethical one. One of the effects of the attempt to conceal a participant's identity is that they are thereby denied the very voice in the research that might originally have been claimed as its aim. It confirms one of the prevalent images of those who are researched by psychologists as fragile beings needing to be protected by others (McLaughlin, 2003, p. 17).

Each of the five youths participating wrote a brief biography that was included in the dissertation. All statements from the inquiry process used in the text were attributed to the youths who made them.

I introduced the idea of having them contribute by generating some questions that they would like to speak to and that would help organize the conversations. They were not particularly interested in generating questions, preferring to "just have a conversation." We talked about what a queer methodology might be, and I explained that there really wasn't much about that in the literature. We agreed that what we would be venturing into together would indeed be queer in method, if for no other reason than "queer doesn't follow the rules" (Tilsen, 2010, p. 70).

Setting

At the initial meeting, I checked to see whether they would be comfortable meeting at my house, and whether the location was accessible for them. They agreed to meet at my house. I told them that I would compensate them financially and that I would feed them each time we met. Although I fully believed that "compensation" would be experienced through meaningful change for each individual (myself included), I also knew that I was the one who would walk away with at least two things that carry economic value in our culture: an advanced degree and a publishable document. It was important to me, as a practice of accountability, to respect their time and contributions in a similar way.

Meeting at my house (cats curled up on the couch), sharing food, and lingering in conversation after each inquiry session created a warm, friendly, and queer experience that I came to love and now remember with affection. It also disrupted conventional power relations, and this did not go unnoticed by the team. Below are some of their comments about how they experienced the setting:

- It's a really relaxed setting. I'm really comfortable.
- I was thinking about this earlier as I was sitting in a café. If we weren't doing this here, like this, there's probably a lot of things I wouldn't say.
- I'd probably censor myself.
- Or, if we were at the university, doing it more traditionally, or if we were at a therapist type setting, like all of that can change the dynamic of it. I think this is an interesting way to queer it.
- I didn't feel like all day, 'oh my god I have to go and do this thing where I have to sit and talk.' I think it's energizing that we're eating and drinking and I'm happy to be here. (Tilsen, 2010, pp. 72–73)

These comments reflect how the relationship between the setting and the methodology were mutually influential and supportive of each other: The setting was both facilitated by and facilitative of a conversational space of inquiry that featured a methodology reliant on transparency, shared reflexivity, and a coconstructed dialogical process committed to flexibility and embracing uncertainty.

Process of Inquiry

So, what *did* we do? What did we talk about and how did we talk about it? For the most part, the six meetings were guided by the research question and the "topic of the day." As previously discussed, topics were generated in the preliminary meeting I had with Sophie and Carly. I often would reflect before the meeting on some considerations from the literature and experiences that I've had with queer youths to help me generate a few initial questions. Typically, these questions were to invite participants to talk about their experiences with or thoughts about the topic at hand. I would start with these, opening the floor for anyone to respond, and usually, a lively conversation ensued. Essentially, this is the dialogical research process described in Part 1. This process features the following:

- Interviewees positioned as coresearchers
- Interview content and process negotiated with coresearchers
- Moving from individualized accounts to collective co-participation
- A process that emerges relationally and is constituted in the interview process (Parker, 2005)

Each member of the Q-Squad was sent a copy of the transcript of each meeting to review, and I began every meeting by asking whether there was anything from the previous meeting's transcript that they wanted to follow up on or adjust. At times, when I had a particular idea that I wanted to ask about, or if I felt that we had drifted too far afield from the questions that were relevant to the research focus, I would attempt to be transparent and situate my question and comment for the team as I worked our way back. In this way, I attempted to balance cocreation and fluidity with the assertion of leadership and purpose.

Impact of the Inquiry Process

The efforts to re-methodologize the research were not lost on the Q-Squad. In our final meeting, I asked about their experience of the process, what stood out for them, and in what ways they saw it contributing to their participation. In the following excerpt from our last meeting, a discussion of safety serves to highlight what stood out for them around the process of this inquiry:

- Hanging out before helped.
- I think that it wouldn't have been possible to talk in that way if we had been just sitting down and go, go, go.

- I feel like I can remember points where we all interacted with someone else's comment . . . instead of someone saying 'this is what I think' and then someone else, 'this is what queer is to me' . . . it created its own life.
- I think that we met at your home and you were comfortable enough to have these strange people in your home.
- The way that you've been very welcoming and down to earth and personable, rather than being very closed off, and like, analyzing things. I think that really helps because it brings a really human level to it. (Tilsen, 2010, pp. 75–76)

The team's observations about how safety emerged without a formal discussion of it[14] may be understood in many ways. From my position as the researcher and facilitator of the process, their experience of the inquiry as safe enough is evidence that the efforts to re-methodologize the inquiry process and create a relational, responsive conversational space were successful—not only because of my efforts but also because of theirs.

IN-QUEERY: DOING JUST RESEARCH

From Dialogue to Written Word

How did I use the words of my coresearchers? What did I do to ensure that the values and analysis of power relations that informed the project from the beginning are reflected in my treatment of the conversations? It was never my intention to collect data, analyze them, and render some kind of authoritative interpretation. In fact, I believe that the stories shared by the members of the Q-Squad *are* the analysis of their experience. I told the participants from the beginning that my plan was to pepper the dissertation with excerpts from the conversations. By placing their comments alongside the theoretical arguments I was making, I was hoping to bring forward the relationship between queer theory and lived experience, demonstrating how two discursive frames may articulate similar concepts very differently. The value of theory is found only when it serves to elevate the lived experiences and insider knowledges of marginalized people. I wanted to honor the authority of participants' perspectives by including their comments directly in the text.

My interpretation would take place in my selection of some excerpts and in my use and placement of them in certain sections of the document. I made these decisions primarily by choosing things that stood out for me as particularly poignant, provocative, or representative of a perspective that may not be available for many practitioners. I chose articulations of Q-Squad members' experiences and ideas that made queer theory more available and real and that brought to life the process of relationally engaged identity construction. Finally, I queered the scholarship process and destabilized conventional power relations by including the written reflections of Carly and Sophie in the body of my dissertation.

---

[14] Carly, Sophie, and I did talk about safety considerations when we met and talked about the forming of the team. This was previously discussed.

What was learned from this research? I learned that by inviting queer youths into a conversational space, new ideas for therapeutic practice emerge. These ideas include using queer theory as a theoretical resource that respects nonnormative identities, engaging in reflexive conversations, undoing conventional notions of development and interiority, and decentering adult/professional expertise. Conversations influenced by these practices provide rich discursive soil for the cultivation of power, as they produce a bounty of possibilities.

Just Research

Why do we do research? I do research—and I do it as I have described it here—to engage in scholarship that challenges the norms that legitimate certain forms of knowledges and knowledge production over others. I do this research because it allows me to stay grounded in my relational ethic of inclusive justice, experience embodied participation (mine and others), and participate in an "effort to resist the process of assimilation" (Diversi & Moreria, 2009, p. 178). Re-methodologizing research premised on queer theory principles of resisting normativity and allowing for the proliferation of ways of being makes social science inquiry a project of social justice. It is just research.

As such, the process of in-queery can serve to disrupt reductionistic and essentializing representations of marginalized people, confront the privileging of academic literacies over insider knowledges, and reconnect the stories of people's lives with their rightful authors: themselves. In this way, queering the research process is not for queers only.

REFERENCES

Austin, J. L. (1962). *How to do things with* words. Cambridge, MA: Harvard University Press.

Bakhtin, M. (1981). *The dialogical imagination.* Austin: University of Texas Press.

Bruner, E. (1986a). Ethnography as narrative. In V. Turner & E. Bruner (Eds.), *The anthropology of experience* (pp. 139–155). Chicago: University of Illinois Press.

Bruner, E. (1986b). Experience and its expression. In V. W. Turner & E. M. Bruner (Eds.), *The anthropology of experience* (pp. 3–20). Chicago: University of Illinois Press.

Deleuze, G., & Guattari, F. (1987). *A thousand plateaus: Capitalism and schizophrenia* (B. Massumi, Trans.). Minneapolis: University of Minnesota Press.

Diversi, M., & Moreria, C. (2009). *Betweener talk: Decolonizing knowledge production, pedagogy, and praxis.* Walnut Creek, CA: Left Coast Press.

Duggan, L. (2002). *The incredible shrinking public: Sexual politics and the decline of democracy.* Boston: Beacon Press.

Epston, D. (1999). *Co-research: The making of an alternative knowledge in narrative therapy and community work: A conference collection.* Adelaide, Australia: Dulwich Centre Publications.

Foucault, M. (1965). *Madness and civilization: A history of insanity in the age of reason.* New York: Random House. (Original work published in 1961)

Foucault, M. (1970). *The order of things: An archeology of the human sciences.* New York: Pantheon Books. (Original work published 1966)

Foucault, M. (1973). *Birth of the clinic: Archeaology of medical perception.* New York: Pantheon Books. (Original work published in 1963)

Foucault, M. (1978a). *Discipline and punish: The birth of the prison.* Middlesex: Peregrine Books. (Originally published in 1963)

Foucault, M. (1978b). *The history of sexuality, Vol.1: An introduction.* New York: Pantheon Books. (Originally published in 1976)

Foucault, M. (1985). *The use of pleasure: The history of sexuality, Vol. II.* New York: Pantheon Books.

Foucault, M. (1986). *The care of the self: The history of sexuality, Vol. III.* New York: Pantheon Books.

Freire, P. (1999). *Pedagogy of the oppressed* (3rd ed.). New York: Continuum.

Geertz, C. (1973). Thick description: Toward an interpretive theory of cultures. In C. Geertz (Ed.), *The interpretation of cultures* (pp. 3–30). New York: Basic Books.

Geertz, C. (1985). *Local knowledge: Further essays in interpretive anthropology.* New York: Basic Books.

Gordon, C. (Ed.). (1980). *Power/knowledge: Selected interviews and other writings 1972–1977 by Michel Foucault.* New York: Pantheon Books.

Halberstam, J. (1998). *Female masculinities.* Durham, NC: Duke University Press.

Harding, S. (Ed.). (1987). *Feminism and methodology: Social science issues.* Bloomington: Indiana University Press.

Hartsock, N. (1987). The feminist standpoint: Developing the ground for a specifically feminist historical materialism. In S. Harding (Ed.), *Feminism and methodology: Social science issues* (pp. 283–310). Bloomington: Indiana University Press.

hooks, b. (1994). *Teaching to transgress: Education as the practice of freedom.* New York: Routledge.

Jagose, A. (1996). *Queer theory: An introduction.* New York: NYU Press.

McLaughlin, K. (2003). Agency, resilience, and empowerment: The dangers posed by a therapeutic culture. *Practice, 15*(2), 45–58.

McNamee, S. (1988). Accepting research as social intervention: Implications of a systemic epistemology. *Communication Quarterly, 36*(1), 50–68.

McNamee, S. (1989). Challenging the patriarchal vision of social science: Lessons from a family therapy model. In K. Carter & C. Spitzack (Eds.), *Doing research on women's communication: Perspectives on theory and method* (pp. 95–117). New York: Ablex.

McNamee, S. (1994). Research as relationally situated activity: Ethical implications. *Journal of Feminist Family Therapy, 6*(3), 69–83.

McNamee, S. (2000). The social poetics of relationally engaged research: Research as conversation. In K. Deissler & S. McNamee (Eds.), *Philosophy in therapy: The social poetics of therapeutic conversation* (pp. 146–156). Heidelberg, Germany: Carl Auer Systeme Verlag.

McNamee, S., & Hosking, D. M. (2012). *Research and social change: A relational constructionist approach.* New York: Routledge.

McNamee, S., & Tomm, K. (1986). Research as intervention. *American Family Therapy Association Newsletter, 25,* 18–19.

Morris, M., & Patton, P. (Eds.). (1988). *Michel Foucault, politics, philosophy, and culture: Interviews and other writings, 1977–1984.* New York: Routledge.

Norman, J. (2001). Building effective youth–adult partnerships. *Transitions, 14*(1), 10–18.

Parker, I. (2005). *Qualitative psychology: Introducing radical research.* Maidenhead, England: Open University Press.

Rowbotham, S., Segal, L., & Wainwright, H. (2013). *Beyond fragments: Feminism and the making of socialism* (3rd ed.). London: Merlin Press.

Ryle, G. (1949). *The concept of mind.* London: Hutchinson.

Smith, L. T. (1999). *Decolonizing methodologies.* London & New York: Zed Books.

Tilsen, J. (2010). *Resisting homonormativity: Therapeutic conversations with queer youth* (Doctoral dissertation, Tilburg University, Tilburg, the Netherlands).

Tilsen, J. (2013). *Therapeutic conversations with queer youth: Transcending homonormativity and constructing preferred identities.* Lanham, MD: Rowman & Littlefield.

Warner, M. (1999). *The trouble with normal: Sex, politics, and the ethics of queer life.* Cambridge, MA: Harvard University Press.

Wilson, S. (2008). *Research is ceremony: Indigenous research methods.* Halifax, Canada: Fernwood Publishing.

Woolgar, S. (Ed.). (1996). *Psychology, qualitative methods and the ideas of science.* Leicester, UK: BPS Publications.

Zeldin, S., McDaniel, A., Topitzes, D., & Lorens, M. B. (2001). Bringing young people to the table: Effects on adults and youth organizations. *CYD Journal, 2*(2), 20–27.

Zeldin, S., & Petrokubi, J. (2006). Understanding innovation: Youth–adult partnerships in decision making. *Prevention Researcher, 131,* 11–15.

17

Conclusion and Syllabus

Vanessa Jackson, Elaine Pinderhughes, and Patricia Romney

Elaine Pinderhughes has spent over six decades exploring power. This book builds on her work and explores the many ways that power expresses itself. We hope that we have provided rich examples of how power operates and have shared some of the novel ways in which clinicians, researchers, and consultants are thinking about power and working toward emancipatory practice. We challenged ourselves to edit a book that would offer guidance to new and veteran social workers regarding the process of coming into consciousness and taking action relative to power positions. We look forward to seeing how others build on our work.

We want to stress the importance of defining power and creating a process for analyzing power dynamics in social work practice. The narrative tradition invites us to externalize and question problems, and we have found this to be a useful process in understanding power. These are some questions we have found useful to consider:

- How do I define power?
- How does power show up in my work?
- How is power talked about and addressed in my organization, community, or clinical sessions?
- How would my work be different if it were grounded in an analysis of power?
- What would it mean for me to be "power literate?" What would it mean for my clients to be "power literate?"
- Where do I feel most threatened in my use of power?
- Where do I feel powerless in my personal life? In my professional life?
- Where do I feel powerful in my personal life? In my professional life?
- What have been my most positive professional experiences in sharing power?

These questions can be explored individually, in supervision, in staff in-services, and in social work training programs. We invite you to develop additional questions that will support an increased understanding of how power manifests and affects the social work field.

Our goal is to help readers develop a power-literate practice, one in which the practitioner pays close attention to power dynamics and is attentive to power sharing. The goal of a power-literate practice is enhancement of clients' ability to recognize the power they have, to build power within themselves, and to engage in equitable and growth-enhancing use of power in themselves and in their contexts. Building on Tew's (2006) concept of emancipatory practices, we offer the following attributes of a power-literate practice.

- Requires a basic understanding of power and its multilevel operations.
- Is an ongoing process of analysis and dialogue
- Is grounded in power as a relational experience and not a thing or static state of being.
- Requires honesty and personal inquiry into one's own uses of power
- Operates from a foundation of power together and power with
- Is compromised by denial of power and/or surplus powerlessness
- Is creative, ever changing, and results in growth and authentic healing

In spite of all of the funding directed to so-called empowerment programs over the past few decades, few social workers have been trained to analyze power dynamics, and even fewer have been given the space to struggle with power—power to, power over, power within, and power with—on a personal level as part of their professional training. This leaves us vulnerable to frustration and power abuses as we attempt to ameliorate conditions for our clients without having a full understanding of how the problems were laid down, what maintains them, and what collaborative actions need to be taken to remedy the power inequities. One editor (Vanessa Jackson) recounted her experience talking with the director of a state mental health agency about the importance of understanding power. When the issue of power was raised, this individual immediately stated, "I have no power." This was a stunning admission by one of the most powerful mental health professionals in the state, but it reflects the complexity of power, especially in institutional settings. One can have actual power in the form of authority, control of resources, and professional knowledge but can engage in surplus powerlessness by minimizing or denying that power or by fixating on points of powerlessness and not fully using the power available to them. As writer Alice Walker noted, "The most common way people give up their power is by thinking they don't have any" (Martin, 2004, p. 173). Once we are able to stand more consistently in our own power, we will be better prepared to support individuals, families, communities, organizations, and institutions in negotiating and freeing themselves from power constrictions.

Understanding power requires a willingness to struggle, to appear foolish, to be open to feedback, and often to accept angry or frustrated correction by individuals and communities that have experienced the burden of inequity and oppression. The BICAP chapter invites us into the emotionally fraught space of risking relationships, being misunderstood, and being challenged and held accountable for unconscious privilege. Understanding power is a lifelong quest, but we can create a clear vision for right use of power and commit to manifesting that vision. We challenge ourselves and our colleagues to continually look for ways to expand our knowledge and practices related to power. Many of the authors of the chapters included in this book are activists, and although they may not explicitly discuss their activism, it is evident in the many ways that they engage clients and communities related to social justice. Social workers need more opportunities to talk about how we integrate or, better yet, center our work in political change or macro level, power shifting rather than spending our resources on helping people adapt to the social, political, economic, and emotional fallout of power inequities. We stand at a crucial point in history. We need to decide whether we will offer bandages to the wounded or work to transform societies by making power visible, understandable, and available for transformation.

How would our work look if we centered it in power from within and power with and used that position to transform power over in ways that reflect power in the service of justice and human dignity? Starhawk (1987), activist, therapist, and Witch (a term which she uses deliberately) said, "So, if our work is to evoke power-from-within, we must clearly envision the conditions that would allow that power to come forth, we must identify what blocks it and create the conditions that foster empowerment. Given a world based on power-over, we must remake the world" (p. 8).

In April 1988, I (Vanessa Jackson) submitted to Professor Pinderhughes a paper in which I described my work with local Job Corps staff on program development for low-income African American young adults. I wrote:

> It seemed that out of their own feelings of helplessness and possible anger toward their clients, they were willing to write their clients off as lost causes. I have seen this scene replayed numerous times, and have personally experienced the despair and frustration. It is important for me to be able to distinguish between my feelings of powerlessness and the reality of my clients' situation and their motivation for solving their problems. Only then will I be able to develop intervention strategies which might actually benefit my clients.

The long and laborious process of writing this book was fueled by the understanding that we sometimes must write the books that we most need to read. This is part of the process of reclaiming power, honoring marginalized voices, and challenging power over in our field by stepping up and believing that we can all make powerful contributions to this discourse on power. There are so many areas to explore. We trust that the examples in this book will inspire you to assess your practice, organization, community, and society to better understand how power functions in the constriction and expansion of opportunities within our society.

This book will help readers engage in a process of analyzing power and how it affects our own mental health and well-being. We want to stress that personal clarity is a prerequisite to creating and sharing healing strategies for individuals and communities that have experienced violence (economic, physical, sexual, emotional, cultural, and so on), oppression, daily microaggressions, and economic underinvestment and are manifesting emotional difficulties as a result of these experiences. We can build sustainable and effective programs by engaging root causes of distress, understanding context, and increasing our ability to identify and disrupt power transactions that compromise individuals and communities. We can invest our energy in cocreating prevention, early intervention, and healing programs in collaboration with mental health consumers/survivors and affected communities to support emotional well-being.

The following two appendices on developing your own Power Manifesto and a suggested syllabus on power for social work programs are two tools that can help you bring power into the center of your work. We hope you find them useful. Together, we have the power to transform our communities.

QUESTIONS TO GUIDE THE DEVELOPMENT OF YOUR POWER MANIFESTO

- What values are reflected in your right use of power?
- What actions reflect your commitment to right use of power?
- Where do you feel most challenged in your commitment to right use of power?
- What are three behaviors, attitudes, or beliefs that you would need to release (especially related to your work) to live out your commitment to right use of power?

MY POWER MANIFESTO

Use the space below to write out your Power Manifesto, or the values and commitments that you embrace to support you in walking through the world conscious of the power that you hold. This statement will also serve as a vision statement for your work in the wellness and emotional well-being field to ensure that you engage in power-conscious interactions with the individuals and families who come to you for support.

The syllabus that follows presents our ideas for a potential course on power in schools of social work. It is our conviction that all social workers must understand power to work effectively with clients toward their own empowerment or emancipation. It is also our conviction that power is the concept that underlies all forms of oppression and inequality. This preliminary syllabus draws primarily on the writing in this volume. It is just a beginning. Please read it as a stimulus to your own creative thinking, and, if you are an instructor, consider offering a course on power in your institution.

POWER IN SOCIAL WORK: TEACHING, PRACTICE, AND RESEARCH

Course Description

Basic facts about how power operates must be understood by social workers who (as therapists, researchers, teachers, and leaders) are charged with helping people with issues and problems that are directly or indirectly connected with the way power has operated in their lives. Indeed, Bertrand Russell (2004) called power, "the fundamental concept in social science . . . in the same sense in which energy is the fundamental concept in physics" (p. 4). The perspective in this course is on helping students to become power literate and assisting them in developing emancipatory perspectives and emancipatory uses of power for themselves and those they serve. We will explore power as an entity, a force, and a dynamic relationship between people.

Our examination of power is intended to help social work students connect power to social work theory, social work practice, and issues of policy and research. The course is divided into four parts. The first part involves a preliminary analysis of the concept of power. We do this by examining the literature on power followed by developing self-awareness through an examination of power and powerlessness in ourselves and in our families. The second portion of the course looks at power in teaching and training. The third part of the course looks at power in social work practice at micro, mezzo, and macro levels. At the micro level, we consider work with individuals and families. At the mezzo level, we consider power in larger groups and organizations. At the macro level, we analyze power in larger systems and national and international contexts. We then move to the fourth and final part of the course and look at power in the process and practice of research. Particular attention is given to the role of power in racism, in poverty, and in oppression more generally.

Course Goals

This course is designed to address five of the 10 areas of competency listed in Council on Social Work Education (CSWE) accreditation standards. The relevant competency is listed below each course goal, and the designated measure of each competency is provided.

Course Goal 1. By the end of the course, students will be able to understand power's role in human functioning. CSWE Competency 5: Advance human rights and social and economic justice. Measures: class participation, first assignment.

Course Goal 2. By the end of this course, students will be able to understand their role as professionals in helping clients to become power literate and how to engage in emancipatory uses of power. CSWE Competency 3: Apply critical thinking to inform and communicate professional judgments. Measures: class participation; Assignment 3: the Power Manifesto.

Course Goal 3. By the end of this course, students will be able to recognize and manage personal and professional values around power in a way that allows professional values to guide practice. CSWE Competency 1: Identify as a professional social worker and conduct oneself accordingly.

Course Goal 4. By the end of this course, students will be able to identify and apply strategies and techniques to build power use in their professional roles. CSWE Competency 1: Identify as a professional social worker and conduct oneself accordingly.

Course Goal 5. By the end of this course, students will have a clear picture of how values and structures may oppress, marginalize, alienate, or create or enhance privilege and power in terms of race, social class, sexual orientation, and other forms of oppression. CSWE Competency 4: Engage diversity and difference in practice.

Format

This course will rely on the reading, reflection, discussion, and writing.

Readings

Required Text:

Pinderhughes, E., Jackson, V., & Romney, P. (Eds.). (2016). *Understanding power: An imperative for human services.* Washington, DC: NASW Press.

PART 1: POWER: DEFINITIONS, THEORIES, AND SELF-REFLECTIONS

Week 1: Power in Human Functioning: Definitions and Concepts

(1) Introduction and course overview, (2) power definitions and concepts, (3) emancipatory power in social work practice, and (4) power and advocacy

Required Readings

Foucault, M. (1982). The subject and power. In H. L. Drefus & P. Rabinow (Eds.), *Michael Foucault: Beyond structuralism and hermeneutics* (pp. 208–226). Brighton, UK: Harvester.

Miller, V., VeneKlasen, L., & Reilly, M. (2006a). *Making change happen: Power. Concepts for revisioning power for justice, equity and peace. #3.* Retrieved from https://www.justassociates.org/sites/justassociates.org/files/mch3-concepts-for-revisioning-power-2011upd.pdf

Miller, V., VeneKlasen, L., & Reilly, M. (2006b). *Making change happen: Power. Concepts for revisioning power for justice, equity and peace. #4*. Retrieved from http://www.justassociates.org/en/resources/mch3-power-concepts-revisioning-power-justice-equality-and-peace

Oxfam. (2009). *A quick guide to power analysis*. Retrieved from http://www.powercube.net/wp-content/uploads/2009/11/quick_guide_to_power_analysis_external_final.pdf

Pinderhughes, E. (2016a). Conceptualization of how power operates in human functioning. In E. Pinderhughes, V. Jackson, & P. Romney (Eds.), *Understanding power: An imperative for human services* (pp. 1–24) Washington, DC: NASW Press.

Pinderhughes, E. (2016b). Preface. In E. Pinderhughes, V. Jackson, & P. Romney (Eds.), *Understanding power: An imperative for human services* (pp. xix–xx) Washington, DC: NASW Press.

Tew, J. (2006). Understanding power and powerlessness: Towards a framework for emancipatory practice in social work. *Journal of Social Work, 6*(1), 33–51.

Week 2: Theories of Power

(1) Learning several theories of power, (2) assessing the strengths and limitations of different theories, (3) understanding power's omnipresence, (4) understanding power's complexity, and (5) understanding the relationship between theory and practice.

Required Readings

Foucault, M. (1982). The subject and power. In H. Dreyfus & P. Rabinow (Eds.), *Michel Foucault: Beyond structuralism and hermeneutics* (pp. 208–228). Chicago: University of Chicago Press.

Freeman, D. (2008). Kenneth B. Clark and the problem of power. *Patterns of Prejudice, 42*(4–5), 413–437.

Hunjan, R., & Petit, J. (2011). *Power: A practical guide for facilitating social change*. Dunfemine, Scotland: Carnegie UK Trust. Retrieved from http://www.carnegieuktrust.org.uk/publications/power-a-practical-guide-for-facilitating-social-change/

Lerner, M. (1986). *Surplus powerlessness: The psychodynamics of everyday life and the psychology of individual and social transformation*. Atlantic Highlands, NJ: Humanities Press International.

Lord, J., & Hutchinson, P. (1993). The process of empowerment: Implications for theory and practice. *Canadian Journal of Community Mental Health, 12*(1), 5–22.

Week 3: Self-Reflections on Power

(1) Exploring feelings, (2) developing empathic awareness, and (3) self-reflection and developing a deep and nuanced understanding of power

Required Readings

Boston Institute for Culturally Affirming Practice (BICAP). (2016). Deconstructing power to build connection: The importance of dialogue. In E. Pinderhughes, V. Jackson, & P. Romney (Eds.), *Understanding power: An imperative for human services* (pp. 195–218). Washington, DC: NASW Press.

Conklin, W. (2008, Winter). Latinos and blacks: What unites and divides us? *The Diversity Factor, 16*(1), 20–28.

McAdams-Mahmoud, V. (2016). Racial shaming and humiliation: Tools of oppressive power. In E. Pinderhughes, V. Jackson, & P. Romney (Eds.), *Understanding power: An imperative for human services* (pp. 41–54) Washington, DC: NASW Press.

Sue, D. W., Capodilupo, C. M., Torino, G. C., Bucceri, J. M., Holder, A.M.B., Nadal, K. L., et al. (2007). Racial microaggressions in everyday life. *American Psychologist, 62,* 271–286.

Tawa, J., & Suyemoto, K. L. (2010). The influence of race and power on self-construal in bicultural Asian Americans. *Asian American Journal of Psychology, 1*(4), 275–289.

PART 2: TEACHING

Week 4: Undergraduate Teaching

(1) Methods of teaching about power, (2) practices that empower, and (3) understanding self and others in the context of diversity and intersectionality

Required Readings

Davis, N. J. (1992). Teaching about inequality: Student resistance, paralysis, and rage. *Teaching Sociology, 20,* 232–238.

Deal, K. H., & Hyde, C. A. (2004). Understanding MSW student anxiety and resistance to multicultural learning: A developmental perspective. *Journal of Teaching in Social Work, 24*(1/2), 73–86.

Jackson, V. (2016). Power-based therapy: Transforming powerlessness into power. In E. Pinderhughes, V. Jackson, & P. Romney (Eds.), *Understanding power: An imperative for human services* (pp. 55–70) Washington, DC: NASW Press.

Kliman, J. (2010, Winter). Intersections of social privilege and marginalization: A visual teaching tool [Special issue], *AFTA Monograph Series* (pp. 39–48). Washington, DC: American Family Therapy Academy.

Tawa, J., & Tauriac, J. J. (2016). Teaching power beyond black and white: Recognizing and working with resistance in diverse classrooms. In E. Pinderhughes, V. Jackson, & P. Romney (Eds.), *Understanding power: An imperative for human services* (pp. 165–178) Washington, DC: NASW Press.

Week 5: Training Professionals

(1) Exposure to program development, (2) considering training methodology, (3) distinguishing difference and power, (4) seeing the intersections of difference and power

Required Readings

Llerena-Quinn, R. (2001). How do assumptions of difference and power affect what and how we teach? *Newsletter of the American Family Therapy Academy, 82,* 22–26.

Mostow, C. (2016). Discovering and building RESPECT: A relational model addressing power and difference in medical training. In E. Pinderhughes, V. Jackson, & P. Romney (Eds.), *Understanding power: An imperative for human services* (pp. 179–193) Washington, DC: NASW Press.

PART 3: SOCIAL WORK PRACTICE

Week 6: Clinical Work with Individuals

(1) Diagnosis and treatment planning, (2) empowerment and therapeutic approaches, and (3) role of racism

Required Readings

Gutiérrez, L. (1990). Working with women of color: An empowerment perspective. *Social Work, 35,* 149–153.

Lord, J., & Hutchinson, P. (1993). The process of empowerment: Implications for theory and practice. *Canadian Journal of Community Mental Health, 12*(1), 5–22.

Proctor, G. (2008). CBT: The obscuring of power in the name of science. *European Journal of Psychotherapy and Counselling, 10*(3), 231–245.

Thomas, S., & Gonzalez-Prendes, A. (2009). Powerlessness, anger, and stress in African American women: Implication for physical and emotional health. *Health Care for Women International, 30*(1–2), 93–113.

Week 7: Clinical Work with Families and Other Groups

(1) Working with families, (2) working with groups, (3) strengths perspectives, (4) relational empowerment, (5) difference and power, and (6) children and power

Required Readings

Fishbane, M. (2011). Relational empowerment. *Family Process, 50,* 337–352.

Fraenkel, P. (2009). The therapeutic palette: A guide to choice points in integrative couple therapy. *Clinical Social Work Journal, 37*(3), 234–247.

Grant, J. G., & Cadell. S. (2009). Power, pathological worldviews and the strengths perspective in social work. *Families in Society, 90,* 425–430.

Jones, L. V. (2016). The power to recover: Psychosocial competence interventions with black women. In Pinderhughes, E., Jackson, V., & Romney, P. (Eds.), *Understanding power: An imperative for human services* (pp. 87–100) Washington, DC: NASW Press.

Pinderhughes, E. B. (1997). The interaction of difference and power as a basic framework for understanding work with African Americans: Family theory, empowerment and educational approaches. *Smith College Studies in Social Work, 67,* 322–347.

Prilleltensky, I., Nelson, G., & Peirson, L. (2001). The role of power and control in children lives: An ecological analysis of pathways towards wellness, resiliency and problems, *Journal Community and Applied Social Psychology, 11,* 143–158.

Week 8: Power in Organizations

(1) Leadership, and (2) consultant's role

Required Readings

Romney, P. (2008). Consulting for diversity and social justice: Challenges & rewards. *Consulting Psychology Journal: Practice and Research, 60*(2), 139–156.

Romney, P. (2016). The power to create equity and justice. In E. Pinderhughes, V. Jackson, & P. Romney (Eds.), *Understanding power: An imperative for human services* (pp. 129–138) Washington, DC: NASW Press.

Week 9: Power and Communities

(1) Facilitating action, (2) use of self, and (3) working with larger systems

Required Readings

Aiyer, S. M., Zimmerman, M. A., Morrel-Samuels, S., & Reischl, T. M. (2015). From broken windows to busy streets: A community empowerment perspective. *Health Education & Behavior, 42*(2), 137–147. doi:10.1177/1090198114558590

Akinyela, M. (2016). Culture, power and resistance: Testimonies of hope and dignity. In E. Pinderhughes, V. Jackson, & P. Romney (Eds.), *Understanding power: An imperative for human services* (pp. 101–113) Washington, DC: NASW Press.

Mahoney, K. J., & McGaffigan, E. E. (2016). Cash & Counseling: Empowering elders and people with disabilities to make personal care decisions. In E. Pinderhughes, V. Jackson, & P. Romney (Eds.), *Understanding power: An imperative for human services* (pp. 155–164) Washington, DC: NASW Press.

Rojano, R. (2016). The joy of sharing power and fostering well-being in community networks. In E. Pinderhughes, V. Jackson, & P. Romney (Eds.), *Understanding power: An imperative for human services* (pp. 139–154) Washington, DC: NASW Press.

Romney, P. (2005). The art of dialogue. In P. Korza, B. Schaffer Bacon, & A. Assaf (Eds.), *Civic dialogue, arts & culture: Findings from animating democracy* (pp. 57–79). Washington, DC: Americans for the Arts Press.

Tawa, J., Suyemoto, K. L., & Tauriac, J. J. (2013). Triangulated threat: A model of black and Asian race-relations in a context of white dominance. In S. Pinder (Ed.), *American multicultural studies* (pp. 229–247). Thousand Oaks, CA: Sage Publications.

PART 4: RESEARCH IN SOCIAL WORK

Week 10: Power and Research

(1) The place of research, and (2) re-imaging research

Required Readings

Davis, S. K. (2016). Power and research. In E. Pinderhughes, V. Jackson, & P. Romney (Eds.), *Understanding power: An imperative for human services* (pp. 219–233) Washington, DC: NASW Press.

Tilsen, J. (2016). Re-methodologizing research: Queer considerations for just inquiry. In E. Pinderhughes, V. Jackson, & P. Romney (Eds.), *Understanding power: An imperative for human services* (pp. 235–250) Washington, DC: NASW Press.

ASSIGNMENTS

Assignment 1: My Relationship to Power

Recording project. (assignment method inspired by Beverly Daniel Tatum; questions derived from Vanessa Jackson's Power Cards)

The purpose of this project is for you to do an initial assessment of your own ideas and attitudes about power. To do this project, you will need the questions below and a recording device. Instructions:

1. Answer each of the questions as though you were being interviewed by someone else. Try to make your answers as complete as possible so that if someone else were listening, she or he would understand what you meant by your response.
2. Be sure to record all of your responses.
3. Turn in or send the recording, labeled with your name or other identifying information by _____.
4. Although the recording will be collected, you will be the only person who will listen to it. Your confidentiality is assured. Feel free to be as candid in your response as possible. The recording will be returned to you near the end of the course. At that time, you will be asked to listen to your own tape and do a written analysis of it according to guidelines that will be provided at that time.

Please respond to these questions:

- How do you define power?
- What is your earliest memory about power? How does it influence you today?
- What is your earliest memory about powerlessness? How does it influence you today?
- What messages did you receive about power from your family?
- How, if at all, is your sense of power influenced by your spiritual beliefs and practices? Are there other values that influence your sense of power?
- How do you exercise power with integrity?
- Have you ever used power in less than constructive ways?
- Who/what are your models for right use of power?
- What situations, people, or emotions tend to trigger a sense of powerlessness for you?
- What are some ways in which you give up your power?
- What is your best experience of sharing power with others?

Assignment 2: Power and Your Client

Discuss the usefulness of understanding the operation of power in clients' problems. Choose a case; track the operation of power in terms of kinds, levels, and role in the creation and maintenance of problems. Identify at least two "choice points" for intervention: places and approaches that you believe can change the client's sense of powerlessness into power. Identify which choice point and which intervention approach you believe will have the best chance for success and discuss why. Your client can be an individual, a family, an organization, or a community.

Assignment 3: Power Manifesto

Using the aforementioned guidelines, complete your own Power Manifesto.

REFERENCES

Martin, W. P. (2004). *The best liberal quotes ever: Why the left is right.* New York: Perseus Books Group.

Russell, B. (2004). *Power: A new social analysis.* New York: Routledge.

Starhawk. (1987). *Truth or dare: Encounters with power, authority and mystery.* San Francisco: Harper & Row.

Tew, J. (2006). Understanding power and powerlessness: Towards an emancipatory practice in social work. *Journal of Social Work, 6,* 33–51.

Index

In this index, *n* denotes note, *t* denotes table